Making Democratic Gov

How Regimes Shape Prosperity, Welfare, and Peace

This book focuses on three core questions. Is democratic governance good for economic prosperity? Has this type of regime accelerated progress toward achieving the Millennium Development Goals, social welfare, and human development? Does it generate a peace dividend and reduce conflict at home?

Despite the importance of understanding these questions and the vast research literature generated, remarkably little consensus has emerged about any of these issues. Within the international community, democracy and governance are widely advocated as intrinsically desirable and important goals. Nevertheless, alternative schools of thought continue to dispute their consequences – and thus the most effective strategy for achieving a range of critical developmental objectives. Some believe that human development is largely determined by structural conditions in each society, such as geographic location, natural resources, and the reservoir of human capital, so that regimes have minimal impact. Others advocate promoting democracy to ensure that leaders are responsive to social needs and accountable to citizens for achieving better schools, clinics, and wages. Yet others counter that governance capacity is essential for delivering basic public services, and state-building is essential in postconflict reconstruction prior to holding elections.

This book advances the argument that both liberal democracy and state capacity need to be strengthened in parallel to ensure effective development, within the constraints posed by structural conditions. Liberal democracy allows citizens to express their demands; to hold public officials to account; and to rid themselves of incompetent, corrupt, or ineffective leaders. Yet rising public demands that cannot be met by the state are a recipe for frustration, generating disillusionment with incumbent officeholders, or, if discontent spreads and becomes more diffuse, with the way that the regime works, or even ultimately with the promise of liberal democratic ideals. Thus governance capacity is also predicted to play a vital role in advancing human security, so that states have the capacity to respond effectively to citizens' demands.

The argument is demonstrated using systematic evidence gathered from countries worldwide during recent decades and selected cases illustrating the effects of regime change on development.

Pippa Norris is the Paul F. McGuire Lecturer in Comparative Politics at Harvard University and an Australian Research Council (ARC) Laureate Fellow and Professor of Government and International Relations at the University of Sydney. She is the author of a dozen related books published by Cambridge University Press, including *Driving Democracy* (2008) and *Democratic Deficit* (2011). Her contribution to the humanities and social science has been recognized most recently by the award of the 2011 Johan Skytte Prize (with Ronald Inglehart) and the 2011 Kathleen Fitzpatrick Australian Laureate Fellowship.

Also from Cambridge University Press by the Author

Political Recruitment: Gender, Race and Class in the British Parliament. Pippa Norris and Joni Lovenduski (1995)

Passages to Power: Legislative Recruitment in Advanced Democracies. Pippa Norris, editor (1997)

A Virtuous Circle: Political Communications in Postindustrial Societies. Pippa Norris (2000) (Awarded the 2006 Doris Graber Award by political communications section of the American Political Science Association [APSA])

Digital Divide: Civic Engagement, Information Poverty, and the Internet Worldwide. Pippa Norris (2001)

Democratic Phoenix: Reinventing Political Activism. Pippa Norris (2002)

Rising Tide: Gender Equality and Cultural Change around the World. Ronald Inglehart and Pippa Norris (2003)

Electoral Engineering: Voting Rules and Political Behavior. Pippa Norris (2004)

Radical Right: Voters and Parties in the Electoral Market. Pippa Norris (2005)

Driving Democracy: Do Power-Sharing Institutions Work? Pippa Norris (2008)

Cosmopolitan Communications: Cultural Diversity in a Globalized World. Pippa Norris and Ronald Inglehart (2009)

Sacred and Secular: Religion and Politics Worldwide, second edition. Pippa Norris and Ronald Inglehart (2011) (First edition [2004] awarded the 2005 Virginia A. Hodgkinson Prize by the Independent Sector)

Democratic Deficit: Critical Citizens Revisited. Pippa Norris (2011)

Making Democratic Governance Work

How Regimes Shape Prosperity,
Welfare, and Peace

PIPPA NORRIS
Harvard University

CAMBRIDGE
UNIVERSITY PRESS

CAMBRIDGE
UNIVERSITY PRESS

32 Avenue of the Americas, New York NY 10013-2473, USA

Cambridge University Press is part of the University of Cambridge.

It furthers the University's mission by disseminating knowledge in the pursuit of education, learning, and research at the highest international levels of excellence.

www.cambridge.org
Information on this title: www.cambridge.org/9781107602694

First published 2012
Reprinted 2013

A catalog record for this publication is available from the British Library.

Library of Congress Cataloging in Publication data
Norris, Pippa.
Making democratic governance work : how regimes shape prosperity, welfare, and peace / Pippa Norris.
  pages cm
Includes bibliographical references and index.
ISBN 978-1-107-01699-6 (hardback) – ISBN 978-1-107-60269-4 (paperback)
1. Democracy – Economic aspects. 2. Economic development – Political aspects.
3. Political science – Economic aspects. I. Title.
JC423.N675 2012
321.8–dc23   2012004308

ISBN 978-1-107-01699-6 Hardback
ISBN 978-1-107-60269-4 Paperback

Contents

Tables and Figures

Preface and Acknowledgments

This book has followed a lengthy period of gestation. The original stimulus for writing this volume was my experience five years ago directing the work of the democratic governance practice within the United Nations Development Programme (UNDP), where I was frequently confronted by the practical challenges of development. On many occasions, colleagues from related agencies and bureaus asked how the United Nations' commitment to strengthen the institutions and processes of democratic governance contributed toward other urgent priorities facing the organization, from achieving the Millennium Development Goals to overcoming the challenge of enduring poverty, mitigating the effects of climate change and environmental degradation, peace building and reducing the grievances leading to armed conflict, and combating HIV-AIDS. We were engaged in writing the UNDP's strategic plan, which sought to express a coherent vision demonstrating how the work of all parts of the organization tied together. At the time, I, like many colleagues in the organization, remained frustrated that we struggled to provide a plausible response to these requests. Of course, we offered anecdotal stories and illustrations from common practices, but little that could be regarded as conclusive evidence. How did improving electoral administration in Liberia, strengthening parliaments in Burundi, expanding the capacity of public sector management in Ukraine, or advising on anticorruption strategies in Guatemala actually help deliver clean water, reduce hunger, expand growth, or prevent humanitarian crises?

After a long period of reflection, this book seeks to provide at least a partial answer to these puzzling questions. I learned a tremendous amount from these discussions with UNDP colleagues, especially Pauline Tamasis, and also from collaborating with many other international development agencies over the years, including the World Bank; the National Democratic Institute (NDI); the United Nations Educational, Scientific, and Cultural Organization (UNESCO); the International Institute for Democracy and Electoral Assistance (IDEA); the Council of Europe; the European Union (EU); and the Organization for Security and Cooperation in Europe (OSCE).

The intellectual foundations for this book also build upon my previous research. Earlier books have compared democratic institutions, culture, and processes, including studies about value change and societal modernization, public support for democratic principles and practices, patterns of political engagement and activism, the distribution of religious and secular values, women's representation and gender equality, the impact of political communications and new digital technologies, and the design of power-sharing constitutions. As the next step, it seems timely and important to turn from analyzing the multiple causes of democratization to understanding some of the potential consequences.

I was also encouraged to do so by many Harvard students who have taken my classes on democracy and democratization over the years, as well as by colleagues from economics and other disciplines, who frequently urged me to address the consequences of political reform for achieving many other development objectives. In my classes, students learned about theories of democratization and measures of the quality of democratic governance, the principles of electoral design, the options for power-sharing constitutions, the ways that countries reduce corruption and expand access to justice, and so on. They were curious to learn about these issues, but, they often asked, would democratic governance actually help confront the challenges they faced back home – in Nigeria and Ghana, Burma and Pakistan, Afghanistan and Ethiopia, Mexico and Brazil? Would elections help overcome endemic problems of poverty and inequality? Would power-sharing reduce violence and instability? Would inclusive parliaments prove more responsive to social needs? Would good governance help development aid reach clinics and food banks rather than enriching the bank accounts of elites? They were natural skeptics. In many ways, based on my reading of the research literature, so was I.

Well, maybe, I usually responded. Possibly. Under certain conditions. But instead of puzzling about the instrumental consequences, I answered more confidently, democratic governance can and should be valued as intrinsically good, in and for itself. Citizens should be able to choose their own representative governments, exercising the basic right to determine their own fates, irrespective of any impact on other dimensions of development. After all, as specified in Article 21(3) of the 1948 Universal Declaration of Human Rights: "The will of the people shall be the basis of the authority of government; this will shall be expressed in periodic and genuine elections which shall be by universal and equal suffrage and shall be held by secret vote or by equivalent free voting procedures." Students often wanted to be convinced, but this answer was only partially persuasive. Many continued to express the hope that, in addition to its intrinsic value, democratic governance would also deliver concrete instrumental benefits to improve people's lives in the world's poorest societies. Whether these connections can be demonstrated to skeptics is challenging, however, and irrespective of our personal values and beliefs, the empirical evidence deserves to be thoroughly and systematically examined, with an open mind about the final conclusions. I was still reluctant to go down this road, realizing how far this would force me to travel ill equipped into disciplinary territories well beyond the familiar and comfortable tribal boundaries of comparative political science. Given my initial skepticism, and my commitment to democracy, I was also concerned that the evidence might run counter to my own values, providing fodder to support democracy's critics and to prop up illiberal regimes. In many ways, the journey has proved difficult but worthwhile, and this book reflects my long-delayed response to my students, colleagues, and UNDP practitioners.

Contemporary headlines around the world also reinforced the importance of understanding the issues considered in this book, not least the unfolding developments in the "Arab uprisings." The Tunisian regime transition proved relatively peaceful, after ousted leader, Zine al-Abidine Ben Ali, fled in January 2011. Morocco introduced reforms to the monarchy and held elections in late 2011 in which the moderate Islamist Justice and Development Party (PJD) won the most seats. By contrast, elsewhere in the region, the events toppling the regime of President Hosni Mubarak in Egypt were characterized by sporadic outbreaks of violence and street protests before the Muslim Brotherhood and Salafi Nour won the first post-transition elections. Libyans experienced an outright civil war, Yemen saw prolonged instability, and unrest has simmered in Jordan, while brutal suppression of protest movements occurred in Syria and Bahrain. The uprisings, like the transformation of postcommunist Central and Eastern Europe in the early 1990s, have been carried out in the name of promoting democracy, although survey evidence suggests that a democratic regime may be desired for its assumed instrumental consequences, and thus the potential benefits for growth and peace, as much as for its intrinsic value.

The final catalyst for this project arose from participating in the American Political Science Association Taskforce on Indicators of Democracy and Governance, under the leadership of Henry Brady and Michael Coppedge. Meetings at the University of California, Berkeley, and the Annenberg Public Policy Center in Philadelphia, and continuing our debates in floods of emails, forced us all to think harder about the core concepts and measures in this subfield. A broad consensus was quickly established about concepts and standard indices of liberal democracy, but our search to identify equally coherent ideas and measures of good governance proved more challenging and frustrating.

As always, this book also owes immense debts to many friends and colleagues. Research for the project was generously supported by the award of the Kathleen Fitzpatrick Australian Laureate from the Australian Research Council, for which I am immensely grateful. The project also draws heavily on the work of the Quality of Governance (QoG) Institute at the University of Gothenburg, including their shared datasets and ideas generated at an early workshop at the Institute. The theme of the book started to be developed following conversations over the years with colleagues at Harvard's Kennedy School (HKS) of Government and the Department of Government at Harvard University. I also greatly appreciate the academic hospitality offered by the

Department of Government and International Relations at the University of Sydney, and I am deeply indebted to Michael Spence, Duncan Ivison, and Simon Tormey for facilitating the arrangement of my visit, as well as to all colleagues in the department. Sydney provided a welcoming home for completing the book manuscript.

I am also most grateful to all colleagues and friends who provided encouraging comments on this project during its gestation, including Michael Coppedge, Ivor Crewe, Larry Diamond, David Ellwood, Francis Fukuyama, Graeme Gill, Kristian Skrede Gleditsch, Ben Goldsmith, Simon Hug, Elaine Kamarck, Danny Kaufmann, John Keane, William Keech, Phil Keefer, Alex Keysaar, Stephen Krasner, David Laitin, Margaret Levy, Jane Mansbridge, Lant Pritchett, Robert Putnam, Richard Rose, Bo Rothstein, and Jan Teorell. I also always appreciate the invaluable help and assistance from Camiliakumari Wankaner at HKS. I received invaluable feedback from presentations of draft chapters at various professional meetings, including the Western Political Science Association meeting in San Francisco in 2010; faculty seminars at HKS; the European Consortium Joint Workshops in St. Gallen in April 2011; seminars in the Department of Politics at the University of Brisbane and the University of Queensland in May 2011; the conference on "Democracy in East Asia and Taiwan in Global Perspective" held in Taipei, Taiwan, in August 2011; and annual meetings of the American Political Science Association held in Washington, D.C., in September 2010 and in Seattle in September 2011. Finally, as always, the support of Cambridge University Press has proved invaluable, particularly the patience, efficient assistance, and continuous enthusiasm of my editor, Lew Bateman, as well as the helpful comments of the reviewers.

PART I

INTRODUCTION

Does Democratic Governance Determine Human Security?

This book focuses on three core questions. Is democratic governance good for economic prosperity? Has this type of regime accelerated progress toward achieving the Millennium Development Goals, social welfare, and human development? Does it generate a peace dividend and reduce conflict at home? Prosperity, welfare, and peace are core components of human security, reflecting critical risks and interrelated threats facing an increasingly complex and globalized world.[1] Despite the importance of understanding these questions, and despite the vast research literature generated on each of these topics, remarkably little consensus has emerged about any of these issues. Within the international community, democracy and good governance are widely advocated as intrinsically desirable and important goals. Nevertheless, several alternative schools of thought continue to dispute the consequences of democratic governance, each presenting contrasting visions about the most effective strategy for expanding human security. This book seeks to develop a more unified theory and to examine systematic empirical evidence throwing fresh light on this debate.

During recent decades, the *democracy-promotion* perspective has become increasingly popular, championed by commentators such as Thomas Carothers, Larry Diamond, Morton Halperin, Michael McFaul, Joseph Siegle, and Michael Weinstein, among others. This perspective emphasizes that deepening and consolidating the principles and procedures of liberal democracy will have intrinsic benefits, reinforcing human rights around the globe, as well as instrumental payoffs, by improving human security.[2] Through constraining predatory leaders, expanding voice and participation, and empowering citizens to rid themselves of incompetent rulers, democracy-promoters hope that this type of regime will make elected officials more accountable to ordinary people and thus more responsive to social needs and political grievances. In places undergoing transitions from autocracy – exemplified by developments in Egypt, Myanmar/Burma, and Tunisia – democracy-promoters argue that it is essential to strengthen human rights and fundamental freedoms for their own sake. In addition, however, commentators such as Halperin, Siegle, and

Weinstein argue that this process also delivers concrete benefits by reducing poverty, expanding educational opportunities and building the conditions for lasting peace in developing societies. Carothers identifies a standard template that the international community seeks to foster in transitions from autocracy and the consolidation of democracy. The early stages of this process include developing constitutional frameworks respecting human rights, strengthening competitive political parties, and holding competitive elections that meet international standards. The process moves on with a series of initiatives designed to strengthen the capacity of effective and inclusive legislatures, professionalizing independent judicial bodies and the courts, decentralizing decision making for local government, and also expanding participation in civil society organizations, nongovernmental organizations (NGOs), and the independent media.[3] Yet it is striking that the standard democracy template that Carothers recognizes as practiced by most democracy aid programs is not also directed toward state-building, with relatively little attention devoted toward activities such as strengthening public sector management in the civil service and central government ministries, establishing civilian control of militia, and training security forces. The power of the core executive is commonly regarded by democracy-promoters as part of the problem, not part of the solution to achieving developmental goals for meeting social needs.

Despite the popularity of democracy promotion, these initiatives have come under growing challenge from alternative viewpoints. Where basic human security is lacking, diverse commentators such as Simon Chesterman, James Fearon, Francis Fukuyama, Samuel Huntington, Stephen Krasner, David Laitin, and Roland Paris have all advocated *state-building* in postconflict societies.[4] From the state-building perspective, the poorest developing societies – places such as Somalia, Chad, Timor-Leste, and Southern Sudan – can be understood as "weak" or "failed" states emerging from a long legacy of conflict and anarchy where the central authorities have limited capacity to maintain order and manage the delivery of many basic public goods and services.[5] Governments struggle to guarantee conditions of public safety (such as in Côte d'Ivoire, Somalia, and the Democratic Republic of Congo), to protect against the worst effects of humanitarian and natural crisis (such as following the devastating earthquake in Haiti, floods in Benin, and famine in Niger), and to provide universal access to schooling and healthcare for their citizens (such as in Liberia). There is no single understanding of the concept of state-building, but it is commonly thought to include public sector reforms designed to strengthen the core functions of executive agencies, government ministries, the civil service, the courts, security services, local government agencies, and public sector management. The core functions of the state restored through this process including the capacity to maintain security and rule of law; to provide basic services, such as emergency relief, schools, and healthcare; to formulate and administer budget plans; and to collect taxation revenues.[6] Cases such as Timor-Leste, Kosovo, Afghanistan, Liberia, and Southern Sudan exemplify the complex dilemmas raised by attempts by the international community to rebuild government capacity.[7] The state-building school of thought generally acknowledges the normative value of democracy as an abstract ideal, but recognizes the pragmatic benefits of strengthening governance institutions as the overarching priority. In the strongest version of this argument, state-builders contend that in "weak" or "fragile" states, democracy-promotion should be deferred, with the postponement of multiparty elections or attempts to strengthen civil society organizations. This idea has also been increasingly reinforced by several agencies in the international community, led by the World Bank, which emphasize the developmental benefits thought to accrue from strengthening the institutions of "good governance," reflecting the principles of transparency, accountability, and rule of law.

Lastly, the claimed beneficial consequences of both democracy-promotion and state-building for development are questioned by the *structural* view, emphasizing the role of deep drivers of human security reflecting fixed and enduring conditions, irrespective of the type of regime in power.[8] From this perspective, countries are poor because, like Liberia, they are land-locked and stranded at the periphery of international trade markets. Or, like Somalia, they lack investment in human capital, new technologies, and physical infrastructure (transportation, communications, factories, clinics, and schools). Or, like Bangladesh, they are located in an area vulnerable to tropical diseases and susceptible to natural disasters such as floods and droughts. Or, like the Democratic Republic of Congo, they are plagued by the scourge of violent conflict, deepseated social inequality, and ethnic divisions. Or perhaps states confront "all of the above." For all these reasons, no matter the most heroic attempts by the international community and national leaders to strengthen and transform democratic governance, it is thought Panglossian to dream that through the process of regime change, a Niger could thereby rise up the ladder of development to become a Nigeria or a Nicaragua, much less a Norway. Structuralists emphasize that the type of regime has minimal impact on human security, in part because political institutions are themselves the *product* of deep-seated socioeconomic and geographic conditions (the classic "Lipset thesis") rather than functioning as an independent cause of development.[9] From this viewpoint, it is naïve and foolish at best, and dangerous at worst, to hope that complex political processes of regime transition and democratization can generate immediate economic payoffs, reductions in poverty, or peace processes that improve the lives of ordinary people and thereby transform societies. In the words of a saying popularized by Jacob Zuma, "You can't eat democracy."[10]

Arguments about these rival claims are commonly heard in contemporary foreign policy circles in Washington, Paris, Berlin, and London when debating the most effective interventions for the world's trouble spots. In some cases, one side or the other wins the argument; after the fall of the Berlin Wall, it seemed to many self-evident that democratic elections, multiparty competition, and initiatives strengthening human rights, civil society, and the independent media were the most urgent priorities facing the reconstruction of postcommunist societies in Central and Eastern Europe. In other cases, such

as newly independent postconflict Timor-Leste and Kosovo, it seemed equally
self-evident to many observers that the basic structure of the new government
had to be created, including security services and justice, central ministries, and
public sector management.

But in many other countries around the world lacking the institutions for
both liberal democracy and for effective state capacity – in Iraq and Afghanistan,
Egypt and Libya, or Southern Sudan and Yemen – the choices about strategic
priorities are far from self-evident. In a situation of limited resources – and
there are always limited resources – if you were determining priorities, do you
choose to invest aid into parliaments – or courts? Do you train police – or journalists? Do you hold elections – or rebuild government agencies? Do you "do
it all"? Or do you instead choose to bypass governments by investing directly
in humanitarian aid, blue-helmet security, clean water wells, anti-malaria nets,
child immunization, girls' schools, health clinics, antiretroviral drugs, rural
food collectives, microfinance, demilitarization job training, and de-mining
programs, where the international community works in partnership directly
with local civil society organizations, on the grounds that these types of initiatives are more likely to generate an immediate, concrete payoff in people's
lives than attempts to strengthen democratic governance? These are not simply
abstract scholarly questions; debate about these sorts of dilemmas commonly
divides donor agencies, NGOs, think-tanks, national governments, and multilateral organizations in the international development community.

The claims and counterclaims are often framed in the context of particular
cases currently in the headlines, exemplified by the world's fascination with dramatic events unfolding during the Arab uprisings in Tahrir Square, the battle for
Tripoli, or protests and bloody repression in Homs, Manama, and Damascus.
Understanding these issues has much wider and deeper resonance beyond specific cases, however, including for the ongoing violence in Democratic Republic
of Congo, the stirrings of liberalization in Myanmar/Burma, and the famine in
Somalia, with debates about priorities dividing scholars among diverse disciplines within the social sciences as well as practitioners.

As reviewed in subsequent chapters, by now an extensive econometric literature in comparative politics, developmental economics, and international
studies has tested the impact of democratization and governance for the attainment of multiple developmental goals, employing empirical indices of income
growth, social welfare, and conflict. Some studies of the empirical evidence do
indeed report detecting significant linkages, where regimes influence human
security. Yet the direction of causality is usually complex to interpret due to
potential interaction. Cross-national and time-series data often prove messy
and untidy. Research on regime effects has been fragmented across different
subfields and indices. Models often suffer from omitted variables or countries. Cherry-picked cases have limited generalizability due to selection bias.
Theories about the underlying mechanisms supposedly linking regimes and
development remain underdeveloped. For all these reasons, overall this rich
body of research has failed to demonstrate robust and consistent confirmation

of many core claims, disappointing the hopes of proponents. The lack of consensus weakens the ability of social scientists to offer rigorous evidence-based policy advice useful for the practitioner community.

It is important to attempt to construct a unified and comprehensive theory from these claims and counterclaims, building on each of these incomplete perspectives but going beyond them to synthesize our understanding about the impact of regimes on diverse dimensions of human security. The current debate reflects an unfortunate intellectual schism and an artificial division of labor among various disciplines in the social sciences. It also arises from divergent normative values. These intellectual blinkers are reinforced by the varied mandates of development agencies within the international community, such as the United Nations Development Programme (UNDP), the World Bank, and the European Union. Each argument presents an incomplete and partial vision, often deriving plausibility from certain particular cases but limited in its broader generalizability. Like scattered pieces of a jigsaw puzzle, the alternative perspectives become more coherent and comprehensive, and the supporting evidence becomes clearer and more convincing, if synthesized into an integrated theoretical framework.

THE UNIFIED THEORY OF DEMOCRACY + GOVERNANCE

Accordingly, the unified theory at the heart of this book predicts that the institutions of both liberal democracy *and* state capacity need to be strengthened in parallel for the most effective progress deepening human security, within the broader enduring fixed constraints posed by structural environments. Democracy and governance are rightly regarded as separate and distinct phenomena, both conceptually and empirically. This book contends that regimes reflecting *both* dimensions are necessary (although not sufficient) for effective development. These dimensions function separately, rather than interacting; thus, as discussed fully in later chapters, today certain types of states, exemplified by China and Singapore, are particularly strong in their capacity for governance, but they continue to fail to protect basic human rights. Others, such as Ghana, El Salvador, and Mali, have registered significant gains in democracy during recent years, but these regimes continue to be plagued by weak governance capacity to deliver public goods and services. Certain contemporary regimes are strong on both dimensions – not simply established Western democracies in affluent societies such as Canada, Germany, and Sweden, but also many diverse third wave democracies and emerging economies, including Chile, Slovenia, and Taiwan. Still other regimes around the world – exemplified by Somalia, Zimbabwe, and Azerbaijan – display an exceptionally poor performance on both democratic rights and state capacity. The book develops a new conceptual typology based on sharpening these general ideas and then focuses on identifying the impact of regimes on a series of vital developmental goals, including economic growth; social welfare, such as education and health; and reductions in interval armed conflict.

The unified theory assumes that development is most effective where regimes combine the qualities of democratic responsiveness *and* state effectiveness. The argument is based on several premises.

The first is that the institutions of liberal democracy encourage elected officials to pay attention to human security, principally where procedures allow citizens to express their demands; to hold public officials accountable for their actions; and to rid themselves of incompetent, corrupt, or ineffective leaders. These mechanisms encourage leaders to be responsive to social needs and concerns. In practice, liberal democracies often prove imperfect in each of these procedures, particularly where party competition is limited, electoral systems are manipulated, or channels of participation are skewed toward money more than people. But, at best, liberal democracies should make leaders procedurally accountable to citizens for their action. Democratic regimes strengthen downward electoral accountability and develop institutions providing multiple horizontal and vertical checks and balances so that vote-seeking politicians have strong incentives to pay attention to public concerns and to deliver services and programs meeting social needs.

But the unified theory also assumes as the second premise that by themselves, democratic institutions are insufficient to achieve development goals. The institutions in liberal democracy can limit the abuse of power, but curbing Leviathan does not ensure that leaders will necessarily have the capability to implement effective public policies addressing social needs. Indeed, excessive checks and balances may even prove counterproductive for the developmental state, bogging down decision making over urgent challenges in a morass of partisan interests and mutual veto points. Elected politicians do not, themselves, build schools, run clinics, or dig latrines. Moreover, the initial move from autocracy, and the rhetorical promises commonly made by leaders during transitional elections, often encourages rising expectations among ordinary citizens. If these cannot be met by elected officials, due to limited state capacity, this can be a recipe for frustration. Among critical citizens, this process can generate disillusionment with incumbent officeholders, and, if discontent spreads upward to become more diffuse, with the way that the regime works or even, ultimately, with the promise of liberal democratic ideals.[11]

For all these reasons, the third premise of the unified theory suggests that the quality of governance – particularly state capacity – will also play a vital role in achieving developmental goals, by bolstering state effectiveness and thus allowing responsive officials to deliver things that citizens want: better security, schools, healthcare, and living standards. If unconstrained by democratic procedures and principles, however, in the long term, strong states are unlikely to serve the general public interest. Like the ancient concepts of Yin and Yang, the seemingly contrary forces of democratic responsiveness and governance effectiveness are conceptualized here as interconnected and interdependent in the world, balancing each other's strengths and weaknesses.

Lastly, and equally importantly, the central argument acknowledges that the quality of both democracy and governance is not isolated phenomena; regimes are assumed to reflect, as well as shape, the enduring structural conditions and the broader environment in each society. Thus the fourth premise is that deep drivers of development function to restrict or facilitate progress in strengthening regimes based on democratic governance. These fixed conditions are exemplified by each state's physical size and regional location, their degree of integration into global markets, their pool of natural resources and physical capital, the human capital and skills of its labor force, the existence of deep-rooted ethnic divisions and destructive civil wars, the impact of deep-rooted religious cultural values, and also colonial legacies. All these fixed structural conditions need to be incorporated as controls in comprehensive models analyzing the effects of regimes on human security.

By itself, it could be argued that these claims are hardly novel, bold, nor indeed startlingly original. Yet, for several reasons, this argument needs to be forcefully reiterated and the evidence carefully scrutinized.

The previous literature commonly fails to acknowledge and test the importance of both democracy and governance, with scholars from different disciplines preferring to emphasize one or the other of these twin phenomena. In particular, the vast bulk of the literature has focused on the impact of democracy irrespective of state capacity. Moreover, previous research has failed to present robust and consistent evidence using multiple indices of human security and a comprehensive battery of controls; too often there is potential selection bias in the narrow choice of dependent variable. Much research has focused on income and wealth, but rich nations can still be vulnerable to a broad range of risks and threats, whether from social inequality; lack of education, healthcare, and provision for children and the elderly; or violence and armed conflict. Thus the robustness of any regime effects need to be tested against multiple indices.

In addition, the notion of the "quality of governance" is a complex and slippery concept, open to several interpretations and meanings. Indeed, "good governance" is now such a catch-all term that it has become a Humpty Dumpty Rorschach ink blot test meaning whatever the commentator likes it to mean. This is useful for diplomatic language in realpolitik, but lacks the precision necessary to make the term valuable for social science. The way that the notion of governance is conceptualized and measured in this book as reflecting 'bureaucratic state capacity' will be clarified and carefully unpacked and measured in subsequent chapters. Regimes most successful in achieving a wide range of developmental goals, the unified theory predicts, reflect a delicate balance between the effective mechanisms of *democratic accountability* (restricting the autonomy of rulers) and the effective mechanisms of *bureaucratic state capacity* (expanding the ability of public officials to implement policies serving the general public interest). This claim is subjected to rigorous scientific tests against a diverse range of developmental indicators, within the limits of the available evidence and analytical techniques, to see whether it holds water.

Before critics jump into the fray and attack the simple theoretical propositions presented in the unified theory, however, several important qualifications need to be emphasized.

First, trade-offs among value choices are often encountered in the transition from regimes based on patronage autocracy toward those reflecting the principles of democratic governance; the initial stages of this process can expand electoral choice, human rights, and political freedoms while simultaneously weakening the capacity of the state to maintain order and stability. Only in subsequent stages do governance and democracy come together again in a more balanced trajectory. As Charles Tilly theorizes, tensions exist between state capacity and democracy, so that countries such as Libya and Egypt face regime transitions with difficult trade-offs.[12]

Secondly, this book does not prescribe a simple "one-size-fits-all" set of practical political reforms; instead, attention needs to be paid to diagnosing the particular weakness of regimes in each country on both these dimensions. Hence, in autocracies that have restricted political rights, the most urgent priorities should be focused on encouraging transitions from autocracy and promoting the principles and institutions of liberal democracy, typically through interventions seeking to implement legitimate and competitive multiparty elections meeting international standards of integrity, strengthening effective and inclusive legislatures with the capacity of government scrutiny, and bolstering independent and professional judiciaries to improve access to justice, within an overarching constitutional and legal framework respecting minority rights. In other democratic states, however, where the key challenge remains lack of governance capacity to deliver, international agencies should prioritize initiatives designed to address these issues, commonly through programs professionalizing training, budgeting, and management in the public sector; strengthening the capacity of local service delivery agencies; and reducing incompetence, malfeasance, and corruption in public life. The idea that one set of programs is effective in all social contexts should be abandoned in favor of a more accurate diagnosis of the key needs-based priorities, and thus more effective and targeted policy interventions tailored to local conditions.

Finally the empirical evidence available to test core propositions in each of the alternative accounts remains complex to analyze due to many technical challenges. Scholars in each subfield – comparative politics, economics, welfare development, and international relations – have developed specialized analytical techniques and concepts that may well differ from the approach used here. This book attempts to overcome these limitations by adopting a mixed method design, but nevertheless the interpretation of the results remains sensitive to the particular selection of indices, country coverage, and model specifications. We have to adopt an honest and dispassionate perspective, acknowledging in the conclusions that the evidence lends strong support for several of the core theoretical propositions, as expected, but not to all. The book therefore contributes to our knowledge about these issues, but further work needs to explore the remaining puzzles in understanding the underlying linkage mechanisms connecting regimes and development, using alternative approaches, case studies, and analytical techniques.

The Lessons of Regime Change for Human Development

What evidence allows us to weigh and evaluate each of the arguments in the contemporary debate? As structural theorists argue, do enduring drivers of human security – such as each country's natural resources, access to global markets, ethnic divisions, and cultural traditions – outweigh any impact arising from regime institutions? Or do processes of democratization promote development, as democracy promoters claim? Alternatively, as the state-building perspective suggests, is effective governance vital? Or else is it more important to understand how democracy and governance develop in parallel, within the context of structural conditions, as the unified theory proposes?

The "third wave" of democratization is conventionally thought to have occurred, following Huntington's periodization, during the mid-1970s.[13] The Arab Uprising is only the most recent of successive waves of regime change. Thus today processes of democratization can now be observed over almost four decades. The diverse trajectories of regime transitions occurring during these years – with some states flourishing as stable liberal democracies, while others have faltered or fallen back – put us in a far better position now than ever before to unravel the complex relationship between regimes and development. Establishing robust and convincing evidence to resolve the debate presents formidable challenges, however, not least due to the way that income, welfare, and peace are reciprocal conditions that can also affect processes of democratization and governance. The voluminous empirical literature assessing these issues presents an inconclusive, scattered, and contradictory body of findings. This is hardly surprising given the complexity of the issues, deep disciplinary boundaries, and uncertainty about the most appropriate analytical techniques, well-specified models, and choice of indicators.

Standard econometric techniques are invaluable, and central to the research design used in this book, but analysts are quickly confronted by the serious limits in this methodology. Thus these methods ideally need to be supplemented by an alternative narrative approach examining historical processes occurring within specific cases of regime change. Examples are commonly highlighted in popular arguments to provide anecdotal support for certain claims; hence the emerging economies of South Africa, Brazil, and India are seen to exemplify rising prosperity, growth in investment and trade, domestic security, and improved living standards experienced since the mid-1990s under democracy. In selected cases, such as Indonesia, Chile, and Rwanda, a plausible narrative story can be constructed about how improvements in a series of multiparty competitive elections, as well as capacity building in the public sector, strengthened the state's management of the economy and the delivery of basic healthcare, schools, jobs, and clean water and also reduced the underlying grievances fostering violent conflict. But many counterexamples are also cited, hence state-builders emphasize China's remarkable economic growth lifting millions out of poverty or Singapore's orderly and affluent society under one-party rule, as well as marked progress in human development (defined as gains of twenty points or more in the one hundred–point Human Development Index [HDI] since 1980) under some authoritarian regimes, such as in Hosni Mubarak's Egypt and King Mohammed VI's Morocco.[14] Cases are an invaluable way to provide additional insights into the observed statistical regularities, but this approach raises important challenges about their selection. In this book, several paired cases are highlighted, such as Haiti and the Dominican Republic, two nations sharing the Caribbean island of Hispaniola, chosen to display diverse trajectories of regime change *and* human security, yet sharing common geographic, cultural, and historical roots, to help control for structural conditions.

THE CASE OF KOREA

The core questions at the heart of this book can be vividly illustrated by the contrasting fates of the peoples living on either side of the thirty-eighth parallel in the divided Korean peninsula. The Korean Republic made substantial progress in human development; indeed, out of all countries worldwide, during the last twenty years the country registered the second-largest net gains in the UNDP HDI, beaten only by China. Yet during the same years, poverty and hunger north of the thirty-eighth parallel severely worsened. What explains the divergent trajectories?

For much of its history, Korea was one kingdom with a common culture and language, and a religious heritage drawn from Buddhism and Confucianism. Following the end of World War II, the country was partitioned into zones of U.S. and Soviet occupation. In 1948, new governments were established; the Republic of Korea in the south and communist Democratic People's Republic of Korea (DPRK) in the north, divided at the thirty-eighth parallel. In 1950, the unresolved tensions of division surfaced in the Korean War, after northern forces invaded the Republic of Korea. The founder of North Korea, President Kim Il Sung, ruled through the manipulation of nationalist fervor and a charismatic following devoted to the cult of the Great Leader, as well as through the draconian repression of dissidents and the support of the military. The country's borders remained hermetically sealed and deeply isolated from the international community; the main foreign policy ties were with China and the Soviet Union. The president's son, Kim Jong Il, was officially designated as his father's successor in 1980, assuming a growing political and managerial role until his father's death in 1994, when he inherited the role of supreme leader.[15] In 2011, Kim Jong Il's youngest son, Kim Jong-Un, was promoted to become his heir, creating a modern dynasty. As Human Rights Watch summarizes the contemporary record: "Human rights conditions in North Korea remain dire. There is no organized political opposition, free media, functioning civil society, or religious freedom. Arbitrary arrest, detention, and torture and ill-treatment of detainees and lack of due process remain serious issues."[16] In November 2009, the United Nations General Assembly adopted a resolution criticizing "systematic, widespread and grave" human rights violations in North Korea, condemning the use of torture and "all-pervasive and severe restrictions on the freedoms of thought, conscience, religion, opinion and expression, peaceful assembly and association, the right to privacy and equal access to information."[17]

During the early years, South Korea was also ruled by a series of oppressive autocratic governments, backed by the military, beginning with the government of Syngman Rhee, with presidents governing with the façade of fraudulent and manipulated elections. The country was initially highly protectionist, based on state-planning agencies, but following popular demands for reform, it eventually transitioned during the 1990s to become a market-oriented economy.[18] The democracy movement, launched by students in the 1960s and championed by opposition parties in the 1970s, delivered reforms the following decade. In 1987, the country initiated the Sixth Republic, with the regime transitioning to a multiparty presidential democracy. Trends in the Polity IV constitutional democracy index jumped sharply upward (see Figure 1.1).[19] In 1993, the first civilian president was elected to power. Since then, the country has held a succession of presidential and legislative multiparty elections meeting international standards of integrity and resulting in peaceful transitions rotating power between the government and opposition.[20] Gains have also been registered in the quality of governance; for example, corruption rankings have improved.[21] The state had a long tradition of merit-based bureaucracy in the public sector.[22] The democratic transformation of South Korea has by no means been smooth and stable; scandals associated with crony capitalism continue to afflict the presidency, while disruptive outbreaks of "people power" street protests remain common and the legislature and executive branch are often gridlocked. North Korea's nuclear capacity raises security concerns and strains attempts to repair diplomatic relationships with its neighbor. Nevertheless, progress in democratization in South Korea during the last quarter century has been substantial.

The record of economic growth in both regions also illustrates stark contrasts; until the 1970s, both countries were poor, with per capita gross domestic product (GDP) of around $330. Today, the population in the North continues to suffer from prolonged food shortages and poor living conditions, with recurrent outbreaks of flooding causing severe famine, killing millions of people.[23] The World Food Programme estimates that a third of North Korean women and children are malnourished. Recent monetary "reforms" have wiped out modest household savings and thus destroyed a safety net protecting against hard times. In its starkest terms, the average Korean lives roughly fourteen years longer in the South than across the border in the North. Instead of supporting agriculture or industry, in North Korea state resources are poured into the military, representing by some estimates the second-largest military expenditure as a percentage of GDP worldwide.[24] In 2011, per capita GDP in the North was estimated at around $1,900.[25] By contrast, since the 1970s, South Korea has achieved a remarkable record of modernization and global integration to become a high-tech industrialized economy based on export-led growth. As Figure 1.1 shows,

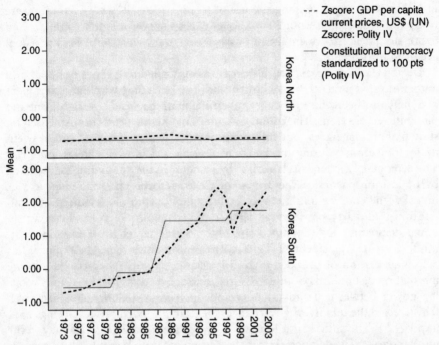

FIGURE 1.1. Trends in economic and democratic development, North and South Korea.
Note: The graph illustrates changes in per capita GDP in current prices, and the
Polity IV Constitutional Democracy scores, standardized around the mean (z-scores).
For more details, see the appendix.
Sources: United Nations; Polity IV.

steady growth was evident even before the 1987 democratic transition, accompanying modest political liberalization. But the economy accelerated dramatically
in the decade following this watershed event, with average income quadrupling.
Having recovered from the 1997 Asian economic crisis, South Korea currently
boasts a $1.356 trillion GDP, which is among the world's twenty-largest econ-
omies. Four decades ago, GDP per capita in North and South Korea was comparable with the poorer countries of Africa and Asia. By 2011, however, South
Korean GDP per capita had leapfrogged to $31,700, fifteen times as high as in
the North. Rapid industrialization and societal modernization have resulted in
indicators such as longevity, education, and literacy, as well as income, rising
substantially; South Korea ranks twenty-eighth highest worldwide in the UNDP
Human Development Index, similar to Greece and Israel.

The links connecting democracy, governance, and human security – illustrated by these dramatically contrasting paired cases – are the puzzle central to
this book. What caused both sides of the Korean border to diverge so sharply
that two peoples now live in different worlds? Standard structural conditions

commonly offered to account for advances in human security in equivalent cases elsewhere in the world are unsatisfactory explanations for these twin societies – such as contrasts in enduring cultural values and religious traditions, geographical location (determining access to global markets and climates), the "natural resource curse," or path-dependent historical legacies. So has the process of democratization been the key factor driving the contrasting levels of development? Or was it, instead, the skills, effectiveness, and capacity of these countries' state bureaucracy? Or were both important? More broadly, is it possible to generalize the lessons derived from these divergent pathways on the Korean peninsula to understand regime effects on human security in societies around the world?

Plan of the Book

I. Introduction

To address contemporary debates about these issues among scholars and policy makers, Part I of the book develops the theoretical argument presented in this book. *Chapter 2* considers the claims in the debate. Building on these ideas, and synthesizing the separate viewpoints, the chapter presents the unified theory of democratic governance.

II. Comparing Regimes

Based on these arguments, Part II operationalizes the main concepts, develops a fourfold typology to classify regimes both around the world and over time, and illustrates these by contrasting case studies. *Chapter 3* presents the regime typology at the heart of this book. This focuses on two components. The first concerns *liberal democracy*, understood here, most simply, to reflect the capacity of people to influence regime authorities within their nation-state. Democratic states are expected to provide elected leaders with strong incentives to respond to social needs. Drawing on the ideas of Robert Dahl, the concept of liberal democracy is understood to reflect the principles of contestation, participation, and human rights.[26] To operationalize this concept, the book uses measures of democratization provided by Freedom House and Polity IV, which have become standard in comparative research, allowing regimes to be categorized as autocracies or democracies. The second dimension of the regime classification concerns *state capacity*, shaping how public sector officials have the competencies, skills, and resources to respond to social needs. State capacity is closely related to the idea of "governance," which has become intellectually fashionable in recent years, yet it remains a complex and contested concept that is open to multiple meanings, often with a long and ever-growing shopping list of potential attributes.[27] State capacity is understood in this study as the ability of regime authorities to perform functions essential for collective well-being, including, most essentially, maintaining security and managing the delivery of public goods and services, measured by the quality of bureaucracy, lack of corruption, and rule of law. The chapter operationalizes and applies measures of state capacity derived from the International Country Risk Guide Quality of Governance indicators.[28] Alternative conceptualizations and measures are also considered.

Often it is assumed, falsely, that democracy and governance are interchangeable concepts, or that, at a minimum, they go hand in hand. When the regime typology is applied, however, it reveals a complex relationship between these twin phenomena; instead of a linear relationship, a logistic curve exists between indices of liberal democracy and state capacity.[29] The classification is applied to compare regimes worldwide and over time, highlighting selected cases to understand the essential features of each ideal type in more depth.

Bureaucratic democracies, such as Chile, are predicted to prove most likely to achieve the universal developmental goals of income growth, social welfare, and peaceful stability. By contrast, *patronage autocracies,* exemplified by Somalia, combining the worse features of both, are expected to prove least successful in delivering human security. The other two categories of regimes – *bureaucratic autocracies* (illustrated by Singapore) and *patronage democracies* (such as Ghana) – are expected to display a mixed and less consistent record, where developmental performance is heavily contingent on many structural conditions, including the existence of prior economic and social conditions, patterns of ethnic heterogeneity and conflict, the geographic locations and natural resources of states, reservoirs of human and physical capital, and the enduring historical legacy of previous colonial rulers and predominant religious cultures.

Chapter 4 discusses the research design used to determine regime effects. Those more interested in learning about the results, rather than the technical and methodological details, may choose to skip ahead to the next chapter. It is important to explain the approach, however, because many arguments in the research literature revolve around alternative model specifications and case selections. No single analytical approach is wholly satisfactory and reliable, so comparative evidence is tested through mixed quantitative and qualitative methods. Longitudinal comparisons spanning countries worldwide during the third wave era, starting in the early-to-mid-1970s, provide a broad overview of general trends and global patterns. Evidence is based on a panel of time-series cross-sectional (TSCS) data, where the unit of observation is each country-year (Afghanistan-1984, Afghanistan-1985, ... Afghanistan-2010, and so on). Models testing the main effects use least squares regression analysis with panel-corrected standard errors, an approach widely adopted in political science.[30] This method generates easy-to-interpret results and accurate estimates for testing rival hypothesis, yet it avoids some common problems associated with panel data. Models using alternative techniques, indicators, and specifications, including fixed effects, are also employed for robustness checks.

What else causes the stark contrasts in human security observed in Botswana and Somalia? India and Pakistan? Croatia and Belarus? Turkey and Libya?

Obviously development does not rest on institutions alone; hence properly specified analytical models need to control for multiple factors. The impact of different variables is expected to vary across each of the dimensions of human security, but the core battery includes, at a minimum, several sets of controls:

(i) The role of *geography* (and hence the fixed effects of location, climate, distance to global markets, the size of physical terrain, regional influences, and the endowment of natural resources);

(ii) *Economic conditions* (including prior levels of economic development and trade flows);

(iii) *Social structure* (including ethnic fractionalization, human capital, levels of economic development, and population size);

(iv) *Cultural traditions* (exemplified by the influence of predominant religious faiths and the type of colonial legacy in each society); and lastly,

(v) *Global trends* (such as the impact of the steady reduction in interstate conflict following the end of the Cold War, or the global financial crisis and economic downturn).

Based on the previous research literature, further specific controls are introduced selectively into several models in each chapter, depending on the dependent variable, to avoid omitted variable bias. The impact of democratic governance is thus compared against many other common alternative explanations of why countries expand their economies, lift citizens out of enduring poverty, and protect their citizens against internal conflict.

Convincing studies need to tackle several major challenges, however, not least in disentangling what causes what, where there are complex and reciprocal processes of change. The concept of human security encompasses many issues, so to make headway, just a few central dimensions need to be selected for analysis. Annual changes in the core dependent variables, monitoring economic growth, welfare, and internal conflict, are examined in subsequent chapters. Models test the potential effects of liberal democracy and state capacity (measured the year before) on subsequent changes in the dependent variables, controlling for structural conditions. Problems of endogeneity arising from reverse causation are mitigated (although not wholly excluded) by using lagged indicators, where democratic governance is measured one year prior to the dependent variables, such as the outbreak of armed conflict or the onset of recession. The chapter also discusses the pros and cons of alternative specifications and techniques and considers potential problems arising from omitted variable bias, lack of robustness, poor conceptual validity, measurement errors, and systematic biases in country coverage arising from missing observations. The technical appendix at the end of the book describes the construction of the democratic governance indices in more detail.

Even the best research designs encounter the limitations of what can and cannot be established via econometric techniques. Accordingly, our understanding is enriched by selected case-oriented studies illustrating divergent pathways and historical trajectories of development in greater depth. The wide range of regime transitions occurring during the third wave era provides the backdrop for this book, offering multiple "natural experiments" to monitor the systematic effects of institutional change on societies during recent decades. There are a number of alternative ways to pick country cases – for example, selecting those nations that most closely exemplify the results of the large-N regression models or examining outliers that might illuminate other factors not included in the statistical models.[31] The strategy used in this book selects paired case studies to compare particular societies – such as North and South Korea, Haiti and the Dominican Republic, and Botswana and Zambia – which are similar in certain important regards – including being neighboring countries sharing common borders, cultural traditions, regional influences, and ethnic compositions – while differing in their regime institutions and their developmental pathway. This process alone cannot determine the general consequences of democratic governance, due to case-study selection bias, but historical narratives thicken theories and the observed generalizations concerning pathways of development. Cases also throw light on more actor-centric approaches, highlighting how leaders and elites play a role when responding to the context of broader structural conditions. The combination of large-N and case-oriented approaches in a mixed research design serves to increase confidence in identifying causal relationships.

III. Regime Effects

Building on this foundation, subsequent chapters proceed to test empirical evidence for the core propositions concerning the predicted effects of regimes on economic prosperity, social welfare, and peace.

Chapter 5 addresses the classic debate about the impact of democratic governance on economic prosperity, income growth, and living standards. The structural view suggests that regimes have minimal effect on rates of income growth, whether positive or negative, compared with the impact of many other largely fixed conditions.[32] This includes processes of industrialization and the adoption of new technologies, the introduction of mechanized agriculture, the availability of capital and investments in infrastructure, trade location and openness, the existence of natural endowments (such as iron ore, oil, gas, and coal), the availability of human capital (education and a skilled workforce), conditions of social equality, and the impact of colonial legacies. Given these conditions, the recent transition from autocracy in Egypt, Tunisia, and Libya is not expected to transform people's lives overnight, or indeed even in the medium term. Considerable empirical evidence supports this view; Hristos Doucouliagos and Mehmet Ali Ulubasoglu compared a wide range of eighty-four published democracy-growth studies, reporting that the findings of these studies are far from robust, with the results varying due to the use of different data sources, estimation methodologies, country comparison, time periods, and control variables. Once these differences are controlled for, however, the authors concluded that democracy had a zero direct effect on growth, although a positive *indirect* effect was still evident, through democratic states having a superior record of human capital accumulation.[33]

This argument is challenged by the democracy-promotion perspective, however, suggesting several reasons why these types of regimes are expected to grow faster than autocracies. One argument emphasizes leadership turnover: Theories of retrospective voting suggest that in democracies, citizens will punish politicians and parties that fail to deliver income, jobs, and prices, providing a strong electoral incentive for effective economic performance.[34] Over successive contests, governing parties more capable of managing the economy can be expected to be returned to power, while incompetent leaders are relegated to the opposition. By contrast, no similar fail-safe mechanisms exist to rid autocratic states of venal, self-serving, and ineffective leaders. A second argument emphasizes that liberal democracies invest more in human capital (literacy, educational qualifications, and employment skills).[35] This process, in turn, is thought to generate a more productive and skilled workforce and thereby expand economic growth.[36] Lastly, the "Lijphart thesis" suggests that the type of constitutional arrangement conditions any economic effects arising from democracy. Along similar lines, Persson and Tabellini report that constitutions matter for economic performance; thus presidential regimes induce smaller public sectors, while proportional elections lead to greater and less targeted government spending and larger budget deficits. They find that electoral rules (including proportional representation, district magnitude, and ballot structures) influence both corruption and the structural economic policies facilitating growth.[37] Consensus or power-sharing democracies are also believed to generate stable, moderate, and predictable macroeconomic policies, avoiding the "top-go" abrupt policy reversals of majoritarian regimes.[38] For all these reasons, consensus democracies are expected to demonstrate a superior economic record.

Yet several leading scholars emphasize that the initial process of regime transition from autocracy toward democracy generally hinders, rather than benefits, economic growth. Guillermo O'Donnell argued that the expansion of mass politics in Latin America during the 1960s and 1970s exacerbated instability, stoked inflationary pressures on the state, and raised distributional conflict in the region. By contrast, he suggested that bureaucratic authoritarianism laid the foundation for more stable states and thus for the process of industrialization and economic growth.[39] Democratic governments are believed to be vulnerable to growing demands for redistribution to middle- and lower-income groups, implying higher levels of progressive taxation. Democratic governments may also prove less capable of suppressing social instabilities arising from ethnic, religious, and class struggles. To support their arguments, contemporary statebuilders commonly cite case studies of societies achieving exceptional economic growth despite lacking completely, or even partially, competitive multiparty democratic elections. Singapore and China exemplify the East Asian "authoritarian advantage" model, both experiencing annual growth rates of 9 percent or more during recent decades, leading state-builders to posit a sequential process of "economic development first, democracy second."[40] At the same time, however, as Francis Fukuyama notes, many other autocracies have spectacularly failed to develop, notably the rising poverty and humanitarian disasters experienced under Robert Mugabe in Zimbabwe and under Kim Jong-Il in North Korea.[41] An alternative viewpoint presented by the unified theory at the heart of this book suggests that the debate between democracy-promoters and state-builders involves a false dichotomy and that in fact both democracy and governance should be strengthened simultaneously and in parallel for the most effective economic performance. This chapter therefore reexamines the cross-national time-series evidence concerning the impact of democratic governance on indicators of economic prosperity, and then compares the contrasting cases of Haiti and the Dominican Republic in the Caribbean, twin nations sharing one island, to illustrate the underlying processes at work.

Even if the national economy expands, and even if middle-income sectors benefit, it is by no means guaranteed that this process necessarily trickles down to benefit the poor or disadvantaged sectors of society, thereby "raising all boats" out of extreme poverty and insecurity and thus affecting broader concerns of human development. *Chapter 6* therefore examines the impact of regimes on human development, social equality, poverty, and welfare. Theorists provide many reasons why democracy *should* improve the welfare of the poor. Median voter theory suggests that disadvantaged social sectors are empowered and mobilized through the spread of the universal franchise and freedom of association, thus strengthening public demands for comprehensive welfare services and redistributive economic policies.[42] Democracies provide electoral incentives for elected representatives to respond to social needs and popular demands.[43] In this view, the link between the type of regime and welfare outcomes runs through mechanisms of democratic accountability, where the fate of elected officials ultimately lies with citizens at the ballot box. Consociationalists theorize that not all types of constitutions are similar, however, as power-sharing democracies are more inclusive of all interests in society and thus more likely to generate "kinder, gentler" policy outcomes than majoritarian democracies.[44] For these reasons, compared with autocracies, democracies are expected to produce a more egalitarian distribution of public goods and income and more generous welfare policies, with the result that the poor live longer, healthier, or more productive lives in these states.

If democracy benefits development, all other things being equal, this should be apparent through comparing the performance of democratic and autocratic regimes measured in terms of policy *outputs*, such as levels of public spending on healthcare, education, and social security, as well as through comparing policy *outcomes* on indices such as the Millennium Development Goals (MDGs), including the record of democratic states in reducing infant and child mortality, achieving universal literacy, and expanding longevity. Yet the large body of research that has examined the empirical evidence for the impact of regimes types on levels of social policy spending and developmental outcomes generally reports mixed or inconclusive empirical confirmation of these core claims.[45]

Any effects arising from the regime–welfare relationship may also prove relatively weak compared with fixed structural conditions commonly believed to improve welfare directly, including the role of geography, the impact of internal violence and conflict, environmental degradation, the simple lack of economic resources, or limited access to information and communication technologies. Chapter 6 therefore revisits this long-standing debate by analyzing the record of democratic governance in achieving several of the MDGs, the set of universal targets that the world's governments pledged to achieve by 2015. The chapter also contrasts the paired cases of Botswana and Zambia in Southern Africa to illustrate the underlying processes linking the type of regime to processes of human development.

Chapter 7 turns to examine the influential claim that democracy reduces the dangers of civil war and armed insurrection. Theories focus on issues of grievance, limits on state repression, and the adoption of global norms. Unless regimes are founded on competitive elections meeting international standards, as a minimum, democracy promoters argue, rulers will fail to be regarded as legitimate by citizens, thus fostering enduring grievances, suppressing but not mitigating the deeper causes of conflict. Democracies provide participatory outlets for the expression of discontent, disarming the triggers for extreme violence and coercion and building trust and tolerance. Moreover, some human rights scholars argue that democratic political institutions also reduce the dangers of state repression, preventing a wide range of actions that governments use against their own citizens, ranging from curtailments of fundamental freedoms and the imprisonment of dissidents to outright violence and even genocide.[46] The leaders of democratic states are typically constrained from using violence against their own citizens, especially in power-sharing democracies with multiple checks and balances and separation of powers. These states avoid reckless confrontations or the use of excessive force.[47] Lastly, cultural argument suggests that the predominant norms and values in democratic states emphasize the belief that it is appropriate to use negotiation, bargaining, and compromise, rather than force, to settle internal political disputes.[48] Democratic states are also more likely to be affected by globalization – including the integration of countries into international and regional organizations.[49] This process is thought to bind democratic states to accept international norms, encouraging rulers to resolve internal disagreements through the ballot box rather than the bullet. Violation of these standards also carries the risks of international actions, such as the threat of sanctions by the International Criminal Court or by regional organizations.

State-building theorists dismiss these claims. In particular, Edward D. Mansfield and Jack Snyder provide a strong counterpoint by claiming that the process of transition from autocracy increases, not reduces, the risks of internal conflict and civil war.[50] They argue that elections are particularly risky if held early in any transition process, before the mechanisms of political accountability, institutional checks and balances, and a tolerant culture have had time to develop. In this context, they believe, politicians seeking to mobilize popular support have strong incentive to heighten tribal and nationalistic appeals. Mansfield and Snyder's arguments reflect many of the claims made decades earlier by Huntington, and they are reinforced by several contemporary authors.[51] Yet an attempt to replicate Mansfield and Snyder's evidence and findings concluded that, far from proving robust, the results are heavily contingent on measurement issues.[52] The empirical evidence therefore deserves to be reexamined, especially in deeply divided societies that continue to struggle with this challenge.

IV. Conclusions

Finally, the conclusions presented in Chapter 8 summarize the main findings and consider their implications for understanding the consequences of regime change and for several practical policy interventions that could help the international community to strengthen both democratic governance and human security. Unraveling the complex links among democracy, governance, and human security is not only important for the world of academe, it is also critical for determining policy priorities and thus the agenda within the international development community. The lack of consensus in the research literature limits the practical policy advice that can be offered with any degree of certainty. Hence many general recommendations are made to strengthen the quality of democracy and governance, and a standard menu of reforms has become fairly common.[53] Beyond this abstract level, however, far less accord surrounds what consequences will flow from each and thus how countries should determine developmental priorities to decide which interventions are most urgent and most effective. As Merilee Grindle argues, the "good governance" shopping list is lengthy and ever expanding.[54] For the international community, however, it is vital to understand how far strengthening democratic governance contributes toward many other challenges of human security facing the world. The unified theory developed in this book suggests that, within the limits of fixed structural conditions, regimes combining the institutions of liberal democracy with those strengthening state capacity provide the most successful conditions for responsive and effective states and thus contribute most effectively toward sustainable progress in human security. The empirical evidence provides considerable support for the argument that regimes matter, even with multiple structural controls, although the results presented in each chapter vary across the three dimensions of prosperity, welfare, and peace. Accordingly, the final chapter identifies a range of effective strategies and policies that have been tried and tested in developing societies and that are useful for policy makers struggling to strengthen democratic governance and to improve the living conditions, security, and well-being of citizens.

2

Theories of Regime Effects

This chapter addresses the ongoing debate in the international community about the role of regimes as one of the underlying drivers of human security. Four alternative viewpoints are contrasted: *democracy-promoters*, advocating deepening and consolidating the institutions of liberal democracy and human rights; the *state-building* perspective emphasizing the importance of governance capacity; and the *structural* viewpoint, suggesting that regimes are the product of growth and societal modernization, not the primary cause. By contrast, the *unified theory* developed by this book suggests that the institutions of both liberal democracy and state capacity need to be strengthened in parallel for effective progress in human security. There is nothing particularly novel about any of these claims, which have echoed through the ages. Contemporary debates became more heated following the third wave of democratization and in the context of America's engagement in Iraq and Afghanistan, particularly the efforts of the administrations of President George W. Bush and President Barack Obama to establish strategic goals that could define successful outcomes in these wars. Debate intensified following events in Tunisia, Egypt, Yemen, Syria, Bahrain, and Libya, as the "Arab uprisings" continue to unfold. This issue is central to many long-standing challenges facing the international development community, however, and the ideas have wider resonance beyond any particular contemporary cases.

THE DEBATE ABOUT REGIME EFFECTS

Structural Perspectives

Traditionally most analysts have been highly skeptical about the impact of regimes for processes of human security compared to the influence of structural determinants.[1] For many years, textbook accounts of development emphasized the importance of certain enduring or "fixed" conditions that are believed to affect the capacity of countries to expand their economies, alleviate deep-rooted poverty, and reduce conflict. Thus human security in any society has been thought to benefit from connections to modern communication and information technologies, the distribution of natural resources, the physical terrain and types of agricultural production, access to global markets for trade-led growth, the reservoir of human and physical capital, the existence of internal conflict or interstate wars spilling over from neighboring states, and the role of cultural values. Economists who have examined the empirical evidence have commonly proved skeptical about the significant impact of democracy on growth, detecting neither positive nor negative effects.[2] Similarly, other scholars, such as Michael Ross, doubt whether democracy has the capacity to improve welfare outcomes, such as achieving lower levels of infant, child, and maternal mortality.[3] The debate about the impact of regimes on internal violent conflict and civil wars still remains unresolved.[4]

Moreover, even where a correlation is established linking regimes with certain developmental indices, interpreting the direction of causality can be tricky. Regimes have long been regarded as a *product* of structural conditions, not an independent cause; the "Lipset thesis" suggests that democratization is due to societal modernization, not the reverse. This perspective derives from Seymour Martin Lipset's seminal work on the social requisites of democracy, published in 1959, which suggests a sequential developmental process. Processes of industrialization, the expansion of literacy and education, urbanization, rising living standards, and the growth of the professional middle class, Lipset argued, lay the social foundations for subsequent processes of democratization. These social conditions are believed to strengthen the chances that an active civil society will flourish, heterogeneous economies and the diffusion of wealth and power will develop, the educated middle class will act as a buffer between rich and poor, and thus stable democracies will be more likely to persist. In the classic Lipset proposition: "The more well-to-do a nation, the greater the chances that it will *sustain* democracy."[5] Lipset acknowledged that poorer countries could still be democratic, as exemplified by the cases of Costa Rica, India, and Botswana. Social conditions generate probabilities, not universal laws. Nevertheless, liberal democracy was thought most likely to endure and flourish in wealthier countries. The claim that democracies are likely to persist once they reach a certain level of economic development has been reinforced by the findings of a widely cited study by Adam Przeworski and his colleagues.[6] Despite the renewed emphasis on regimes and state institutions, therefore, in fact many other enduring social conditions may outweigh regime effects.[7]

THEORIES OF DEMOCRACY PROMOTION

During the third wave of democratization, however, the social determinism underpinning early modernization theories gradually fell out of fashion. During the late 1980s and early 1990s, many lower- and middle-income countries saw the ending of decades or even centuries of repressive autocracy based on military dictatorships (in Chile), one-party states (in Russia), elite control (in South Africa), and strongman rule (in the Philippines) and their replacement by governments coming to power through multiparty elections. In these circumstances, it seemed politically unacceptable, or even foolhardy and churlish, to advise reformers to wait cautiously until "the conditions were right" before realistically seeking to build democratic regimes in poorer societies such as Mali and Ghana. Instead, the international community sought to support and strengthen fledgling democratization movements, providing technical assistance and developing local capacity for elections, parliaments, and civil society organizations, even under inhospitable conditions, such as in Afghanistan and Iraq. The Lipset thesis continues to shape contemporary thinking, however, reflected in the assumption that successful regime transitions from autocracy, and the subsequent processes of democratization, are most likely to succeed in emerging economies while often struggling to take root in the poorest developing societies.

During the last two decades, it has become increasingly common for the international community and for scholarly research to emphasize the impact of "institutions" on human security, referring to the formal procedures and informal social norms that govern human behavior. "Formal" rules include the constitutional framework in each state, as embodied in founding documents and basic laws. These are buttressed by legal statutes, customary codes of conduct, and administrative procedures, authorized by law, enforceable by courts, and reinforced by cultural norms. It is neither necessary nor sufficient for institutions to be embodied in law to be effective; social norms, informal patterns of behavior, and cultural values also create mutual expectations among political actors. Studies have focused attention on formal rules as these represent the core instruments of public policy interventions, open to reform and amendment by the political process, whether by legislation, executive order, constitutional revision, administrative decision, judicial judgment, or bureaucratic decree.[8] Although there is a "gray" overlapping area, by contrast cultural norms are altered gradually by informal mechanisms, such as social pressures, media campaigns, and processes of value change located largely outside of the formal political arena.

Within this general conceptual framework, alternative theories posit several diverse reasons why specific formal institutions are expected to matter for human security; hence many economists have emphasized the importance of rule of law, anticorruption measures, and property rights for economic growth.[9] Political scientists have repeatedly stressed the role of left-wing political parties representing urban labor and the rural poor; trade union organizations; and working-class mobilization for redistributive taxation policies, welfare states, and social policy spending.[10] Similarly, international relations scholars have commonly highlighted the role of executive constraints in democratic states for curtailing the headlong rush to war.[11] But theorists differ in a long-standing debate about the underlying mechanisms connecting the type of regime to development.

The most influential perspective about the role of democratic institutions, generating an enormous literature over the years, derives from theories emphasizing that the accountability and transparency flowing from democratic practices have the potential capacity to cure many of the world's ills, ranging from poverty, economic growth, and social inequality to problems of corruption, minority rights, conflict, and insecurity. Where citizens have a voice in determining their own affairs and holding leaders to account, democratic theory suggests, then policies will reflect social needs. Michael McFaul provides a forthright and unambiguous summary of these kinds of claims when arguing that American foreign policy needs to be fully committed to democracy promotion abroad, holding elections and strengthening civil society even under challenging circumstances:

> As a system of government, democracy has clear advantages over other kinds of regimes. Democracies represent the will of the people and constrain the power of the state. They avoid the worst kinds of economic disasters, such as famine, and the political horrors, such as genocide, that occur in autocracies. On average, democracies also produce economic development just as well as other forms of government. Democracies also tend to provide for more stable government and more peaceful relations with other states compared to other regime types. Finally, most people in the world want democracy.[12]

Nor is this statement an isolated view; similar claims are echoed by Joseph T. Siegle, Michael M. Weinstein, and Morton H. Halperin, who conclude that democratic regimes have overwhelming instrumental advantages for developing societies:

> Poor democracies have grown as fast as poor autocracies and they have significantly outperformed the latter on most indicators of social well-being. They have also done better at avoiding catastrophes. Development can also be measured by social indicators such as life expectancy, access to clean drinking water, literacy rates, agricultural yields, and the quality of public health services. On nearly all these quality-of-life measures, low-income democracies dramatically outdo their autocratic counterparts.[13]

If human security is understood more broadly, in terms of internal conflict and interstate war as well, it is a commonly held belief that democratic states generate an important "peace dividend" at home and abroad. International relations scholars claim that democracies are unlikely to fight each other. One of the most widely cited studies, by Bruce Russett, argues that the spread of the democratic peace occurred toward the end of the nineteenth century, and this pattern has been enduring ever since then: "There are no clear-cut cases of sovereign stable democracies waging war with each other in the modern international system."[14] Moreover, Christian Davenport suggests that democracies prevent the excesses of domestic repression and abuses of human rights directed against their own citizens, such as minority groups.[15] Arend Lijphart has long emphasized that power-sharing democracies, in particular, are essential for peaceful accommodation and stability in deeply divided communities.[16]

How does democracy generate these beneficial consequences? Commentators differ on the relative importance of different institutions.

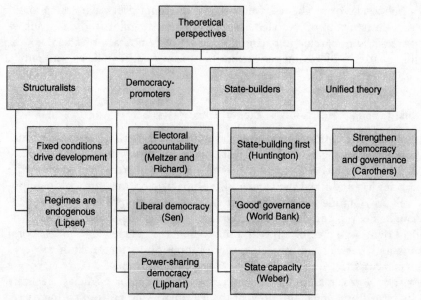

FIGURE 2.1. Perspectives and seminal thinkers within the theoretical debate.

Alternative perspectives include theories focused on electoral accountability (the A. H. Meltzer and S. F. Richard thesis), the broader panoply of liberal democratic institutions (the Amartya Sen thesis), and the role of power-sharing arrangements (the Lijphart thesis). Each view, associated with a seminal theory, is depicted schematically in Figure 2.1.

Electoral Incentives and Median Voter Theory: Meltzer and Richard

For scholars adopting a minimalist or Schumpeterian notion of representative democracy, periodic competitive multiparty elections, which meet international standards for integrity, are the key accountability mechanism. These institutions let citizens exercise choice over their leaders and, where necessary, throw them out.[17] Working within this perspective, Meltzer and Richard offered one of the most influential and widely cited arguments, based on median voter theory, emphasizing the importance of elections for social and economic equality.[18] Where there are multiparty elections and a universal franchise, Meltzer and Richard predict that the pressures to appeal to the median voter will favor politicians and parties advocating income redistribution, progressive taxation, and welfare spending, as well as those demonstrating a superior track record of delivering public goods and services. They reason that in countries with a highly skewed income distribution, the median voter will earn less than the mean income. Politicians in democratic states with genuinely competitive multiparty contests therefore have a strong electoral incentive to adopt policies favoring the less well-off (although not necessarily the poor) if they seek to return to office. Median voter theory has influenced much subsequent scholarly research comparing the impact of democracy on social goods, including patterns of income redistribution, social welfare policies, and public spending.[19]

The Institutional Constraints of Liberal Democracy: Sen

Meltzer and Richard's theory was developed within the context of long-established democracies, and thus rests on assumptions about the existence of a broader framework of political rights and civil liberties. Yet today many autocracies have adopted the façade of multiparty elections but with manipulated results violating the principles of electoral integrity.[20] Electoral competition can be uneven and deeply flawed due to practices that fail to respect basic political rights and civil liberties and undermine the independence of electoral commissions, restrict ballot access, repress opposition forces, limit fair and balanced access to campaign finance resources, disenfranchise citizens, coerce voters, buy votes, manipulate election rules, limit campaign news, generate fraudulent ballot counts, and prevent the legitimate victors from taking office. Where electoral competition is restricted through these practices, this limits the capacity of citizens to monitor and evaluate government performance, to mobilize and organize, to learn from alternative sources of information, and to replace failing leaders with an alternative team. Elections, even under these imperfect conditions, still provide opportunities for opposition forces to mobilize and thus for advances in human rights and democratic practices.[21] But elections alone are insufficient for government accountability without the broader institutions of liberal democracy.

Moreover, developmental theorists argue that elections need to be supplemented by a range of checks and balances counteracting executive power within a framework safeguarding political rights and civil liberties. Sen's work exemplifies this position when emphasizing that in liberal democracies such as India, the threat of electoral defeat gives elected officials a strong incentive to be responsive to citizens, but the independent media are an essential part of this process. Political leaders become more informed about urgent social needs, he argues, where reporters provide extensive coverage of news stories about humanitarian crisis and natural disasters, such as problems of local crop failure, draught or floods, health emergencies, or environmental problems. If politicians fail to respond to urgent local needs, under conditions of electoral competition and transparency, public dissatisfaction expressed at the ballot box can lead to their removal from power. In this context, elected officials have every reason to seek to avoid preventable humanitarian catastrophes, such as by distributing supplies to mitigate periods of food shortage.[22] By contrast to India, Sen observes, famines have occurred far more frequently, and with more disastrous consequences, in countries such as China, where public officials face no such electoral sanction.[23] It follows that states need elections plus other democratic mechanisms to ensure leadership accountability and government responsiveness to social priorities.

Consensus or Power-Sharing Democracy: Lijphart

Alternative theories based on ideas of "consociational" or "consensus" democracy, long championed by Arend Lijphart, emphasize that power-sharing arrangements in democratic states are critical both for welfare and for peace.[24] Power-sharing democracies are characterized by multiple democratic checks and balances designed to ensure that power is widely dispersed vertically and horizontally, typified by the adoption of proportional representation electoral systems, decentralized and devolved governance, and prime ministerial executives accountable to parliament. This type of regime is typified by countries such as Switzerland and Belgium, and it is regarded as the polar opposite of "majoritarian," "Westminster," or power-concentrating regimes. According to Lijphart, by incorporating and empowering a diverse range of interests, power-sharing democracies generate "kinder, gentler" policy outcomes, including producing more egalitarian economic policies and more generous welfare states.[25] Empirical evidence provides some support for these claims; political institutions such as types of electoral systems, executives, and federalism have been found to influence economic performance, including levels of growth, taxation, and public spending.[26] Consociational theory has also long claimed that power-sharing constitutional settlements serve to dampen down armed conflicts in deeply divided multi-ethnic societies and thereby produce durable peace settlements, political stability, and the conditions under which sustainable development and growth flourish.[27]

To summarize, therefore, democratic theories suggest that desirable goals for human security, including prosperity, welfare, and peace, are most likely to be achieved where citizens can hold their governments to account and thus make leaders responsive to social needs. Theorists differ in their interpretation of the underlying mechanisms through which this process is thought to work, whether (i) (for minimalists) through the mechanisms of competitive elections alone (the Meltzer and Richard thesis); (ii) through elections that are buttressed by other strong and effective democratic institutions (the Sen thesis); or (iii) through power-sharing arrangements that disperse decision making widely among multiple interests (the Lijphart thesis). There are no absolute guarantees that any of these mechanisms will work; transitions from autocracy are risky and uncertain processes, just like attempts at peace building. Without any of these institutional safeguards, however, democratic theorists emphasize that venal, incompetent, or self-serving autocrats remain unaccountable. Without the risk of immense bloodshed, or even civil war, it remains difficult, or impossible, for citizens to rid themselves of repressive leaders such as Alexander Lukashenko in Belarus, Bashar al-Assad in Syria, or Muammar Gaddafi in Libya. Thus there is no effective institutional incentive for autocratic leaders to serve and protect the public interest.

OR STATE-BUILDING FIRST?

Yet the beneficial consequences of democracy promotion have long been challenged by alternative theories emphasizing the pragmatic need for sequential
development. The "state-building" school also contains a broad and diverse
group of thinkers and draws on different disciplines in economics, international
relations, and comparative politics. The common view among scholars who
share this perspective is the assumption that effective development requires a
series of strategic steps, although theorists within this school of thought also
differ in their view about the underlying institutional mechanisms: whether
emphasizing that development requires either (i) well-functioning states capable of maintaining order and security against internal and external threat (the
Huntington thesis); (ii) classical liberal modern notions of "good governance,"
especially property rights and rule of law (the World Bank); or (iii) Weberian
notions of state capacity, especially the quality of bureaucratic governance.
These alternative perspectives are also depicted schematically in Figure 2.1.
Only further down the road, once these initial preconditions are met, commentators suggest, should societies seek transition to the next stage by developing
democratic regimes.

State-Building: The Huntington Thesis

Ideas of state-building have become fashionable again in American foreign
policy circles and in Bretton Woods institutions such as the World Bank. The
intellectual roots of these ideas within contemporary political science can be
traced back to the original arguments of Samuel P. Huntington in his 1968
work *Political Order in Changing Societies*.[28] Huntington's account was seared
by the experience of decolonization during the late 1950s and early 1960s and
the failure of the institutions of representative democracy to take firm root
when transplanted into many newly independent developing societies, such as
in many former British and French colonies in West and East Africa. He was
also challenging early theories of modernization, put forward by leading scholars such as Lucian Pye, Edward Shils, and Daniel Lerner, which had assumed
that the process of industrialization, the expansion of mass democracy, and the
growth of the modern bureaucratic state could occur simultaneously in many
developing societies.[29] Yet if social mobilization outpaced the establishment
of democratic institutions and processes of industrial growth, Huntington
cautioned, this raised the risks of social disorder, insurgency movements, and
fragile regimes. Thus he predicted that newly independent postcolonial states
would be destabilized by "premature" increases in mass participation, typically
by mobilizing new groups and holding elections early in any regime transition
process. In support, his study cited the history of growing political instability
during the 1950s and 1960s, including a series of coups d'états experienced
throughout Latin America; revolutionary violence, insurrection, and guerrilla
warfare in Indonesia, Thailand, and the Philippines; and ethnic tensions or

communal violence in Nigeria, Burundi, and Sudan. What caused this violence and instability? Huntington blamed the rapid mobilization of new groups into politics coupled with the slow development of political institutions: "Social and economic change ... extend political consciousness, multiply political demands, broaden political participation. These changes undermine traditional sources of political authority and traditional political institution."[30] The result is anarchy. Instead, Huntington recommended that regimes should first establish the foundation of legitimate authority, social order, and rule of law by modernizing authoritarianism, as exemplified by leaders such as Lee Kwan Yew in Singapore, Park Chung-Hee in Korea, or Suharto in Indonesia. Once these foundations were stable, he argued, countries would be ready for the expansion of mass participation.

Contemporary debate about the Huntington state-building thesis revived again during the mid-2000s, following the experience of the Bush administration's efforts at democracy-promotion in post-Saddam Iraq and in Afghanistan under President Hamid Karzai. Troubled by continued violence and instability in these countries, several thinkers within international relations have argued that enthusiasm for democracy-promotion should be tempered by other considerations. Most commentators do not question the normative claims about the importance of democracy for human rights; rather, they usually share these liberal values, but they believe that the most effective way to achieve these long-term goals is indirect. Echoing Huntington, sequentialist theories suggest that the international community needs to establish the foundations of a well-functioning state in countries afflicted with deep-rooted conflict before rushing headlong into elections. "Premature" democratic experiments before the conditions are ripe, in this view, are, at best, irrelevant and, at worst, dangerous and costly. This perspective has been forcefully expressed by diverse commentators; hence the journalist Robert Kaplan articulated many reasons for pessimism about democracy-promotion, arguing that population increases, urbanization, and resource depletion were undermining fragile governments in West Africa and Asia.[31] Fareed Zakaria expressed concern about the election of a new generation of autocrats, suppressing human rights in countries as diverse as Peru, Kazakstan, and the Philippines, and establishing "illiberal democracies."[32] In a long series of articles, Edward Mansfield and Jack Snyder warn that instead of benefiting from a peace dividend, democratizing states in the process of transition are far more susceptible to ethnic conflict, through the encouragement of nationalist rhetoric in the pursuit of popular electoral support.[33] Reflecting on the international community's peace-building record in Haiti, Cambodia, and Bosnia, Francis Fukuyama argued that important trade-offs exist between governance and democracy. In particular, state-building in multicultural societies often requires authorities to use force to disarm militia and to establish legitimate control over national territorial borders. By contrast, liberal democracies constrain the power of the central authorities. If elections are held prior to the completion of this process, Fukuyama claims, then internal conflicts may be frozen, prolonging instability.[34] Similarly, Simon Chesterman analyzed the history of internationally run transitional administrations, arguing that peace-builders had not devoted sufficient attention to the process of building sustainable institutions, such as the need for effective law enforcement and a judicial system in Bosnia and Kosovo.[35] Moreover, a popular book by Amy Chu argued that the pursuit of democracy and market reform in countries with predominant minorities is destabilizing because it encourages ethnic conflict.[36] Similar claims also echo in the rhetoric surrounding American foreign policy; for example, in August 2010 the Obama administration signaled retreat from the more muscular attempts at promoting democracy in Afghanistan, adopting the more modest strategic goals of fighting al Qaeda terrorists operating in the region.

Thus commentators differ in many important regards, but many believe that the most effective and coherent strategy for peace builders is to follow a step-by-step sequential process, where the first priority in many societies that have long experienced instability and conflict is state-building and establishing effective governance. The recipe calls for stamping out malfeasance and corruption, disorder and chaos, through demobilizing warring factions and private militia, strengthening police and the courts, training and professionalizing the civil service, building an effective central and local state, and deregulating the state-controlled economy. Once the foundations of order and security are established in any society, then, it is hoped, this will be followed eventually by stable processes of societal development, economic growth, and democratic elections.

"Good Governance" for Human Development: The World Bank Thesis

Moreover, these ideas are not simply confined to the concern about security within international relations and applied to the major postconflict peace-building operations led by the United Nations in cases such as Sudan, Cote d'Ivoire, Burundi, and Afghanistan. Instead, the related claim is that "good governance" is essential for improving economic growth and poverty alleviation has now become pervasive throughout the international community; in the words of Kofi Annan, secretary-general of the United Nations, "Good governance is perhaps the single most important factor in eradicating poverty and promoting development."[37] This is a relatively new concern, however; during the 1980s and early 1990s, global financial institutions pushed for a minimal role for the state in the drive for unfettered markets, regarded as the route to economic efficiency. During this era, the standard "Washington Consensus" promoted free markets through privatization and deregulation, fiscal austerity and disinflationary policies, tax reform, trade liberalization, currency devaluation, and open labor markets.[38] These policies were designed to shrink the scope and role of the central government, thereby dispersing state powers to a wide range of actors within the local community, the private sector, and civil society. During the mid-1990s, however, the intellectual tide gradually turned against the first-generation Washington Consensus, and radical structural adjustment nostrums became less fashionable. Many Latin American countries, which had adopted the liberalization policies recommended by the Washington Consensus, experienced high or growing problems of inequality during the 1990s while failing to achieve sustained economic growth.[39] Neoconservative free-market ideas were further undermined during this era by the Asian economic crisis in 1997–8, by trenchant criticism from neo-Keynesian economists such as the Nobel Prize winner Joseph Stiglitz, and by political pressures from the antiglobalization movement.[40]

During the last decade, this shift in philosophy gradually led to the "augmented" Washington Consensus championed by the Bretton Woods institution of global finance.[41] This added several "second-generation" prescriptions to the original list, including prescriptions for "good governance."[42] It was argued that national governments that reflect these principles function as an effective partner for development by managing the delivery of public goods and services and regulating the market economy.[43] The augmented Washington Consensus emphasizes the importance of establishing rule of law as a precondition for effective development, including access to justice, an independent judiciary, and professionally trained security forces. Rule of law is thought to facilitate economic growth by encouraging social stability, legal contract compliance, and business confidence, and thus attracting international investment.[44] Similarly, James Wolfensohn's leadership at the World Bank prioritized integrity, transparency, and lack of corruption in the public sector, to ensure that aid improves public goods and services and thus reaches poor people rather than ending up in the pockets of political and economic elites. Democracy has sometimes been regarded as one necessary component of "good governance," among others, but most agencies have treated these components as separate and distinct phenomenon.[45] Regional multilateral organizations also came to reflect these changing priorities, including the European Union, the African Union, and the Latin American Development Bank, as well as bilateral donors. Government transparency and accountability have also been championed by an array of NGOs, notably Transparency International, the Global Integrity Project, and the Rights to Information movement.[46]

Bureaucratic Capacity

"Good governance" remains an ambiguous notion, however, and it does not necessarily need to reflect classical liberal assumptions about the limited role for the state. Within public administration, a long tradition has theorized that the expansion of state capacity is critical for achieving many developmental objectives, whether through sound economic management, the provision of basic public goods and services, or maintenance of domestic security. Thus in this view development is thought to be hindered if states lack technical capacity, impartial processes of decision making, and a clear process of professional career advancement in the civil service in central and local government; if the justice system has inadequate legal training for judges and lawyers; or if

ministers and elected politicians are unable to implement practical solutions
to meet societal needs. The "good governance" thesis from the Weberian perspective emphasizes that well-functioning states – implicitly those that meet
standards of impartiality, effectiveness, legality, efficiency, transparency, and
integrity – are a more effective national partner for international developmental agencies. To examine the evidence, a pioneering study of the quality of
bureaucratic governance was developed by Peter Evans and J. E. Rauch based
on expert assessments of meritocratic recruitment and predictable career ladders in the public sector. The survey gathered data during the early 1990s in
around three dozen middle- and low-income countries.[47] Evans and Rauch
analyzed the links between the quality of bureaucratic governance and economic growth, concluding that in the selected countries under comparison,
state bureaucracies characterized by meritocratic recruitment and rewarding
career ladders generated higher rates of economic growth. More recently, Bo
Rothstein has examined the impact of the quality of government, conceptualized in terms of the concept of impartiality, on several diverse variables,
including institutional trust, economic growth, corruption, welfare outcomes,
and life satisfaction.[48] Therefore, the claim that bureaucratic state capacity is
important for human security is often heard, although evidence supporting this
view has still not been widely demonstrated. The "good governance" agenda
proposed by these commentators has been framed in terms of emphasizing (i)
state-building (the Huntington thesis) by those agencies concerned with peace
building; (ii) classical liberal notions of "good governance," emphasizing private property rights and rule of law, by those seeking economic development,
growth, and prosperity (termed here the World Bank thesis); or (iii) Weberian
concepts of state capacity, impartiality, and the quality of bureaucratic governance (termed the Weberian thesis).

THE COMBINATION OF DEMOCRACY + GOVERNANCE

The democracy-promotion and state-building viewpoints offer persuasive
reasons that regimes should have important consequences for development.
Nevertheless, an alternative perspective developed in this study suggests that
each provides only partial insights. A unified theory is needed to provide a
more holistic and comprehensive view. Some have acknowledged the need
to combine these dimensions; for example, when debating with Fukuyama,
Thomas Carothers has suggested that the process of gradually strengthening
democracy needs to accompany state-building initiatives, recognizing that both
components are necessary for successful development.[49] Nevertheless, the analysis of systematic evidence supporting this view has been unduly neglected.
The terms "democracy" and "governance" are also often employed so loosely
in practical language that it is widely assumed that these separate and distinct
phenomena are, in fact, the same thing; an example is where it is thought a pri-
ori that "good governance" must necessarily reflect the values and principles
of liberal democracy.[50] The division of labor among different disciplines in

the research literature has also encouraged an intellectual schism; scholars of public administration and management have commonly regarded the issue of the effective delivery of public goods and services as their bailiwick. By contrast, international relations scholars have focused on the capacity of the state in terms of military security and the prevention of interstate and civil conflict. Similarly, developmental economists have emphasized the effects of governance on prosperity, including the role of property rights. By contrast, academics in comparative politics have long placed processes of democratization and regime transitions at the heart of their subfield. The disciplinary divisions are not iron-clad, as academic subfields certainly overlap, but specialization within the social sciences has commonly reinforced intellectual rifts.

Unfortunately, this division is also reflected in the work of many organizations within the international community; hence the agencies of the global economy, exemplified by the World Bank and International Monetary Fund (IMF), as well as Transparency International and the Global Integrity Project, have commonly devoted their energies to promoting "good governance." Many other agencies have also focused their mission primarily on strengthening democratic institutions and processes, as exemplified by the International Foundation for Electoral Systems (IFES) and International IDEA's work improving electoral processes and management, the efforts of Amnesty International and Human Rights Watch to bolster human rights, and the Open Society Institute's programs designed to expand civil society and the role of the independent media. Too few development agencies have sought to span the gulf by investing in both dimensions of democratic governance, although there are some notable exceptions, exemplified by the United Nations Development Programme, the U.S. Agency for International Development, and the UK's Department for International Development (DFID).

Rather than presenting a false choice between democracy and governance, therefore, the core argument at the heart of this book suggests that a more integrated synoptic approach and a unified theory that understands the need for both democracy and governance are likely to pay dividends. The book posits that development is most often achieved and sustained in societies where the formal institutions of both liberal democracy and bureaucratic governance are simultaneously strengthened in parallel.

To help understand the basis for this claim, Figure 2.2 illustrates the standard sequential stages identified in the policy-making process. The schematic figure draws loosely on systems models developed in the 1960s by David Easton, as well as the idea of distinct steps in the public policy-making cycle, developed by John Kingdon, Thomas Dye, and many other scholars.[51] The standard policy-making model is useful for highlighting the underlying reasons why either electoral accountability or improvements in good governance, alone, are expected to be insufficient for achieving developmental outcomes. The cyclical model identifies multiple actors as players in a sequential policy-making process, illustrated in Figure 2.2, with several distinct sequential steps: (i) the *agenda-setting* stage in the public sphere, engaging the public, political parties, the media, and NGOs,

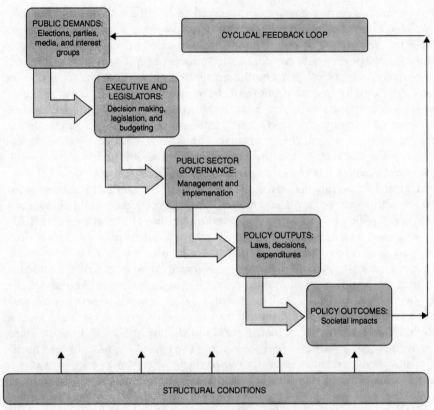

FIGURE 2.2. Sequential stages in the policy-making process.

which heightens the salience of the key problems to be addressed on the policy agenda; (ii) the *policy-making* stage in the state, where policy options are formulated, coalitions are built, and policies are adopted to address these perceived problems, directly engaging decisions by actors in the legislature and the executive; (iii) the *implementation* stage, where policies are put into practice, involving public sector bodies; (iv) policy outputs, reflecting the decisions, regulations, and expenditures made by governing bodies; (v) the policy outcomes, representing the social impacts of these decisions; and, finally, (vi) the *feedback* evaluation loop, when learning about the consequences of public policies shapes either satisfaction with the status quo or further demands for subsequent actions. All this activity is understood to occur within a broader environment in each country, including the role of path-dependent historical traditions, the social structure and culture, and the economic structure. This cycle regards the policy-making process as a series of activities – involving problem identification, agenda setting, formulation, legitimation, implementation, evaluation, and feedback.

The general model is sufficiently flexible to apply to any major dimension of public policy making, rather than generating *sui generis* explanations of development, while recognizing significant factors common to diverse contexts. It also has the advantage of identifying a more comprehensive range of actors and a broader series of stages than accounts of liberal democracy that focus solely on the role of electoral accountability or than accounts of good governance that focus only on the capacity, integrity, or impartiality of the public sector. The model remains agnostic, however, about the precise impact of each type of actor in the policy-making process – for example, the relative weight of the public, NGOs, and the news media in agenda-setting, and whether economic elites or international agencies influence the legislature and executive. The process of determining priorities that need to be addressed by the state starts in this model with the perception of social problems, generating public demands on the regime, whether articulated through elections (in liberal democracies with competitive multiparty contests) or channeled through the other institutions that are part of the complex agenda-setting process in any regime, including political parties, the mass media, and organized groups. Demands on the regime are directed toward the core executive, legislative, and judicial bodies, the authorities responsible for processes of policy making, legislation, and the allocation of resources. The institutions of liberal democracy are designed to expand the opportunities for public participation, strengthening the accountability of elected officials to all citizens, as well as providing checks and balances among the branches of government that limit the autonomy of the core executive. But the core executive and legislative officials can implement decisions only through public sector governance, thus the effectiveness and efficiency of the policy-making process depend on the capacity of the public sector to manage resources and oversee the delivery of public goods and services. In turn, policy outputs will ultimately affect societal outcomes and the achievement of developmental goals, making a difference to citizens' living standards, welfare, and security. Perceptions of how well policies work are expected to feed back into perceptions of social problems, shaping subsequent public demands in a cyclical process. In addition, the policy process does not work in an isolated bubble; instead, it occurs within the complex set of constraints and opportunities set by enduring structural conditions within each society, including the reservoir of resources available to each state from economic development; natural resources; human and physical capital; the integration of states into global and regional networks; the types of social and ethnic cleavages that divide communities within national borders; and the path-dependent legacies of historical, cultural, and colonial traditions.

Within this policy process, the most common and recognizable feature of liberal democracy is the holding of competitive multiparty elections. These contests are now a standard component in negotiated settlements for divided societies emerging from conflict, as part of the international peace-building process.[52] Yet this strategy ultimately elects governments to fail, and thus has the capacity to spread long-term public discontent with the regime, or even disillusionment with liberal democracy, in states where regime authorities lack the governance capacity to implement effective public policies that can improve the lives of their citizens. Many weak states have rulers who lack the ability to manage basic public services. It is potentially problematic to expand the institutions of representative democracy, which facilitate the expression and mobilization of citizens' demands, in states where regimes lack basic governance capacity.

This does not imply that efforts by the international community to strengthen liberal democracy should be downplayed by any means, for example, where state-building is prioritized and there are delays or the postponement of competitive elections and political reforms to executive legislative bodies. It is equally – or perhaps even more – inappropriate to expand regime capacity – for example, by strengthening the public sector bureaucracy, bolstering tax collection agencies, or equipping the security forces – without first establishing the accountability mechanisms and safeguards over executive power provided by liberal democratic institutions. Once installed securely in office, autocracies may prove benevolent, because of ideological commitments to serve the public interest and improve the lives of citizens. But there is no guarantee whatsoever that these rulers will necessarily subsequently relinquish power voluntarily; indeed, based on past experience, there is every expectation that they will not. Transitions from autocracy may fail to lead toward stable democratic regimes, but this does not mean that they should not be attempted. The history of democratization in Western Europe was one of erratic and uncertain steps, with many false starts and regressions, rather than trajectories showing steady linear progress.[53] Waiting for "ideal" timing may be naïve and foolish. Instead, the thesis suggests that the core challenge for reformers is to strike a careful and delicate balance between *simultaneously* strengthening both the institutions of liberal democracy *and* public sector governance in tandem. The idea that these dimensions are most effective when developed in parallel is an extremely simple proposition, especially when understood in a unified theory as sequential steps in the policy process, yet this notion is commonly underestimated, or overlooked, both by scholars and practitioners.

To develop these ideas further, Figure 2.3 illustrates the basic analytical regime typology used in this book, as expanded and measured in the next chapter. The theoretical framework is based on the proposition that development will be advanced most effectively under two conditions: first, in nation-states where liberal democratic institutions strengthen voice and accountability (depicted schematically on the horizontal axis), so that all citizens have the capacity to express their demands and to hold elected officials to account; and, secondly, in nation-states where bureaucratic governance is strengthened (on the vertical axis), so that regime authorities have the capacity to implement policies, including maintaining security, raising public revenues, and managing the delivery of public goods and services. Expanding either the demands of democracy or the supply of governance alone is regarded as insufficient; instead, the combination of both factors working in tandem is predicted to provide the conditions most conducive to prosperity, welfare, and peace. The next chapter operationalizes both dimensions of the conceptual framework, classifying and

		DEMOCRACY	
		RESTRICTED VOICE AND ACCOUNTABILITY	INCLUSIVE VOICE AND ACCOUNTABILITY
GOVERNANCE	EXPANDED CAPACITY	Bureaucratic autocracies (Mixed performance)	**Bureaucratic democracies (Most effective performance)**
	LIMITED CAPACITY	**Patronage autocracies (Least effective performance)**	Patronage democracies (Mixed performance)

FIGURE 2.3. Regime typology in equilibrium theory.

comparing regimes worldwide and over time. To test these core propositions, subsequent chapters in Part II analyze cross-national time-series evidence, as well as examining specific cases, drawn from many countries around the globe during the third wave era. In fact, as we shall observe, there is no linear relationship between liberal democracy and bureaucratic governance; instead, in many contemporary regimes, democracy has advanced ahead of governance, while elsewhere in other countries, governance capacity has expanded more than democracy.

CONCLUSIONS

Debate about the most important route to development continues, with divisions among structural theories doubting the independent effects of regimes, others emphasizing state-building and good governance, and those scholars advocating establishing the institutions of democracy. By contrast, theory in this book suggests that the central issue is not about choosing between liberal democracy and elections *or* state-building and good governance, but instead how practical steps toward democracy and governance should be timed, sequenced, and combined in parallel. Rival accounts can be analyzed and tested to see whether this theory provides the best fit to the evidence concerning the predicted links between regimes and development. Establishing convincing proof remains challenging, however, both theoretically and empirically. The next chapter turns to defining and operationalizing the core concepts, developing the regime typology, applying the classification to regimes worldwide, and illustrating the ideas through selected case studies.

PART II

COMPARING REGIMES

3

The Regime Typology

The unified theory outlined in the previous chapter predicts that human security will be advanced most effectively where inclusive and effective democratic institutions and procedures empower all citizens, so that they can express their demands and hold elected officials accountable for their actions, and, secondly, where state capacity is strengthened, so that the regime authorities can implement their policies and respond to public demands, including managing security, tax revenues, and the supply of public goods and services. It is argued that strengthening either liberal democracy or state capacity alone is insufficient; instead, it is proposed that the combination of both factors will provide the conditions most likely to generate effective and durable development outcomes, defined here in terms of prosperity, welfare, and internal peace. The next challenge is therefore to unpack these broad concepts, to consider how they can be operationalized, and then to apply the measures to classify regimes around the world and over time.

THE CONCEPT OF GOVERNANCE

To clarify our terms, following the Eastonian conception of a political system, three levels can be distinguished: the nation, the regime, and the incumbent authorities.[1] The *nation-state* represents the community to which people belong. The *regime* constitutes the basic framework for governing the nation-state within its territorial boundaries. This includes the overarching constitutional arrangements and the core government institutions at national, regional, and local levels, reflecting the formal and informal rules of the game. Lastly, the *authorities* represent the elected and appointed actors holding office and the key decision makers in the public sector. Of these elements, nation-states are the most stable, although they can be dissolved and break up into their component parts, as in the case of Yugoslavia, Czechoslovakia, and Sudan, and new nation-states can succeed them, such as in Timor-Leste. Regimes are moderately durable, although they can also change, whether in response to conquest by an external power, popular revolution, elite coup d'état, or the dissolution of the nation-state, or through processes of reconstruction and peace building, such as a negotiated constitutional settlement following civil war. Regimes also fall into distinct eras, as occurred, for example, with new constitutions introduced in states following the breakdown of the Soviet Union, the downfall of Saddam Hussein's regime in Iraq, or the end of apartheid in South Africa. It is more difficult to classify cases of regime transition where an incremental or evolutionary process gradually modifies major components of the state's existing institutions, as occurred, for example, following the major electoral reform that produced an enduring shift in patterns of party competitions in New Zealand or following the passage of laws expanding the constitutional powers of the executive and abolishing the monarchy in Nepal. In general, however, it requires a wholesale constitutional settlement altering many institutions to produce clear-cut cases of regime change.

How should regime institutions be conceptualized and measured? The idea of "governance" has become intellectually fashionable in recent years, yet this complex notion is open to multiple meanings. Governance is widely understood as more diffuse than simply "government," including a broader range of actors, but scholars differ in their understanding of this term.[2] This book seeks to remain neutral about *what* goals states seek to achieve, and their policies, and thus normative judgments about the most appropriate range, size, or scope of governance. State capacity is also treated as distinct from the effects of the state on society, which the research seeks to establish empirically. Unfortunately, many studies mix all these elements together conceptually, including a long and ever-growing shopping list of qualities.[3] The term "governance" is often modified in recent usage by heavily value-laden but highly abstract terms of approval, notably the World Bank's notion of "good' governance,"[4] as well as vague normative terms of approval, such as the "quality of governance."[5] This kitchen-sink approach is problematic and conceptually muddled, however, since the most appropriate role, functions, size, and scope of the state remain a matter of intense ideological debate, especially the degree of government intervention in economic markets.

This book focuses primarily on state capacity, specifically conceptualized in classical Weberian terms. State capacity determines *how far regime authorities can achieve their goals and perform functions essential for collective well-being,* including maintaining order and security within the nation's territorial boundaries, improving welfare outcomes for its population, and expanding prosperity.[6] This conception closely follows Michael Mann's argument, focusing on the "institutional capacity of a central state ... to penetrate its territories and logistically implement decisions."[7] The broadest function of state capacity concerns protecting the safety and security of citizens through maintaining sovereignty against external threat, exercising a monopoly over the use of military force, and establishing social order. This understanding is consistent with the Weberian definition: "The state is a human community that (successfully) claims the monopoly of the legitimate use of force within its given territory."[8] At the most extreme, the antithesis of "governance" is "anarchy," reflecting concern about "fragile" states, where the governments lack the capacity to maintain order within its territorial boundaries, reflecting the breakdown of central authority. Fragile states, where the regime is persistently challenged through revolutionary insurgencies, political violence, and rival factions, are exemplified by the long-running civil conflicts in Colombia, Sri Lanka, and the Democratic Republic of the Congo. Anarchy is a situation where regime authorities are unable to control military forces or to maintain security and rule of law within their borders, illustrated most dramatically by cases such as the al Shabaab insurgents in Southern Somalia and the Waziristan region in northwest Pakistan. The U.S.-based Political Instability Task Force provides estimates of the number of incidents of instability from 1955–2003, reporting that the highest number of cases occurred in Sub-Saharan Africa, followed by the Middle East and South Asia.[9] In countries in which the state's failure is most extreme, independent movements seeking succession and cultural autonomy, rebel factions, and local warlords or criminal cartels roam freely and without check. Sovereignty and the maintenance of security comprise the most basic form of governance that is essential for any functioning nation-state. Lack of security is clearest in extreme cases such as Somalia, Sierra Leone, and Sudan, where the state is largely ineffective in maintaining sovereignty and exercising the legitimate use of force within its national borders, including preventing rebel incursions. The second dimension of state capacity reflects how far the regime authorities can implement public policies, collect revenues, and manage the delivery of basic goods and services. State capacity can be strong or weak irrespective of whether the delivery of public goods and services is implemented through the public sector, nonprofit civil society organizations, or private sector corporations.

Drawing on Weberian conceptions, we can divide state capacity into two ideal types.[10] *Bureaucratic* forms of governance refer to a particular type of organizational structure, which Weber argued was one of the institutional foundations for capitalist growth and the modern nation-state. Bureaucracies exert control through instrumental forms of legal-rational authority, following the principles of impartiality, effectiveness, efficiency, transparency, and integrity.[11] Legal-rational authority rests in the office, whether the holder is recruited through election or appointment, not personal ties to the individual. Bureaucrats are responsive to elected authorities and yet somewhat autonomous from undue partisan pressures, with established mechanisms for recruitment and training based on formal qualifications and technical expertise. Moreover, meritocratic procedures extend well beyond the core civil service; public sector employees such as teachers, scientists, healthcare officials, and social workers use professional standards involving processes of peer review for accreditation, appointment, and promotion. During the mid- to late-nineteenth century, industrialized nations gradually came to reflect notions of Weberian rational bureaucracy. Just as factory machines gradually replaced craftsmen, bureaucracy was seen as the ideal form of public administration for managing large, complex organizations in modern states. Bureaucracy has been regarded as instrumentally rational and efficient, reflecting the top-down command-and-control way to manage the delivery of organizational goals, just as the production line transformed the manufacturing industry. Bureaucratic rules and regulations, in particular, are designed to ensure that even lowly functionaries follow standardized procedures in each government department, so that all citizens receive equitable treatment. Impartiality is thus a central principle of Weberian bureaucracy, but it is only one of many related characteristics, and thus it should not necessarily be elevated as its defining feature.[12] In the Weberian conception, bureaucracy implies that an efficient, effective, and accountable public sector requires the following characteristics:[13]

- *Meritocratic processes of recruitment, training, and career promotion*: These processes are based on technical qualifications, expertise, and formal education, skills, conduct, experience, and knowledge. Human resource policies are based on open competition and transparency and often administered by independent civil service commissions.
- *Hierarchical and centralized decision-making authority within large-scale organizational structures*: A clear and coordinated chain-of-command links subordinate, politically neutral bureaucratic officials to superior authorities and ultimately to elected politicians, allowing effective processes of government oversight, decision making, and political accountability.
- *Functional specialization*: Officials have clearly specified fixed salaries, pensions, ranks, duties, obligations, roles, and supervisors.
- *Standardized procedures:* Actions are guided by transparent formal and impersonal rules, written regulations, and legal codes designed to provide consistent, equal, and impartial treatment of all citizens and employees, rejecting administration on a case-by-case basis.
- *Strict firewalls separating private and public interests*: Public officials are full-time, salaried career professionals with considerable job security, receiving rewards from their salary, status, and condition of service, not benefiting by financial gain from clients, rent seeking, or personal favors from partisan politicians.

Modern states started to transition into Weberian rational bureaucracies only following reforms in the public sector. A series of developments in European states during the mid- to late-nineteenth century gradually brought elements of bureaucracy into practices of public administration. In Britain, for example, a permanent, unified, meritocratic, and politically neutral civil service was introduced following the Northcote-Trevelyan report of 1854. An independent civil service commission was created by William Gladstone along with a requirement for technical competence for appointment in the public sector. Open competitions for appointment were adopted in the civil service in India in 1853 and became the rule throughout British government in 1870. A similar tide of reform to get rid of the spoils system swept through the post–Civil War United States government; the civil service was established in 1872 and the Pendleton Act (1883) implemented meritocratic appointments and the civil service commission. Although public administration reflects cultural traditions within each society, particularly the legalistic tradition in Continental Europe, parallel reforms were adopted in many other modern states and at subnational levels, reflecting the need to manage the growing size and technical complexity of government activities and to reduce corruption, inefficiency, and malfeasance.[14] Through colonial administrative practices, bureaucratic structures and procedures were also exported to many countries worldwide.

By contrast, there are many other ways of arranging administrative functions and responsibilities in the public sector and implementing public policies. The chief positions can be allocated based on class, caste, ethnicity, or honorary status. The principle antithesis to bureaucracy is conceptualized in this book as *patronage* states, understood as those where leaders gain compliance primarily through the use of personal networks, traditional prerogatives, and social privileges, delivering goods and services selectively to clientalistic groups of loyal supporters. In patronage states, personal relations, social status, nepotism, ad hoc favors, and corruption, rather than merit-based criteria, commonly determine recruitment and promotion processes, while legal, judicial, and administrative agencies are far from impartial and independent of political pressures. Patronage through the allocation of spoils helps rulers gain the loyalty and allegiance of clans, tribes, and followers and also the support of the security forces, and thus maintain control of the general population through threat of force. Patronage relationships essentially emphasize *personal* connections between particular leaders and subjects, or patrons and clients, exemplified by rule by monarchs, sultans, dictators, and emirs, where authority rests in the individual rather than the office.[15] Decision making is not standardized and instead ad hoc rulings are made on a case-by-case basis. Rulers gain compliance directly through the allocation of rewards, reinforcing their personal status, informal social ties, and deference to traditional loyalties, as well as indirectly through use of force and outright repression. Traditional forms of patronage were common in most states during the eighteenth and early-nineteenth centuries, as exemplified in the United Kingdom by the purchase of army commissions and naval and civil service appointments based on personal or family recommendations (rather than by merit, open competition, and formal qualifications), and in the United States by "machine" party politics. Patronage politics can still prove effective for those who directly benefit by personal gain, and the spoils system generates loyalty among followers, but in general it usually undermines the capacity of the public sector to serve the broader public interest; weakens the legitimacy of the authorities; and violates widely accepted norms of integrity, impartiality, transparency, and rule of law. In patronage states where public sector jobs are allocated as a way to reward loyalists or on the basis of kinship ties, the civil service tends to be poorly skilled, underpaid, and politicized. Senior cadres lack professional and technical expertise and often fail to provide any chain of continuity in government decision making over the longer term. As a result, delivery of public services tends to be inefficient, at best, and, at worst, beset by venality and corruption. Problems of patronage politics and lack of administrative capacity are illustrated most vividly today by poor states such as Haiti and Cote D'Ivoire, where the central authorities are incapable of fulfilling core governance functions, such as raising revenues through regulatory tariffs and taxation, providing essential services such as emergency relief and basic healthcare, curbing criminal activities, and policing "no-go" lawless areas. By contrast, during the third wave era, states as diverse as South Korea, the Czech Republic, South Africa, Mauritius, and Brazil have a relatively successful record in maintaining security, expanding national living standards, and improving human development.

Bureaucracy is often seen negatively today, implying organizations characterized by "red tape," inefficiency, and rigid procedural rules, rather than by more flexible agencies that provide incentives for managers to respond effectively to contemporary challenges of governance. Bureaucracy in the public sector has been regarded as old-fashioned and inappropriate for the twenty-first century, compared with the potential advantages of governance by networks or markets and reforms in the public sector associated with the "new" public sector management.[16] The assumption that bureaucracies are the most efficient organizations for governing the modern state has come under growing challenge. It is widely believed that this form of organization suffers from numerous dysfunctional flaws, including excessive rigidity, inflexibility, and lack of innovation in identifying new solutions to complex social challenges. The use of written rules as mechanisms of control has been seen as cumbersome and inefficient (red tape), slowing decisions. The chain-of-command division of responsibilities and the culture of official secrecy has reduced the accountability of subordinate officials for poor performance. Bureaucratic organizations have grown in size and complexity, including in the number and cost of public sector employees. Moreover, bureaucratic structures have rewarded employees based on standardized procedures, fixed rewards, and career promotions, irrespective of their performance in delivering substantive results, thereby generating perverse incentives. By the early 1980s, ideas of performance management became increasingly popular in corporations, involving the construction of new metrics of service quality and customer satisfaction. These doctrines spread to the public sector as well, popularized in books such as David Osborne and Ted Gaebler's *Reinventing Government* (1993).[17] Political leaders sought new ways to limit the growth of public expenditure while also making governance more efficient, flexible, and responsive.

These developments encouraged the rise of *new public management* (NPM), transforming public sector management in leading countries – including the United Kingdom, the United States, New Zealand, and Australia, as well as gradually diffusing to many other societies and types of organizations.[18]

As a general philosophy, moreover, NPM has not yet altered traditional public administration in many European states, such as Germany, Belgium, and France, with an alternative Rechtsstaat tradition and culture of governance, still less transformed than the public sector in most developing nations.[19]

Moreover, the fundamentals of Weberian bureaucratic public administration, in its original meaning, remain essential for governance capacity in much of the developing world. For Max Weber, bureaucratic organizations are understood to reflect the principles and values of impartiality, effectiveness, efficiency, transparency, and integrity, where public policy making has a clear chain of command through processes of legislation, regulation, and budgeting. Administrative law governs civil service procedures and decisions, where individual citizens have transparent processes to appeal against specific bureaucratic decisions. The absence of these qualities is evident in many countries, as exemplified by problems of corruption, maladministration, and malfeasance in the public sector. Even where the appropriate scope of the state is regarded as limited, public sector agencies reflecting these qualities are still needed, for example, to regulate the process of privatization of state assets so that it is transparent, fair, and well managed.

Measuring State Capacity

The Weberian framework thus continues to provide the core concepts to distinguish two ideal types of state capacity. Nevertheless, these concepts are difficult to operationalize empirically, especially for consistent comparison of worldwide patterns and trends over time.

Typically, the capacity of the state to maintain security has often been operationalized by the strength of military personnel, whether measured on a per capita basis, as a proportion of the total labor force, or as a proportion of GDP or total government outlays.[20] Nevertheless, studies have found that these indicators are poorly, or even inversely, correlated with other measures of governance.[21] Not surprisingly, levels of military expenditure may in fact be a proxy for insecurity; states that perceive external or internal threats may well decide to boost spending on the armed forces.

An alternative indicator is government spending on public order and safety (on a per capita basis or as a proportion of total outlays), including expenditure on the police and other law enforcement agencies. This measure is particularly important in lawless regions, where the state lacks the capacity to limit criminal activity, and standardized international data on government outlays for this function are compiled for some countries by the IMF and derived from National Accounts.[22] Yet reliable time-series data are unavailable in many countries, especially many developing societies, and again spending on domestic security could also be expected to rise following a resurgence of criminal activity, exemplified by the Mexican government's war on drug cartels.

Another measure assessing bureaucratic governance is the World Bank's Resource Allocation Index, which estimates the contemporary quality of public administration, based on its annual Country Policy and Institutional Assessment exercise, but data are limited to seventy-six developing countries. The International Monetary Fund has also compiled general and central government revenues and outlays by function, based on standardized data from national accounts.[23] Nevertheless, the IMF data cover few developing countries and, in addition, it cannot be assumed that the size of the state – or, indeed, high government revenues and expenditures – is indicative of state capacity.

A pioneering study of the quality of bureaucratic governance was developed by Peter Evans and J. E. Rauch, based on expert assessments of meritocratic recruitment and predictable career ladders in the public sector. The survey gathered data during the early 1990s in around three dozen middle- and low-income countries.[24] Evans and Rauch analyzed the links between the quality of bureaucratic governance and economic growth, concluding that in the selected countries under comparison, state bureaucracies characterized by meritocratic recruitment and rewarding career ladders generated higher rates of economic growth. This suggests an important proposition, explored further in Chapter 5, but evidence needs to be examined by comparing a far wider range of countries and time periods to have confidence in the robustness of the results. A new cross-national dataset is under development, using expert surveys to measure several dimensions of bureaucracy in over one hundred countries, but unfortunately this is unable to provide comparisons over time.[25]

The most comprehensive geographic and longitudinal coverage that is designed to assess state capacity is available from the Political Risk Service's Group (PRSG) International Country Risk Guide. This series covers more than one hundred nation-states over time, with observations based on expert assessments since 1984. The PRSG indicators have been used in the previous research literature.[26] The PRSG's Quality of Government index combines three components: bureaucratic quality, corruption, and law and order.[27] *Bureaucratic quality* measures how far the country's public sector is characterized by (i) regular processes of meritocratic recruitment and career advancement, (ii) independence from political pressures, and (iii) the ability to provide continuous administrative services during government changes.[28] *Corruption* in the regime is measured by actual or potential corruption from excessive patronage, nepotism, and secret party funding, as well as demands for special payments or bribes in financial transactions with public sector employees. Lastly, *law and order* is assessed by the strength and impartiality of the legal system, including how far there is popular observance of the law or whether the law is routinely ignored without sanction. Thus the conceptual framework and the core components underlying the PRSG's Quality of Government index closely mirror the Weberian distinction between patronage and bureaucratic forms of governance, which are at the heart of this book.[29] This measure lets us classify states worldwide and over time to compare bureaucratic state capacity. Most importantly, the data allow us to investigate whether bureaucratic state capacity is consistently associated with a more effective performance in managing the delivery of public goods and services, exemplified by levels of prosperity, welfare, and peace.

At the same time, it is important to establish whether the results of the analysis are robust or whether they are sensitive to measurement issues. Accordingly, this book compares the PRSG Quality of Governance indicators with several of the World Bank Institute (WBI) "good governance" indices. These provide broader geographic coverage worldwide, although the estimates are only available for a shorter time period, from 1996 to 2009.[30] The World Bank composite indices seek to measure "government effectiveness," "political stability," "rule of law," "voice and accountability," "regulatory quality," and "control of corruption." Several of these indicators can be selected to check the robustness of the findings from the PRSG's Quality of Governance measure.

THE CONCEPT AND MEASUREMENT OF DEMOCRACY

All states require state capacity to maintain security and to implement policy decisions. Only some regimes, however, are governed according to the principles of "liberal democracy." The complex notion of "democracy" is open to multiple conceptualizations and the employment of many alternative modifiers, such as "participatory," "liberal," "social," "direct," "effective," and "deliberative" forms of democracy.[31] Liberal democracy is understood here, most simply, to mean *the capacity of people to influence regime authorities within their nation-state.*[32]

Following the Schumpeterian tradition, minimalist notions of democracy focus on the provision of competitive elections. In this perspective, leaders in democratic regimes are recruited on the basis of free and fair multiparty elections that meet international standards of integrity. Nevertheless, Joseph Schumpeter offers a relatively narrow definition that fails to take account of the many other institutions required to ensure that democratic elections work effectively, including the provision of freedom of expression and respect for civil liberties, checks and balances among the core regime institutions, an independent judiciary, and an effective legislature.[33] Reflecting the long tradition of classical liberal theories, following Robert Dahl's conception, liberal democracy is understood in this book to rest on the principles of contestation, participation, and human rights.[34] Dahl suggested that, in practice, liberal democratic regimes (or "polyarchies") can be identified by the presence of certain key political institutions: (1) elected officials; (2) free and fair elections; (3) inclusive suffrage; (4) the right to run for office; (5) freedom of expression; (6) alternative information; and (7) associational autonomy.[35] Liberal democracies use competitive multiparty elections to fill offices for the national legislature and the chief executive. Contests in this type of regime are free and fair, with an inclusive suffrage allowing widespread voting participation among all citizens, and citizens having the unrestricted right to compete for elected offices. Competitive elections alone, even if conducted according to international standards of electoral integrity, are insufficient to establish liberal democratic states. For electoral competition to be meaningful, other conditions need to be established, including freedom of expression, the availability of alternative sources of information (freedom of the media), and associational autonomy (freedom to organize parties, interest groups, and social movements).

It should be noted that Dahl's conception reflects classical liberal notions emphasizing the importance of *negative* freedoms, restricting the potential abuse of state power. Based on these ideas, *liberal democratic* regimes are conceptualized in this book as those where legitimacy is derived from periodic multiparty elections that meet international standards, as well as guarantees of a broader range of political rights and civil liberties, including those recognized worldwide in the Universal Declaration of Human Rights. This is essentially a procedural definition that focuses on the processes and institutions for decision making. The standard indicators that have been most commonly used to measure and compare levels of liberal democracy include Polity IV's scale of democracy–autocracy (from 1800–2007) and the Freedom House Gastil index of political rights and civil liberties (from 1972 to the present). Although forming the basis for many large-N comparative studies, each has certain strengths and weaknesses.

Freedom House: Liberal Democracy

One of the best-known measures of liberal democracy, and one of the most widely used in the comparative literature, is the Gastil index of civil liberties and political rights, produced annually by Freedom House. The measure has been widely employed by practitioners; for example, its results are incorporated into the benchmark data employed by the U.S. Millennium Challenge Account to assess the quality of governance and award aid for poorer nations. It has also been employed by many comparative scholars, such as in recent publications by Larry Diamond, Robert J. Barro, and Ronald Inglehart and Christian Welzel.[36] Freedom House, an independent think-tank based in the United States, first began to assess political trends in the 1950s with the results published as the *Balance Sheet of Freedom*. In 1972, Freedom House launched a new, more comprehensive annual study called *Freedom in the World*. Raymond Gastil developed the survey's methodology, which assigned countries political rights and civil liberties ratings and categorized them as "free," "partly free," or "not free." The survey continued to be produced by Gastil until 1989, when a larger team of in-house survey analysts was established. Subsequent editions of the survey have followed essentially the same format, although specific items have been amended over the years,[37] and in recent years more details have been released about the coding framework used for each assessment and about disaggregated data for specific components.

The index monitors the existence of political rights in terms of electoral processes, political pluralism, and the functioning of government. Civil liberties are defined by the existence of freedom of speech and association, rule of law, and personal rights. The research team draws on multiple sources of information to develop its classifications based on a checklist of questions, including ten separate items monitoring the existence of political rights and fifteen on civil liberties. These items assess the presence of institutional checks and balances constraining the executive through the existence of a representative and inclusive legislature, an independent judiciary implementing the rule of law, and the existence of political rights and civil liberties, including reasonable self-determination and participation by minorities and the presence of free and fair election laws.[38] Each item is allocated a score from 0 to 4 and given equal weight when aggregated. The raw scores for each country are then converted into a seven-point scale of political rights and a seven-point scale for civil liberties, and in turn these are collapsed to categorize each regime worldwide as either "free," "partly free," or "not free." As a result of this process, the survey estimates that in 2009, out of 193 nations, almost half, or 89 (46 percent), could be classified as free, while 58 nations could be classified as "partly free."[39] This represents a remarkable net advance during the third wave era, but nevertheless Freedom House estimates that the balance of regime types has largely stabilized during the last decade; for example, the survey reports that the total number of "not free" states was exactly the same in 1999 and a decade later. The emphasis on a wide range of civil liberties, rights, and freedoms means that this measure most closely reflects notions of liberal democracy. The index has the advantage of providing comprehensive coverage of nation-states and independent territories worldwide, as well as establishing a long time series of observations conducted annually since 1972.

Despite these virtues, the index has been subject to considerable criticism on a number of conceptual and methodological grounds.[40] The procedures used by the team of researchers employed by Freedom House lack transparency, so scholars cannot double-check the reliability and consistency of the coding decisions, nor can the results be easily replicated. The questions used for constructing the index often involve two or three separate items within each sub-category, allowing ambiguous measurement and aggregation across these items. The process of compositing the separate items is not subject to systematic factor analysis, so it remains unclear whether the items do indeed cluster together into consistent scales of political rights and civil liberties. The multiple dimensions included in the index provide a broad-ranging attempt to monitor human rights; such dimensions, for example, concern property ownership, freedom of religious expression, choice of marriage partners, and the absence of economic exploitation. These are all widely regarded as important dimensions of human rights, with intrinsic value, but it is not clear that these are necessarily essential components or valid measures of democracy per se. The concepts of freedom and democracy are not equivalent. It remains an empirical question whether democratic regimes promote these sorts of values – for example, whether they are associated with free-market capitalist economies or whether some prefer protectionist economic policies and a greater role for the government in economic planning and the welfare state.[41] Moreover, because it contains such a broad range of indicators, the index is less useful as an analytical tool for policy makers; for example, if it is established that the Freedom House measure of democracy is consistently linked to the protection of human rights, economic growth, peace, or the provision of more generous welfare services, it remains unclear what particular aspect of the index is driving this relationship.[42] It is argued that a neoliberal bias is built in to the measure, reflecting the mission of the organization.[43] The construction of the measure therefore suffers from certain problems of conflation and redundancy, and although it is widely used, it essentially reflects liberal notions of democracy, and other approaches emphasize alternative concepts.

Polity IV: Democracy–Autocracy Scale

Another approach commonly used in the comparative and international relations literature is the classification of constitutional democracy provided by the Polity project.[44] This was initiated by Ted Robert Gurr in the 1970s and it has evolved over the past three decades. The latest version, Polity IV, provides annual time-series data in country-year format covering 161 countries from 1800 to 2007.[45] Coders working on the Polity IV project classify democracy and autocracy in each nation-year as a composite score of different characteristics relating to authority structures. Democracy is conceived of conceptually as reflecting three essential elements: the presence of institutions and procedures through which citizens can express preferences about alternative policies and leaders; the existence of institutionalized constraints on the power of the executive; and the guarantee of civil liberties to all citizens (although this is not actually measured). The classification emphasizes the existence or absence of institutional features of the nation-state. For example, competitive executive recruitment is measured by leadership selection through popular elections contested by two or more parties or candidates. The openness of recruitment for the chief executive is measured by all citizens having the opportunity to attain the position through a regularized process, excluding hereditary succession, forceful seizure of power, or military coups. By contrast, autocracies are seen as regimes that restrict or suppress competitive political participation, in which the chief executive is chosen from within the political elite, and, once in office, leaders face few institutional constraints on their power. The dataset constructs a ten-point democracy scale by coding the competitiveness of political participation (1–3), the competitiveness of executive recruitment (1–2), the openness of executive recruitment (1), and the constraints on the chief executive (1–4). Autocracy is measured by negative versions of the same indices. The two scales are combined into a single democracy–autocracy score varying from −10 to +10. Polity has also been used to monitor and identify processes of major regime change and democratic transitions, classified as a positive change in the democracy–autocracy score of more than three points.

The Polity IV scores have the virtue of providing an exceptionally long series of observations stretching over two centuries, as well as covering most nation-states worldwide. The provision of separate indices for each of the main dimensions allows scholars to disaggregate the components. The emphasis on constitutional rules restricting the executive may be particularly valuable for distinguishing the initial downfall of autocratic regimes and the transition to multiparty elections. Unfortunately, the democracy–autocracy score also suffers from certain important limitations. Polity IV emphasizes the existence of constraints on the chief executive as a central part of its measure. As Geraldo L. Munck and Jay Verkulian point out, however, there is a world of difference between those restrictions on the executive that arise from democratic checks and balances, such as the power of the elected legislature or an independent judiciary, and those that arise from other actors, such as the power of the military or economic elites.[46] Although more information is now released in the user's codebook, the processes that the Polity team uses to classify regimes continue to lack a degree of transparency and therefore replicability by independent scholars. Moreover, although acknowledging the importance of civil liberties as part of its overall conceptualization of democracy, Polity IV does not actually attempt to code or measure this dimension. Gurr originally conceived the Polity IV index for very different purposes, to monitor notions of political stability and regime change, and the growing use of this measure to assess constitutional forms of democracy represents a newer development.

It should be emphasized, however, that the democratic mechanisms that empower citizens, allowing them to participate and express their preferences, are complex, and alternative democratic theories emphasize different institutional procedures and processes. Theories that emphasize "participatory," "deliberative," or "social" democracy provide alternative visions about the core principles and values underpinning regimes, so the concept of liberal democracy provides only one perspective on the issues at the heart of this book. For example, Amy C. Alexander and Christian Welzel emphasize the concept of "effective democracy," combining both liberal democracy (measured by Freedom House) combined with control of corruption.[47] Nevertheless, this seems to mix two distinct phenomena, making a conceptually unclear indicator, because control of corruption does not necessarily deepen democratic qualities per se. Liberal democratic theories focus on the existence of a broad range of political and civil rights that protect and guarantee an inclusive franchise, processes of collective organization, informed deliberation, and freedom of choice, all of which seek to constrain and restrict the state, protecting citizens from the potential abuse of power. Liberal democracy therefore includes a broader range of criteria than minimalist accounts of representative democracy, reflecting Schumpeterian notions. Electoral autocracies hold multiparty contests for the effective head of government, but competition is limited, to a lesser or greater extent, so that these contests are flawed or manipulated. Absolute autocracies are the most restrictive types of states, without even the fig leaf of fake elections to legitimate rule.

Given these notions, several indices are selected to provide alternative measures of the quality of democratic governance, as listed in Table 3.1. The analysis of multiple measures allows us to check whether the results remain robust or whether they are sensitive to the specific indicator that is chosen for analysis. Thus the analysis draws on the International Country Risk Guide (ICRG) measures of the bureaucratic quality of governance (combining bureaucratic quality, anticorruption, and law and order). This series is

TABLE 3.1. *Selected indices of democratic governance*

Indicator	Source	Scale	Years Available	Countries	Number of Observations
Rule of law	World Bank Institute		1996–2010	177	2,077
Control of corruption	World Bank Institute		1996–2010	177	2,037
Government effectiveness	World Bank Institute		1996–2010	177	2,090
Regulatory quality	World Bank Institute		1996–2010	177	2,066
Political stability	World Bank Institute		1996–2010	177	2,070
Quality of bureaucratic government	Political Risk Service Group, International Country Risk Guide	100 pts	1984–2010	136	3,272
Liberal democracy	Polity IV democracy-autocracy index standardized	100 pts	1800–2007	149	4,783
Liberal democracy	Freedom House political rights and civil liberties scale, standardized	100 pts	1972–2010	191	3,822

Source: Quality of Government Institute, University of Gothenburg. 2011. *Quality of Government Dataset*. http://www.qog.pol.gu.se.

available annually for a smaller range of 136 countries, but it has the important advantage of extending over a longer period (1984–2010), thus capturing the dynamics of change during the third wave era. The ICRG estimates are also more narrowly conceptualized and thus their meaning is easier to interpret conceptually. These indices are supplemented by comparing five of the World Bank Institute estimates of "good governance," namely measures of the rule of law, control of corruption, government effectiveness, regulatory quality, and political stability, all aspects closely related to Weberian conceptions of the characteristics of bureaucratic governance.[48] The broader global coverage provided by the World Bank Institute estimates is advantageous, and because they include the ICRG indices, both sources are expected to be closely related. For liberal democracy, this book draws on the Freedom House estimates of political rights and civil liberties, available annually since 1972, and the Polity IV democracy–autocracy index available since 1800. These are used in alternative models to cross-check the results.

To analyze whether the selected indices form one dimension or whether they fall into two distinct dimensions, as theorized, the technique of principle component factor analysis can be employed. The results in Table 3.2 confirm that the indices present two distinct dimensions, reflecting the underlying concepts

TABLE 3.2. *Components of democratic governance*

	State Capacity Index	Liberal Democracy Index
Rule of law (WBI)	.945	
Control of corruption (WBI)	.933	
Government effectiveness (WBI)	.915	
Quality of government (ICRG)	.915	
Regulatory quality (WBI)	.836	
Political stability (WBI)	.826	
Liberal democracy standardized (Polity IV)		.970
Liberal democracy standardized (Freedom House)		.869
% variance 62.5	62.5	28.5

Notes: Principal component factor analysis with varimax rotation and Kaiser normalization, excluding coefficients less than 0.45. Years: 1984–2012.
Source: See Table 3.1; Quality of Government Institute, University of Gothenburg. 2011. *Quality of Government Dataset*. http://www.qog.pol.gu.se.

of bureaucratic governance and liberal democracy. Thus the World Bank indices measuring rule of law, control of corruption, government effectiveness, and political stability as well as the ICRG measure of the quality of bureaucratic governance fall into the first dimension. By contrast, the Freedom House and the Polity IV measures fall into a second, distinct dimension. The results provide empirical confirmation that these are indeed different phenomenon rather than two aspects of the same underlying type of regime.

APPLYING THE REGIME TYPOLOGY

So how are types of regimes distributed around the world? Figure 3.1 illustrates the contrasts that can be observed based on the analytical typology at the heart of this book, operationalized and compared in 2008, using a standardized one hundred–point index of liberal democracy drawn from annual estimates provided by Freedom House, and the Quality of Governance index generated by the ICRG. As the pattern in Figure 3.1 shows, instead of a linear relationship, one or the other dimension commonly dominates in different countries. Curve fit tests show that the regression line providing the best fit to the data is cubic (R^2= 0.579 ***). The scatterplot of countries suggests a curvilinear relationship, a pattern observed elsewhere in previous studies.[49] For comparison, Figure 3.2 illustrates a snapshot of historical developments that have occurred during the third wave era, in the mid-1980s and the mid-1990s. It is apparent that processes of democratization and the expansion in state governance capacity have not necessarily evolved hand in hand in many countries around the world, by any means. Let us examine the characteristics and development of the regimes found in each quadrant of these scatterplots.

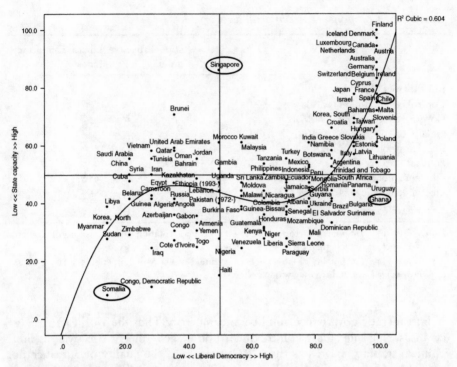

FIGURE 3.1. Democratic governance, 2008.

Notes: State capacity standardized to a one hundred–point scale is measured by the ICRG Indicator of Quality of Governance, Political Risk Service Group, International Country Risk Guide; liberal democracy standardized scale is measured by the Freedom House Political Rights and Civil Liberties index.

Sources: See Table 3.1 for all sources. For more details and the Quality of Government Dataset, see Quality of Government Institute, University of Gothenburg. 2011. *Quality of Government Dataset.* http://www.qog.pol.gu.se.

Bureaucratic Democracies: Chile

Bureaucratic democracies are located in the top-right quadrant, including many affluent post-industrial societies where the expansion of the mass franchise and the growth of the professional civil service evolved roughly simultaneously during the mid- to late-nineteenth century. Scandinavian nations show the strongest performance of democratic governance in Figure 3.1, along with many of the most affluent European and Anglo-American societies. The position of these leading countries has also remained relatively stable over time. But not all the regimes falling into this category are long-established Western democracies; a diverse range of emerging economies and third wave democracies from different world regions are also located here, including Namibia, Hungary, the Czech Republic, Croatia, Costa Rica, Botswana, South Korea, and Taiwan.

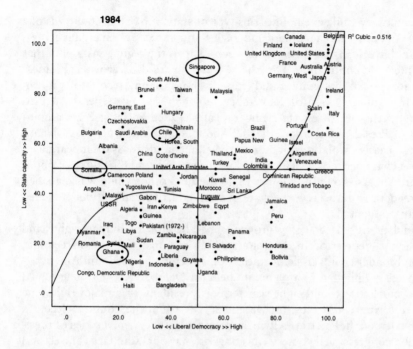

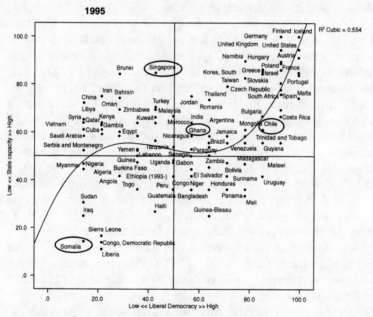

FIGURE 3.2. Democratic governance over time.

Sources: See Table 3.1 for all sources. For more details and the Quality of Government Dataset, see Quality of Government Institute, University of Gothenburg. 2011. *Quality of Government Dataset.* http://www.qog.pol.gu.se.

Contemporary Chile exemplifies this type of state; today this country is one of South America's most stable democracies and successful emerging economies.[50] Yet historically this country has not escaped the regime instability that has blighted the continent.[51] The 1960s were a period of growing political polarization, social intolerance, and class divisions among sectors of Chilean society. The military coup on September 11, 1973, led by General Augusto Pinochet Ugarte, overthrew the democratically elected Socialist Party administration of President Salvador Allende. The Pinochet era, which lasted until 1989, saw massive violations of human rights, including mass disappearances, attacks on civil liberties, the widespread use of torture, and the killing of opposition forces.[52] As shown in Figure 3.2, in the mid-1980s Chile was classified as a bureaucratic autocracy; the state exerted effective control, but it lacked democratic credentials.

The end of this decade saw growing liberalization of human rights and a reduction of repression in the country, such as expanding press freedoms, reflecting broader trends in democratization sweeping across Latin America.[53] This process culminated in a plebiscite held on October 5, 1988, that denied General Pinochet a second eight-year term as president. In a major milestone toward restoring democracy, on December 14, 1989, the country elected a Christian Democrat, Patricio Aylwin, as president. Since then, a series of presidential and congressional contests, meeting international standards of electoral integrity, have seen peaceful multiparty competition and both center-left and center-right coalitions in power. By 1995, the regime in Chile could be classified as a bureaucratic democracy. The bicameral Congress consists of a 38-seat Senate and a 120-member Chamber of Deputies. Senators serve for eight years with staggered terms, while deputies are elected every four years. The most recent national congressional elections were held on December 13, 2009, concurrently with the presidential election. The lower house – the Chamber of Deputies – is currently divided fairly evenly between the governing center-right coalition and the center-left opposition, plus a few independents and members from small parties. This type of party system and coalitional politics is encouraged by the unique electoral system which uses a closed party list majority system with small districts for the lower house. In these contests, if the majority party obtains more than two-thirds of the valid votes cast, it is entitled to the two seats of the constituency. If it obtains less than two-thirds, it is entitled to one seat, and the second seat goes to the second-place party. The party system is based on structural cleavages, such as class and income, as well as divisions between democratic and authoritarian values.[54] The Pinochet-era constitution was revised, limiting presidential terms of office to a single four-year period, and the judicial system was overhauled to make it more independent.

Thus Chile has emerged in recent decades as one of the most stable democracies in the region, even though important challenges remain concerning the expansion of minority rights, reductions in socioeconomic inequality, student and labor unrest, and levels of popular disenchantment with democracy.[55] This relative success story of the regime has occurred despite the authoritarian legacy of the past and contemporary problems facing a number of other Latin American countries, notably in the Andean region, where the quality of electoral integrity has eroded in Colombia and Venezuela and a trend toward the concentration of executive power is evident in Bolivia and Ecuador.[56] Moreover, the Chilean state ranks well not just in democracy and human rights, but also on most of the indicators of governance, rating in the top seventy-five percentile worldwide in control of corruption, rule of law, and government effectiveness.[57] During the Pinochet era of the 1970s and 1980s, GDP per capita lagged well behind the Latin American average. From the early 1990s, however, during the democratic era, the economy has surged well ahead of the average growth in the region. Indeed, the country had Latin America's fastest-growing economy during the 1990s and it has weathered recent regional economic instability and natural disasters, with strong foreign trade and a reputation for effective financial institutions and sound regulatory policies. Average GDP per capita (in purchasing power parity [PPP]) is $15,400 today, with solid growth in recent decades lifting millions out of poverty, although socioeconomic inequality remains high.

Patronage Democracies: Ghana

Elsewhere in the world, however, during the third wave era, processes of representative democracy and the state's governance capacity have commonly achieved far less balanced development. Some of the starkest disjunctions today come from countries scattered in the bottom-right quadrant, such as South Africa, El Salvador, and Ghana, which have experienced substantial gains in competitive elections and representative democracy in recent years, yet where the state continues to lack the capacity and resources to manage the delivery of many basic goods and services, such as schooling, health clinics, and economic growth.

The case of Ghana illustrates this category most clearly. A half-century ago, Ghana was the first African state to achieve independence following colonial rule. A new constitution, approved on April 29, 1954, established a cabinet comprised of African ministers drawn from an all-African legislature chosen by direct election. After independence was granted in 1957, the Convention People's Party government under Nkrumah sought to develop Ghana as a socialist state. A new constitution in 1960 replaced parliamentary government with a republic headed by a strong president. In 1966, its first president and pan-African hero, Kwame Nkrumah, was deposed in a coup, heralding years of mostly military rule. In 1981, Flight Lieutenant Jerry Rawlings staged his second coup. During the late 1980s, the country began to move toward economic stability and democracy. In April 1992, a constitution allowing a multiparty system was approved in a referendum, ushering in a sustained period of democracy under the fourth republic. Since then, Ghana has experienced periodic multiparty contests that international observers have regarded as free and fair. As shown in Figure 3.2, the classification indicates that Ghana shifted from a patronage autocracy in the mid-1980s to a bureaucratic democracy a decade later. The current constitution specifies that presidential elections are held using the second-ballot majoritarian system, while the 230 parliamentary members are elected for a four-year term in single-member constituencies using a first-past-the-post election system. The two largest political parties that dominate contemporary politics in Ghana, the liberal democratic New Patriotic Party (NPP) and the social democratic National Democratic Congress (NDC), have both enjoyed two consecutive terms in presidential office and majorities in parliament, the NDC from 1992 to 2000 and the NPP from 2000 to 2008. In December 2000, John Kufuor was elected as president, succeeding Jerry Rawlings in a peaceful transition of power.[58] Reelected in 2004, President Kufuour stepped down voluntarily four years later, observing the constitutional two-term limit.

In the run-up to the December 7, 2008, presidential and parliamentary elections, parties campaigned freely across the country on policy-driven issues such as social welfare and the economy, and they published comprehensive manifestos. The campaign environment was lively and the parties canvassed voters door to door, holding a series of peaceful local rallies and town-hall meetings across Ghana, with the presidential candidates of the NPP and NDC touring the country. A series of independent polls were published in the media. Debates between the presidential candidates of the four parties with parliamentary representation were broadcast live via the major media outlets. Public and private sector broadcasting channels offered extensive news reporting about the campaign, especially coverage of the major parties and presidential candidates and a large number of discussion programs. Newspapers provided a diverse range of views and covered all of the major events organized by the parties during the campaign, although as was the case with broadcasters, they focused their coverage on the larger political parties. There were also many paid political advertisements in the media and at times these were used to openly criticize opposing parties. The absence of any legal campaign spending limits meant that political parties were free to use unlimited resources. Both the NDC and NPP organized highly developed campaign strategies.

In the first round of the presidential contest, the governing party candidate was Nana Akufo-Addo, one of the founding members of the New Patriotic Party when multiparty democracy returned to Ghana, and an advocate of human rights. He faced the opposition candidate, Professor John Atta Mills, a social democrat heading the National Democratic Congress Party, and six other minor party candidates who also threw their hat into the ring. The first-round election among all contestants ended on a knife-edge; the popular vote was evenly divided between Akufo-Addo (49.1 percent) and Atta Mills (47.9 percent), with scattered support for others. As no single candidate gained an absolute majority, the outcome was decided by the second-round contest between the two leading candidates. This round saw an extremely close contest where Atta Mills won a slender lead (50.23 percent) over the governing party's Akufo-Addo (49.77 percent). The parliamentary elections, held on December 7, 2008, under plurality single-member rules, proved equally competitive. The result saw the governing

New Patriotic Party fall to 107 parliamentary seats with 49 percent of the popular vote. The NPP was overtaken in a tight race by the opposition National Democratic Congress, gaining 114 seats, with a more efficient distribution of support, as it won only 47 percent of the national popular vote. Two minor parties and four independents were also returned as members of parliament.

The European Union was among a host of institutions observing these contests, including the Carter Centre, the Economic Community of West African States (ECOWAS), African Union, and over four thousand representatives from the Coalition of Domestic Observers (CODEO). The EU reported that the electoral commission that administered the contests proved impartial, professional, and independent, ensuring the transparency of the process. Electoral observers and party agents were able to observe all stages of polling, vote counting, and aggregation. There were clear legal channels for complaints and appeals challenging the results, and the commission worked to ensure conciliation and acceptance of the process among the major stakeholders. There were some minor administrative irregularities experienced on polling day, but the electoral commission apologized for these and sought to rectify the situation. A series of public forums, organized by the National Peace Council (NPC), brought together all major stakeholders and parties to discuss the polling process, to defuse any discontent, and to offer recommendations for future contests. Disputes followed the second round of presidential voting, and tensions rose in the tight contest with some slight delays in announcing the vote, but these were eventually resolved peacefully. The governing NPP stood down and President Atta Mills assumed office.

The outcome is all the more remarkable because Ghana lacks many of the social and economic conditions that are commonly associated with stable democracies. An ethically divided society, by languages and religions, the country is home to more than an estimated one hundred distinct groups, including the Akan, Ewe, Mole-Dagbane, Guan, and Ga-Adangbe.[59] Ghana is also one of the poorest countries in the world, with an average per capita GDP of $1,400, one-tenth the level of Belarus. One-third of the population live on less than $1.25 a day.[60] Francophone West Africa is one of the least well-off and most unstable regions of the world; autocracies in Mauritania, Chad, Cameroon, and the Central African Republic coexist with fragile states engaged in peace building after protracted conflict, including Sierra Leone, Liberia, and Cote d'Ivoire. Within a few days after Ghanaians went to the polls, in Guinea the death of a dictator triggered a chaotic military coup. Overall, the Ghanaian elections have been judged by domestic and international observers to be a considerable success, with another largely orderly and peaceful contest further consolidating Ghana's successive steps toward sustainable democracy under the Fourth Republic. In 2009, Freedom House rated Ghana 1.5 on its seven-point index of political rights and civil liberties, classifying it as a liberal democracy comparable to Greece, Israel, South Korea, and Bulgaria.[61]

Beyond the ballot box, however, the capacity of many other political institutions in Ghana still require strengthening to build a more effective state, ensuring that parliament can effectively carry out its independent oversight and budgetary role, that access to justice and human rights is open to all sectors, and that local governance has the capacity to deliver basic public services, healthcare, and education to alleviate poverty.[62] The economy is heavily based on natural resources and agriculture, with an expected windfall following discovery of offshore oil, but nevertheless in 2010 per capita GDP in purchasing power parity in Ghana was only $2,500. Roughly four out of ten Ghanaians are below the poverty level. Moreover, if measured against the global yardstick of progress toward achieving the 2015 targets of the Millennium Development Goals, Ghana continues to lag behind on many indicators, including cutting child mortality and improving maternal health while at the same time reducing overall levels of extreme poverty and expanding primary education for all.[63] The capacity of the public sector remains limited, despite many attempts to strengthen the civil service, public sector management, and financial services, for example, by use of budget planning systems, information technologies, and computerized public expenditure management systems. Hence an official assessment of governance in Ghana concluded, "It is questionable whether value has been obtained from the massive investments made in public sector reform over the last twenty years."[64] Under the Fourth Republic, citizens can therefore freely express demands through electoral channels, with a choice of parties in government, but this does not mean that elected leaders can necessarily deliver effective public services or raise millions of Ghanaians out of poverty.

Patronage Autocracies: Somalia

The patronage autocracies located in the bottom-left corner vary a great deal, but this typically includes many of the world's poorest developing countries and so-called failed states, such as Haiti, the Democratic Republic of Congo, Sudan, and Somalia, lacking effective governance. The most problematic cases are those where enduring, deep-rooted, ethnic conflict has eroded the authority and capacity of the central authorities to maintain social order and rule of law, the most basic functions of the state, as well as to manage the economy so as to alleviate poverty, disease, and malnutrition.

Somalia exemplifies these cases, a country without an effective central government since President Siad Barre was overthrown in 1991. Years of fighting among rival warlords and an inability to deal with famine, droughts, floods, and disease led to the deaths of up to one million people. The UN also estimates that another one million Somalis are internally displaced after fleeing violence. Life expectancy for the average Somali is fifty years, one of the lowest in the world. In East Africa, bordering the Gulf of Aden and the Indian Ocean, with a current population of about 10 million people, Somalia was created in 1960 as a result of merging a former British protectorate and an Italian colony. Today Somalia is one of the poorest countries in the world, with an estimated

per capita GDP of $600 (in purchasing power parity). The country's econ-
omy is largely agricultural, with livestock, hides, fish, charcoal, and bananas
Somalia's principal exports. Predominately Sunni Muslim, the population is
mainly Somali, although one-sixth are Bantu and other non-Somali, including
Arabs.

In 1969, Somalia's President Abdirashid Ali Shermarke was shot dead by one
of his own bodyguards. His assassination was quickly followed by a bloodless
military coup d'état led by the head of the army, Major General Mohamed
Siad Barre. In 1970, Siad Barre proclaimed a socialist state, paving the way for
close relations with the USSR. The revolutionary army spearheaded large-scale
public works programs and rural literacy campaigns. The regime maintained
stability for more than two decades until 1991, when President Barre was overthrown by opposing clans. After the regime's overthrow, the clan leaders failed
to agree on a replacement and thus plunged the country into a decade of lawlessness, turmoil, factional fighting, and civil warfare.

In 2000, clan elders and other senior figures appointed a moderate Islamist,
Abdulkassim Salat Hassan, as president at a conference in Djibouti. A transitional government was set up with the aim of reconciling warring militias, and
Ethiopian troops withdrew. But as its mandate drew to a close, the administration had made little progress in uniting the country, and Islamist insurgents
are keeping up their almost daily attacks. The main fighters in opposition to
the government are al-Shabab, a radical faction that emerged from the rem-
nants of the Union of Islamic Courts. Maintaining links with al-Qaeda, the
group now controls much of southern and central Somalia and it has imposed
strict Sharia law in those areas. A rival group of Islamist fighters struggling for
power against the government – Hisbul-Islam – is regarded as more moderate,
although it also wants to impose Sharia law on the population.

In December 2010, *Jane's* Country Stability Ratings reported that Somalia
was one of the world's least stable environments, alongside Gaza, the West Bank,
Haiti, Chad, Afghanistan, Guinea, Central African Republic, Sudan, Zimbabwe,
and Guinea-Bissau. Somalia's ranking reflected the country's continued fighting between the government and Islamic militia, the near-continuous armed
conflict in Mogadishu, the presence of pirates threatening international shipping, and difficulties in brokering an agreement between the government and
opposition factions. Two years of drought in East Africa triggered widespread
famine and a humanitarian crisis in 2011, but only limited aid got through to
alleviate the crisis in areas of Somalia controlled by al-Shabab. Reflecting all
these challenges, the indicators under comparison for Somalia show no change
in autocracy and the gradual marked deterioration in the quality of bureaucratic governance over successive decades (see Figure 3.3).

Bureaucratic Autocracies: Singapore

In contrast to the situation two decades earlier, few cases of bureaucratic autocracy are evident today, although China exemplifies this type of regime, located

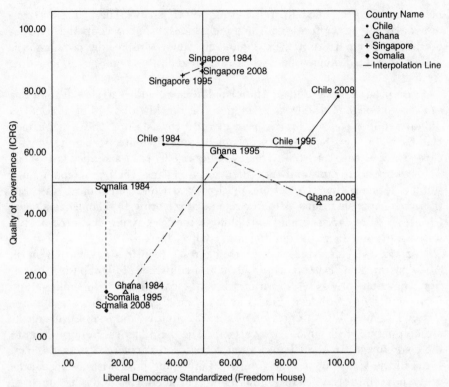

FIGURE 3.3. Trajectories of democratic governance in the four case-study countries.
Sources: See Table 3.1 for all sources. For more details and the Quality of Government
Dataset, see Quality of Government Institute, University of Gothenburg. 2011.
Quality of Government Dataset. http://www.qog.pol.gu.se.

in the top-left corner of Figure 3.2. Governance is also rated relatively highly in
other bureaucratic autocracies, such as Brunei, Qatar, and Saudi Arabia, which
continue to be ruled by absolute monarchies.

Singapore illustrates this category, as a one-party autocracy where many
fundamental human rights are restricted, yet where governance works well,
judged by relatively clean and efficient public services supported by substantial
economic growth.[65] As one of the East Asian "four tigers," along with South
Korea, the economy has forged ahead to make the nation one of the most
prosperous in the world. The economy has been built on high-tech electron-
ics and the service sector, particularly finance, banking, investment, and trade.
In 2005, Singapore produced a per capita GDP of around $25,000 (in PPP),
similar to Italy and even more affluent than South Korea. The compact island
nation contains just over 4 million people (compared with 48 million South
Koreans), three-quarters of whom are ethnic Chinese, while the remainder are
mainly Malay and Tamil Indian. The country is multilingual, divided among

Malay, Chinese, Tamil, and English. In terms of wealth and size, therefore, the underlying conditions for democratic consolidation are promising.

Yet the island-state remains a one-party predominant autocracy, which Freedom House rates as only partly free.[66] Indeed, some observers suggest that the country has become more repressive of human rights even as it has become more prosperous.[67] Given the underlying conditions, Singapore should be ripe for democracy: It is a compact island-state without any threats to its borders, an ex-British colony with low-to-moderate ethnic fractionalization. During the nineteenth century, the island grew in population and prosperity as a major port controlled first by the British East India Company and then, after 1867, directly from London as a crown colony as part of the Straights Settlement. After the end of World War II, demands for self-rule grew as part of the decolonization wave affecting the British Empire. In 1959, Singapore was granted full self-governance by the British authorities. In the parliamentary elections held in 1959, the People's Action Party (PAP), founded and led by Lee Kuan Yew, swept into power by winning 47 percent of the vote and three-quarters of all seats. Despite a regular series of multiparty contests challenging its hegemonic status, PAP has ruled continuously ever since, winning eleven successive general elections over almost half a century.[68] The PAP has controlled parliament without effective challenge to its power, winning on average two-thirds of the vote but a remarkable 95 percent of all parliamentary seats in the series of parliamentary general elections held from 1959 to 2001. This has effectively squeezed out any opposition members of parliament (MPs) beyond an occasional token representative from one of the parties of the left. The share of the vote won by PAP eroded slightly from 1984 to 1997, but the party strengthened again in 2001. A majority of PAP candidates continue to be returned unopposed.

One reason for the ruling party's hegemony lies in the majoritarian electoral system that translates the PAP's share of the vote into an overwhelming majority in parliament. The unicameral parliament uses a combined-independent electoral system.[69] In the current parliament, nine members were elected from simple-plurality, single-member constituencies (a first-past-the-post system). In total, seventy-five other MPs were elected in a block vote system (termed locally Group Representation Constituencies) from fourteen multimember districts, where parties field a list of three to six candidates. In these, the party with a simple plurality of votes in the district wins all the seats. The block vote system is designed to ensure the representation of members from the Malay, Indian, and other minority communities, as each party list must include at least one candidate from these communities, encouraging parties to nominate ethnically diverse lists. Another nine members of parliament can be nominated by the president from among the opposition parties without standing for election. Another factor contributing to the ruling party's predominance is alleged gerrymandering and the redrawing of electoral districts just a few months before the general election. In particular, constituencies where the PAP did relatively badly in one contest have sometimes been systematically removed from the electoral map by the next election.[70]

The 1965 constitution established a Westminster-style parliamentary democracy where the president, elected by parliament, used to be a largely ceremonial head of state. The 1991 constitutional revision introduced a more powerful president, where the office is directly elected through a simple plurality vote. A contested election was held in 1993, but in 1999 and in 2005 the position was filled by President Sellapan Ramanathan, as all other nominated candidate were declared ineligible by the presidential election committee. Candidates can be ruled out of the contest if the committee judges that they are not "a person of integrity, good character and reputation," among other stringent criteria. Nominees also must not be a member of the government or a current member of a political party. The president appoints the prime minister, the head of government, government ministers from among the members of parliament, and key members of the civil service, as well as exercising veto budgetary powers and other responsibilities. After leading the PAP in seven victorious elections since 1959, Lee Kuan Yew stepped down as prime minister in 1990, remaining "Minister Mentor" in an advisory position but handing over his executive office to his PAP successor, Goh Chok Tong. After a series of PAP prime ministers, in 2004 the elder son of Lee Kuan Yew, Lee Hsien Loong, took office as part of a planned handover of power.

Another way in which PAP maintains control is through its influence over the judicial system, including suing opposition members for libel, interring opposition politicians without trial under the Internal Security Act, and requiring police permits to hold any kind of public talk, exhibition, or demonstration. The government also exercises strong control of the press and news media; for example, the leading newspaper of Singapore, the *Straits Times*, is often perceived as a propaganda newspaper because it rarely criticizes government policy and covers little about the opposition. The owners of the paper, Singapore Press Holdings, have close links to the ruling party and the corporation has a virtual monopoly of the newspaper industry. Government censorship of journalism is common, using the threat or imposition of heavy fines or distribution bans imposed by the Media Development Authority, with these techniques also used against articles seen to be critical of the government that are published in the international press, including *The Economist* and *International Times Herald Tribune*. Internet access is regulated in Singapore, and private ownership of satellite dishes is not allowed. Due to this record, the Reporters without Borders assessment of Press Freedom Worldwide in 2005 ranked Singapore 140th out of 167 nation-states.

Singapore is governed by the rule of law. Thus the island-state has not suffered the violent repression of opposition movements. Human rights agencies do not report cases of ballot stuffing, polling irregularities, tinkering with the electoral roll, or voter intimidation conducted in fraudulent elections by security forces. The administration of elections is widely regarded by election observers as free, fair, and well organized, within the rules.[71] Indeed, the government of Singapore can be admired as a model of technocratic efficiency, delivering effective public services such as housing and transport without the widespread corruption and abuse of public office that are characteristic of many autocracies. Singapore is ranked relatively positively on the World Bank measures of government effectiveness, political stability, regulatory quality, control of corruption, and rule of law. Thus the country exemplifies a type of regime where bureaucratic governance is exceptionally strong and the public sector works efficiently, even though basic human rights continue to fail to meet democratic standards in the one-party predominant state.

CONCLUSIONS

The cases highlighted in this comparison illustrate the major contrasts among regimes that are evident around the world today. The differences observed among Chile, Somalia, Ghana, and Singapore are not simply confined to these countries; instead, these can be understood as reflecting broader general patterns and types of regimes. Clearly each of the countries starts from a different position, in terms of levels of human development and processes of political change. Nevertheless, the annual changes and the trajectories summarized in Figures 3.3 and 3.4 illustrate divergent pathways taken by each country. Bureaucratic democracies are most common among affluent post-industrial societies, but post-Pinochet Chile exemplifies the successful development of this type of regime during the third wave era in an emerging economy. By contrast, in Ghana during the same years, democratic processes and institutions have strengthened over successive elections, improving human rights, but the state administrative capacity and resources to provide basic public services meeting social needs have actually worsened in recent years. Singapore reflects the opposite challenge, with efficient and effective public services and political stability, but without effective checks and counterbalances on executive one-party rule. Somalia exemplifies the worst case of a failed state, where the regime has gradually lost its capacity to deliver security or to lift its population out of enduring poverty. Rather than looking only at either democracy or governance, the new typology provides insights into the importance of understanding the interaction of these phenomena. Building on this foundation, the task addressed in the next chapter is to consider how to apply this regime typology to analyze its effects on human security.

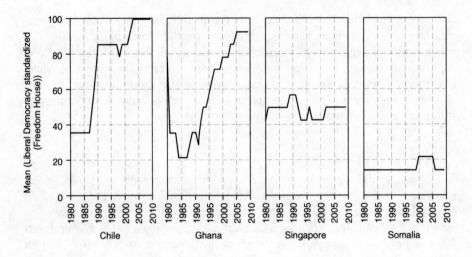

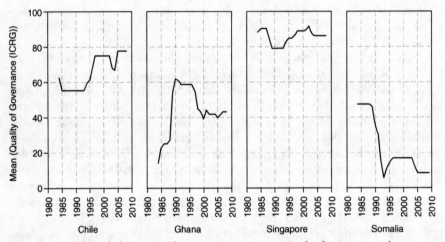

FIGURE 3.4. Annual changes in democratic governance in the four case-study countries, 1980–2010.

Sources: See Table 3.1 for all sources. For more details and the Quality of Government Dataset, see Quality of Government Institute, University of Gothenburg. 2011. *Quality of Government Dataset* http://www.qog.pol.gu.se.

4

Analyzing Regime Effects

Establishing convincing proof about the consequences of democratic governance for core components of human security is challenging. Over the years, an extensive research literature has sought to determine the impact of regime institutions (variously defined and measured) on a series of developmental indicators (also variously defined and measured). Scholars drawn from multiple disciplines have employed increasingly sophisticated analytical techniques, typically examining the separate effects of either liberal democracy or else the impact of "good" governance on standard indicators of economic growth, income inequality, welfare spending, social policy outcomes, human rights violations, environmental degradation, and levels of interstate and internal peace and security.

Nevertheless, the accumulated body of research findings that emerges from this scientific research has usually frustrated the hopes of practitioners seeking unambiguous, reliable, and robust evidence-based recommendations that could inform decision making. Research seeking to demonstrate the impact of institutions on human security has been challenged on the grounds of conceptual vagueness, analytical problems in establishing the direction of causality and dealing with endogeneity, poorly specified models lacking important controls, measurement errors, systematic bias arising from missing data and limited country coverage, and lack of precision in identifying the specific channels and mechanisms through which institutions affect policy outcomes.[1] An extensive literature has questioned the operationalization of the core concept of liberal democracy and the coherence of "shopping-list" notions of "good governance."[2] Advocacy of deeply held normative values can also color the interpretation of the evidence and the selection of cases rather than confronting uncomfortable evidence that not all good things necessarily go together. Moreover, diverse disciplines concerned with the challenges of human security – including developmental economics, international relations, public sector management, developmental sociology, public administration, security studies, and comparative politics – have commonly talked past each other in the overly fragmented and specialized research literature rather than establishing a shared consensus. If a general logic underpins the effects of democratic governance on human security, then robust results should be consistently observed, irrespective of the particular scientific methodology, research design, model specification, and the specific types of policy outputs and outcomes under analysis. Despite the burgeoning body of research, therefore, we continue to lack robust generalizations that are useful for policy makers and capable of withstanding the effects of different model specifications, controls, and time periods when replicated in different scientific studies.

This book therefore revisits the evidence, adopting a multimethod research design seeking to overcome some of the technical shortfalls in the previous literature by combining both large-N quantitative studies with small-N qualitative cases. Readers wishing to move directly on to see the results could choose to skip this chapter, but it is important to understand debates about the technical issues in order to evaluate and interpret the evidence. To develop the research design used in this study, the first part of this chapter clarifies the concept of human development and considers whether democracy should be regarded as an integral part of this broader notion. It then goes on to discuss and evaluate the developmental indicators available to measure prosperity, welfare, and peace and selects the core dependent variables. The chapter concludes by summarizing the mixed-method research design, including the cross-national time-series data, the analytical techniques suitable for handling this type of data, and the cases illustrating the arguments presented in the remainder of the book.

THE CONCEPT AND MEASUREMENT OF HUMAN SECURITY

Is there a clear conceptual distinction between "human security" and "democratic governance"? Or are these phenomena so closely intertwined that it is not possible to distinguish the independent and dependent variables in this book? The concept of human security emphasizes the welfare of ordinary people against a range of complex, interconnected, and interdependent threats rather than just the territorial defense of nation-states.[3] The intellectual roots of the United Nations' work in promoting general ideas of human security can be traced back to the 1940s.[4] The concept came to the world's attention following publication of the seminal United Nations Development Programme's 1994 *Human Development Report*: "The concept of security has for too long been interpreted narrowly: as security of territory from external aggression, or as protection of national interests in foreign policy or as global security from the threat of nuclear holocaust .... Forgotten were the legitimate concerns of ordinary people who sought security in their daily lives."[5] Under the vision formulated by the lead editor, Dr. Mahbub ul Haq, this report proposed seven major components of human security: (1) economic security; (2) food security; (3) health security; (4) environmental security; (5) personal security (safety from such things as torture, war, criminal attacks, domestic violence, drug use, suicide, and traffic accidents); (6) community security (the survival of traditional cultures and ethnic groups); and (7) political security (the enjoyment of civil and political rights and freedom from political oppression).[6] Human security was also envisaged in the report as *universal* (applying to all people and societies), *interdependent* (where diverse types of threats are linked together), *preventative* (where the primary concern is to ameliorate and reduce the causes of insecurity), and *people-centered* (focusing on individuals, not just relationships among nation-states). The report also introduced the important notion of *subjective* security – what makes people feel safe – referring to "Human Security as people see it" in contrast to objective indicators of income inequality or armed violence.

The core idea therefore expands the concept of security beyond narrow conceptions of state defense against external military threats. Human security recognizes the complex links between "freedom from fear" and "freedom from want," anticipated decades earlier in Franklin D. Roosevelt's State of the Union address of 1941.[7] In this regard, the revisionist conception seeks to reintegrate separate scholarly disciplines focused on economic growth, military security, and international development. By focusing on economic growth, social developmental indices, and internal conflict as the core dependent variables, this book therefore adopts this idea of the interdependent threats and complex risks facing ordinary people in a globalized world.

The need for a broad understanding of human development was also strongly reinforced by the ideas of Amartya Sen, the distinguished economist and Nobel Prize winner, who advocated the concept of human development focusing on the general well-being of the population at large, including the capacity for people to exercise basic freedoms and choice in how they want to live, work, save, worship, politic, organize, and create. The human capacities approach goes beyond the pursuit of material income and financial wealth by emphasizing the importance of individuals being able to achieve broader developmental goals, including well-being, life satisfaction, self-determination, and happiness.[8] Money may help attain these goals – but not necessarily. If we accept this vision, then democratic states that ensure the capacity of people for self-determination, participation, and emancipation are, by definition, intrinsically more conducive to human development than autocratic regimes. The public's choice of leaders, laws, and public policies is regarded as similar to decisions over other important dimensions of life, such as enlarging people's choices over their livelihoods, healthcare, or education. As the 1991 UNDP *Human Development Report* put it, "It has to be development of the people, by the people, and for the people."[9] This conceptualization can be persuasive and attractive for those already sympathetic toward democratic values and human rights, as it suggests that there can be no trade-off among these goals. Thus, for Sen, "Freedom and development are inextricable."[10]

The capacity development vision has proved increasingly influential, especially among groups and theorists seeking to unite development, participation, and human rights.[11] In the early 1990s, the UN Development Programme moved away from income-based notions of poverty and increased its emphasis on broader concepts and measures of human development, recognizing the need for poor people in local communities to be empowered to make choices affecting their own lives and well-being.[12] As the 2010 *Human Development Report* encapsulates this understanding: "Human development is about putting people at the centre of development. It is about people realizing their potential, increasing their choices and enjoying the freedom to lead lives they value."[13] The core idea was that countries could be financially prosperous, measured by gross domestic product per capita, and yet still plagued by deep-rooted social problems, such as social alienation, AIDS, homelessness, crime, drugs, and alcoholism. By contrast, low-income societies could achieve relatively high levels of human well-being if people had the capacity to live long and healthy lives, acquire knowledge, and achieve a decent standard of living. Mahbub ul Haq, one of the founders of the *Human Development Report*, expands these claims further:

> The basic purpose of development is to enlarge people's choices. In principle, these choices can be infinite and can change over time. People often value achievements that do not show up at all, or not immediately, in income or growth figures: greater access to knowledge, better nutrition and health services, more secure livelihoods, security against crime and physical violence, satisfying leisure hours, political and cultural freedoms and sense of participation in community activities. The objective of development is to create an enabling environment for people to enjoy long, healthy and creative lives.[14]

In this conception, the capacity to participate in community decisions, which is at the heart of democracy, cannot be disentangled from other fundamental freedoms enabling progress on alleviating poverty, improving health, or strengthening human security. The UNDP's *Human Development Report* has expounded this philosophy now for over two decades.[15]

Despite these arguments, traditional concepts of income-based development often continue to prevail within the international community and scholarly studies, where the institutions of democratic governance are treated as instrumentally valuable primarily for achieving concrete material improvements in economic growth and human security. In turn, it is hoped that prosperity and peace are basic conditions that will in turn facilitate human security by lifting the bottom billion out of extreme poverty and hunger; getting children into primary schools; addressing the challenges of AIDS, malaria, and child health; preserving sustainable environments; and reducing conflict, war, and violence. This traditional understanding of development remains widespread, and in this context the human capabilities approach is unlikely to persuade skeptics about the intrinsic value of democracy. The most authoritative universally accepted statement of development, for example, comes from the 2000 UN World Summit, where the world's government pledged to achieve the Millennium Development Goals (MDGs) by 2015.[16] Targets include halving poverty head counts, achieving universal primary school completion, and cutting child mortality rates by two-thirds. The 2000 Millennium Declaration passed by the UN

General Assembly does explicitly recognize the value of "democratic and participatory governance based on the will of the people" as a way to guarantee other fundamental freedoms and rights.[17] This commitment is nothing new; the statement echoes, in diluted form, the language used in the 1948 Universal Declaration of Human Rights.[18] Yet at the 2000 World Summit, the international community failed to incorporate a specific MDG target for strengthening democratic governance.[19]

The emphasis on expanding material prosperity and economic growth as the overarching priority for development is not confined to the MDGs; rather, this vision is also commonly deeply ingrained today in the Bretton Woods institutions of global finance and also reflected in much of the traditional political economy literature. Economists deeply dispute the most effective means and strategies to achieve prosperity, particularly the role of markets and the state. But they rarely question the centrality and desirability of this goal as the central focus of development, based on the assumption that growth will, in turn, translate into poverty reduction, health clinics, nutrition, clean water, and schools.

In this regard, either "democratic" or "good" governance is usually recognized by the development community as an important exogenous or external "driver of change" that can help strengthen human security. A clear statement typical of this common perspective comes from the Department for International Development (DFID) in the UK:

> The Drivers of Change approach is a way of understanding the political economy of poverty reduction in developing countries. It directs attention to the underlying and longer-term factors that affect the political and institutional environment for reform in different countries, as well as factors that more directly affect the incentives and capacity for change that is likely to benefit the poor.... DFID understands pro-poor political and institutional change to be a move from systems where power is heavily concentrated and highly personalised, and where poor people have to seek benefits as clients, to systems where power is more widely distributed, institutions more rules-based, and poor people have incentives and opportunities to organise as citizens, able to claim access to assets and services as a right. In other words, a transition from "clients" to "citizens".[20]

From this perspective, democratic governance continues to be conceptualized as exogenous and instrumental to development. The low-income nation emblematic for successful development, from this perspective, is China, with its remarkable economic growth lifting millions out of poverty, famine, and disease, not democracies in some of the world's poorest societies that have experienced substantial gains in human rights, exemplified by Mali, Ghana, and Benin. If development is understood as the goals of prosperity, welfare, and peace, then it makes sense to ask whether the institutional foundations of democratic governance are among the underlying conditions that facilitate development, alongside other factors such as geography and climate, access to markets and trade, societal levels of ethnic fractionalization, and the distribution of natural resources.

In addition, in practice, even if lip service is paid to the human capacities conception of development, the goal of strengthening democratic governance can conflict directly with other strategies adopted by development agencies. For example, aid conditionality has been used by the World Bank, the International Monetary Fund, and the World Trade Organization, as well as by the U.S. Millennium Challenge Account. This strategy has required countries to implement a given set of policies as a quid pro quo for receiving loans, debt relief, or trade agreements. The logic underlying conditionality is that aid works most effectively when targeted toward countries with certain policies and institutions.[21] Hence the U.S. Millennium Development Corporation specifies certain selection criteria that poor countries have to meet before being eligible for assistance, including demonstrating a record of promoting political and economic freedom, investment in education and health, the sustainable use of natural resources, control of corruption, and respect for civil liberties and the rule of law.[22] Leading American commentators have argued that a muscular approach should be adopted where countries are required to demonstrate progress on governance as a general precondition for *all* U.S. development aid and technical assistance.[23]

The use of aid conditionality may be well meaning in intent; the promise of grants and loans may indeed incentivize some leaders to strengthen democratic practices and good governance, although reports suggest that the evidence remains mixed.[24] Yet the process of using aid conditionality imposes top-down technocratic solutions to poverty that can undermine channels of democratic accountability within the nation-state, violating the principles of national self-determination.[25] Through conditionality, as William Easterly has argued, governments in the least-developed nations, even if democratically elected, become accountable to the priorities of Western donors rather than downwardly responsive to the social needs and priorities of their own citizens.[26] Critical policy choices, such as levels of public spending on healthcare, welfare benefits, and schools, come to be determined by international agencies based in Washington, Geneva, and New York, not by local communities, citizens, elected officials, or leaders within each of the recipient countries. Moreover, international officials are not directly accountable to countries if the recommended policies fail to alleviate, or may even worsen, poverty. Policies promoting democratic elections, which increase public demands on the state while weakening state capacity to meet public expectations and social needs through neoliberal reforms, are a combustible and unstable mix.

For all these reasons, therefore, this book – instead of simply accepting the intrinsic claims about the value of democratic governance – treats the type of regime as potentially *instrumental* to human security. This approach is the standard practice in the extensive empirical research literature that seeks to establish the relationship between some measure of democracy or governance and some indicator of economic development, welfare, or peace.

MONITORING THE CONSEQUENCES OF DEMOCRATIC GOVERNANCE

Over the years, an extensive body of research has sought to establish the consequences of democratic governance for a broad range of challenges facing the world. Prosperity is obviously important, but, in addition to material income and wealth, does this type of regime serve as a driver for welfare that helps efforts to feed the hungry, shelter the homeless, or prevent diseases? Does it generate a peace dividend for the world and diminish the risks of humanitarian crisis, civil wars, and repression of minorities at home? These sorts of consequences are usually treated separately by separate disciplines in the research literature – as well as by policy analysts in the international community – but it is important to reintegrate and synthesize our knowledge to provide a more comprehensive understanding of the complex linkages.

Providing convincing evidence determining plausible answers to the core questions addressed by this book with any degree of confidence is far from a simple undertaking, especially establishing the causal direction of any interactive association based on observed data, given the limits of standard econometric techniques and case-study methods. These questions are addressed in this book mainly by contrasting the diverse trajectories of change occurring during the late twentieth century. These pathways provide a wide range of "natural experiments." Countries such as Chile, the Republic of Korea, South Africa, and Mongolia have made rapid strides in democratization, all improving their score on the Freedom House liberal democracy standardized one hundred–point index by double or more from 1980 to 2010.[27] As a result, after undergoing processes of regime change, did these states experience subsequent gains in per capita GDP? Longevity, healthcare, and schooling? Peace and security? Trajectories can be used to understand the dynamic relationship between *prior changes* in regimes and *subsequent changes* in human security (broadly understood), controlling for many "fixed" and enduring characteristics that evolve sluggishly in the short term or may not change at all, such as in each society's geographic location, natural resources, physical terrain, pool of physical and human capital, ethnic composition, and deep-rooted cultural and religious values.

Progress in Human Security

The trajectories in human welfare that have occurred in recent decades can be illustrated by achievement of the MDGs. In September 2000, the United Nations adopted the Millennium Declaration, out of which emerged the set of universally agreed-on goals that the world's governments pledged to attain by 2015. The United Nations Millennium Summit agreed on eight targets for reducing extreme poverty and hunger, improving health and education, empowering women, and ensuring environmental sustainability. The MDGs embody powerful normative claims, encouraging a global consensus about what objectives development should seek to achieve. Yet they are silent about the more contentious issue: What policy strategies are most effective for achieving these objectives?[28] Some charge that the MDGs are not sufficiently ambitious, and that more radical initiatives need to be implemented for effective and inclusive development.[29] Despite these potential criticisms, the MDGs provide suitable yardsticks to evaluate developmental progress, and the targets have become accepted international norms.

Since 1990, the UN reports that some of the world's poorest countries have registered impressive gains in the fight against poverty, with measurable improvements in school enrollments, child mortality, deaths from malaria and HIV-AIDS, and access to clean water.[30] In recent decades, some societies have enjoyed steadily growing living standards; rising levels of literacy, school enrollments, and healthcare; and more secure conditions within their national borders. The most successful emerging economies and rising world powers – such as Brazil, China, South Africa, Turkey, Indonesia, and India – have lifted millions out of poverty. Diverse smaller states, including Nepal, Tunisia, Mauritius, and Botswana, have also successfully strengthened human development during recent years. Yet advancement worldwide has been uneven, with substantial gaps among and within countries. The least developed countries still lag behind in efforts to improve living standards. Persistent food shortages, high energy costs, and the global economic recession threaten progress. National income has expanded in many societies, but inequality has also grown. The most vulnerable populations, including women and children, rural dwellers, and the disabled, also continue to be marginalized. Sustained progress remains a distant dream for many people.

The clearest single indicator of overall progress in human development is provided by the UNDP index, which monitors trends since 1980 in three basic dimensions: whether people enjoy a long and healthy life, knowledge, and a decent standard of living.[31] Development is often a complex process of fluctuating and erratic steps forward and backward, but Figure 4.1 illustrates the accumulated net changes occurring from 1980 to 2010. The UNDP estimates that substantial gains in human development have occurred during the last two decades in places as diverse as China, El Salvador, South Korea, Chile, and Indonesia. By contrast, during this period it has also worsened, or stagnated, in some of the world's poorest societies, such as Zimbabwe, the Democratic Republic of Congo (DRC), Zambia, and Liberia.

Security encompasses living in peaceful and secure conditions, safe from natural and manmade disasters and humanitarian crises, as well as improving material standards of living. Recent decades have also witnessed significant but uneven progress in reducing civil wars around the globe. According to estimates in the 2010 *Peace and Conflict* report, provided by Ted Gurr and his colleagues at the University of Maryland, the overall number and severity of internal armed conflicts have decreased worldwide from their peak in 1990, following the end of the Cold War.[32] Enduring peace settlements in El Salvador, Cambodia, and Liberia contributed toward the cession of deep-rooted violence,

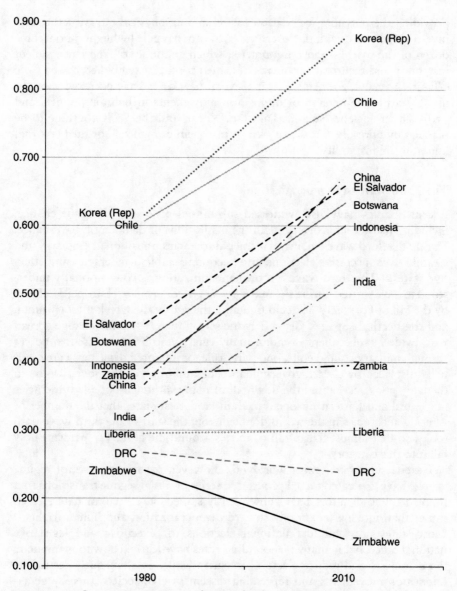

FIGURE 4.1. Contrasting progress in human development, 1980–2010.

Note: Change is monitored through the UNDP one hundred–point Human Development Index.

Source: United Nations Development Programme. 2010. *Human Development Report 2010.* New York: UNDP

providing the potential foundation for rebuilding physical infrastructure and investing in human capital. Nevertheless, the 2010 report highlights about three dozen of the world's poorest countries, which continue to experience violent instability and recurrent outbreaks of armed conflict, exemplified by the Cote d'Ivoire, Somalia, and Afghanistan. Several new cases have occurred recently, notably armed repression of opposition movements in Bahrain, Yemen, and Syria. Other societies such as Pakistan, Nepal, and the DCR continue to be plagued by unresolved tensions, which put them at high risk of further social and political instability.

The Third Wave of Democratization

Recent decades have also witnessed substantial processes of regime change, including marked improvements in the institutions of democratic governance. During the third wave era, many former autocracies transitioned gradually and steadily over successive elections into becoming stable democracies and effective states.[33] The third wave era of democratization is conventionally understood to have started during the mid-1970s in Mediterranean Europe, catalyzed by the fall of Portugal's Marcelo Caetano, the end of the Greek military junta, and the death of Spain's General Francisco Franco.[34] Regime change spread worldwide in subsequent decades; many rulers who had first risen to power through military coup d'états, one-party rule, or inherited dynasties were gradually displaced by elected governments. The implosion of the Soviet Union in the late 1980s accelerated the downfall of many, although not all, autocracies in Central and Eastern Europe. Freedom House estimates that the number of "free" democracies in the world doubled from the start of the third wave until today, so that almost half of all countries around the globe (45 percent) now fall into this category.[35]

Despite substantial gains worldwide, however, recent processes of regime change have generated mixed progress; a series of initial regime transitions that toppled ruling dictators have subsequently stalled, stagnated, or deteriorated rather than moving inexorably toward democratization and human rights.[36] Most states now conduct national elections for executive and legislative national office, but in many places ruling elites have learned how to manipulate these contests and reduce electoral integrity while simultaneously restricting opposition movements and repressing dissent in civil society, thereby generating "electoral autocracies" or "competitive authoritarianism."[37] Elections held under these conditions can occasionally provide unexpected openings for a transition of power to opposition forces.[38] In many other cases, however, contests reinforce the power of ruling elites while simultaneously deflecting criticism of their country's human rights record behind a façade of multiparty competition. Freedom House estimates that in 2011 forty-seven countries remain "not free" – that is, these states continue to repress their citizens and abuse human rights.[39] Some examples of the worst "not free" states include Alexander Lukashenko's grip over Belarus, Nursultan Nazarbayev's iron rule over Kazakhstan, or the military junta in Myanmar/Burma. Many other states continue to be governed by fragile and poorly consolidated regimes, as exemplified in Sub-Saharan Africa by instability, violent protests, and unrest following recent elections in Cote d'Ivoire and Kenya and coup d'états in Guinea, Mali, Madagascar, and Niger. The "Arab uprisings" revived hopes for a fourth wave of democracy; the sudden collapse of long-standing autocratic regimes in Tunisia and Egypt fueled democratic dreams that these events would provide openings for the peaceful expansion of reform movements, multiparty elections, and human rights in these societies as well as elsewhere in the region. Progressive reform became more uncertain by summer, with slow change in Egypt and bloodshed in Libya. In Syria, Yemen, and Bahrain, repressive regimes did not hesitate to bring the military out of their barracks, using force against their own civilian populations in an attempt to stamp out opposition movements and dissenters.

Several examples illustrating contrasting trajectories of regime change are shown in Figure 4.2, using a one hundred–point standardized index of liberal democracy derived from Freedom House's estimates in 1980 and 2010. Clearly many ups and downs can occur over the years, in trendless fluctuations, and processes of regime change and democratization are often the results of gradual and uncertain steps. Nevertheless, the figure summarizes the accumulated *net* political changes in these years. Countries as diverse as Mongolia, Turkey, the Republic of Korea, and South Africa illustrate cases of rapid strides in democratization during the last two decades, exemplifying some of the success stories of the third wave era. Many other countries around the world have seen important gains in human rights and multiparty competitive elections. By contrast, countervailing trajectories can be observed in cases as different as Venezuela, Sudan, Gambia, and Zimbabwe, all states that Freedom House estimates to have become more autocratic during the same period. In 1989, the fall of the Berlin Wall encouraged Francis Fukuyama to envisage the end of history, or at least the final closure of Cold War ideological debates.[40] Hopes for the steady triumph of democratic ideals have been tempered in recent years by more skeptical and realistic views; Huntington cautioned that past successive waves of democratic advance were usually followed by subsequent periods of retreat.[41]

Similarly, changes in the quality of governance in the public sector also show diverse pathways; hence states such as Chile, South Korea, and Turkey have improved professional standards of public administration and expanded capacity in local and national government. These states have pursued reforms by actively reducing corruption, malfeasance, and incompetence; expanding skills and training in appointments and processes of career advancement in the civil service; and improving modern techniques of public sector management. Yet elsewhere other states, exemplified by Haiti, Afghanistan, and Somalia, continue to be plagued by problems of patronage, malfeasance, and lack of technical capacity in the public sector, so that officials lack the capacity to deliver basic services such as schools and clinics, alleviate humanitarian and natural disasters, or maintain conditions of local security.

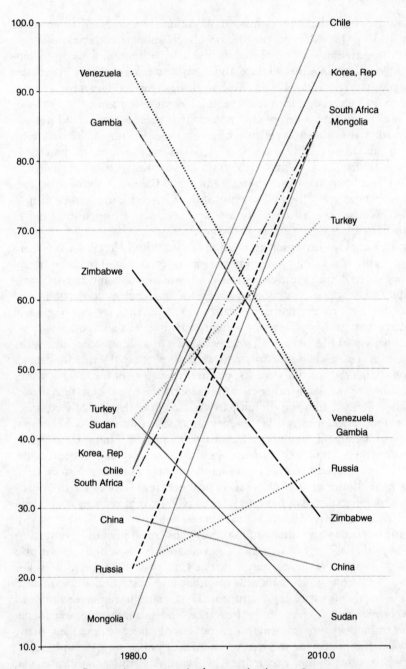

FIGURE 4.2. Contrasting progress in democratization, 1980–2010.
Note: Change is monitored through the Freedom House liberal democracy standardized index.
Source: Freedom House. http://freedomhouse.org.

Thus diverse trajectories of change help to analyze the relationship between democracy and development. Numerous empirical measures are now widely available to gauge growth, welfare and peace, however, and the choice of appropriate indicators needs to overcome certain common challenges, including avoiding *measurement errors* arising from missing observations and systematic bias in cross-national coverage; *conceptual validity*, so that indicators match the underlying concepts that we are seeking to gauge; *reliability*, so that internationally standardized indices are consistent across countries and over time; and *robustness*, to make sure that the results are not sensitive to minor modifications in the analytical models.

Selecting Outcome Indices

There is also no consensus about which indicators of human security should be selected for analysis. Comparative studies have typically focused on policy *outputs*, such as the proportion of GDP, the public sector budget, or the total outlays devoted to spending on healthcare, social protection, and defense. The International Monetary Fund and the Organization for Economic Cooperation and Development (OECD) collect and publish internationally standardized public audit data, monitoring government accounts, tax and social contribution receipts, and a breakdown of general government outlays by function.[42] These data provide important insights into government priorities, to see, for example, which types of democracies typically offer more generous welfare and employment policies. Unfortunately, audited public accounts, harmonized to monitor expenditure by function, are unavailable in many emerging and developing economies. Moreover, even where available, output data (expenditure) tell us little about the effectiveness of public sector expenditure on social outcomes; in places where politicians adopt generous budgets for schools or immunization programs, this does not mean that the resources actually improve the lives of children, by any means. Specific public policies can also change relatively quickly when, for example, the governing party leaves office and a new team takes over the reins of power. But processes expanding the reservoir of wealth, expanding welfare services, and reducing conflict are typically long-term and cumulative phenomena, especially on a sustainable basis.

Several studies have attempted to construct a composite index based on the concept of human security by combining a range of standard indicators available at the national level, exemplified by levels of battle-related deaths, average longevity, rates of infant mortality, and estimates of poverty.[43] Gary King and Christopher J. L. Murray argue that Human Security is potentially open to operationalization, within the limits of the available data, by focusing on the most severe threshold of a range of life-threatening risks.[44] They offer a definition of Human Security that is intended to include only essential elements that are "important enough for human beings to fight over or to put their lives or property at great risk." King and Murray identify five key indicators of human security: poverty, health, education, political freedom, and democracy.

Yet attempts to construct composite indicators suffer from several problems. First, it remains unclear which macro-level indicators should be included or excluded, how these should be combined and weighted, and what level or threshold constitutes a "severe" threat.[45] Thus a general consensus surrounds many internationally standardized measures of human development, such as those used to monitor progress toward meeting the Millennium Development Goals; examples include levels of child mortality, rates of tuberculosis or measles, and levels of per capita GDP.[46] Similarly, the scholarly literature has developed standard measures of the severity of intrastate and internal armed conflict, monitored by battle-related deaths and casualties, such as those collected by the Uppsala Conflict Data Program (UCDP) for the Peace Research Institute Oslo (PRIO) Armed Conflict Dataset 1946–2009.[47] But there is a serious aggregation problem in any broader measure: It still remains unclear how to combine separate macro-level indicators into a rigorous, coherent, and valid composite measure reflecting the underlying concept of human security. King and Murray select certain dimensions as representing human security without offering a clear justification for doing so. Why is political freedom included but not, say, the threat of environmental degradation or, indeed, the severe risks of natural and humanitarian disasters arising from floods, famine, earthquakes, or tsunamis? If measured by the risk of fatalities, disasters arguably have more severe effects than lack of political freedoms. Composite indices also lose much of the fine-grained detail that is essential for accurate policy diagnosis and prescription; if a particular country is low in human security, is this due to natural disasters, military aggression, or endemic poverty? We would not know from the overall rating. For all these reasons, this book, instead of using a composite scale for the dependent variables, will therefore focus on analyzing separate *outcome* indicators measuring the achievement of three central components – prosperity, welfare, and internal peace – reflecting the underlying concept of human security.

To monitor economic prosperity, this book uses per capita gross domestic product, the market value of all final goods and services produced within a country in a given period, adjusted to account for purchasing power parity (PPP), or the estimated cost of goods and services in different societies. Data are drawn from the Penn World Tables, because this source provides comprehensive cross-national coverage for 189 independent nation-states from 1950–2009.[48] Per capita GDP in PPP is the standard variable used in the research literature. Similarly, economic growth is measured as annual change in per capita GDP in PPP and is derived from the same source.

Because social welfare is a multidimensional phenomenon, it is not clear whether to select outcome indices of health (such as child or maternal mortality or incidence of diseases such as measles, malaria, or HIV-AIDS), educational attainment and literacy, estimates of economic inequality and poverty, or alternative measures of development, such as access to clean water. Scholars choose different indicators in the literature, but the selection is often somewhat arbitrary or based on data availability rather than on conceptual validity.

Accordingly, for a more systematic perspective this book analyzes several of the core indices monitoring achievement of the MDGs. This is the most comprehensive set of indices because it reflects the universal targets that the world government agreed to strive to achieve by 2015. The MDGs provide a widely agreed-on and comprehensive set of yardsticks covering all important dimensions of human welfare. Although there remain many problems of missing data, standardized international indicators monitoring annual progress since 1990 on each of these goals have been compiled by the United Nations.[49] Data analysis comparing trends over time and cross-national comparisons requires the careful choice of control variables, however, because multiple factors well beyond government institutions in each country contribute toward achieving these goals. The September 2010 UN summit concluded that progress on reaching the MDGs has been uneven across indicators, both among regions and among countries.[50]

To compare civil war, violence, and stability, standard indices are drawn from the Uppsala Conflict Data Program. The UCDP/PRIO Armed Conflict Dataset Version 4.0 provides a widely used source classifying interstate and internal armed conflict in 183 countries since 1946.[51] The dataset provides a comprehensive accounting of all forms of major armed conflicts in the world over the contemporary period: 1946–2007. UCDP defines conflict as "a contested incompatibility that concerns government and/or territory where the use of armed force between two parties, of which at least one is the government of a state, results in at least 25 battle-related deaths."[52] The analysis in this book focuses on incidents of "internal armed conflict," or civil wars, defined as conflict that occurs between the government of a state and one or more internal opposition groups without intervention from other states. The UCDP measure is coded on a four-point ordinal scale depending on the incidence and magnitude of conflict (depending on the number of battle-related deaths): 0 represents no intrastate conflict, 1 a minor intrastate armed conflict, 2 an intrastate intermediate armed conflict, and 4 an intrastate war. Each of these data sources and indicators is discussed further in the subsequent chapters where they are analyzed.

RESEARCH CHALLENGES

As observed earlier, scholars and practitioners continue to debate the relative weight and priority that should be given to governance and democracy – and, in particular, to address whether there are trade-offs between these values and whether there is a sequential process for peace-building interventions in states emerging from poverty and deep-rooted conflict. How can alternative theories be investigated using the empirical evidence?

Case Studies

One common approach to studying the evidence has focused on detailed and rich historical case studies within particular countries or regions, using qualitative research. As illustrated in the previous chapter, cases can help us to understand the impact of processes of administrative reform within the public sector or the downfall of autocratic leaders and subsequent transition processes toward electoral democracy. This approach allows researchers to develop richer and more complex theories, derive new hypotheses, and identify potential causal mechanisms. This approach is particularly useful when examining outliers, such as Singapore, that deviate from a generally observed pattern. Unfortunately, it remains difficult to establish broad generalizations from particular cases, no matter how vivid and persuasive the narrative stories, because scholars can usually always suggest counterexamples that support alternative arguments. For example, claims that autocracies deliver a better instrumental performance than democratic states gain plausibility by citing the record of China's remarkable economic growth compared against the historical performance of the Indian economy during the 1970s and 1980s. The argument that autocracies provide greater predictability and stability for international investors can be illustrated by contrasting the turbulent and disorderly democratic politics characteristic of the Philippines or Taiwan with Singapore's record of stable, clean, and efficient government.[53] Democratic theorists can cite alternative cases to challenge these claims, exemplified by the economic growth rates enjoyed before and after the transitions from authoritarian rule experienced in Hungary or the Czech Republic. Single-nation historical studies can thus generate important insights and deepen our understanding of the underlying factors behind observed regularities.[54] There are potential problem of bias in case selection, however, so cases need to be carefully chosen. In this book, cases are selected that share many structural characteristics in common, such as their geographic location, historical backgrounds, and type of social composition, but which differ in developmental outcomes and types of regimes. This approach can still only be illustrative, and ideally this needs to be combined with systematic cross-national time-series evidence that allows us to establish reliable generalizations about the underlying relationships across multiple contexts. A mixed research design combines the virtues of large-N quantitative models with richer and detailed narrative studies of contrasting paired cases.[55]

Global Comparisons

Global comparisons have employed large-N time-series cross-sectional (TSCS) panel datasets, utilizing econometric models that draw on an extensive range of quantitative economic, social, and political indicators that have become available during recent decades.[56] The standard unit of analysis is a country-year panel, with repeated annual observations of each nation. Occasionally, five-year panels have also been used to overcome problems of missing data.[57] Large-N comparisons are most effective for establishing the generalizability of relationships and identifying outliers to the observed patterns. In this book, chapters use a panel of repeated annual observations for 130 to 192 independent nation-states (depending on missing data in the variables under analysis) during the third wave era, usually for the period from 1984 to 2008 (twenty-four years). The country-year is the basic unit of analysis. The number of countries dominates the number of time periods, and the number of countries is large enough to generalize across regions and continents with some reliability, making the dataset suitable for econometric techniques. The data are an unbalanced panel, meaning that they include new countries, such as the Czech Republic, Slovakia, and Macedonia, that became independent nation-states during the third wave era. This avoids biases arising from including only countries that existed throughout the entire period. At the same time, it also includes a few exceptional cases, such as Czechoslovakia and Yugoslavia, which disintegrated as nation-states during this period, and unified Germany, which merged after the Berlin Wall fell.

The analysis of cross-sectional time-series data faces certain important challenges, however.[58] Multivariate analysis commonly uses ordinary least squares (OLS) regression analysis, but this technique generates estimates based on the assumption that errors are independent, normally distributed, and with constant variance. Cross-sectional time-series data violate these assumptions, however, and thus the use of OLS estimates raises potential problems. Heteroskedasticity is produced if the range of variations in the scatter of nation-states around the regression line is not uniform and linearly distributed across different levels of democratic governance, such as would occur if there were a "stepped" pattern or an S- shaped curve. Autocorrelations are generated, because with time-series data, the same countries are being counted repeatedly every year and the additional observations do not provide substantially new information. The danger is that OLS will fail to identify the lack of independence between cases and will subsequently reach false conclusions. The beta coefficients in any regression estimates will remain unbiased, but the disturbance terms from the errors (that is, omitted variables) are likely to be correlated. The use of ordinary least squares regression models would lead to estimates of standard errors, used for evaluating the significance of any relationships and testing rival hypotheses, which are less accurately measured than they appear. In other words, OLS with this type of dataset is likely to generate Type I errors (false positives); the results would suggest a statistically significant coefficient exists when, in truth, there is no statistical difference.

OLS Regression Models with Panel-Corrected Standard Errors

Various options are available to overcome the problem of both autocorrelated and heteroskedastic disturbances typically found in cross-sectional time-series datasets. Feasible generalized least squares can be used that estimate errors with an AR1 model, or robust regression can be employed.[59] OLS models can also seek to control for national variations by using a pooled model, including dummy variables for each country, but this quickly becomes inefficient with the coverage of many nations. Alternatively, OLS can be run with no pooling, where separate models are run for each nation, but this is also clumsy.

For a more efficient approach to estimating the impact of levels of democratic governance on the development indices across countries and time, following the advice of Nathaniel Betz and Jonathan Katz, this book uses ordinary least squares linear regression with panel-corrected standard errors (PCSE).[60] Beck and Katz argue that feasible generalized least squares (FGLS) models are less accurate and efficient than OLS with PCSE. This approach is particularly suited to the type of dataset, as the number of countries under comparison worldwide is far greater than the number of years. When computing the standard errors and the variance-covariance estimates, OLS regression analysis models with PCSE assume that disturbances are, by default, heteroskedastic and contemporaneously correlated across panels. One important advantage of this approach is that the results of OLS regression models are relatively easily interpretable as a widely familiar statistical technique in the social sciences. The use of panel-corrected standard errors is the most appropriate approach where the data contain most contemporary countries worldwide rather than a sample of units drawn from a larger universe, where estimating the random effects may be more suitable.[61] Moreover, with a large time series, the results of fixed and random effects models usually converge, so there is no substantial difference in the use of either approach. The use of fixed effects has its costs, however, because it forces us to drop independent variables from the model that are unchanging attributes of each country, such as region. Fixed effects models also make it hard for any slowly changing variables to appear substantively or statistically significant, making a rigorous test for estimating the impact of any incremental regime change.[62]

Before and after Fixed Effects

Even the most rigorous OLS regression models with PCSE have difficulty in establishing the direction of causality in any relationship, due to the complex interaction effects of the social phenomena under analysis. In the relationship between institutions and developmental indicators, causality can run both ways. Thus well-run states can be expected to manage the economy more effectively and thereby strengthen national income. On the other hand, wealthier economies can afford to invest in public sector management.[63] Similarly, by delivering effective social services and an outlet for public disaffection, the mechanisms of bureaucratic democracy can be expected to reduce the causes of grievance and thereby minimize one of the prime sources of societal conflict. Stable and peaceful societies can also be expected to build more effective state institutions. The Lipset thesis has long claimed that processes of economic development and societal modernization are some of the key drivers for processes of democratization, through expanding literacy, cognitive skills, media access to alternative forms of information, and the professional middle class.[64] Yet democracy can simultaneously help to explain human development, if associated with higher investment in human capital, spending more on education, healthcare, and welfare.

Given these complex reciprocal relationships, any observed correlation linking democratic governance and development indicators can be challenged on the grounds of the causal direction of the linkage.[65] Conclusions therefore need to be carefully double-checked for robustness using different specifications, alternative indicators, and diagnostic sensitivity tests.[66] One potential problem is that the explanatory variable (the type of regime) is correlated with the error terms. Such correlation may also occur due to poorly specified models that fail to omit relevant explanatory factors, suggesting spurious and false relationships; for example, a model might seek to explain economic growth but fail to control for levels of ethnic fractionalization, civil violence, the predominant type of religious culture, or geographic location, all of which may simultaneously influence *both* the type of regime *and* the developmental outcomes of growth, welfare, and peace.

To mitigate issues arising from simultaneous observations, time lags are normally employed for the dependent variable, by measuring the type of regime at one-to-five-year intervals before the subsequent occurrence of the outcome variables, such as subsequent levels of literacy, poverty, or conflict. Nevertheless, models can prove sensitive to the choice of interval, and it remains unclear theoretically what precise lag is most appropriate; if democracy and governance institutions are sticky phenomena, should democratic and governmental reforms be expected to bear fruit immediately after they are introduced, for example, or only after an extended historical period of stabilization and consolidation?[67] Regime transitions provide particularly valuable analytical leverage, however, analogous to diverse "natural experiments" in the social sciences, allowing us to evaluate the "before" and "after" effects of regime change (shocks) on policy performance. The case studies described in the earlier chapter suggested that certain decisive transitions or historic watersheds can sometimes be identified in retrospect, notably processes strengthening democratization in Chile following the end of the Pinochet era in 1989 and in Ghana with the introduction of the 1992 constitution. Similarly, the overthrow of Somalia's President Barre in 1991 was decisive for plunging the country into conditions of lawlessness, anarchy, and violence, weakening the central government. The outbreak of particular interstate and civil wars also provides specific historical events where it is possible to determine periodicity with some confidence. Many political transitions are gradual, however, cumulating slowly or wavering back and forth over the years, rather than one-off steps in a progressively linear direction.

Multiple variables can also be expected to generate complex processes of regime change and development, meaning that it becomes difficult to control for all these without quickly encountering major difficulties arising from missing observations in the series (and, by implication, potential systematic bias in the selection of countries contained in models) and serious problems of multicollinearity. Given the complexity of the underlying processes, no matter how many variables are contained in comprehensive models, there are always challenges arising from alternative specifications.

One potential way to overcome some of these challenges is to supplement OLS regression models with fixed effects models, which test for within-country changes over at least two points of time.[68] This approach is analogous to the experimental method, the "gold standard" for causal inference in scientific research, where certain treatments are administered (for example, changes in levels of democratic governance) and the effects are monitored (the mean change in development indices, measured before and after the treatment is introduced). This type of model assumes that some features of countries will not alter during the period of the third wave era under analysis. For example, in Ghana and Chile, during the third wave era there was no change in each country's geographic location, colonial inheritance, ethnic heterogeneity, spatial size and type of terrain, and the predominant religious and cultural traditions in each society. The extent to which these should be treated as stable during the period under study is a matter for interpretation; for example, the geographic location of countries is fixed, if measured simply by distance from the equator. Yet the most recent wave of globalization and technological developments in transportation and communications during the late twentieth century, which tie places together, substantially shifted the meaning of a society's geographical location by shrinking space and time. Similarly, the distribution of "natural resources" is often treated as stable (the existence of copper reservoirs in Chile), although the discovery and production of these minerals change substantially over time (such as Ghana's discovery of off-shore oil). Constructivist accounts emphasize that even ethnicity within each society, usually regarded as fixed, can be manipulated in its political meaning and significance, as well as in its composition, through migration policies. A fixed effects model is most useful in controlling for each country's stable characteristics while focusing only on the within-country mean change over time in levels of democratic governance and development. If democracy-promotion claims are true, then the transitions to democracy in Chile and Ghana that occurred during the early 1990s should have sharply accelerated progress in development in each society, as observed two decades later, controlling for each country's fixed characteristics. In this regard, geography or national culture is treated as equivalent to individual-level race, sex, or intelligence. Controlling for all the stable characteristics of any country, when examining changes in democratization and in income, eliminates a potentially large source of bias.

Nevertheless, certain well-known disadvantages arise from fixed effect models. In particular, these cannot generate coefficients for stable variables with no within-country variation. This can be problematic for estimating the effects of institutions in countries, such as Singapore, that we have already observed change sluggishly, if at all, in their levels of bureaucratic autocracy over successive decades during the third wave era. The danger of fixed effects models in this context is Type II errors – rejecting an effect arising from bureaucratic autocracy that really does matter for developmental performance. Fixed effects models are mainly useful for this book in estimating the effects of countries that experienced regime transition during the third wave era. Random effects models, on the other hand, estimate the effects of within-country and between-county variations, including stable characteristics (such as whether or not countries such as Canada or Norway were liberal democracies throughout the third wave era). This between-country variation provides important information, allowing analysts to generalize beyond the cases (countries and years) under comparison. Comparison of both random and fixed effects models provides a double-check on the analysis, and, if the estimates appear similar in both, then this process increases confidence in the interpretation of the results.

Instrumental Variables

An alternative approach seeking to overcome some of these analytical challenges is to use an instrumental variable, if available, as consistent estimates may then still be obtained using OLS regression. An instrument is a variable that does not belong in the explanatory equation (it is not part of the explanation) yet is correlated with the type of regime (as the endogenous explanatory variable), conditional on other factors. However, it is difficult to establish satisfactory instrumental variables to measure prosperity, welfare, and conflict that should also have no effect on the quality of democratic governance.[69]

For example, in an influential study, Darron Acemoglu, Simon Johnson, and James A. Robinson suggest that in European colonies, colonial settler mortality rates serve as a proxy for contemporary political institutions.[70] In particular, they argue, the conditions in the colonies were vital for early institution building, and these early efforts laid the foundations for modern institutions. European settlers who arrived in colonies relatively free of the risks of disease could develop subsistence farming, such as in Australia and Canada. In this context, settlers also invested in building institutions, including contract law, secure property rights, and human capital, which created the foundations for flourishing markets and effective states. By contrast, in extractive states – such as in West Africa and Latin America, where colonists profited from the slave trade, gold, and ivory commodities – settlers did not build these institutions. Instead, the primary aim of the colonizers was to transfer resources back to Europe but not to settle in these countries, due to the high risk facing European colonists who lacked immunity and were thus vulnerable to such fatal diseases as malaria and yellow fever. The measure of historical mortality rates is estimated from the record of soldiers, bishops, and sailors living in the colonies from the seventeenth to nineteenth centuries. The strongly negative relationship between historical colonial mortality rates and contemporary patterns of GDP is theorized to run through the institutions developed by the European colonizers. But at the same time, it cannot be suggested that contemporary levels of economic development *caused* levels of settler mortality experienced centuries earlier. Based on this instrument, Dani Rodrik, Arvind Subramanian, and Francesco Trebbi conclude that institutions matter for growth, outweighing the impact of geography and trade integration.[71]

Instrumental variables require strong assumptions, however, about the underlying narrative and the reasons given for their conceptual validity and meaning. For example, Edward L. Glaeser and his colleagues argue that the Europeans who settled in the New World may have brought with them their human capital rather than their institutions. Because human capital (skills and capacities derived from literacy and schooling) is a strong predictor of economic growth, they suggest that predictors of settlement patterns are not valid instruments for institutions.[72] Limited cross-national coverage also restricts the utility of these data; for example, historical estimates of settler death rates given by Acemoglu, Johnson, and Robinson are available only for sixty-four countries worldwide. The policy implications arising from their analysis also seem ambiguous; countries need effective institutions to generate growth, the argument suggests, but the foundations of property rights and rule of law lie in earlier colonial eras, and thus they are not necessarily amendable to contemporary reforms. It is thus extremely challenging to find appropriate instruments that are correlated with democratic governance (relevant) but unrelated to development (exogenous). For all these reasons, this book adopts OLS regression with panel-corrected standard errors for the panel data analysis.

Country Selection Bias

Another important problem to overcome is any sample bias arising from country selection. The United Nations currently recognizes 195 independent nation-states.[73] Yet most studies are based on a far smaller subset of states where standardized cross-national data are available, perhaps drawing on around half to two-thirds of all countries. This practice can introduce systematic measurement error as reliable data are most often missing in fragile states and in low-income countries that lack the capacity to gather reliable official statistics from census or household surveys, and the exclusion of these states can seriously limit the generalizability of any findings. Dependent territories are also usually excluded from comparison prior to achieving statehood. Survivorship bias is also evident in studies that exclude independent nation-states that have fallen apart during recent years, such as Yugoslavia, as well as new states that have emerged, such as Timor-Leste. In all these situations, ordinary linear regression can produce biased and inconsistent estimates.

The importance of selection bias can be illustrated by one of the most widely used datasets in the research literature, Polity IV, which excludes microstates with a population below a minimum threshold. The Polity IV series therefore covers 164 nations, but it leaves out at least three dozen of the world's independent nation-states. Because smaller societies are often also more democratic,[74] this process systematically underestimates the global trends in democratization and also generates unintentional regional biases (for example, excluding almost three-quarters of all Pacific and Caribbean island states). Compared with the global average, the countries excluded from the Polity IV dataset also have a higher per capita income (real GDP per capita in PPP in 2007 was $15,523 in the excluded nations compared to $12,416 in the Polity IV countries), better growth rates (real GDP per capita grew by 2.47 percent from 1984 to 2007 in the excluded countries, compared to 2.02 in the Polity IV nations), and a higher level of democracy (the standardized Freedom House Gastil one hundred–point index estimates in 2007 were 85 in the excluded nations, compared to 63 in the Polity IV countries). More than half of the nations excluded from Polity IV were ex-British colonies, and Polity also excluded more than 70 percent of the island microstates located in the Pacific and Caribbean. Thus what may appear to be unimportant technical decisions about the size threshold for including countries in the dataset can in fact generate serious bias in any global comparisons based on Polity IV. Therefore, in general, the more comprehensive the country coverage, the more reliable the worldwide comparisons.

Omitted Variable Bias and Controls

Although state institutions have been widely emphasized in the recent literature, the extensive body of research suggests that the complex interaction of many other factors contribute toward prosperity, welfare, and peace. Omitted variable bias arises if important variables are not included in the regression models. Accordingly, subsequent chapters discuss the most appropriate controls to include when analyzing each of the different topics. This includes the role of geography, which is thought to matter because of its consequences for climate, agricultural production, distance to trade markets, transportation costs, vulnerability to disease, integration into regional networks, cross-border conflicts, and the global diffusion of cosmopolitan ideas.[75] The endowment of natural resources such as oil, gas, precious minerals, diamonds, and gold is often regarded as critical for prosperity and conflict, whether positively through generating export-led trade and economic growth or, more commonly, like Midas, the "resource curse" may encourage rent-seeking behavior, the predatory state and elite capture of public goods, as well as the fueling of civil wars over the plunder.[76] Similarly, ethnicity – including the existence of linguistic, racial, and religious divisions – is expected to play a major role in development, with the most fractionalized societies commonly plagued both by extreme poverty and social inequality (as noted by William Easterly) as well as by internal conflict and instability (as Edward D. Mansfield and Jack Snyder document).[77] Cultural attitudes, including the residual historical legacy of religious traditions, colonial histories, and the strength of either traditional or self-expression values, have also been emphasized as influential for human development.[78] Another issue to consider in the analysis concerns exogenous global trends, such as the reduction in armed conflict experienced since the early 1990s or global improvements registered in some of the Millennium Development Indices during the same era. Unless these trends are controlled for, any improvements in development and security may be incorrectly attributed to the simultaneous growth of democratic governance during these years. Properly specified models therefore need to control, at a minimum, for the role of geography, natural resources, ethnic fractionalization, cultural values, and global trends, as well as for many other variables. Based on this foundation, subsequent chapters need to examine the arguments and evidence, starting with debates about the effect of regimes on economic prosperity.

PART III

REGIME EFFECTS

5

Prosperity

Does democratic governance expand wealth and prosperity? This question has long been at the heart of intense debate in the social sciences and among policy makers. In recent decades, international organizations have devoted growing resources to strengthening regimes; hence the World Bank now emphasizes that countries with "good governance" are more likely to attract investment in human and physical capital and thus generate the conditions thought favorable to long-term prosperity.[1] The Bank's programs have worked with country partners to reinforce mechanisms designed to strengthen the transparency of decision making and the accountability of public officials, including control of corruption, legal mechanisms securing property and contractual rights, the independent media and civil society organizations, the conditions of basic security and order, and capacity building of public sector management.[2] Elsewhere this perspective has influenced development agencies, notably the United States Millennium Challenge Account, which uses the quality of governance as a condition for the allocation of additional aid.[3] Similarly, the assumption that democratic governance generates both growth and welfare (and thus potential achievement of the Millennium Development Goals) has strongly influenced strategic priorities within many United Nations agencies and bureaus.[4] Hence the United Nations Development Programme used to focus on providing technical assistance and capacity building for public administration reform; since 2002, however, work on democratic governance has expanded in scope and size to the point that it absorbs almost half the organization's total budget. UNDP supports one in three parliaments in the developing world and an election every two weeks. In 2010, UNDP helped more than 130 countries and devoted US$1.18 billion in resources to democratic governance, making this organization the world's largest provider of democratic governance assistance.[5]

Given this investment of resources, it is vitally important to understanding the role of regime institutions in spurring economic growth, improving living standards, and alleviating poverty. For more than half a century, rival theories about the regime–growth relationship have been repeatedly tested against the empirical evidence, using a variety of cases, models, and techniques. Scholars have examined evidence throughout the third wave era, and a substantial research literature has now emerged investigating this relationship, both in regional studies as well as comparisons of global trends.[6] Despite repeated and imaginative attempts, many technical challenges arise when seeking to establish conclusive proof about core theoretical claims. Partial agreement is starting to emerge about some of the observable empirical regularities, but even here the complex reciprocal linkages between regime institutions and growth mean that consensus is far from complete. For some, neoliberal "good governance" institutions such as property rights and rule of law (but not democracy) do indeed facilitate growth in per capita GDP.[7] For others, however, growth is regarded as the key driver of the quality of democratic governance.[8] For still others, any relationship is modified by certain conditions, whether the type of constitutional design, the length of time that institutions have been established, a specific threshold level of development, or the type of societal structure and culture within which institutions are embedded. Empirical studies of the relationship between democracy and growth generate results that are highly sensitive to technical specifications and the comparative framework, hence findings have failed to prove robust when replicated with a different range of nations or with models employing alternative indicators and methods.[9] Moreover, claims that "institutions matter" are constructed at a highly abstract level, and theories identifying the intermediate mechanisms linking regimes and growth, and thus our capacity to offer policy-relevant recommendations, remain underspecified and poorly understood. Equally importantly, most studies have analyzed the impact of either democracy or governance, but the comparison of both of these twin phenomena has been neglected. For all these reasons, previous research needs to be revisited to establish more robust and precise generalizations.

The structure of this chapter proceeds as follows. The first section reviews and summarizes theories positing why regimes are expected to influence economic growth directly, either positively or negatively. After considering these debates, the second section discusses the technical challenges facing research on this topic and how it is proposed to overcome these. The third section presents the results of the comparative analysis for the main effects of democratic governance on economic growth during recent decades. The descriptive results illustrate the main relationship between regimes and growth. The multivariate models check whether these patterns remain significant after controlling for other factors associated with growth, including geography, economic conditions, social structural variables, cultural legacies, and global trends. The evidence supports the book's core thesis suggesting that regimes combining both liberal democracy and bureaucratic governance in parallel are most likely to generate growth, while by contrast patronage autocracies display the worst economic performance. The underlying processes that help to explain the patterns are illustrated in more depth by comparing the paired case studies of Haiti and the Dominican Republic, conjoined twin societies sharing one Caribbean island, with similar histories during earlier centuries and similar geographic resources, yet illustrating contrasting types of regimes and trajectories of economic development during recent years.

I. THEORIES LINKING REGIMES WITH ECONOMIC GROWTH

Skeptics believe that regime institutions are unable to exert significant independent effects on growth (the null hypothesis) compared with standard factors, such as trade, technology, and geography, commonly emphasized in the research literature. Although societal modernization is expected to strengthen processes of democratization and investment in the quality of governance institutions, in the skeptical view the reverse relationship does not hold. These views are challenged by this book's theory, which posits that economic growth is strengthened by regimes combining liberal democratic institutions (reinforcing channels of electoral accountability) with bureaucratic governance (and thus state capacity for effective macroeconomic management). The claims are compared against those of other scholars who offer a number of reasons that the institutions of either governance or those of liberal democracy are expected to influence income. As discussed earlier, there is no single perspective within these schools of thought. Several potential linkage mechanisms are suggested in the previous literature, each emphasizing a different underlying connection. After reviewing the arguments, the cross-national time-series evidence allows us to test each of these accounts, comparing the book's theory against its rivals.

The Skeptical Null Hypothesis

The traditional economics literature seeking to identify the "deep" or "fundamental" determinants of economic performance suggests that growth is affected by a multitude of complex structural conditions. Economists typically emphasize levels of investment in human and physical capital, societal infrastructure (schools, roads, communications, and so on), openness to trade (and thus export-led growth of goods and commodities), geography (climate, location, type of agriculture, risk of tropical disease, and access to neighboring markets), the diffusion of access to technological innovations, the distribution of natural resources (such as minerals, oil, and gas), social structure (including the size of the labor force, levels of social inequality, and ethnic divisions), and the cultural values that predominate in any society.[10] Countries that invest more, develop new technologies, and have better infrastructures are usually expected to flourish more successfully.

By contrast, the precise role of regimes as part of this process, and which particular types of institutions are important, remains under dispute in the contemporary research literature. Ever since Douglas North's seminal contribution, it has become fashionable for economists to claim that "institutions rule."[11] In particular, many emphasize that growth is strongly shaped by institutions strengthening rule of law, private property rights, and control of corruption. An influential study by Darron Acemoglu, Simon Johnson, and James A. Robinson argues that in former European colonies, colonial settler mortality rates serve as a proxy for the quality of contemporary political institutions.[12] The conditions in the colonies, they reason, were vital for early institution building, laying the foundations for modern contract law, secure property rights, and human capital, all of which provide the groundwork for flourishing markets and effective states. Yet several scholars reverse their interpretation of the relationship on the grounds that institutions such as effective and clean administration in the public sector, rule of law, and respect for property rights are probably the consequence, rather than the cause, of economic growth.[13] As noted earlier, Glaeser and his colleagues argue that the Europeans who settled in the New World may have brought their human capital with them (the skills and capacities derived from literacy and schooling) rather than their legal institutions. Because human capital is a strong predictor of economic growth, they argue that historical settlement patterns are not valid instruments for contemporary political institutions.[14] Similarly, Nicholas Charron and Victor Lapuente argue that any relationship runs from growth to governance; growing prosperity is thought to expand the resources available to invest in the quality of bureaucratic governance and the administration of public services, as well as encouraging public demands for these services.[15] Therefore, although "good governance" has now become fashionable in the international development community, the robustness of the empirical findings claiming that institutions matter for growth continues to be debated, especially compared with many other deep drivers of economic development.

At the same time, skeptics doubt whether democracy exerts a significant independent effect on economic prosperity; democratic regimes can be rich (Sweden) or poor (Benin). Similarly, autocracies vary from the resurgent growth experienced by China and Vietnam to the economic stagnation or decline evident in North Korea or Zimbabwe. Support for the skeptical perspective can be found in much of the empirical evidence. Thus, although some research reports that the institutions of liberal democracy have a positive impact on economic growth, most studies suggest a negative relationship or indeed no significant relationship at all.[16] A widely cited early study by Robert Barro reported that growth was strengthened by maintenance of the rule of law, free markets, small government consumption, and high human capital. Once models control for these kinds of variables, and the initial level of real per capita GDP was held constant, then the overall additional effect of liberal democratic regimes on growth proved weakly negative.[17] The skeptical perspective was reinforced by one of the most comprehensive studies, by Adam Przeworski and his colleagues, which compared the experience of economic and political development in 141 countries from 1950 to 1990.[18] Democratic and autocratic regimes were classified according to Schumpeterian rules of electoral contestation. The study concluded that according to this measure, democracies proved no better (but also no worse) than dictatorships at generating economic growth. Among poor countries as well, the type of regime made no difference for growth:

> In countries with incomes below $3000, the two regimes have almost identical investment shares, almost identical rates of growth of capital stock and of labor force, the same production function, the same contributions of capital, labor, and factor productivity to growth, the same output per worker, the same labor shares, and the same product wages... Regimes make no difference for growth, quantitatively or qualitatively.[19]

The most recent comprehensive review of the research literature, by Hristos Doucouliagos and Mehmet Ulubasoglu, compared and summarized eighty-four studies published on the regime–growth relationship.[20] Not surprisingly, their meta-analysis noted that estimates of the regime–growth relationship differed across this range of studies due to varied data sources, techniques, control variables, country coverage, and time periods. Overall, however, the study concluded that liberal democracy exerts no *direct* impact on prosperity, either positively or negatively. Some indirect regime effects were observed, however, as liberal democracies invest more in human capital and have greater political stability, both of which strengthened growth. If the skeptical view is indeed correct, then the empirical evidence should demonstrate that the direct effect of the prior type of regime makes little significant difference, positive or negative, to subsequent levels of economic growth.

The Effects of Governance on Growth

The skeptical view about the positive role of regimes for growth was not confined to academic studies; it also used to permeate the international development community. During the 1970s and 1980s, the first-generation Washington Consensus advocated by the agencies of global finance, based on neoclassical theories in political economy, explained prosperity as a product of market forces; countries seeking to expand production output and export-led growth were advised to end protectionism and open borders to international trade, attract investment capital, allow competitive exchange rates, develop human capital, adapt to technological progress, deregulate the economy, and enlarge the labor force. In the neoclassical view, the state was regarded as hindering growth in the private sector if it ventured beyond strictly minimal Smithsonian functions of providing security, infrastructure, and protection of property rights. The predatory or bloated state was seen as problematic for growth, especially macroeconomic policies involving public sector ownership of industry, massive budget deficits, negative interest rates, protectionist restrictions on free trade, overregulation, endemic corruption, and inadequate basic public services.[21] Tax reform, privatization, trade liberalization, anticorruption measures, and fiscal austerity were the prescribed medicine to cure these ailments. It was believed that the state had to get out of the way to let unfettered markets achieve growth most efficiently. In the rush to liberalize public sector ownership and shrink the size of the state, little attention was paid to the capacity of the government, whether to regulate the privatization process and prevent the emergence of new oligopolies, maintain security, manage the delivery of basic public goods and services, plan and implement policies, or enforce laws. The first-generation Washington Consensus therefore held that good economic performance required liberalized trade, macroeconomic stability, and getting prices right.

In subsequent years, however, the revised second-generation Washington Consensus came to acknowledge the important positive role of the state in development and the dangers of radical structural adjustment, growing social inequality, market failures, and corruption.[22] Many factors contributed toward this revised philosophy. Latin American countries, which had embraced the menu of liberalization, often failed to achieve stable and equitable economic growth. Economists in the region started to address the institutional reforms needed to tackle social inequality and substantial improvements in living standards for the poor.[23] Experience in Eastern Europe, especially Russia, demonstrated that shock therapy and the selling off of public sector assets in countries lacking rule of law and control of corruption merely transferred state power to business oligarchs and reinforced crony capitalism. The fall of the Berlin Wall, and transitions from autocracy elsewhere in the world, spurred renewed interest in understanding the economic consequences of processes of democratization and constitutional arrangements, as well as providing new opportunities for reforming regimes. The 1997 Asian economic crisis in countries that had liberalized their economies created new challenges to the standard prescriptions.[24] Most recently, doubts about the wisdom of unregulated markets have been reinforced by the financial downturn catalyzed by the bursting housing bubble and banking crisis in the United States, which quickly infected debt-ridden economies in Mediterranean Europe and beyond.[25]

Neoliberal Claims for "Good Governance"

The second-generation Washington Consensus, emerging during the early 1990s, recognized that effective state institutions and the quality of governance can function as deep drivers that supplement markets and thereby also contribute positively toward economic growth.[26] "Institutions" are commonly understood, following North, as both formal legal regulations and informal patterned social interactions, cultural traditions, and social norms determining mechanisms of social cooperation and the way in which authority is exercised.[27] The substantial body of empirical literature that has emerged in economics in recent decades has claimed that certain types of neoliberal governance institutions are critical for economic development. Research started to explore some of the empirical evidence, including a seminal paper by Paulo Mauro documenting the links between corruption and growth.[28] This study stimulated a substantial body of work replicating and expanding the core findings, using many types of economic indices and measures of corruption.[29] Another early study by Stephen Knack and Philip Keefer reported that the ICRG ratings of the quality of governance were directly related to growth of per capita income.[30]

This work highlighted the need for cross-national and time-series indicators capable of monitoring institutional quality. From 1996 onward, Daniel Kaufmann, Aart Kraay, and Massimo Mastruzzi at the World Bank Institute developed composite estimates for all countries worldwide covering six dimensions of "good governance," including perceptions of rule of law, control of corruption, voice and accountability, regulatory quality, government effectiveness, and political stability; these perceptions were measured by expert polls and public opinion surveys conducted by multiple organizations.[31] This evidence seemed to provide empirical support for the importance of good governance institutions, especially those strengthening control of corruption, property rights, and rule of law. In a series of papers, Kaufmann, Kraay, and Mastruzzi have drawn on the World Bank Institute indices as evidence to argue that "good governance" generates substantial payoffs for the economy: "A country that improves its governance from a relatively low level to an average level could almost triple the per capita income of its population in the long-term."[32] Similarly, Rodrik, Subrahanian, and Trebbi also conclude that rule of law and security of property rights are both deep determinants of economic growth, controlling for the effects of geography and trade.[33] These particular institutions are believed to underpin free markets, investor confidence, and contract enforcement. Neoliberals therefore emphasize that income growth is facilitated by specific types of institutions that are thought to reduce the risks and barriers that investors face in the marketplace. If this claim is true, then *growth should be strongly linked with several specific indices of "good governance,"* in particular the WBI estimates of rule of law, property rights, and control of corruption.

The Effects of State Capacity on Growth

Yet governance is an abstract and vague term that is open to alternative interpretations. Following the "institutional turn" in economics, other leading scholars have renewed the emphasis on the role of formal rules, but governance has been interpreted from a more Keynesian or social democratic perspective. Hence the Nobel Prize–winner Joseph Stigletz advocated a more interventionist role for the state in the economy, using the strategic levers of regulatory institutions, social insurance programs, and fiscal and monetary policies, above and beyond ensuring the conditions for free markets through protecting private property rights and rule of law.[34] Francis Fukuyama has emphasized the urgent need for state-building and well-functioning public administration, on the grounds that weak states are the source of many of the world's problems, from poverty to AIDS, terrorism, and drugs.[35] Public sector reform was critical for effective state capacity, Fukuyama argues, even though the scope and functions of the state need to be limited. By contrast, Fukuyama did not regard democracy and human rights as deserving equal priority for the international development community, except perhaps as a way to legitimize states.[36]

If it is recognized that governments need to play an effective role in economic development – through regulating the market economy, implementing laws and policies, planning budgets, and managing the delivery of public goods and services – then their ability to do so rests, in large part, on the professional skills, procedural culture, and technical capacity of the public sector. Presenting empirical support for this view, Peter Evans and J. E. Rauch documented the link between estimates of the quality of "Weberian bureaucracy" and economic growth. The study compared almost three dozen developing societies from 1970 to 1990, measuring perceptions of the quality of bureaucratic governance from an expert survey. After controlling for initial levels of per capita GDP and human capital, the results of their analysis showed that greater economic prosperity was common in states where the civil service in the core economic agencies had meritocratic recruitment processes and predictable career ladders.[37]

Many case studies are also often cited to support the claim that the implementation of effective development policies requires competent public administration and a strong and effective state. This argument is believed to be supported by the remarkable growth and rapid industrialization enjoyed in the East Asian tiger economies of Taiwan, Singapore, China, and South Korea, leading some observers to posit a sequential process of "economic development first, democracy second."[38] The case of Singapore is commonly thought to illustrate the Asian model of development, combining both economic success and social stability, and thus the presumed advantages of bureaucratic autocracies. Singapore has become one of the most affluent nations around the world, ranked twenty-third highest on the 2009 Human Development Index, just behind Germany and ahead of Greece, Israel, and Portugal. The Singapore economy, built on the service sector, particularly finance, banking, investment, and trade, has forged ahead despite a lack of natural resources. In 2009, Singapore produced a per capita GDP of around $37,000 (in PPP), similar to Italy and Japan. Bureaucratic governance in the island-state, an autocracy ruled by one predominant party and with limited political rights and freedoms, is widely regarded as both efficient and effective.[39]

China is an even more striking case, enjoying an average annual growth rate of 10 percent over the last three decades, a level that was maintained despite the 2008 global financial crisis that has afflicted the United States and the euro zone. In 1980, the average per capita income in China was $251 (with the nation ranked fourth to last worldwide).[40] By 2010, this figure had risen to $7,240 (ranked eighty-ninth from the bottom). China is widely regarded as challenging the standard neoliberal conventional wisdom that free markets, state deregulation, and secure private property rights are vital for growth.[41] The Chinese Communist Party has also developed internal mechanisms for regular leadership succession, as well as maintaining meritocratic processes for bureaucratic recruitment and career advancement. The political stability found in bureaucratic autocracies is believed to encourage the process of rapid industrialization and thus facilitate sustainable economic growth. Yet the evidence for administrative competence in East Asian states does not always tell a consistent story supporting these claims; the Republic of Korea, for example, experienced serious problems of corruption and crony capitalism for many decades during its long period of economic development, although in recent years these problems have greatly diminished.[42] If the core argument is correct, however, it suggests that *the quality of bureaucratic governance in any country should significantly affect subsequent levels of economic growth.*

The Effects of Democracy on Growth

In this section, we explore how democracy encourages accountability and what types of regimes promote growth. Claims that democracy fails to exert an independent effect on economic development, compared with other structural determinants, are also challenged by those emphasizing the instrumental consequences of democracy promotion.

Accountability: Elections Reward Competent Economic Management

The most common argument from this perspective suggests that democracies are usually more successful at generating economic growth because competitive elections provide an automatic fail-safe mechanism for removing incompetent leaders; governing parties perceived by citizens as successful at managing the economy are usually returned to office, while ineffective administrations are kicked out. Morton H. Halperin, Joseph T. Siegle, and Michael M. Weinstein suggest that in this regard democracies have a "self-correcting mechanism."[43] By contrast, no such regular and peaceful channel exists in autocracies to remove inept, repressive, or venal leaders. As Francis Fukuyama points out, autocracies have variable economic performance; states may be ruled by a Lee Kwan Yew, but they may also be run by a Mobutu or a Marcos or a Gaddafi.[44]

The accountability argument builds on several well-established theories in the literature, including (i) the Schumpeterian conception of democracy, emphasizing the role of elections as core mechanisms in democracy for the expression of public preferences, government accountability, and political responsiveness; (ii) Downsian theories suggesting that rational voters cast ballots seeking to maximize their utility; and (iii) theories of retrospective voting, emphasizing that in democratic states citizens evaluate the economic performance of the governing party and leader, rewarding or punishing them accordingly at the ballot box.[45] This last line of thought suggests that particular elections in each country can revolve around the government's record on a wide range of issues on the policy agenda, but overall many contests are thought to be won or lost based on public evaluations of the governing party or parties' competence in managing bread-and-butter economic conditions.[46] Poor government results at the ballot box have commonly been attributed to conditions of unemployment, inflation, or poor growth, in contests where "it's the economy, stupid."[47] Vote-seeking politicians thus have a strong incentive to manage the economy effectively and to offer alternative policies that appeal to the majority of the electorate.[48] Parties and leaders demonstrating a competent record are expected to be most consistently returned to steer the nation's economy, while those with a poor performance are usually less successful in gaining power. By contrast, autocrats face no such electoral sanction; citizens have little power to get rid of ineffective leaders, short of violent means, in countries such as Zimbabwe, Somalia, and Equatorial Guinea, despite public disaffection with declining incomes, endemic poverty, and worsening living standards.[49] If these claims are true, when tested against the empirical evidence, *levels of democratization should predict subsequent levels of economic growth*.

Some limited evidence supports this claim; for example Halperin, Siegle, and Weinstein compared the economic performance of poorer societies (defined as those below $2,000 per capita) from 1960 to 2005 and found that democracies usually enjoyed higher per capita growth rates than autocracies. Moreover, when all countries are considered, they report that democracies have realized consistently higher levels of economic growth than autocracies during the last five decades.[50] Yet many other characteristics of democratic societies, not controlled in their models, may be driving these observations. The claim that democratic regimes are more positive for growth has also been strongly challenged. Hence drawing on the experience of development in Latin America, Guillermo O'Donnell argued that the early stages of any democratic transition in the region were often characterized by weaker governance capacity, and thus greater instability and uncertainty, inflationary pressures on the state, and a rise in distributional conflict, heightening the risks facing international investors.[51] By contrast, he emphasized that states with effective bureaucracies and strong executives had the capacity to respond promptly and decisively when managing the economy, especially during crisis conditions.

Do Democracies Strengthen Human Capital with Indirect Effects on Growth?

Another reason that the type of regime may affect growth indirectly, scholars suggest, is through investment in the labor force. Human capital is widely regarded as important for growth; higher levels of literacy, schooling, and vocational training produce a more productive workforce, a process that is thought especially important given the demands of modern technologies and the need for skills in service sector jobs.[52] Several studies have now reported that liberal democracies invest more in primary and secondary education and vocational training – and they also achieve better attainment outcomes.[53] According to Halperin, Siegle, and Weinstein, for example, among low-income economies, democracies have typically realized secondary school enrollment levels 40 percent higher than autocracies.[54] Moreover, studies relate education with growth; based on a panel study of one hundred countries from 1965 to 1995, Barro reports that growth is affected by the average years of school attainment of adult men at secondary and higher levels.[55] The human capital argument focuses on schooling attainment, literacy, and tertiary training, all thought important for a productive and skilled labor force. If liberal democracies do invest more in human capital, and if this process has an indirect effect on prosperity, as several studies suggest, then *the type of regime combined with the gross enrollment rates of secondary-level education should expand wealth*. Nevertheless, this claim also remains under debate in the literature. In particular, questions remain when determining the direction of causality in any relationship, because the classic Lipset thesis claims that the expansion of education and literacy is a key feature of industrial societies that facilitate democratization. Barro confirmed that access to primary schooling and a smaller gender gap in educational attainment both strengthened the propensity for democracy.[56] Hence it is critical to try to disentangle any complex correlations linking the type of regime, levels of human capital, and income growth.

Do Power-Sharing Democracies Promote Growth?

Several scholars emphasize that beyond the regime, the specific type of democratic institutions matters for accountability. Constitutional arrangements vary among democracies, and major contrasts include those arising among majoritarian-plurality, mixed, or proportional electoral systems; presidential, mixed, or parliamentary executives; single-party or coalitional-party governments; and federal or unitary states. Each of these categories also contains many important variations; for example, proportional representation (PR) electoral systems differ in their use of open or closed lists, the level of any formal vote threshold, and the type of vote formula.[57] Similarly, the constitutional powers and responsibilities of presidents and prime ministers vary substantially, especially in "mixed" executives that combine both roles. Rather than focusing on the type of regime, several scholars emphasize that the particular constitutional arrangements matter for economic performance.[58] In a series of studies, Torsten Persson and Guido Tabellini suggest that constitutional variations such as states with presidential or parliamentary executives influence economic performance, including fiscal policies, trade policies, and levels of public spending, and thus have an indirect effect on growth. They conclude that the type of electoral system does not affect economic performance, but parliamentary government is associated with growth-promoting policies, such as open trade and property protection rights.[59] By contrast, Carl Henrik Knutsen reports that proportional and semiproportional electoral rules do produce substantially higher annual per capita growth rates than do plural-majoritarian rules.[60]

If types of institutional arrangements affect prosperity, however, the exact reasons behind any observed regularities still need to be established. One argument emphasizes that parliamentary executives and majoritarian elections commonly produce single-party governments, where management of the economy rests in the hands of the leader of the governing party.[61] This process has certain advantages for establishing a clear chain of electoral accountability, where the team of cabinet ministers for the governing party is collectively responsible for economic performance while individual representatives of the governing party are also accountable to local single-member constituencies. This arrangement facilitates public evaluations ("the buck stops here") and thus retrospective economic voting at the ballot box.

Similarly, unitary and centralized states also strengthen the direct chain of electoral accountability.[62] By contrast, electoral accountability is weakened in presidential and mixed executives, in proportional electoral systems that usually generate coalition governments, and in federal states. Where party control is divided among the major branches of the legislature and executive, it becomes more difficult for citizens to attribute clear praise or blame for management of economic performance.[63] The attribution of responsibility is further reduced under conditions of multilevel governance and economic globalization; problems with American subprime mortgages triggered the banking crisis in 2008, so who should citizens in Greece, Ireland, and Iceland blame for their economic woes: their own leaders, or those in the United States, or indeed the major multinational financial corporations and international agencies? According to this view, power-concentrating constitutional arrangements (with plurality or majoritarian electoral systems, parliamentary executives, and unitary states) should produce the clearest chain of responsibility and the strongest electoral incentives for governing parties to manage the economy competently and well.

At the same time, however, an alternative line of reasoning suggests that power-sharing democracies may promote greater macroeconomic policy stability. Arend Lijphart suggests that under these arrangements, decision making requires greater compromise establishing agreement among the multiple coalition parties in government.[64] This is predicted to generate greater stability, moderation, and continuity in medium- and long-term macroeconomic policy, which in turn is expected to expand business confidence, reduce investment risks, and improve prosperity.[65] By contrast, majoritarian democracies with single-party governments are thought more vulnerable to abrupt policy reversals following major shifts in party fortunes. Under these arrangements, such as historically in the United Kingdom and Australia, sudden "stop-go" reversals in macroeconomic policies – such as switches in fiscal policy and public spending, trade union bargaining rights, or economic deregulation – are possible when the major parties on the left and right rotate in government office. Abrupt macroeconomic policy reversals and instability are thought to be problematic for investors, creating uncertainty and thereby heightening risk.

Thus there are several plausible reasons that power-sharing institutions may matter for growth, but debate continues about the underlying mechanism and the predicted effects. Theories identify rival pathways, but it is not clear whether electoral accountability or political stability is more important for income. If democratic effects on growth are conditional, then *growth should be observed to vary by the type of institutional arrangements* (including whether states are federal or unified, whether electoral systems are proportional or not proportional, and whether the type of executive is parliamentary or not). Nevertheless, the state of knowledge about these relationships does not allow us to predict the direction of any effects with any degree of confidence. Moreover, the complexity of alternative constitutional arrangements and diverse channels of electoral accountability means that coding institutions into proxy dichotomous categories loses much fine-grained detail about how institutions work in practice.

The Unified Theory and Democratic Governance

Lastly, in counterbalance to all these claims, the book's argument suggests that previous claims need to be synthesized into a unified theory where both liberal democracy and governance capacity developed in parallel are understood as contributing toward economic growth. In particular, electoral accountability increases the pressures on governments to deliver effective performance. Voters demand jobs, cheaper food, and better homes. But elected officials can respond only if the state has the technical capacity and skills to manage macroeconomic policies. Politicians, by themselves, cannot pay wages, export goods, or build factories. If government leaders are thrown out of office for failing to improve the economy, but opposition parties are similarly unable to reduce levels of inflation and unemployment, then the result is likely to be deepening disillusionment with the political process. Moreover, if economic malaise continues over successive administrations, then disenchantment may spread so that the public comes to lack confidence in the regime and ultimately faith in democratic ideals and principles. On the other hand, if state officials are competent and effective at managing economic growth and expanding the country's GDP but government leaders are not responsive and accountable to citizens, then there is no mechanism that ensures that wealth trickles down to benefit the living standards of the general public rather than the Swiss bank accounts and Cayman Island tax havens of economic elites. For these reasons, this book's thesis suggests that *the combination of liberal democracy and governance capacity developed in parallel will prove the most effective recipe for growth,* within the constraints of structural conditions.

II. CHALLENGES IN RESEARCH DESIGN

The previous body of research therefore suggests several propositions that can be tested in this chapter. The empirical evidence needs to be reexamined cautiously, however, due to the series of technical challenges facing any systematic study of the regime–growth relationship. This includes issues of reciprocal causality, omitted variable bias, invalid conceptualization, measurement errors, and bias arising from missing data.

First, major difficulties arise from complex issues of *reciprocal causality*; regimes may facilitate growth. But economic development is also widely believed to provide conditions conducive both to processes of democratization and to strengthening investment in the quality of governance.[66] A large body of economic and sociological research has observed that wealthy societies have usually been more democratic. The political sociologist Seymour Martin Lipset laid the groundwork for this perspective, specifying that, "The more well-to-do a nation, the greater the chances that it will sustain democracy."[67]

Greater affluence consolidates democracy, Lipset theorized, by expanding levels of human capital (literacy, schooling); widening media access; broadening the middle classes; dampening the effects of extreme poverty; facilitating intermediary civil society organizations, such as labor unions and professional associations; and promoting the cultural values of democratic legitimacy and social tolerance.[68] Acemoglu, Johnson, and Robinson argue that in the short term, the direction of causality runs from development to governance rather than the reverse, controlling for country fixed effects, although they acknowledge that in the long term (over the last five hundred years) there is a positive correlation between economic development and processes of democratization.[69] To mitigate the effects of reversed causation, the measures for the independent variables are taken for the year before the annual measure of economic growth. I also include measures of levels of economic development from previous years; this makes sense if growth is understood as a sticky phenomenon that is not invented anew every year. Past growth can be expected to strengthen future growth. The measure of income also helps to capture all the accumulated factors that have expanded growth until the current observation and that are unobserved in the models.

In parsimonious but underspecified models, *omitted variable bias* may also prove problematic; another independent variable, not included in controls, may determine simultaneously both the type of regime and levels of economic growth. For example, developing societies meeting international standards of "good governance" and democracy are more likely to attract international aid as well as international private sector investment.[70] As a result, states with well-governed democracies may experience faster growth than those with autocratic regimes, but this should not be attributed directly to how different types of regimes manage their economies. Many studies of economic growth analyze the importance of institutions, trade, and geography but fail to control for social structural factors, such as levels of ethnic fractionalization or income inequality, as well as the potential role of civil wars and interstate conflict, all of which can be expected to depress growth. Econometric studies of democracy also commonly fail to distinguish the role of power-sharing and power-concentrating democratic institutions, which can be expected to differ in their economic effects.[71] Many parsimonious economic models are elegant but underspecified. To guard against this tendency, by contrast this book uses a battery of items to control for several sets of factors: constitutional arrangements, prior economic conditions, geography, social structure, cultural traditions, and global trends (see Table 5.1). Moreover, many models examine the impact of either democracy or governance, but not the combination of both phenomena.

Thirdly, other difficulties arise from *poor conceptualization and measurement errors*; a growing consensus has arisen today about standard indicators of liberal democracy, using the Gastil Index from Freedom House and the Polity IV democracy–autocracy scale.[72] Notions of "good governance" still remain vague and poorly defined, however, and the available empirical indicators may well be invalid measures of the overarching concepts.[73] The World Bank

TABLE 5.1. *The impact of governance on economic growth*

Models	Economic Growth Correlations		1a Good Governance Institutions			1b Bureaucratic Governance			1c Democratic Governance		
	R	p	b	p	PCSE	b	p	PCSE	b	p	PCSE
Regime Effects											
Liberal democracy (FH)	.038	***							.023	*	.014
Bureaucratic governance (ICRG)	.083	***							.032	*	.016
Good governance (rule of law, property rights, and control of corruption)			-.188		.143	-.003		.007			
Controls											
Economic											
Trade flows	.092	***	.032	*	.014	.029	***	.006	.029	***	.006
Income (per capita GDP)	.040	***	.001		.000	.001		.000	-.001		.000
Geographic											
Location (latitude)	.063	***	6.75	***	.642	2.36	**	.633	3.13	***	.798
Area size (sq.km)	-.018		-.001		.000	.001		.000	-.001		.000
Natural resources (oil/gas rents)	.008		-.001		.000	.001		.000	-.001		.000
Social Structure											
Linguistic fractionalization	-.039	***	-.244		.854	-.575	*	.203	-.259		.227
Religious fractionalization	.000		.681		.793	-.125		.424	-.026		.427
Human capital (secondary schooling)	.053	***	.001		.011	-.008		.005	-.005		.005
Logged population size	-.005		.247		.380	.714	***	.149	.672		.147
Internal conflict	-.058	***	.238		.453	-.104		.242	-.077		.249

(*continued*)

TABLE 5.1. (cont.)

Models	Economic Growth Correlations		1a Good Governance Institutions			1b Bureaucratic Governance			1c Democratic Governance		
	R	p	b	p	PCSE	b	p	PCSE	b	p	PCSE
Cultural traditions											
Muslim society	-.038	***	1.45	*	.779	.282		.461	.319		.434
British colonial legacy	-.012		.959	***	.290	.611	***	.130	.580	***	.129
Global trends											
Year	.042	***	-.094		.105	-.004		.030	-.009		.031
R-²			.085			.030			.030		
Number of observations	5767		508			1769			1769		
Number of countries	95		103			95			95		
Years	20		5			20			20		

Note: The models present the unstandardized beta coefficients and the statistical significance of ordinary least squares linear regression models with panel-corrected standard errors. The dependent variable is income per capita in purchasing power parity from the chain series index of the Penn World Tables. Alan Heston, Robert Summers, and Bettina Aten. 2011. *Penn World Table Version 7.0.* Philedelphia: University of Pennsylvania, Center for International Comparisons of Production, Income and Prices. http://pwt.econ.upenn.edu/php_site/pwt_index.php. *** p < 0.001, ** p < 0.001, * p < 0.05. For details of all the variables, see the technical appendix.

Institute good governance indices are widely employed in both theoretical and applied policy research, but they have been criticized as suffering from problems of perceptual biases, adverse selection in sampling, and conceptual conflation with economic policy choices.[74] For example, the WBI indices include "regulatory quality" based on the assumption that minimal intervention is optimal, yet this conflates specific controversial policy prescriptions with the quality of governance. Many of the indices are actually outcome measures of good governance rather than "input" or process measures; for example, control of corruption is widely recognized as important for growth, but estimates arising from broad and abstract measures do not tell us anything about what government procedures, institutions, or policies actually work to minimize corruption. There are potential problems arising from all perceptual measures of governance performance, especially those based on unrepresented groups of elites such as businesspeople, academics, and journalists, because favorable outcomes (such as conditions of economic growth) can color evaluations of the quality of governance. This can prove particularly problematic with the analysis of cross-national data, because growth rates may be spuriously correlated with perceptions of good governance. Longitudinal analysis is needed, but the WBI indices only started to be estimated in 1996. Many studies have also emphasized the importance of "rule of law" for development, but this abstract and vague idea contains multiple components.[75] If "rule of law" matters, it is still unclear whether policy makers heeding these lessons should seek to strengthen the independence of the courts and judiciary, develop procedures and institutions designed to control corruption, expand professional training and capacity building for lawyers, prioritize police protection of person and property, expand access to transitional justice, engage in the demilitarization of security forces, or "all of the above." The underlying institutional mechanisms, and the policy implications arising from the governance research literature, thus remain underspecified and poorly understood. To overcome problems of measurement error, this book tests the robustness of key relationships by using alternative measures of liberal democracy and good governance.

Lastly, potential problems of systematic bias arise from *missing data* in the longitudinal and cross-national analysis of development indices. Moreover, the missing data are often not randomly distributed; instead, they are most common in poorer nations, in societies deeply divided by conflict, and in patronage autocracies. In these contexts, national statistical offices often lack the resources, technical capacity, or political independence to gather reliable internationally standardized statistics from official statistics, regular household surveys, or census data, even for basic indices monitoring progress for the MDGs. Unfortunately, other systematic biases can also arise from standard social science datasets; for example, one of the standard indicators of democracy is provided by the Polity IV series classifying regimes since 1800, but this dataset excludes all microstates around the world (states with populations of less than half a million). Polity IV covers 164 independent nation-states worldwide, with the biases already noted arising from the exclusion of microstates. International statistics also rarely monitor data from dependent territories, such as Montenegro, Kosovo, and Timor-Leste, so that time-series data of past trends are lacking when these societies gain independent statehood. Consequently, major problems can arise from the limited country coverage included in cross-national and time-series comparisons, as the independent nation-states included in the analysis are not a random sample of all countries in the world. Many of the governance indices are also relatively recent in origin, covering the period since the mid-1980s (ICRG) or since the mid-1990s (WBI), hence long-term processes are difficult to determine. To mitigate problems arising from systematic bias, this book compares the robustness of the results using alternative indices with different country coverage.

To examine the evidence, this book uses a mixed research strategy. First, we can examine the descriptive statistics to observe the general patterns. Multivariate models can then analyze cross-national time-series panel data for countries worldwide to determine the predicted impact of liberal democracy and bureaucratic governance on changes in economic growth, incorporating a wide range of controls. Change in per capita GDP is measured in purchasing power parity, derived here from the chain series provided by the Penn World Tables.[76] Models examine the effects of the Freedom House Gastil index of democracy, providing the most comprehensive country coverage of all independent nation-states. The quality of bureaucratic governance is gauged using the ICRG annual estimates, which are available for a more restricted range of 134 countries since 1984. Both these indices are standardized to one hundred–point scales, for comparability and ease of interpreting the results. To monitor conditional effects arising from particular types of power-sharing constitutions, the models also classify whether countries are federal or unitary states, whether the electoral system used for the lower house of the national parliament is proportional representation or not, and whether the type of executive is presidential or parliamentary.[77] As discussed in earlier chapters, a series of comprehensive controls (see Table 5.1 and the appendix) are introduced for the effects on growth arising from economic factors, geographic characteristics, social structural variables, cultural traditions, and global trends. The panel models employ ordinary least squares (OLS) regression with panel-corrected errors, to correct the problem of serial correlation arising from repeated observations of the same countries over time. Robustness checks replicate the models to compare the results by using the alternative Polity IV scale of democracy–autocracy. The selected cases then illustrate processes underlying the econometric analysis.

III. THE MAIN EFFECTS OF REGIMES ON GROWTH

First, does growth vary systematically by the type of regime? To look initially at the descriptive data, Figure 5.1 compares mean levels of annual economic growth during the whole period under review (from 1984 to 2007) for each type of regime, without any prior controls. The results confirm that bureaucratic democracies experienced the highest annual rates of per capita growth (2.49 percent), as well as the most stable growth rates (standard deviation

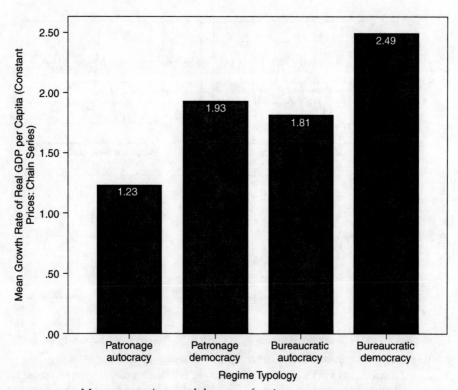

FIGURE 5.1. Mean economic growth by type of regime.
Note: Mean annual growth of income per capita in purchasing power parity from the chain series index of the Penn World Tables, 1984–2007. Alan Heston, Robert Summers, and Bettina Aten. 2011. *Penn World Table Version 7.0.* Philadelphia: University of Pennsylvania, Center for International Comparisons of Production, Income and Prices. http://pwt.econ.upenn.edu/php_site/pwt_index.php. For the regime typology, see the appendix.

[StDev] = 3.92). The book's theory predicts that bureaucratic democracies combine the most effective macroeconomic management by the state, with competent and technically skilled officials steering the economy in the main financial ministries, combined with the accountability that democratic governments face for their performance to the electorate. The initial comparison provides some preliminary support for the claim that this type of regime provides the underlying conditions most conducive for stable and sustained growth. As illustrated in Figure 5.2, trends in the mean growth rate among bureaucratic democracies are relatively steady, providing predictable conditions that are expected to encourage investor confidence, without showing the sharp fluctuations and volatility found among other types of regimes.

By contrast, as also predicted by the argument, compared with all other types of regimes, patronage autocracies usually perform most poorly, displaying mean annual growth of only 1.23 percent during these years, half the rate of

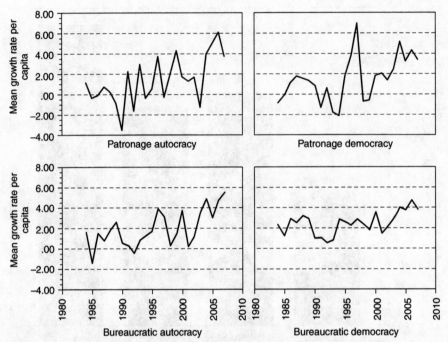

FIGURE 5.2. Trends in economic growth by type of regime, 1980–2010.

Note: Mean annual growth of income per capita in purchasing power parity (constant prices) from the chain series index of the Penn World Tables, 1980–2010. Alan Heston, Robert Summers, and Bettina Aten. 2011. *Penn World Table Version 7.0.* Philadelphia: University of Pennsylvania, Center for International Comparisons of Production, Income and Prices. http://pwt.econ.upenn.edu/php_site/pwt_index.php. For the regime typology, see the appendix.

growth experienced by bureaucratic democracies. Patronage autocracies also display the sharpest peaks and troughs in their growth rate trends (StDev = 9.88); these types of regimes typically occasionally perform very well – or very badly (see Figure 5.2). Thus in the late 1980s and the early 1990s, the global recession depressed all economies. The United States saw soaring unemployment, massive government budgetary deficits, and a slowdown in GDP. But although this downturn almost wiped out growth in bureaucratic democracies, patronage autocracies dipped sharply into deeply negative territory. In particular, oil-dependent autocracies are prone to experience sharp swings in GDP following large fluctuations in the price of energy, such as the volatility evident in Equatorial Guinea, Saddam's Iraq, and Kuwait. Several states transitioning from autocracy and emerging from conflict have also experienced a substantial short-term surge in growth under newly elected regimes, such as Liberia in 1997 and Afghanistan in 2002. Investment in infrastructure and economic recovery, funded partially by international recovery and reconstruction assistance, generates a sudden spike, but long-term growth in these circumstances often proves unsustainable. By comparison, both patronage democracies and bureaucratic autocracies fall roughly midway between the other regime categories, with mean growth rates of 1.93 and 1.81 percent respectively, as well as proving middling in their overall level of growth volatility (see Figure 5.2).

An alternative way to examine the descriptive evidence is to compare rates of growth for states that do not experience any sustained regime change during the period under comparison. This approach holds the type of regime as fixed, which helps to control for the reciprocal effects of growth on regimes. Thus we can compare cases classified as stable regimes, defined as those that fall into the same regime category in both 1984 and 2007; hence Angola, Cameroon, Libya, Syria, Togo, and Zimbabwe, for example, are classified as stable patronage autocracies; Bolivia, and Senegal represent stable patronage democracies; Saudi Arabia, Brunei, Bahrain, and China exemplify stable bureaucratic autocracies; and lastly, stable bureaucratic democracies during this period include states such as Australia, France, Turkey, and Trinidad and Tobago.

Figure 5.3 illustrates the contrasts in income levels and growth rate experienced among each of these types of regimes. In 1984, stable bureaucratic democracies start with the high average levels of per capita GDP ($17,342), and during these decades these states also saw average incomes rise by two-thirds, the largest amount of any category, to reach $29,238 per capita in 2007. In 1984, bureaucratic autocracies were initially even more affluent, with average incomes of $31,885. But far from becoming more prosperous, citizens living under these regimes experienced falling living standards during these years, to reach $26,223 per capita. Patronage democracies started with the lowest average income level of any regime type in 1984 ($3,901) and their average income levels rose slightly, although still to only $5,597. Lastly, patronage autocracies were also poor societies in 1984, with per capita incomes of only $5,232, and their average income levels fell slightly during recent decades. Thus bureaucratic democracies accelerated their lead over all other types of regimes, especially widening the disparities with patronage democracies. In 1984, bureaucratic democracies enjoyed average income levels slightly more than three times the level of patronage autocracies. By 2007, the equivalent gap had grown to roughly six times the level.

But growth is widely recognized to be the product of many factors beyond regime institutions. And in a reciprocal relationship, growing affluence is believed to strengthen the quality of democratic governance. Thus these findings should not be taken to imply that the type of regime necessarily *causes* growth, due to the need for many other controls in multivariate models and the need to address complex issues of endogeneity when interpreting this relationship. Rising incomes have been regarded as a cause of both growing democratization (through the expansion of the middle classes, the Lipset thesis) as well as better governance (through the resources invested in the bureaucracy and public demands for services).[78] For example, both the United States and Mediterranean European countries have been forced to cut public services and

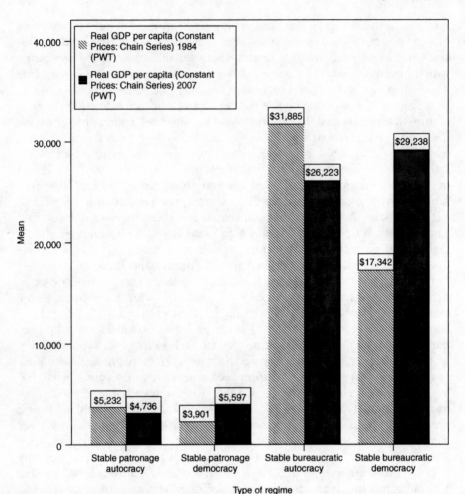

FIGURE 5.3. Economic growth by stable type of regime.
Note: Mean annual growth of real income per capita in purchasing power parity
from the chain series index of the Penn World Tables, 1984–2007. Alan Heston,
Robert Summers, and Bettina Aten. 2011. *Penn World Table Version 7.0.* Philadelphia:
University of Pennsylvania, Center for International Comparisons of Production,
Income and Prices. http://pwt.econ.upenn.edu/php_site/pwt_index.php. For the regime
typology, see the appendix.

shrink the size of the public sector workforce employed at local and national
levels after experiencing an economic downturn, triggered by the 2008 housing crisis in America, global financial pressures, reduced revenues, and growing government budgetary deficits. Thus the recession has had a direct impact
on governance by constraining the provision of basic public services, such as
schools, roads, police, and healthcare.

The simple correlations and the multivariate models presented in Tables 5.1
and 5.2 examine the core propositions arising from theories about the effects of

TABLE 5.2. *The impact of democracy on economic growth*

Model	2a Liberal Democracy			2b Power-Sharing Institutions			2c Democracy and Human Capital		
	b	p	PCSE	b	p	PCSE	b	p	PCSE
Regime Effects									
Liberal democracy (FH)	-.004		.003	.017	**	.005	.016	*	.007
Liberal democracy * human capital							-.001	***	.000
Federal state (1) Unitary (o)				-.543		.587			
PR electoral systems (1)/ Majoritarian or mixed (o)				1.73	***	.007			
Parliamentary Executive (1) Other (o)				4.69	***	1.36			
Liberal democracy * federal state				-.014		.007			
Liberal democracy * PR electoral system				-.014		.006			
Liberal democracy * parliamentary Executive				-.022	***	.013			
Controls									
Economic									
Trade flows	.032	***	.004	.030	***	.004	.030	***	.004
Income (per capita GDP)	.001		.000	.001	*	.000	.001	*	.000
Geographic									
Location (latitude)	1.99	**	.527	1.78	*	.567	2.14	***	.547
Area size (sq.km)	.001		.000	-.000		.000	.001		.000
Natural resources (oil/gas rents)	-.001	***	.000	-.001	***	.000	-.001	***	.000

(continued)

TABLE 5.2. (cont.)

Model	2a Liberal Democracy			2b Power-Sharing Institutions			2c Democracy and Human Capital		
	b	p	PCSE	b	p	PCSE	b	p	PCSE
Social Structure									
Linguistic fractionalization	-.878	***	.242	-.196		.261	-.628	*	.290
Religious fractionalization	-.450		.257	-.448		.331	-.259		.295
Human capital (secondary schooling)	-.011	**	.005	-.011		.005	.008		.101
Logged population size	.568	***	.129	.442	*	.194	.546	***	.127
Internal conflict	-.015	*	.241	-.485	*	.262	-.579	**	.246
Cultural traditions									
Muslim society	.510	*	.344	.300		.359	.013		.336
British colonial legacy	.586	***	.166	.678	**	.208	.549	***	.170
Global trends									
Year	-.039	***	.013	-.050	***	.013	-.040	***	.012
R-²	.027			.031			.029		
Number of observations	3,071			3,038			3,071		
Number of countries	103			102			103		
Years	32			32			32		

Note: The models present the unstandardized beta coefficients and the statistical significance of ordinary least squares linear regression models with panel-corrected standard errors. The dependent variable is income per capita in purchasing power parity from the chain series index of the Penn World Tables. Alan Heston, Robert Summers, and Bettina Aten. 2011. *Penn World Table Version 7.0.* Philedelphia: University of Pennsylvania, Center for International Comparisons of Production, Income and Prices. http://pwt.econ.upenn.edu/php_site/pwt_index.php. *** p < 0.001, ** p < 0.01, * p < 0.05. For details of all the variables, see the technical appendix.

democratic governance controlling for many factors that the literature suggests contribute toward prosperity, including geographic variables, prior economic conditions, social structural factors, cultural traditions, and global trends. The simple correlations suggest that multiple factors are significantly associated with growth, including many structural conditions that are largely fixed or slowly changing. Thus the geographic location of any country (measured by latitude) is strongly correlated with rates of economic growth; because location is fixed, this suggests that geography determines income. Similarly, cultures that are predominately Muslim have negative growth rates, suggesting that religious traditions affect the economy. The levels of liberal democracy (R = .038***) and bureaucratic governance (R = .083***) are also weakly correlated with growth, although here it is not possible to determine the direction of causation in the relationship due to the possibility of reciprocal effects and omitted variable bias. The multivariate regression models lag all the independent variables by one year, as a partial control on endogeneity. The regression models present the unstandardized beta regression coefficients, their significance, and the panel-corrected standard errors, along with the number of observations and countries under comparison.

If we first examine the effects of the controls, factors that are consistently positive and significantly related to growth across all models include the location of countries (measured in latitude or degrees distant from the equator), trade flows, and the legacy of a British colonial background. Latitude is a proxy for many other factors affecting the tropics, from climate and agriculture (the availability of potential crops and animals) to the prevalence of disease.[79] Trade is important for growth via closer integration into global markets for exchanging products and commodities. Negative factors significantly depressing income across many (not all) models include levels of internal conflict; societies experiencing civil wars, domestic violence, and instability can be expected to have conditions deterring investment, while conflict also destroys essential infrastructure and physical capital, increases military expenditure, and reduces the total number of people potentially employed in the civilian labor force. In terms of social heterogeneity, linguistic fractionalization is consistently negatively related to growth whereas religious fractionalization often proves negative, but the coefficient is insignificant. William Easterly and Ross Levine have highlighted the important role of ethnic fractionalization in explaining lack of growth in Sub-Saharan Africa, but the type of ethnic identity and cleavage appears important for its effects.[80] The role of natural resources could potentially function as a blessing (by funding investment) or a curse (by encouraging corruption and inequality).[81] The results in these models confirm the latter interpretation; an extensive literature suggests that income arising from oil and gas natural resources is often captured by predatory elites, as well as being a cause for conflict and instability. Lastly, contra the assumption that human capital contributes toward growth, and in line with Easterly's skeptical view,[82] secondary school attainment was not consistently and significantly linked to prosperity.

Democratic Governance and Growth

After controlling for these factors, what is the impact of governance? Models in Table 5.1 test the main effects suggested by theories of good governance. The results demonstrate that after applying the controls, in Model 1a, *economic growth is not affected by neoliberal measures of "good governance" alone* (including the World Bank Institute's estimates of rule of law, property rights, and control of corruption), *nor in Model 1b by bureaucratic governance alone* (as monitored by the ICRG). These results are contrary to those presented by Peter Evans and J. E. Rausch, but their analysis of Weberian governance was restricted to three dozen developing countries.[83] *When both liberal democracy and bureaucratic governance are entered into Model 1c,* however, *both emerge as significant predictors of economic growth.* The theory in this book posits that it is important to counterbalance the accountability of elected officials for the country's economic performance with the capacity of the public sector to manage the economy effectively, and the results support this argument. This model shows that both of these factors have effects that are similar in strength; an improvement of 10 percent in the one hundred–point scales of liberal democracy and bureaucratic governance increases annual per capita growth in GDP by roughly 0.2 or 0.3 percent higher respectively. This may appear to be a relatively modest impact in itself, but as average growth rates for all countries throughout these years is 1.9 percent, the rise is not inconsiderable.

A similar series of models in Table 5.2 examine the impact of democracy on economic growth, based on the alternative arguments considered earlier. The results in Model 2a demonstrate that after applying the same range of controls, *liberal democracy, by itself, has no direct impact on growth.* A robustness check, replicating the models but substituting the Polity IV standardized democracy scale, produced a similar result.

These results are contrary to the conclusion of Halperin, Siegle, and Weinstein, based on comparing the economic performance of the least developed nations but failing to control for many factors driving both democratization and growth.[84] At the same time, they provide further confirmation for the findings reported in many previous studies that are skeptical about the link between democracy and growth, including those published by Barro, Przeworski and his colleagues, and Doucouliagos and Ulubasoglu.[85] There are many reasons that the assumed mechanism of electoral accountability may fail, so that governments may be returned to office despite a poor economic performance or they may be kicked out despite growing prosperity. In liberal democracies, the chains of accountability linking citizens with representatives are complex. In systems with divided government and power-sharing arrangements, it is difficult to assign praise or blame for macroeconomic management. Government survival during interelectoral periods depends on parliamentary support as well as popular votes. Voters can cast their ballots based on many reasons unconnected with past or future economic performance. The general public may find it difficult, or even impossible, to evaluate more technical and abstract economic conditions (such as the size of the government deficit, the level of any trade imbalance, or the international strength of the currency), still less to attribute praise or blame for these conditions. Citizens' evaluations of many aspects of economic performance, where they lack direct pocketbook experience, are framed by the news media. Parties are accountable to members and partisan supporters, as well as the general public.[86] Given the complexity of assigning responsibility for economic management in long-established democracies, where parties and leaders have established a long track record over successive administrations, it is not surprising if this accountability proves even weaker in many countries where parties and leaders have not yet established a strong reputation that could form a rational basis for retrospective economic voting. Poor economic performance can be blamed on international forces or private sector actors, allowing government officials to duck responsibility.[87] Moreover, even if the chain of accountability works perfectly, so that politicians are accountable for their handling of the economy and they have every intention of serving the public interest, this does not mean, by any means, that they can necessarily deliver on their economic promises if states lack the technical capacity to do so.

Model 2b examines the impact of several of the core institutions associated with power-sharing arrangements. If institutional effects on growth are conditional, then growth is expected to vary according to whether states are federal or unified, whether electoral systems are proportional or majoritarian, and whether the type of executive is parliamentary or presidential, although the direction of any institutional effects is not easy to predict from existing theories. Model 2b in Table 5.2 demonstrates complex results after applying all the prior controls. In particular, the comparison of parliamentary executives in all the countries under comparison shows a strong and significant impact on growth, as Persson and Tabellini have reported.[88] Countries with either mixed executives (combining a presidency and prime minister) or with a pure presidential executive generally have lower prosperity than parliamentary systems. Overall these general findings serve to support the argument that parliamentary executives usually strengthen collective accountability; in these systems, where responsibility for managing the economy rests with the party or parties in government, it is easier for electors to assess economic performance and to "kick rascals out of office." By contrast, in regimes with mixed or presidential executives, when given the opportunity to choose leaders at the ballot box, it is more difficult for citizens to assign clear-cut praise or blame for economic conditions. Similarly, the direct effects of proportional representation electoral systems are also significantly related to income, further confirming Knutsen's conclusions.[89] By contrast, federalism does not appear to have a direct effect on economic performance. Yet the exact reasons for these patterns are not apparent theoretically, because power-sharing theories predict interaction effects, emphasizing the role of *democratic* institutions. Contrary to the direction predicted by consociational arguments, the interaction effect between liberal democracy and parliamentary executives in fact proved weakly negative. The other interaction effects from institutions in power-sharing democracies were insignificant.

Lastly, Model 2c in Table 5.2 tests the argument that democracy has an indirect effect on growth because this type of regime typically makes a greater investment in human capital than autocracies. Human capital has many dimensions and is measured here by gross enrollment (male and female) in secondary schooling. The interaction effect of democracy and human capital on growth emerges as significant but negative, in the contrary direction to that predicted theoretically. There are reasons to be skeptical about the assumed importance of human capital for growth; for instance, Easterly suggests that the dramatic expansion in schooling and literacy experienced in many developing countries during the last four decades have, in fact, proved distinctly disappointing for raising incomes.[90] Creating skills in the workforce is insufficient for prosperity, he argues, if societies continue to lack access to new technologies or if there are few job openings for skilled workers and high levels of long-term unemployment. Moreover, growth may come through alternative strategies; hence Przeworski and his colleagues found that democratic and autocratic regimes achieved prosperity through different routes.[91] The study confirmed that among wealthier nations, democracies were more likely to invest in human capital (including education and training). But this did not necessarily generate a better economic performance, because wealthier autocracies achieve equivalent gains in productivity and growth through the alternative mechanism of higher fertility rates, which expanded the overall size of their workforce population.

Divergent Trajectories: Haiti and the Dominican Republic

Econometric techniques are invaluable when seeking to determine global patterns, but even the most sophisticated techniques have limits in their capacity to determine with any degree of confidence the direction of causality in complex relationships. Narratives can enrich our understanding, especially paired cases that share similar "fixed" conditions, such as in their historical roots, latitude, and natural resources, but that differ during the contemporary era in their regime types. The cases chosen for this purpose in this chapter are Haiti and the Dominican Republic, which share the Caribbean island of Hispaniola (see Figure 5.4).

The countries shared a similar per capita real GDP of around $2,000 in 1960, but, as illustrated in Figure 5.5, their trajectories diverged so far that during the last half-century, income has quadrupled in the Dominican Republic but halved in Haiti. By 2010, per capita GDP was $1,200 (and falling) in Haiti, compared to $8,900 (and rapidly growing) in the Dominican Republic. The Dominican Republic is classified by the UNDP's HDI as a medium developing country, ranked by the HDI as 98th out of 187 societies worldwide in 2011. In this regard, although not as affluent as some of its Caribbean neighbors, such as Trinidad and Tobago or Jamaica, the Dominican Republic is

FIGURE 5.4. Haiti and the Dominican Republic.

roughly comparable in terms of human development with Sri Lanka, Algeria, and China. With the second largest economy in the region, it has become the Caribbean's most popular tourist destination. By contrast, even before the devastating earthquake in 2010, Haiti was one of the least developed countries around the globe, currently ranked 158th lowest worldwide by the HDI, similar to human development in Liberia and Nigeria. In Haiti, real per capita GDP *fell* by an average of 1 percent per year from 1961 to 2000, which resulted in an overall decline of 45 percent over the period.

The key puzzle is determining what produced these divergent trajectories.[92] Are they due to historical legacies? Geographical locations? Social structures? Or institutions?

Their historical roots may be important. The island of Hispaniola was explored by Christopher Columbus on this first voyage in 1492 and claimed by the Spanish, who used it as a base to expand control in the Caribbean and Americas.[93] The French subsequently established a base on the western side of the island, and in 1697 this territory was ceded to them by the Spanish, eventually becoming Haiti. A century later, the western part of the island overshadowed the eastern in population and wealth due to plantations of sugar, coffee, and indigo, worked by African slaves. The twin countries today reflect their colonial heritage in terms of language, although Haiti achieved independence from France in 1804 and the Dominican Republic won independence from Haiti in 1844. The period after independence was marked by extreme political instability: From 1843 to 1915, a succession of twenty-two presidents in Haiti saw twenty-one of them assassinated. The Dominican Republic endured fifty different presidents and thirty revolutions between 1844 and 1930. Acemoglu

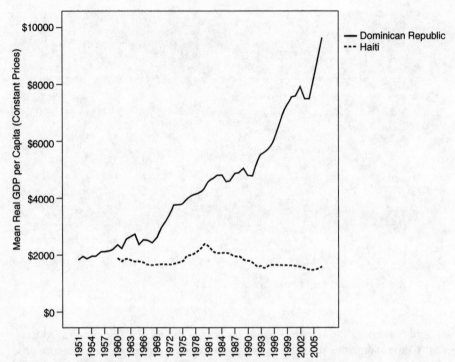

FIGURE 5.5. Economic growth in Haiti and the Dominican Republic.
Note: Real GDP per capita, constant prices, chain series, Penn World Tables. Alan
Heston, Robert Summers, and Bettina Aten. 2011. *Penn World Table Version 7.0.*
Philadelphia: University of Pennsylvania, Center for International Comparisons of
Production, Income and Prices. http://pwt.econ.upenn.edu/php_site/pwt_index.php.

and Robinson suggest that colonial origins matter for growth, with early
patterns of settlement leading to the development of rule of law and governance institutions.[94] The coauthors report that both Haiti and the Dominican
Republic had similar levels of settler mortality, however, so this cannot be the
root cause of modern contrasts in these particular cases. Given the length of
time that each country has been self-governed, and the fact that the economic
divergence has accelerated since the 1960s, it is also implausible to attribute
any contemporary differences in development to their colonial backgrounds in
the early nineteenth century. Moreover, studies that have examined the impact
of colonial legacies on contemporary patterns of economic and political development have reported that British origins do make a difference, for both levels of development and democratization, but no major contrasts have been
detected among other types of French, Spanish, or Dutch colonists.[95]

Geography is often regarded as a deep driver of growth, especially the distribution of natural resources, access to shipping, proximity to trade markets,

and closeness to the equator (and thus vulnerability to tropical diseases, hurricanes and tropical storms, and problems arising from global warming). Yet both parts of Hispaniola are similar in these regards. As small island-states, these nations should be more stable and democratic than their neighbors in South America; ever since Robert Dahl, it has been observed that the size of nations matters for their politics.[96] These societies may differ, however, in physical geography, mountainous terrain, and thus land fertility for agricultural production. Jarad Diamond argues that Haiti suffered from rapid deforestation and loss of soil fertility due to higher population densities and lower rainfall than the eastern part of the island.[97] There has been widespread environmental degradation, destroying fertile land. If crops were poor, this could have prevented growth through exports such as coffee, sugar, and cotton and restricted subsistence farming and the domestic food supply. However, the average annual rainfall in meteorological records is 54 inches in the Dominican Republic, the same as the Haiti total. Both societies have mountainous and rugged terrain interspersed with farming areas; today, arable land constitutes about one-quarter (22.4 percent) of the Dominican Republic but slightly more (28 percent) of Haiti.

The comparative economic and social indicators in Table 5.3 highlight the major contrasts between these conjoined twins. Both countries have populations of almost 10 million, with a predominately Catholic religious background. Easterly and Levine suggest that ethnic fractionalization depressed growth in Sub-Saharan Africa, and deeply divided plural societies are also widely regarded as more vulnerable to instability and violence.[98] Both Haiti and the Dominican Republic have broadly similar ethnic, racial, and religious compositions, however; the indigenous Indian population died out under the Spanish colonists, and both countries developed populations of mixed European and African descent. The early colonists in Haiti relied more on slave labor for sugar production in large plantations, however, while the Dominican Republic was based on a ranching economy and tobacco farming, requiring fewer slaves. By any of the developmental indices, people today living in the east consistently lag far behind the quality of life in the west, whether by unemployment rates, poverty, literacy, infant or maternal mortality, or life expectancy. The Dominican Republic still experiences relatively high levels of social inequality and only moderate levels of average household income, but nevertheless, well before the 2010 earthquake decimated the population and destroyed infrastructure, Haiti had suffered for decades from widespread poverty and social deprivation.

If not history, geography, or social structure, what of political institutions? The record of democratic governance in both nations also shows contrasting paths in recent decades.[99] As shown in Figure 5.6, both countries display some volatility in the measures of liberal democracy and the quality of governance, but nevertheless the Dominican Republic shows a consistently stronger record on both indices.

TABLE 5.3. *Comparative indicators: Haiti and Dominican Republic*

	Haiti	Dominican Republic
Area size (sq km)	27,750	48,670
Natural resources	Bauxite, copper, calcium carbonate, gold, marble, hydropower	Nickel, bauxite, gold, silver
Population		
Population (July 2011)	9,719,932	9,956,648
Language	French/creole	Spanish
Ethnic groups	Black 95%, biracial and white 5%	Mixed 73%, white 16%, black 11%
Religion	Roman Catholic 80%, Protestant 16%, none 1%, other 3%	Roman Catholic 95%, other 5%
Linguistic fractionalization	N/a	.04
Religious fractionalization	.47	.31
Political History		
Colonial background	Became French colony in 1697	Became Spanish colony in 1492
Independence	1804 (from France)	February 27, 1844 (from Haiti)
Regime type (2007)	Patronage autocracy	Patronage democracy
Executive	Mixed executive	Presidential
Legislature	Bicameral National Assembly	Bicameral National Congress
Democracy index, FH (2007)	50/100	85/100
Governance index (ICRG) (2007)	15/100	33/100
Corruption Perception Index (2010)	Ranked 146/178	Ranked 101/178
Economy		
GDP (in ppp) (2010)	$11.48 billion	$87.25 billion
GDP growth rate (2010)	−5.1%	+7.8%
GDP per capita (in ppp) (2010)	$1,200	$8,900
Workforce: % agriculture	38.1%	14.6%
Workforce: % industry	11.5%	22.3%
Workforce: % services	50.4%	63.1%
Unemployment rate (2010)	40.6%	13.3%
Pop. below poverty line (2004)	80.0%	42.2%
Social Indicators		
Human Development Index (2011)	.454 (low)	.689 (medium)
Literacy	53%	87%
Infant mortality rate (2008)	54.02 deaths/1,000 live births	22.2 deaths/1,000 live births
Maternal mortality rate (2008)	300 deaths/100,000 live births	100 deaths//100,000 live births
Life expectancy (2011)	62 years	77 years

Sources: CIA. *The World Factbook.* http://www.cia.gov; World Bank. 2010. *World Development Indicators.*
http://data.worldbank.org/data-catalog/world-development-indicators?cid=GPD_WDI.

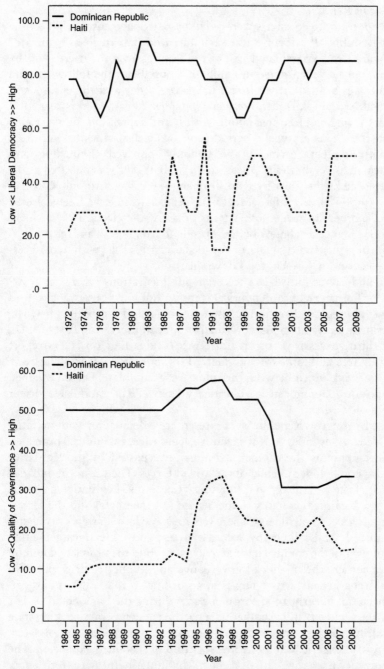

FIGURE 5.6. Trends in democracy and governance in Haiti and the Dominican Republic. *Note:* Liberal democracy is measured by the standardized one hundred–point Freedom House index of political rights and civil liberties. The quality of governance is measured by the standardized one hundred–point ICRG index.

The Dominican Republic

During the 1960s, both countries were ruled by patronage autocracies. In the Dominican Republic, President Rafael Trujillo, who had ruled as a dictator for thirty years, was assassinated in 1961. Elections in 1962 were won by Juan Gavino, but he was toppled in a military coup d'etat the following year. The United States sent in armed forces to restore order and the elections in 1966 returned Joaquín Balaguer. President Balaguer remained in power for a dozen years by rigging elections, jailing critics, and repressing human rights and civil liberties. This era was a period of growing disparities between rich and poor, where the performance of the economy improved, although growth depended heavily on commodity prices. In 1978, Balaguer was defeated at the polls and replaced by the short-lived government of President Antonio Guzman Fernandez (1978–82), the first peaceful transition from one freely elected president to another. In turn, another transition saw the election of President Salvador Jorge Blanco (1982–6) before President Balaguer again returned to power. Political rights and civil liberties eroded under his rule, with two successive rigged elections, before he stood down in 1996.

Since the mid-1990s, however, successive administrations have seen growing respect for human rights and political stability, holding a series of elections that are generally regarded as meeting international standards of integrity. The current president, Leonel Fernandez of the Dominican Liberation Party (PLD), has won a third successive term in office in elections that observers report were relatively free and fair, although marred by sporadic violence. The 2012 presidential race is divided between the ruling PLD candidate, Danilo Medina, and the opposition Dominican Revolutionary Party (PRD) candidate, former president Hipolito Mejia.

Today the Dominican Republic is a representative democracy with national powers divided among independent executive, legislative, and judicial branches. The president appoints the cabinet, executes laws passed by the legislative branch, and is commander in chief of the armed forces. The president and vice president are elected by direct vote for four-year terms. Legislative power is exercised by a bicameral congress – the Senate (32 members) and the House of Representatives (178 members). There remain some human rights problems, notably with unlawful killings by security forces, and issues facing Haitian refugees, but overall the country has moved well beyond the practices common two decades earlier. The quality of governance and public sector reform still need to be strengthened further, however, according to the ICRG index, following a sharp fall in early 2000 through 2002, during the banking crisis. For this reason, the regime is still classified as a patronage democracy, lacking state capacity. During the last fifteen years, as democracy has been consolidated, the economy also experienced its strongest period of sustained expansion. The economy grew at an average rate of 7.6 percent annually from 1996 to 2000, before a banking crisis caused a setback, but growth subsequently recovered, averaging 7.8 percent from 2004 to 2010. The Dominican Republic is part of a free trade area with the United States and Central American partners, and it exports textiles, electronic products, jewelry, tobacco, and pharmaceuticals, as well as cacao, sugar, tobacco, and coffee, as well as benefiting from an expansion of tourism. Thus the strengthening economy coincided with improvements in democratization and the stable transfers of power experienced since the mid-1990s.

Haiti

The political conditions in Haiti present a striking contrast. In 1957, Francois Duvalier (Papa Doc) won in the country's first universal suffrage presidential election. Reelected in fraudulent contests in 1961, he declared himself president for life, ruling with the aid of the paramilitary forces and a predatory state. The Duvalier regime perfectly exemplifies patronage autocracies; the president privatized public funds for his own personal use and to enrich his supporters. His methods included diversion of tax money and foreign aid, contributions from wealthy businesspeople, as well as extortion, theft, and property expropriation from suspected opponents.[100] On his death in 1971, his son, Jean-Claude Duvalier (Baby Doc), took on the mantle and benefits of presidential office. As shown in Figure 5.6, both liberal democracy and the quality of governance were weak during this era. There were two brief attempts at establishing civilian democracy during the mid-1980s and early 1990s, shown by the fluctuating patterns of liberal democracy, but both were crushed by military coups.

A new constitution was ratified in 1987 that provided for an elected, bicameral parliament; a mixed executive with an elected president as head of state and a prime minister, cabinet, ministers, and Supreme Court appointed by the president with the parliament's consent. The constitution also provided for political decentralization through the election of mayors and administrative bodies responsible for local government. In December 1990, Jean-Bertrand Aristide won 67 percent of the vote in a presidential election that international observers deemed largely free and fair. In 1991, just nine months after taking elected office, President Jean-Bertrand Aristide had to flee the country, with the instability causing a sharp economic decline. After a U.S.-led invasion of the country, Aristide was reinstated in 1994. He stood down the next year due to constitutional term limits, to be succeeded by Rene Preval, a close ally. In 2000, Aristide was reelected president amid criticisms of electoral irregularities. In subsequent years, while the Dominican Republic transitioned to a stable electoral democracy and an expanding economy, Haiti experienced successive periods of political deadlock, growing dissatisfaction with the government, deteriorating security, and armed rebellions against the government. On February 29, 2004, Aristide submitted his resignation as president of Haiti and flew on a chartered plane to Africa. The interim government that succeeded him organized free and fair elections, returning Preval to the presidency. Nationwide civil disturbances broke out in April 2008, sparked by sharp increases in food and fuel prices, followed a few months later by a series of tropical storms and hurricanes.

Haiti was beginning the recovery process from these destabilizing events when, on January 12, 2010, Haiti was struck by a 7.0-magnitude earthquake, with its epicenter near Port-au-Prince. The government estimated 320,000 deaths, about 1 million displaced people within the Port-au-Prince metropolitan area. The earthquake was the worst to hit the country in more than two centuries, and it generated an estimated $11.5 billion in damages and reconstruction costs. The capacity of the central authorities to respond with emergency relief was severely hampered by the fact that many government buildings located in the capital, including those for justice officials and police forces, were also severely damaged and personnel were lost. The international community pledged humanitarian aid to help the reconstruction effort, to rebuild essential infrastructure, housing, and public services. The Haitian economy had been growing slowly since 2005, with GDP growth (at 2.9 percent) barely outstripping population growth, but the economy contracted sharply after the earthquake. As shown in Figure 5.6, the trends in democracy and governance in Haiti consistently lag behind those of the Dominican Republic, with a particularly erratic and unstable performance on liberal democracy, and the economy has either flatlined or eroded slightly over time. Haiti remains the poorest country in the Western Hemisphere.

The descriptive comparison of these twin societies cannot prove that it is necessarily the quality of democratic governance per se that is driving the contrasting economic performance and human development in these countries. Indeed, it is also plausible that there is an interaction effect, or a virtuous circle, so that rising prosperity in the Dominican Republic generates government resources that are available for investing in better schools, hospitals, and public services, which also probably encourages greater government satisfaction and thus political stability. But these case studies, combined with the econometric models presented earlier in this chapter, also strongly suggest that in trying to explain the divergent trajectories, we find that the type of regime matters even when we control for many conditions in developing societies arising from their historical legacies, social structure, and geographic location, which these theories suggest also contribute toward poverty and growth. This reinforces the observations of many other scholars who have also concluded that political institutions are critical for the divergent developmental pathways evident in Latin America.[101] And the timing of the improvements in the economy in the Dominican Republic indicates that prosperity started to take off in the late 1960s and early 1970s, when both countries were ruled by patronage autocracies. Sustained growth accelerated most sharply in the Dominican Republic from the mid-1990s onward, however, during the period of democratization, when there were a series of free and fair elections and greater political stability in the peaceful transition from one administration to the next. The transformation in economic fortunes is relatively recent in this state, so it cannot be attributed to the institutional and historical legacy of colonial administration centuries earlier.[102] The econometric models suggest that states that have both growing state capacity and the institutions of liberal democracy are most likely to experience economic growth. By contrast, the continuing political instability, deadlock, armed uprisings, and weak state capacity in Haiti, a patronage autocracy, have been accompanied by no effective alleviation of the severe poverty facing the country.

IV. CONCLUSIONS

Varied thinkers commonly make two core claims favoring democratic governance. Firstly, it is argued on normative grounds that legitimate governance should be based on the will of the people, as expressed through the institutions of liberal democracy. These claims are embodied in international conventions, agreed on by the world's governments, notably Article 21 of the 1948 Universal Declaration of Human Rights: "The will of the people shall be the basis of the authority of government; this will shall be expressed in periodic and genuine elections which shall be by universal and equal suffrage and shall be held by secret vote or by equivalent free voting procedures." Human rights–based arguments reflect universal claims. Rights-based arguments reflect powerful moral arguments that resonate widely among those sharing democratic values. Many also suggest that "good governance" is intrinsically valuable; in this view, states should reflect the Weberian principles of clean, efficient, and effective public administration; rule of law; and impartial decision making. Confronted by those who remain skeptical about these claims, however, the second strand of the argument suggests that democratic regimes are not only of intrinsic value, but they also have instrumental benefits. The way that citizens choose leaders and hold them accountable is thought to have important consequences for whether governments act in the public interest. Similarly, state-builders claim that governments that are more competent, effective, and efficient when steering the economy are more likely to produce stable growth and security, acting as partners for achieving developmental goals in conjunction with the international community.

The evidence that helps to determine institutional effects is complex to analyze, not least due to problems of missing data, reciprocal causation, limited country coverage, and the challenges of conceptual validity for many common indices. This book seeks to throw fresh light on these issues, building on the argument that neither liberal democracy nor "good governance," in isolation, can be expected to generate conditions for sustained growth, although the combination of these characteristics is predicted to prove important for prosperity. The result of the analysis lends confirmation to this argument, while also casting serious doubt on several alternative theories. The core thesis emphasizes that both liberal democracy and governance capacity need to be strengthened simultaneously for effective development, within the constraints posed by structural conditions. Democracy and governance are separate phenomena, but both are necessary (although not sufficient) to achieve progress. Liberal democracy is theorized as critical for development, by allowing citizens to express their demands; to hold public officials to account; and to rid themselves of incompetent, corrupt, or ineffective leaders. Yet rising public demands that elected officials cannot meet is a recipe for frustration – or worse. In this sense, the issue is not simply about providing electoral incentives so that vote-seeking politicians pay attention to social needs but also providing elected leaders with the capacity to implement effective policies. Thus the quality of governance is also predicted to play a vital role in development, where the notion of "good governance" is understood in terms of expanding the capacity of elected representatives and officials to manage the delivery of basic public goods and services so that leaders can respond effectively to citizens' demands. The quality of both democracy and governance are not isolated phenomena, however; regimes reflect, as well as shape, the enduring structural conditions in each society. The international development community, national governments, and civil society organizations have devoted growing resources to strengthening democracy and governance. The difficult and complex challenge facing reformers – including those seeking to apply the lessons of the Dominican Republic to Haiti – is therefore to develop simultaneously both the institutions of liberal democracy and "good governance" within the structural constraints of each society rather than prioritizing one or the other of these twin development goals.

6

Welfare

Earlier chapters illustrated the divergent trajectories of human development evident during recent decades. Countries as diverse as South Korea, Chile, Botswana, and the Dominican Republic have made remarkable strides by lifting people out of poverty, expanding access to education, and extending longevity. In the same years, however, the lives of people living in the Democratic Republic of Congo, Liberia, and Zimbabwe have stagnated, or worsened, according to core developmental indicators (see Figure 4.1). Given the persistence of enduring poverty, disease, and illiteracy around the world, it is critical to understand whether the type of regime is an important determinant of success and failure. Traditional explanations of development have long emphasized the role of economic growth; GDP expands the resources available for investing in schools, clinics, roads, communications, factories, and water wells. But wealth is only part of the answer for achieving human security; many middle-income countries still lag behind in the UNDP's Human Development Index (HDI), and growth may be accompanied by growing inequality within society, while by contrast some low-income societies perform better by ensuring that their citizens live long and healthy lives, have access to knowledge, and have social protection from the worst threats to human security. Other popular explanations focus on long-term determinants arising from physical geography, climate, and natural resources; hence Jarad Diamond argues that some places are blessed with environmental conditions, fertile soils, and mineral deposits that allowed them to evolve methods of food production and technological innovations centuries earlier, turning them eventually into flourishing industrial and post-industrial societies, while others remain stuck in the rut of subsistence rural economies.[1] Yet environmental determinism and evolutionary biology tells us little, if anything, about how to improve the security of poor nations and poor people.

Compared with growth and geography, are political institutions – specifically the type of regime – an important driver of progress in human development? To address this question, the first section of this chapter reviews the debate about the regime–welfare relationship. As in previous chapters, liberal democracy is theorized to strengthen government accountability, making elected officials more responsive to citizens' demands and social needs. Bureaucratic governance is predicted to strengthen the capacity of the state to manage the effective delivery of public goods and services. The two working together – in bureaucratic democracies – are expected to provide the optimal conditions for regimes to meet development goals, strengthening human well-being, long and healthy lives, and knowledge and literacy. Conversely, their absence – in patronage autocracies – is predicted to prove the worst combination. The second section of this chapter considers what data are available to test the evidence for this argument. The section focuses on comparing the record of regimes in achieving several development goals that are closely related to the Millennium Development Goals (MDGs), the set of universal targets that the world government pledged to achieve by 2015. These goals have become accepted international norms by all major stakeholders in the international development community, including national governments, donor agencies, the United Nations and other multilateral organizations, civil society, academics, and the private sector.[2] The section selects six policy outcome indicators: (i) *life expectancy at birth* (the average number of years lived by a group of people born in a particular year, if mortality remains constant); (ii) *child mortality* (the probability of children not living to the age of five years; (iii) *health* (monitored by incidence of tuberculosis); (iv) *gender equality* (measured by the ratio of girls to boys enrolled in primary and secondary education); (v) *education* (monitored by enrollment in secondary schools for girls and boys); and (vi) *human development*, measured by the overall performance of each society on the composite UNDP HDI (combining longevity, income, and education).

The previous research literature has usually analyzed the impact of liberal democracy on a single policy outcome indicator, such as enrollment in primary schools, rates of infant mortality, or maternal mortality.[3] It is important to compare a far broader range of measures, however, to test whether the main findings for the regime–welfare relationship remain robust and consistent irrespective of the particular indicator. Some MDGs are more open to strategic policy interventions than others; it costs less than $5 to provide an insecticide-treated bed-net to protect a child against malaria, a safe and cost-effective solution against a life-threatening disease. It is far more complex to attempt to transform deep-rooted cultural attitudes toward gender equality and the empowerment of women. It is also vital to examine the effects of both governance and democracy, not just one or the other. As in the previous chapter, descriptive results illustrate the average performance of the regime typology, in this case compared against a range of six developmental indicators, without prior controls. In each dimension, as the book's theory predicts, across all societies under comparison, the descriptive results demonstrate that bureaucratic democracies consistently outperform all other types of regimes on human development – often by a substantial amount. By contrast, patronage autocracies display the worst record. In the intermediate categories, bureaucratic autocracies usually slightly outperform patronage democracies. Similar patterns can be observed if the comparison is restricted to developing societies (with per capita GDP of less than $10,000), although development gaps often shrink in size.

Yet many factors such as growth and geography could be driving these contrasts, beyond differences between rich and poor societies. There are also questions about the direction of causality; rising levels of education and human security can be expected to help strengthen stable democratic regimes, whereas poor and deteriorating living conditions may undermine regime stability. The multivariate models check to see whether the main effects of liberal democracy and bureaucratic governance remain significant after including many other structural factors associated with human development, including geography, prior economic conditions, social characteristics, cultural legacies, and global trends. As in earlier chapters, the regression models use lags as a partial control for endogeneity and panel-corrected standard errors to analyze panel data. The results of the regression models presented in the third section of this chapter suggest that both liberal democracy and bureaucratic governance improve performance on three of the six developmental indices, including strengthening the HDI, expanding secondary school enrollments, and improving gender equality in education. This confirms the effects of democracy on schooling, as several previous studies have reported, while also demonstrating the supplementary effects of governance as well.[4] Bureaucratic governance also extends average longevity and reduces child mortality, as predicted theoretically. Yet more mixed and inconsistent results can be observed from analysis of regime effects on the other developmental indicators. Thus the regression coefficients estimating the effects of liberal democracy on child mortality and incidence of tuberculosis (TB) display positive and significant signs, the direction contrary to that predicted by democratic theories. This book considers possible reasons lying behind these results, emphasizing the diversity of MDG objectives.

Finally, the fourth section of this chapter compares contrasting cases in Sub-Saharan Africa, in Botswana and Zambia, to illustrate the underlying processes linking the type of regime to policy outcomes.

I. THEORIES OF DEMOCRACY, GOVERNANCE, AND WELFARE

Early accounts often assumed a strong relationship between processes of democratization and social equity. Thus in nineteenth century Britain, and elsewhere in Europe, the debate over abolishing literacy and property qualifications for the voting franchise revolved around arguments about the potential consequences of this reform for social equality and economic redistribution.[5] Contemporary scholarly arguments about how this relationship works commonly draw on Allan H. Meltzer and Scott F. Richard's median voter theory.[6] In this view, as discussed earlier, in democratic states with multiparty competitive contests with a universal franchise, elections should make governments more accountable to citizens, as governing parties need their votes to stay in office. In any country where the standard distribution of income is skewed in favor of the rich, the income of the median voter will be less than the mean. Based on rational self-interest, the median voter is therefore expected to favor some measure of redistribution. To gain popular support, parties should therefore pledge to reduce social inequality, and the government should therefore allocate more of its resources to social policies that serve the less well-off. Where policies benefit these sectors, governing parties should be rewarded by their return to office. By contrast, in autocracies lacking competitive elections, rulers are unaccountable to citizens (including the poor), and they might safely ignore them. Median voter theory predicts that social welfare spending will probably be higher in democracies than in autocracies, and social outcomes will prove more equitable, thus raising the quality of life of the poor.[7]

Democracy and Welfare

Comparative studies of many countries worldwide have explored the empirical evidence surrounding the claim that democratic states promote the provision of public goods and services, human development, welfare spending, and social equality more effectively than other types of regimes.[8] Some support for this argument has been reported; an influential study by Joseph T. Siegle, Michael Weinstein, and Morton Halperin compared a range of poorer societies, defined as those with per capita GDP below $2,000, in the period from 1960 to 2001. Democracies were defined using the Polity IV index. The study found that even though they did not spend more on public services, poorer democracies are generally better than poorer nondemocracies at delivering education, literacy, and healthcare.[9] This pattern is attributed to more open information access, greater adaptability, and stronger channels of accountability in democratic regimes: "Democracies perform consistently better on a range of social and economic development indicators than authoritarian governments do. They respond more readily to people's needs, they are adaptable, and they create checks and balances on government power that discourages reckless policies."[10]

Siegle and his colleagues are far from alone in these conclusions; several other studies have reported similar patterns linking democracy with several indices of human development.[11] For example, research has compared educational and healthcare policies in Latin America and found that democracy has real, substantively important effects on the daily lives and well-being of individuals, particularly the provision of primary schooling.[12] This pattern has been reported in several other studies of public services provided in the region.[13] In Africa, as well, democratization (particularly multiparty competition) has been found to be associated with greater state provision of primary education and thus the investment in human capital.[14] Development aid has also been found to improve the quality of life when combined with democratization, but to fail when this link is not established.[15] Other scholars comparing infant and maternal mortality also report that democracy is generally associated with better welfare and healthcare outcomes.[16] In addition, the previous chapter has already demonstrated that bureaucratic democracies usually achieved the most successful rates of economic growth, generating the reservoir of resources that, if channeled into schools, clinics, and homes, could potentially lift millions out of poverty. Theories therefore suggest several plausible reasons that democratic regimes are expected to display more generous spending on social welfare policies, achieving policy outputs and outcomes that raise levels of literacy and education, healthcare, and housing, expanding longevity and benefiting the poor.

Or State-Building, Good Governance, and Public Administration?

Yet the median voter thesis may fail for many reasons. Citizens may be unable to judge the record of governing parties or to evaluate the policy promises made by their rivals. The sequential model of the policy-making process depicted schematically in Figure 2.2 presented earlier depicts this as a failure of the feedback loop, connecting societal impacts with public demands. Retrospective judgments about government performance are difficult to estimate with any degree of accuracy for citizens in established democracies, where parties and leaders have established a long performance in office. It can be expected to prove even more challenging to assign responsibility for policy outcomes in newer democracies, where citizens may blame global conditions or private sector actors rather than elected officials.[17] Even if median voters have the capacity to cast a ballot designed to protect their perceived interests, given the substantial socioeconomic skews that are commonly observed in patterns of political participation, this does not imply that the poorest and least educated sectors of society will necessarily cast a ballot. Thus U.S. Democrats and Republicans have an incentive to protect programs – such as Medicare and social security programs protecting the elderly – that benefit large middle-income sectors who vote in America. Yet given the well-established socioeconomic skew in American voter participation, elected officeholders lack equally strong electoral incentives to provide programs such as Food Stamps and Aid for Dependent Families, designed primarily for low-income families. Of course, politicians and parties may also be swayed by many considerations other than pure vote seeking, including their commitment to ideological values and political principles, such as left-wing support for higher social spending, fiscal redistribution, and welfare state institutions designed to ameliorate poverty and reduce social inequality.[18]

Perhaps the most fundamental challenge to median voter theory, however, arises from the observation that the electoral incentives facing politicians do not affect their capacity to implement policies, allocate resources effectively, and manage the delivery of public goods and services that address social needs and alleviate deep-seated poverty and inequality. The sequential model of policy making in Figure 2.2 illustrates the multistep process linking decision making by the executive and legislature with the subsequent process of implementing programs through public sector management, generating policy outputs (laws and regulations, spending allocations, and administrative decisions), and the impact of policies on developmental outcomes. Elected leaders in countries such as Afghanistan, Haiti, and the Democratic Republic of Congo may be committed to achieving the MDGs and improving the lives of local constituents, but they may be powerless to deliver effective programs if confronted by the challenges of endemic problems of corruption and malfeasance draining budgetary resources from their intended uses; limited fiscal revenues and development aid; poor technical skills, human capital, access to technology and professional training limiting the capacity of the public sector when administering budgets and implementing programs; and inadequate transportation infrastructure, communications, and basic security to expand the delivery of public services outside of urban areas and capital cities.

Therefore, arguments advocated by Francis Fukuyama and others emphasize that state-building, good governance, and public administration need to be prioritized for achieving development outcomes, with a potentially stronger impact on the lives of the poor than democratic electoral accountability.[19] Weberian states that are more competent, effective, impartial, and efficient when managing schools, hospitals, and social protection are more likely to expand human capital; reduce diseases; and protect the elderly, women, and children. Such states thus act as effective national partners for achieving developmental goals in conjunction with the work of the international community. Elsewhere, in countries such as Somalia and Haiti, the development community often attempts to bypass the state by dispersing aid and assistance indirectly through a range of grassroots nongovernmental organizations (NGOs), philanthropic agencies, and civic society organizations in the nonprofit sector, but this process can be logistically difficult and complex. Welfare spending and developmental aid can be expected to prove less effective in patronage states, where the public sector lacks the capability to manage resources and deliver public services competently, equitably, and efficiently (at best), and where the distribution of welfare benefits and services is plagued by problems arising from clientalism, lack of transparency, venality, malfeasance, and corruption (at worst). As William Easterley highlights, in weak states, aid resources allocated for development are too often simply wasted, or end up lining the pockets of kleptocratic elites and corrupt public officials, rather than improving the lives of those most in need.[20]

Or the Skeptical Null Hypothesis?

In the substantial research literature that has accumulated on this topic, however, others remain skeptical about the claims of a "democratic advantage." Political economy models show that democracies usually fund public services at higher levels than nondemocracies; nevertheless, Michael Ross argues that this does not necessarily translate into better social outcomes for the poor, evaluated by the yardstick of maternal mortality rates.[21] Indeed, other scholars have argued that in divided societies, democracy may even produce greater inequalities in rates of child and maternity mortality, with dominant elites depriving minorities of access to healthcare services.[22] A comprehensive overview of the evidence by the UNDP *Human Development Report 2002* concluded cautiously that many established democracies, holding a long series of democratic elections based on the universal franchise for more than a century, continue to display highly uneven income distributions, discrimination against minorities, and systematic biases in taxation and spending policies that protect the interests of the rich:

> Social injustices are widespread in democratic and authoritarian regimes alike, whether deliberate or otherwise in the allocation of public services or in discrimination against squatters, street children, migrants, or other socially marginal groups. ... Political incentives to respond to the needs of ordinary people may be offset by incentives to respond to the demands of the powerful or the wealthy.[23]

Affluent nations and long-standing democracies, such as Sweden, the United States, and Germany, display varied indicators of well-being and human security, patterns of longevity, rates of death from cancer and heart disease, child poverty, and levels of long-term unemployment. Instead of finding a common pattern, Gøsta Esping-Andersen theorized that at least three distinct types of welfare states exist in post-industrial societies: social democratic, liberal, and state-corporatist.[24] These generate significant contrasts in social security policies, income inequalities, and employment and welfare programs. A growing literature has also compared affluent post-industrial societies and established democracies to explain divergences in health indices, such as levels of infant and child mortality and low birth weight rates. These patterns are attributed to the ideological orientation of governing parties, welfare state structures, total public coverage for healthcare, and medical expenditures.[25] Similarly, rather than stressing a single convergent model governing the economy and social policies, Peter A. Hall and David Soskice have also emphasized the "varieties of capitalism" found in Western societies.[26]

Among poorer nations, as well, the UNDP *Human Development Report 2002* documented that many democratic and autocratic states display diverse records in achieving key human development targets, such as cutting rates of child mortality or reducing levels of illiteracy. Case studies also suggest that any pattern is far from clear-cut; one-party communist states such as China and Cuba, where the ruling party has been ideologically committed to egalitarian social and economic policies, have invested heavily in clinics, pensions, and schools. By contrast, during the 1980s, many states both in Latin America as well as in postcommunist societies in Central and Eastern Europe introduced multiparty competitive elections in the transition from autocracy while simultaneously cutting expenditure on welfare services as part of the first-generation Washington Consensus reforms, thereby generating growing social inequality.[27] Indeed, some observers attribute growing public disillusionment with the performance of democracy in Latin America and postcommunist Europe to the apparent failure of many newer electoral democracies to deliver greater social equity and welfare services.[28] From the skeptical perspective, structural constraints in society impose serious limits on state capacity to improve living standards and reduce deep-seated poverty, even in regimes with strong mechanisms of both electoral accountability and the capacity for effective public sector management. In this view, even the most effective regime will be unable to improve welfare when confronted with conflict and waves of refugees spilling over national borders, a stagnant economy and global downturn, or the aftermath of major natural disasters such as droughts, famines, and floods.

As with models of economic growth, multiple controls need to be considered when analyzing the regime–welfare relationship, because many intervening conditions are expected to contribute toward linkages between policy outputs and developmental outcomes. This includes the role of a country's geographic location and thus its access to natural resources; connections to global information and communications; vulnerability to tropical diseases; and risks of natural and manmade disasters such as floods, famines, and climate change. It may also prove more difficult for states to cope with the aftermath of natural disasters when this affects a large population or a vast area with difficult terrain; for example, geography may hinder distribution of aid, medical help, and food supplies to remote mountainous regions in Pakistan or the flood plains of Bangladesh. Economic conditions, both levels of per capita economic development as well as changes in GDP, are commonly seen as fundamental where development is strengthened by societal modernization and industrialization as well as by the generation of financial resources that are available for social spending and welfare programs. Social structure can also have a critical impact for human development, notably conflict caused by linguistic and religious fractionalization, the after-effects of humanitarian crisis triggered by civil wars, or an influx of refugees fleeing violence in neighboring states.

II. EVIDENCE AND RESEARCH DESIGN

Clearly at least some of the varying conclusions among empirical studies can be attributed to methodological and technical issues, including the use by different studies of alternative time periods, country and regional coverage, the choice of specific developmental indicators, selected measures of regime types and indices, and model specifications. For example, the yardstick definition of "poorer" societies used by Halperin, Siegle, and Weinstein is set fairly low (per capita GDP less than $2,000), which may have generated an unintended bias by thereby excluding many moderate-income communist societies.[29] The Soviet Union, for example, included many societies with fairly high levels of education and generous social welfare provisions for healthcare, housing, and pensions, although such states lacked democratic rights and freedoms. The choice of control variables for empirical research is also critical to avoid omitted variable bias, irrespective of the type of regime, because patterns of primary school spending, immunization, or access to clean water among the least developed countries in Sub-Saharan Africa can be expected to differ significantly, for all sorts of reasons, from similar indices in Latin America and postcommunist Europe. Moreover, most previous empirical studies have examined separately either the effects of liberal democracy (usually measured by Freedom House or Polity IV) and to a lesser extent the influence of "good governance" (typically measured by the World Bank indicators) rather than testing the impact of both dimensions on human development.

The endogeneity problem also resurfaces; even where it is clearly established that a broad correlation exists between levels of democratic governance and human development, debate continues about the best way to interpret the "chicken-and-egg" direction of the relationship, and the use of lagged indicators is vital for analysis. As the classic Lipset thesis has long suggested, greater schooling and literacy help to provide the social conditions for the growth of a large middle class, thereby underpinning participation in democracy, as well as being a product of the choice of educational and social policies followed by governments.[30] For all these reasons, we need to take a fresh look at the empirical evidence surrounding debates about the regime–welfare relationship.

If democratic governance benefits development, all other things being equal, this should be apparent if we compare the performance of regimes measured in terms of policy *outputs*, such as levels of public spending on healthcare, education, and social security. Yet resources may fail to prove effective. A more rigorous test compares policy *outcomes* on development indices, including the record of states in reducing infant and child mortality, achieving universal literacy, and expanding longevity. One issue that arises in any such analysis concerns the choice of suitable indicators. Many previous studies have focused on the provision of either primary schooling or maternal mortality, both core development indicators, but it is by no means apparent whether it is possible to generalize the results from these sectors to the achievement of other welfare indices. This book therefore compares the record of regimes in achieving several of the MDGs, the set of universal targets that the world government pledged to achieve by 2015. The MDGs cover a wide range of vital development goals, including eradicating extreme poverty and hunger, achieving universal primary education, and ensuring environmental sustainability. The MDGs have exerted a strong impact on the normative ideas of the international development community by combining powerful claims about multidimensional forms of poverty with concrete "results-based" indicators. Nevertheless, there is no international or scholarly consensus about the most appropriate means to achieve these goals, including whether the type of regime is a critical factor; indeed, with the exception of women's empowerment, issues of empowerment, democracy, and human rights, which are central to the human capacities vision of development, are not explicitly addressed in the MDGs.[31] Yet we also need to be selective because reliable standardized annual data are unavailable over an extended period of time for many core targets. The availability of reliable annual data on many basic indicators is remarkably limited, such as measures of poverty, defined by the proportion of the population living with an income of less than $1 per day, or the proportion living below the nationally defined benchmark.[32] Reliable standardized data are also commonly least available in the least developed societies and in states where national statistical offices lack technical capacity or resources needed for gathering household surveys or census data, introducing systematic bias into worldwide comparisons. This book therefore focuses on analyzing regime effects by selecting six indicators that reflect core developmental objectives and where trends from internationally standardized indicators can also be tracked cross-nationally and over time with reasonable reliability and fairly broad coverage of all world regions.

The Human Development Index

The broadest composite measure of the quality of human development is the index estimated by the UNDP. The Human Development Index includes three elements: life expectancy; knowledge (literacy and combined primary, secondary, and tertiary education enrollment); and wealth (the log of per capita GDP in PPP in U.S. dollars). This measure reflects the human capacities approach to development, advocated by Amartya Sen, which goes beyond the pursuit of material income and financial wealth by emphasizing the importance of broader developmental goals, including the capacity for people to live a long and healthy life, to pursue well-being, and to determine their own lives.[33] Sen emphasized that growth in the nation's GDP may help human well-being – but not necessarily. The HDI is widely used to summarize trends and compare cross-national disparities, but it is also useful to disaggregate the component parts in order to understand the impacts of regimes on each of the key components.

Longevity

Longevity, or the average numbers of years that people born in a particular year are expected to live, is perhaps the single most fundamental indicator of human well-being. Cross-national variations in longevity are commonly explained as the product of multiple societal conditions that expose populations to fatal threats and vulnerabilities, including poverty, starvation, disease and health risks, lack of access to clean water, exposure to natural disasters, and the effect of lack of security and war, as well as standard individual-level characteristics, such as sex, ethnicity, and socioeconomic status. Moreover, longevity varies substantially around the globe; hence those born today in affluent societies such as Japan, Switzerland, and Australia can expect to enjoy an average lifespan of about eighty years, living twice as long as those born in Sierra Leone, Afghanistan, and Zimbabwe.

Child Mortality

Longevity is strongly influenced by mortality rates for infants (under one year old) and children (under five years old). The fourth Millennium Development Goal pledged to reduce child mortality, a universally agreed-on target, led by the work of UNICEF. The latest UN estimates suggest that the total number of deaths of children under the age of five declined around the world from

12.4 million in 1990 to 8.1 million in 2009. Yet substantial disparities continue to exist among rich and poor societies, so that a child born in a developing country is more than thirteen times more likely to die within the first five years of life than a child born in an industrialized country. Sub-Saharan Africa accounts for about half the deaths of children younger than five in the developing world. Moreover, despite the importance of this goal, between 1990 and 2006, the UN estimates that about twenty-seven countries – the large majority in Sub-Saharan Africa – made no progress in reducing childhood deaths. In Eastern Asia, Latin America, and the Caribbean, child mortality rates are approximately four times higher than in developed regions. Disparities persist within all regions: Mortality rates are higher for children from rural and poor families and whose mothers lack a basic education. Thus the rate of child mortality is a suitable indicator where systematic data are regularly collected by national statistical offices and standardized by international agencies. The under-five mortality rate is defined as the probability per one thousand that a newborn baby will die before reaching age five. In 2009, the worst cases around the world were Chad, Afghanistan, the Democratic Republic of Congo, Guinea-Bissau, and Sierra Leone, where around one-fifth of all babies (two hundred of every one thousand live births) would probably die before reaching five. By contrast, the rate of child mortality plummets to around three out of one thousand in societies such as Greece, Sweden, and Japan. Child mortality is a core measure of development, affecting perhaps the most vulnerable sector of any society. MDG Target 4A pledged the world's governments to reduce the under-five mortality rate by two-thirds between 1990 and 2015.

Health: Vulnerability to Fatal Diseases

Health can be gauged by multiple indicators, and MDG target 6 pledged the world's governments to combat HIV-AIDS, reverse the effects of malaria, and reduce the prevalence and death rates from incidents of TB, a contagious disease that can be fatal. Unfortunately, due to limits in longitudinal data availability, it remains difficult to monitor global progress in the first two targets, but internationally standardized time-series indicators are available from the World Health Organization (WHO) to monitor trends in TB over successive years. The WHO estimates that about one-third of the world's population is currently infected with the TB bacillus, although only 5 to 10 percent of this group go on to become sick or infectious at some time during their lives. An estimated 1.7 million people died from TB in 2009, and the highest number of fatalities was in Africa. The WHO measures incidence of tuberculosis by the estimated number of new pulmonary, smear-positive, and extrapulmonary tuberculosis cases per one hundred thousand people. Progress against fatal disease is also an area where relatively low-cost interventions, based on well-established medical evidence, have the capacity to make a dramatic difference. For example, the UN *Millennium Development Report 2011* estimates that worldwide, deaths attributed to TB have fallen by more than one-third since

1990. Similarly, between 2000 and 2008, improved immunization coverage led to a 78 percent drop in measles deaths worldwide, especially for children. The distribution of insecticide-treated mosquito nets has also had a major impact on halting the spread of malaria in Africa.

Gender Parity in Education

Another dimension of the MDGs focuses on promoting gender equality and empowering women. The third MDG commits governments to reduce gender disparities in education, which can be monitored by the ratio of girls to boys in primary and secondary schools. The target of gender equality in schooling is an important foundation for achieving equal opportunities in later life, such as women's full participation in the workforce and public sphere, as well as strengthening preventative healthcare through broadening female awareness of contraception, hygiene, prenatal health, and child care. There has been substantial progress toward meeting this goal, but still substantial disparities continue to exist in the ratio of girls' to boys' enrollment. In developing societies, the current overall ratio is ninety-six to ninety-seven girls for every one hundred boys in primary schools, secondary schools, and tertiary education, but still few global regions have achieved gender parity at the highest levels of education, with large disparities in Asia and North Africa.[34]

Access to Education

As discussed in the previous chapter, educational opportunities are important for expanding literacy, knowledge, and technical skills. Schooling is also believed to have instrumental benefits for attaining many other dimensions of development, such as expanding human capital in the labor force and thus strengthening productivity and economic growth.[35] The 2011 UN report on the Millennium Development Goals highlights the way that some of the poorest societies in Sub-Saharan Africa, including Rwanda, Burundi, and Tanzania, have made the greatest strides toward achieving universal primary education, although progress has slowed in recent years so that the target may not be reached by 2015.[36]

III. REGIMES AND DEVELOPMENT

What is the impact of the type of regime on achievement of these developmental goals? Table 6.1 describes the average performance on the six indices across each of the types of regimes in the years and countries under comparison, without employing any prior controls. If we first compare all societies where data are available, the results demonstrate that bureaucratic democracies consistently outperform all other types of regimes on human development – often by a substantial amount. By contrast, patronage autocracies display the worst record. Thus people living under bureaucratic democracies live on average a full fourteen years longer than those in patronage autocracies. Mortality rates

TABLE 6.1. *Social indicators by type of regime, all societies*

Regime Typology	Human Development	Longevity	Child Mortality	Health	Gender Equality in Education	Educational Opportunities
	(Human Development Index)	(average male life expectancy in years)	(mortality rate for under-fives per 1,000 live births)	(incidence of TB per 100,000 people)	(ratio of girls to boys in primary and secondary school enrollment)	(gross enrollment in secondary schools as a proportion of the age group)
Patronage autocracy	.548	56	112	210	83	42
Patronage democracy	.612	60	85	180	94	55
Bureaucratic autocracy	.673	65	49	98	94	63
Bureaucratic democracy	.828	70	23	70	100	89
Total	.706	64	58	127	95	69
Coefficient of association (eta)	.621***	.580***	.559***	.402***	.479***	.587***
N. countries	102–13	100–24	109–22	109–24	67–90	85–95
Years	1984–2007	1984–2007	1990–2007	1990–2007	1984–2007	1984–2007

Definitions and sources: Human development is based on the 0–1 composite Human Development Index, which combines average longevity, income, and education UNDP. *Human Development Report.* http://hdr.undp.org. *Life expectancy* measures average male life expectancy in years. World Bank. World Development Indicators. *Child mortality* is the ratio of deaths for children under five years old per one thousand live births. UN. MDG indicators. *Health* is the incidence of tuberculosis (the estimated number of new pulmonary, smear positive, and extrapulmonary tuberculosis cases per one hundred thousand people). WHO. World Development Indicators. *Gender equality in education* is the ratio of girls to boys enrolled in primary and secondary schools. World Bank, UNESCO. *World Development Indicators.* http://data.worldbank.org/data-catalog/world-development-indicators?cid=GPD_WDI. *Educational opportunities* are measured as the gross male and female enrollment in secondary schools as a ratio of the corresponding population age group. World Bank, UNESCO. *World Development Indicators.* http://data.worldbank.org/data-catalog/world-development-indicators?cid=GPD_WDI.

for children younger than five show even sharper disparities; in bureaucratic democracies, out of every 1,000 live births, 23 children die before reaching five, but in patronage autocracies 112 children die, more than four times as many. Similar disparities can be observed in incidence of TB, gender equality in education, and gross enrollments in secondary school. In the intermediate categories, bureaucratic autocracies usually slightly outperform patronage democracies. Moreover, these cross-national contrasts cannot be attributed simply to levels of economic development, industrialization, and societal modernization; similar patterns can be observed in Table 6.2 if the comparison is restricted to developing societies (with per capita GDP of less than $10,000), although development gaps often shrink in size and some of the differences disappear between patronage democracies and bureaucratic autocracies. Thus if the comparison is restricted to developing societies, the average longevity gap between patronage autocracies and bureaucratic democracies shrinks from fourteen years across all countries to eight years.

When understanding the descriptive comparisons, it also helps to examine the progress over time in achieving several indicators of development by these different types of regimes. If we compare trends in longevity from 1984 to 2007, illustrated in Figure 6.1, it is apparent that bureaucratic democracies have consistently had high levels of average longevity – although gains are apparent during recent years as people live longer, following advances in medicine and care of the elderly. Bureaucratic autocracies see the most substantial gains over time, with average longevity rising by about a decade. By contrast, there are more moderate gains over time in patronage autocracies and fluctuating patterns in patronage democracies.

If we compare secondary school enrollment during this period, as in Figure 6.2, strikingly similar trends can be observed. Thus the bureaucratic democracies start with the highest levels of education and their lead accelerates so that secondary school enrollment becomes almost universal. Bureaucratic autocracies lag slightly behind, but they register steady progress, so that enrollment rises to around 80 percent of the age group for secondary education. Patronage democracies show trendless fluctuations over time. Patronage autocracies start this period with the worst educational performance, although enrollment has risen sharply in recent years.

Multiple factors are believed to contribute to these patterns of human development, however, so multivariate models allow us to see whether the observed contrasts by regime types persist as significant after applying controls. As in the previous chapter, the models presented in Table 6.3 control for prior economic conditions, including level of per capita GDP and GDP growth (except for model 1a, because income is already a component in the composite HDI). Rising income and high levels of wealth are traditionally expected to have a strong impact on attainment of all the MDGs, by providing the reservoir of resources facilitating investment in public and private services. The results of the analysis in Table 6.3 confirm that levels of economic development, measured by per capita GDP, are indeed related to growing longevity, reductions in the incidence of TB, and access to secondary schools. But economic development

TABLE 6.2. *Social indicators by type of regime, developing societies only*

Regime Typology	Human Development (Human Development Index)	Longevity (average male life expectancy in years)	Child Mortality (mortality rate for under-fives per 1,000 live births)	Health (incidence of TB per 100,000 people)	Gender Equality in Education (ratio of girls to boys in primary and secondary school enrollment)	Educational Opportunities (gross enrollment in secondary schools as a proportion of the age group)
Patronage autocracy	.534	55	121	209	81	38
Patronage democracy	.599	60	89	187	93	53
Bureaucratic autocracy	.595	61	73	137	90	53
Bureaucratic democracy	.690	63	52	175	97	61
Total	.615	59	88	183	90	50
Coefficient of association (eta)	.389***	.348***	.383***	.151***	.412***	.376***
N. countries	90–104	86–109	109–22	109–24	67–90	53–95
Years	1984–2007	1984–2007	1990–2007	1990–2007	1984–2007	1984–2007

Definitions and sources: Human development: The 0–1 composite Human Development Index combines average longevity, income, and education. UNDP. *Human Development Report.* http://hdr.undp.org. *Life expectancy* measures average male life expectancy in years.(World Development Indicators); *Child mortality* is the ratio of deaths for children under five years old per one thousand live births. UN. MDG indicators. *Health* is the incidence of tuberculosis (the estimated number of new pulmonary, smear positive, and extrapulmonary tuberculosis cases per on hundred thousand people). World Bank, UNESCO. *World Development Indicators.* http://data.worldbank.org/data-catalog/world-development-indicators?cid=GPD_WDI. *Gender equality in education* is the ratio of girls to boys enrolled in primary and secondary school enrollment. World Bank, WHO. *World Development Indicators.* http://data.worldbank.org/data-catalog/world-development-indicators?cid=GPD_WDI. *Educational opportunities* are measured as the gross male and female enrollment in secondary schools as a ratio of the corresponding population age group. World Bank, UNESCO. *World Development Indicators. Developing societies* are defined as those with per capita income of less than $10,000, measured by income per capita in purchasing power parity from the chain series index of the Penn World Tables. Alan Heston, Robert Summers, and Bettina Aten. 2011. *Penn World Table Version 7.0.* Philedelphia: University of Pennsylvania, Center for International Comparisons of Production, Income and Prices. http://pwt.econ.upenn.edu/php_site/pwt_index.php.

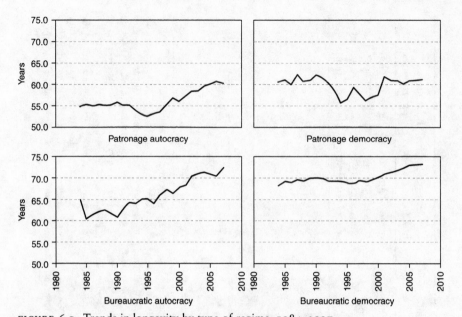

FIGURE 6.1. Trends in longevity by type of regime, 1984–2007.
Note: Average male life expectancy at birth (in years) by type of regime.
Source: World Bank. 2010. *World Development Indicators.* http://data.worldbank.org/
data-catalog/world-development-indicators?cid=GPD_WDI.

does not have the expected positive impact on gender equality in education; there are many oil-rich countries in the Middle East and North Africa where traditional attitudes toward women persist along with disparities in opportunities for girls' education and female employment in the labor force.[37]

By contrast, once we include income and many other conditions, levels of economic growth are unrelated to the achievement of development goals. It has often been observed that countries in Latin America and postcommunist Europe that have achieved substantial growth during recent decades have also experienced growing socioeconomic inequality within society, such as patterns observed in Russia, Brazil, and China. Any linkage is also likely to be complex, nonlinear, and conditional.[38] Robert J. Barro concluded that there is a negative relationship between growth and inequality for poor countries, but a positive relationship for rich countries. In particular, Barro observed a Kuznets curve, whereby inequality first increases and later decreases during the process of economic development.[39] Income generated by growth may be invested in social protection and welfare programs – but not necessarily. Thus there are good reasons to question the pervasive but overly optimistic assumption that growth will automatically "lift all boats."

Physical geography is commonly emphasized as having important fixed effects for industrialization and societal modernization; Jared M. Diamond

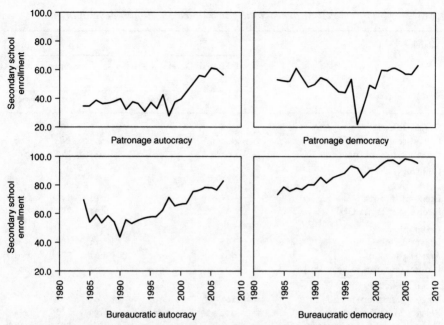

FIGURE 6.2. Trends in secondary school enrollment by type of regime, 1984–2008.
Note: Gross enrollment (male and female) in secondary education.
Source: World Bank. 2010. *World Development Indicators*. http://data.worldbank.org/data-catalog/world-development-indicators?cid=GPD_WDI.

argues that countries closer to the equator share environments and natural endowments hindering the historical evolution of agricultural crop production and animal husbandry that facilitate capital accumulation and thus investment in industrial methods of mass production. The global South is also more vulnerable to tropical diseases and peripheral locations distant from trade markets in core industrial societies, increasing transportation and communication costs.[40] Countries in the tropics are also especially vulnerable to risks arising from climate change, heat waves, floods, and drought. Nevertheless, debate continues about the deterministic role of physical geography; Daron Acemoglu, Simon Johnson, and James A. Robinson argue that institutional development from earlier centuries – and thus history, not geography – caused contemporary patterns of income inequality among nations.[41] Table 6.3 confirms the importance of location on development outcomes, especially for reducing average life expectancy and increasing the risks of child mortality.

Ethnic heterogeneity is also emphasized by William Easterly and Ross Levine as depressing economic growth, as well as potentially increasing the risks of conflict over the allocation of public goods and services. The analysis suggests that countries with high levels of linguistic fractionalization consistently perform more poorly across the range of development indicators under

TABLE 6.3. *The impact of democratic governance on human development*

Model	1a			1b		
	Human Development			Longevity		
	b	p	PCSE	b	p	PCSE
Regime Effects						
Liberal democracy (FH)	.001	***	.001	.007	N/s	.007
Bureaucratic governance (ICRG)	.003	***	.001	.046	***	.013
Controls						
Economic						
Economic growth				.042	N/s	.025
Income (per capita GDP)				.001	***	.001
Geographic						
Location (latitude)	.197	***	.019	−6.12	***	.509
Area size (sq.km)	.001	***	.001	.001	***	.001
Natural resources (oil/gas rents)	.001	***	.001	.001		.001
Social Structure						
Linguistic fractionalization	−.203	***	.003	−7.03	***	.292
Religious fractionalization	.051	***	.005	−3.59	***	.266
Human capital (secondary schooling)				.162	***	.005
Logged population size	−.001	N/s	.002	.858	***	.104
Internal conflict	.044	***	.005	−.030	***	.278
Cultural Traditions						
British colonial legacy	−.022	***	.002	−1.74	***	.185
Global trends						
Year	.003	***	.001	.015		.013
R-²		.71			.77	
Number of observations		652			2290	
Number of countries		128			129	

comparison.[42] Nevertheless, the reasons for this pattern remain to be determined, and it is apparent that indicators of religious pluralism, and the direct impact of internal conflict in a country, do not have consistent effects on the achievement of development goals.

After comparing the effects of these controls, what is the impact of liberal democracy and "good governance" on the attainment of development goals? The parallel theory suggests that both liberal democracy and bureaucratic governance can help to achieve human development by expanding, respectively, both electoral accountability and state capacity in tandem. The results confirm that both liberal democracy and bureaucratic governance consistently improve performance on three of the six indicators: the HDI, enrollment in secondary education, and gender equality in education. Model 1g in Table 6.3 confirms the significant effects of liberal democracy on enrollments in secondary schools,

	1c			1d			1f			1g		
	Child Mortality			Health (TB)			Gender Equality in Education			Education		
	b	p	PCSE	b	p	PCSE	b	p	PCSE	b	p	PCSE
	.091	**	.035	.716	***	.076	.074	***	.003	.168	***	.020
	-.455	***	.087	-.167	N/s	.281	.022	*	.009	.139	***	.045
	-.322	N/s	.179	-.572	N/s	.464	.015	N/s	.019	-.004	N/s	.054
	-.001	N/s	.001	-.004	***	.001	-.001	***	.001	.001	***	.000
	47.62	***	5.38	4.13	N/s	5.87	-15.6	***	1.21	54.1	***	3.29
	-.001	***	.001	-.003	***	.001	-.001	N/s	.001	.001	***	.001
	-.003	***	.001	.009	***	.001	.001	***	.001	-.001	*	.001
	58.3	***	1.71	139.3	***	12.9	-9.8	***	.812	-28.8	***	.827
	4.66	***	1.75	54.7	***	.773	5.4	***	.773	16.0	***	1.59
	-1.29	***	.035	.274	***	.008	.274	***	.008			
	3.15	*	1.59	-1.845	***	.145	-1.84	***	.145	.216	N/s	.355
	-1.73	N/s	1.97	.699	*	.308	.699	*	.308	3.13	***	.958
	13.0	***	.631	.052	N/s	.273	.052	N/s	.273	1.21	N/s	.645
	-.459	***	.093	.072	***	.016	.072	***	.016	.529	***	.059
	.74			.50			.66			.73		
	1654			1696			2338			2338		
	126			129			129			129		

as several previous studies have reported.[43] Model 1f in Table 6.3 also demonstrates the impact of democracy on improving gender equality in primary and secondary school enrollments.[44] These results expand and supplement previous studies, however, by also highlighting the overlooked role of bureaucratic governance for attaining the delivery of educational goals. In addition, bureaucratic governance also seems to strengthen average longevity and to reduce child mortality rates. The remaining developmental indicators present more mixed and inconclusive results, however; thus the effects of liberal democracy on longevity, although positive, are not statistically significant. In addition, the estimated coefficients for the effect of liberal democracy on child mortality and incidence of TB are in the direction contrary to that predicted theoretically.

Inconsistencies in these results may be due, at least in part, to technical issues arising from limited data availability, missed observations, restricted country coverage, and different periods under analysis for each series. But another possible reason that could help to account for these contrasts is that developmental goals differ in how far they are amenable to public policy interventions by regimes. Thus a range of standard policies can be implemented by educational ministries to expand access to primary and secondary schools for both girls and boys, whether by mandating school attendance and investing resources in public sector education (teachers, learning facilities, and schools), reducing or eliminating school fees, and regulating private schools. Similarly, the Bill and Melinda Gates Foundation has prioritized several well-established and low-cost interventions to fight common diseases such as diarrhea and malaria, including vaccination, bed-nets, and better diagnosis.[45] Governments committed to improving the health of their citizens can and do implement similar workable solutions. By contrast, it may prove far more challenging to design effective public policies to extend average life expectancy by a substantial number of years in any society, because longevity is affected by a complex range of long-term and diffuse causes, including the risks of ongoing wars and internal conflict; lack of healthcare; the transmission of contagious diseases; vulnerability to natural disasters such as floods, tsunami, and earthquakes; average living standards; inherited biological characteristics; traditional diet, nutrition, and habitual lifestyles; and fertility rates. Like poverty, longevity is a multidimensional problem with complex causes, subject to major debates about the most effective diagnosis and prescriptive policy interventions. Democratic governance can therefore be expected to have the greatest impact on human development goals where challenges can be addressed by relatively well-established and straightforward policy interventions and where progress can be measured against simple and concrete yardsticks. This situation strengthens accountability for government performance both downward to citizens (through elections, legislative oversight, and civil society NGOs) and upward to the development community (where international agencies and aid donors regularly monitor outcomes). Where developmental challenges are more complex, the goals more diffuse, and the solutions less clear-cut, however, this dilutes government accountability and the capacity for effective policy interventions. It is therefore important to qualify any lessons arising from this evidence; the type of regime does seem to affect several important dimensions of human development and social welfare, but the relationship may vary across different types of developmental goals.

IV. COMPARING BOTSWANA AND ZAMBIA

As in previous chapters, the patterns we have observed around the world can be explored in greater depth with more qualitative narrative case study comparisons. Botswana and Zambia in Southern Africa are selected as the current stark contrasts in economic growth and human development while sharing certain characteristics as neighboring landlocked states, with similar physical size and economies based largely on the extraction of natural

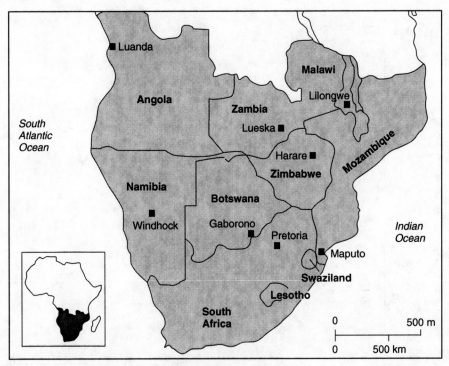

FIGURE 6.3. Botswana and Zambia in Southern Africa.

resources (see Figure 6.3). Both nations achieved independence from Britain in the mid-1960s, part of decolonization movements and the "winds of change" shrinking the British Empire. South Africa is the dominant hegemonic power in the region, although states as politically diverse as Zimbabwe, Namibia, and Angola share borders. Both countries are also multicultural societies, containing a diverse range of languages and ethnic groups based on tribal identities, although Zambia is divided more deeply among Christian, Muslim, and Hindu communities. Despite ethnic fragmentation, both countries also have constitutions embodying majoritarian electoral systems and presidential executives, concentrating power in the hands of the winning party and limiting power-sharing arrangements.

Zambia

The territory of Northern Rhodesia became Zambia on independence in 1964, headed by Kenneth Kaunda, who was elected as its prime minister under the banner of the United National Independence Party (UNIP). Kaunda then became Zambia's first president following a constitutional change. He adopted the principles of African socialism, implementing policies of centralized planning and nationalization of the private sector. Zambia had considerable reservoirs

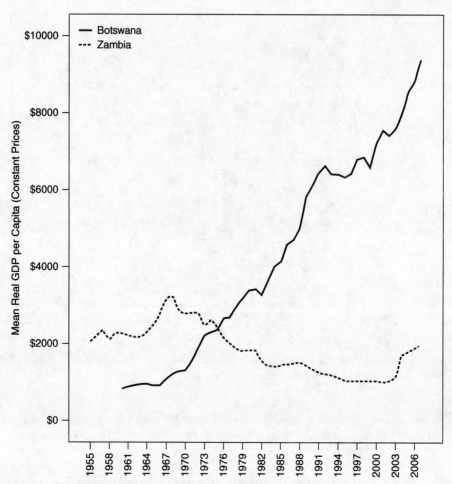

FIGURE 6.4. Economic growth in Botswana and Zambia.
Note: Real GDP per capita, constant prices, chain series.
Source: Alan Heston, Robert Summers, and Bettina Aten. 2011. *Penn World Table Version 7.0.* Philadelphia: University of Pennsylvania, Center for International Comparisons of Production, Income and Prices. http://pwt.econ.upenn.edu/php_site/pwt_index.php.

of mineral wealth as the continent's largest producer of copper, although also with reserves of coal, cobalt, zinc, emeralds, and uranium. At the time of independence, average per capita GDP in Zambia was higher than in Botswana (see Figure 6.4). In 1968, Kaunda was elected unopposed for president and one-party rule was introduced, so that all parties were banned except for the UNIP. The 1973 constitution consolidated strong powers in the hands of the executive, supported by a unicameral National Assembly. Kaunda continued to be elected unopposed as president until the early 1990s, when pressures increased for constitutional reform and moves toward multiparty competition following a series of protests and strikes expressing dissatisfaction with government, rising prices, and the steadily declining economy. The falling price of copper eroded national wealth.

After a new constitution had been drafted, recognizing multiparty competition, elections were held in 1991. These were won by former union leader Frederick Chiluba, leader of the Movement for Multiparty Democracy (MMD). The elections were reported to be free and fair, moving the country toward democracy (see Figure 6.5), but nevertheless the subsequent detention and harassment of political opponents eroded human rights. President Chiluba shifted Zambian policies rightward, in line with the standard menu of reforms under the Washington Consensus, by liberalizing the economy; privatizing state-owned enterprise, such as the copper mining industry; and removing subsidies for different commodities. In 1996, Chiluba was reelected, but the following year saw an attempted coup d'état by the army, triggering a state of emergency and the arrest of those accused of perpetrating the coup, including Kaunda. In 2002, when Chiluba retired as president due to term limits, he was replaced by another MMD candidate, Levy Mwanawasa, who died in office and was succeeded by the vice president, Rupiah Banda. The most recent presidential elections, in September 2011, saw the transition to Michael Sata, leader of the Patriotic Front. Throughout most of the country, polling day was incident-free. In the period after the polls closed and prior to the release of final results, however, tensions rose and violent protests broke out in several areas. Most missions assessed the entire electoral process positively, declaring the voting process as transparent and reflecting the will of the electorate, although unequal campaign funding and access to resources were criticized by observers.[46] Zambia currently has a two-and-a-half party system, with the Patriotic Front and Movement for Multiparty Democracy as the two major rivals, and the United Party for National Development as the minor party contender. Freedom House currently rates Zambia as "partly free" in political rights and civil liberties, the "gray" middle category, similar to regimes in Bangladesh, Kenya, and Papua New Guinea. As shown in Figure 6.5, ratings for the quality of Zambian governance register an improvement during the early 1990s, accompanying the process of democratization, before plateauing. President Mwanawasa launched a strong anticorruption drive that prosecuted several cases, but this initiative was subsequently abandoned. Transparency International's 2011 Corruption Perception Index ranks Zambia as tied at 101st worldwide, similar to the Dominican Republic, Egypt, and Mexico. According to the classifications used in this book, today Zambia can be classified as a patronage democracy, moving ahead of others in the region, such as Zimbabwe, but not yet attaining the position enjoyed by South Africa or Botswana.

Despite opening the economy to foreign investors and experiencing strong growth in recent years, in part reflecting improved copper prices, Zambia is not currently expected to reach many of the Millennium Development Goals

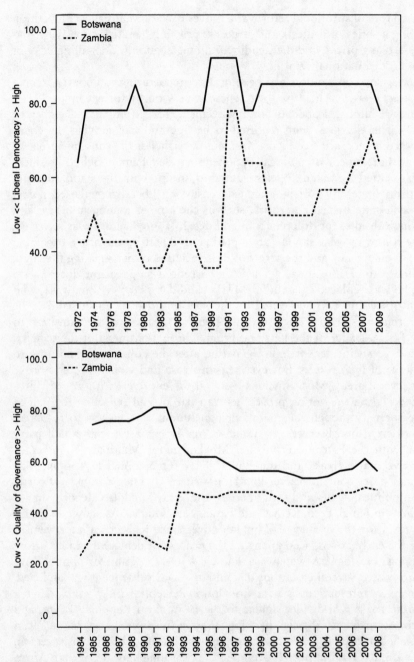

FIGURE 6.5. Trends in democracy and governance in Botswana and Zambia.
Note: Liberal democracy is measured by the standardized one hundred–point Freedom House index of political rights and civil liberties. The quality of governance is measured by the standardized one hundred–point ICRG index.

by 2015, including cutting extreme poverty, reducing maternal mortality, increasing women's voice in decision making, and improving environmental protection.[47] As shown in Table 6.4, average per capita real income in Zambia is only $1,500, with two-thirds of the population estimated to live below the poverty line. The UNDP's 2011 Human Development Index classifies Zambia as low development, ranked 164th out of 187 nations worldwide, similar to Rwanda and Benin. By all the social and economic indices, Zambia scores worse than Botswana – often displaying a massive gap. The HIV-AIDS crisis in the 1980s and 1990s hit the country hard, depressing life expectancy rates. There has been some progress in achieving certain MDG targets, however, including widening access to education (especially for girls) as well as cutting child malnutrition and infant mortality. Net enrollment of children in primary education increased from 80 percent in 1990 to 102 percent in 2009, supported by the increased construction of schools and the removal of school fees. Extreme poverty declined from 58 percent in 1991 to 51 percent in 2006. Nevertheless, although the country is moving in the right direction, Zambia would need to accelerate its rate of progress to meet the MDG targets.

Botswana

By contrast, when Botswana first attained independence from Britain in 1966, the country's economy lagged behind Zambia, but during the mid-1970s Botswana overtook its rival in real per capita income, and since then the emerging economy has grown to become one of the success stories on the continent.[48] Today average GDP per capita (in purchasing power parity) is $1,500 in Zambia but $14,000 in Botswana, the latter similar to Argentina, Latvia, and Chile. Despite the financial crisis in Europe and the United States, the Botswana economy grew by 8.6 percent in 2010. The main source of wealth in Botswana has been minerals, as the world's second largest producer of diamonds, which accounts for one-third of GDP and half the government's revenues. There have recently been some attempts to diversify the economy, however, through extracting coal deposits, as well as through safari-based tourism, financial services, and agriculture. Botswana has also followed sound macroeconomic policies, accumulating budget surpluses and investing in public infrastructure projects, education, and health. For several decades now, steady progress has been registered in rates of literacy, primary and secondary school enrollments, and levels of infant and child mortality. Despite the economic boom, however, one-third of Botswana's people live in poverty, still a high proportion although half the level found among neighboring Zambians. Since the 1980s, HIV-AIDS has also been a widespread epidemic in the country, reducing longevity and wiping out many developmental gains. It has been estimated in 2004 that 17.1 percent of the people of Botswana were living with HIV and AIDS, making the society one of the worst HIV-affected in the world.

On the positive side of the ledger, Botswana is also one of the most stable democracies in Sub-Saharan Africa, holding a series of ten multiparty

TABLE 6.4. *Comparative indicators: Zambia and Botswana*

	Republic of Zambia	Botswana
Area size (sq km)	752,618	581,730
Natural resources	Copper, cobalt, zinc, lead, coal, emeralds, gold, silver, uranium, hydropower	Diamonds, copper, nickel, salt, soda ash, potash, coal, iron ore, silver
Population		
Population (July 2011)	13,881,336m	2,065,398m
Languages	Bemba 30.1%, Nyanja 10.7%, Tonga10.6%, Lozi 5.7%, Chewa 4.9%, Nsenga 3.4%, Tumbuka 2.5%, Lunda 2.2%, Kaonde 2%, Lala 2%, Luvale 1.7%, English 1.7%, other 22.5%	Setswana 78.2%, Kalanga 7.9%, Sekgalagadi 2.8%, English 2.1%, other 8.6%, unspecified 0.4%
Ethnic groups	African 99.5% (includes Bemba, Tonga, Chewa, Lozi, Nsenga, Tumbuka, Ngoni, Lala, Kaonde, Lunda, and other African groups), other 0.5%	Tswana (or Setswana) 79%, Kalanga 11%, Basarwa 3%, other, including Kgalagadi and white 7%
Religion	Christian 50–75%, Muslim and Hindu 24–49%, indigenous 1%	Christian 71.6%, Badimo 6%, other 1.4%, unspecified 0.4%, none 20.6%
Linguistic fractionalization	.41	.59
Religious fractionalization	.87	.74
Political History		
Colonial background	British colony since 1924	British protectorate
Independence	1964	1966
Executive	Presidential	Presidential
Regime type	Patronage democracy	Bureaucratic democracy
Legislature	Unicameral National Assembly	Bicameral National Congress
Democracy index, FH (2007)	64	85
Governance index (ICRG) (2007)	49	60
Corruption Perception Index (2010)	Ranked 101/178	Ranked 33/178

	Republic of Zambia	Botswana
Economy		
GDP (billions, in PPP) (2010)	$20.04b	$28.49b
GDP growth rate (2010)	+7.6%	+8.6%
GDP per capita (in PPP) (2010)	$1,500	$14,000
Unemployment rate (2010)	14%	7.5%
Pop. below poverty line (2004)	64%	30%
Social Indicators		
Human Development Index (2011)	.430 (low)	.633 (medium)
Literacy	53%	81%
Infant mortality rate (2008)	66.6 deaths/1,000 live births	11.1 deaths/1,000 live births
Maternal mortality rate (2008)	470 deaths/100,000 live births	190 deaths//100,000 live births
Life expectancy (years) (2011)	52	58

Sources: CIA. *The World Factbook*. http://www.cia.gov; World Bank. 2010. *World Development Indicators*. http://data.worldbank.org/data-catalog/world-development-indicators?cid=GPD_WDI.

competitive national elections since gaining independence in 1966, more than any other nation on the continent. These elections have also been widely regarded by observers as upholding international standards of electoral integrity. Nevertheless, although opposition parties regularly contest elections and win representation in the National Congress, the Botswana Democratic Party (BDP) has been in government since independence. The BDP is a coalition representing the eight Setswana-speaking tribes that make up nearly 80 percent of the population. The party regularly wins an absolute majority of votes in elections to the National Assembly, which translates under the "first-past-the-post" electoral system into an unassailable government parliamentary majority. Nevertheless, the BDP's vote lead over the opposition has been gradually diminishing over time. Turnout at these contests is also relatively high, with about three-quarters of the registered electorate casting a ballot. The president is indirectly elected by members of parliament; the winning party needs to win twenty-nine of the fifty-seven parliamentary seats to select the new leader. The leader of the BDP, Seretse Khama Ian Khama, became president in April 2008. Despite the predominance of the BDP, Botswana displays a largely positive record in terms of respect for human rights, freedom of the independent press, and rule of law, with Transparency International ranking the country thirty-third highest worldwide in its Corruption Perception Index, the best score in Africa. The government has established extensive procedures for public accounting and transparency and an anticorruption body with the powers to conduct investigations and make arrests.[49] Botswana's laws also establish civilian supervision over the police and an ombudsman process for civilians to lodge complaints regarding police abuse and other human rights violations.

Thus the twin cases demonstrate that democracy and governance have consistently displayed a stronger performance in Botswana than in Zambia. Clearly the reservoirs of natural mineral resources in the former country, especially diamonds, have played a major role in the rapid economic growth that has transformed standards of living during the last three decades and provided the resources for investment in human development as well as lack of government debt. Nevertheless, due to the well-known phenomenon of the "resource curse," many mineral rich states (especially those with easily lootable resources, such as diamonds) suffer from becoming weakened by rent-seeking elites, unbalanced growth, autocratic leaders, internal conflict dividing rival factions, and public sector corruption and malfeasance.[50] The role of "blood diamonds" in fueling continuing conflict in the Democratic Republic of the Congo, destabilizing attempts at peace building and democratic elections, exemplifies these problems.[51] The fact that Botswana has combined substantial economic growth with a long record of democratic stability, human development, sound macroeconomic management, and low corruption makes this case a remarkable success story on the continent.[52]

The case study does not seek to claim that stable and effective democratic governance alone determined this positive outcome; other econometric studies suggest that there is probably a complex interaction or "virtuous circle" linking long-term economic growth, human development, and the institutions of democratic governance.[53] Economic prosperity can fund investment in public sector capacity building, training, and wages, as well as generating the socio-economic conditions (widening literacy, expanding the size of the professional middle classes and civic society organizations, and reducing grievances) that the Lipset thesis has long suggested are most conducive to sustaining democracy, while stable institutions of democratic governance are also likely to attract international investment and to improve the public sector's macroeconomic management. Similarly, the problems of low development facing Zambia can be attributed to a self-reinforcing negative cycle, where decades of dictatorship, weak governance, political instability, and poor macroeconomic policies lead to low or declining growth, especially when coupled with overdependence of export income on the price of copper, while in turn economic malaise and growing poverty weaken political stability and undermine the transition from autocracy. The econometric evidence suggests that multiple structural conditions help to explain progress in human development, not simply the type of regime in power. Achieving the MDGs by reducing child mortality rates, improving health, and expanding opportunities in schools is shaped by fixed or enduring factors such as the location of countries close to the equator, the availability of natural resources, the degree of ethnic fractionalization, human capital, and internal conflict. But the results also indicate that even after controlling for many conditions, the level of democratization and, particularly, the capacity of bureaucratic governance also affect progress on many MDG indicators. The case studies serve to reinforce this story. The contrasting trajectories experienced by the neighboring African countries since independence, however, with Botswana gradually leapfrogging over Zambia, combined with the econometric analysis of global trends presented earlier in this chapter, do lend further support to the argument that both the constraints produced by liberal democracy and the capacity of the state to respond to social needs are important for enabling effective processes of human development.

7

Peace

Human security concerns issues of peace and freedom from fear; indeed, this can be regarded as an even more essential condition for well-being than reductions in poverty and inequality. As the post–Cold War era has seen the decline of wars between nation-states, internal violence has become the most common cause of conflict; thus this chapter focuses on the impact of regimes on civil wars within states. Moreover, in recent decades the international community has expanded peace-keeping operations seeking to contain and prevent conflict.[1] Interventions have broadened in scope well beyond the provision of blue-helmet security to cover complex challenges of overcoming human suffering and humanitarian crisis, supporting economic and social reconstruction, and securing agreement for new constitutional settlements and regime transitions. The expansion has been fueled by widespread concern that weak states in societies deeply divided by conflict and violence are breeding grounds for many global ills, including terrorism, organized crime and corruption, weapons proliferation, humanitarian emergencies, environmental degradation, genocide, and political extremism.[2] Weak states lack the capacity to protect their citizens from rebel violence, private militia, or local warlords. Instability from refugees, ethnic strife, humanitarian disasters, or armed forces can spill over borders into neighboring countries, as exemplified by the massive displacement of refugees and exiles in the Great Lakes region when Rwandans flooded into Tanzania, the Democratic Republic of Congo (DRC), Uganda, and Burundi following the Rwandan Patriotic Front offensive in 1994, where refugee camps developed into militarized bases for opposition forces. Another example concerns the Bosnian war and the destabilizing effects on the Balkans.

Given the complex challenges, UN peace-building operations have had a checkered record of success.[3] In the most positive cases, the outcome has been durable peace settlements and the establishment of legitimate governments, such as in Mozambique, El Salvador, and Croatia.[4] Elsewhere, peacekeeping has often proved less effective, however, and states have continued to struggle, exemplified by continuing conflict, lawlessness, and unrest in Somalia, a humanitarian crisis in Darfur and southern secession in Sudan, renewed violence over disputed presidential elections in Cote d'Ivoire, and marauding militia and instability in the Democratic Republic of Congo.[5] J. Joseph Hewitt, Jonathan Wilkenfeld, and Ted Robert Gurr estimate that of the thirty-nine outbreaks of armed conflict during the last decade, thirty-one were recurrences after violence had been dormant for at least a year.[6] Like Pandora's Box, the evil of war often refuses to be contained.

When confronted with these challenges, both democratic-promoters and state-building schools of thought are common within international relations and comparative politics. As discussed in Chapter 2, these perspectives differ sharply in their strategic priorities and in their understanding of sequential processes of institution building thought necessary to secure an enduring reduction in armed conflict within societies. Hence state-builders emphasize the critical role of starting postwar reconstruction processes with strengthening governance capacity, especially to maintain order and stability, functioning basic services, and budgetary administration. Insurgency, political violence, and civil war are thought less likely under strong states. By contrast, democracy-promoters stress the importance of first establishing the institutional foundations of liberal democracy, and thus competitive elections, institutional checks and balances, and the dispersal of power, limiting executive autonomy, on the grounds that inclusive democracies reinforce the legitimacy of the government, check the dangers of state repression where armed forces are used against their own citizens, and provide channels for expression that reduce the underlying causes of political grievances driving the use of armed conflict. Debate about these alternative priorities is not confined to academe, by any means; rather, similar arguments also resonate among agencies and policy makers within the international community. Moreover, these arguments are open to challenge if they ultimately involve a false dichotomy based on faulty reasoning, particularly if the most effective strategy is strengthening both democracy and governance simultaneously, as the book's theory suggests.

Therefore, what types of regimes reduce domestic conflict? Is expanded governance capacity the first essential step following civil wars, to reestablish order, stability, and security? Or instead should the process of building democratic institutions be the top priority, thereby strengthening regime legitimacy and accountability? Do we need both? Or is internal conflict the result of deep-rooted structural conditions of greed and grievance, so that even the best-designed regimes are powerless to hold back the tide of ethnic violence and intercommunal intolerance? To understand these issues, the first part of this chapter summarizes the theoretical arguments and points of contention in the debate. Part II operationalizes the concepts and selects indices to compare violence within societies. The dependent variable – measures of internal armed conflict – is derived from the Uppsala Conflict Data Program (UCDP) Peace Research Institute Oslo (PRIO) Armed Conflict Dataset from 1946 to 2009. On this basis, Part III examines the cross-national time-series evidence. The conclusion summarizes the main findings and considers their implications.

I. THEORETICAL FRAMEWORK

Establish Democratic Legitimacy First?

The role of formal institutions has long been central to the study of comparative politics, but what types of regime institutions should be prioritized for peace building in the immediate aftermath of civil wars? As discussed earlier in the book, the argument emphasizing the role of democracy in reducing conflict is common in comparative politics and democratic theory. It is essential to restore trust in any divided society following civil war, it is argued, by building regimes that enjoy popular legitimacy based on the institutional foundations of representative democracy. Elections provide a peaceful outlet for the expression of grievances, where rival factions turn from military conflict to campaigns mobilizing popular support and then to decision-making processes involving negotiation and compromise.

Since the early 1990s, the idea that democratic elections are an integral part of any peace-building process has now become standard. Related processes include support for constitutional and legal reform, training for electoral administrators, assistance for political parties, and aid for civil society organizations. Nevertheless, scholars differ in their institutional recommendations. For Schumpeterians, it is sufficient to hold competitive multiparty elections meeting international standards of electoral integrity, at the start of the peace-building and regime transition process, so that elected officials are accountable to citizens through periodic contests and all citizens have an outlet to express their grievances and demands.[7] Following Robert Dahl, ideas of liberal democracy emphasize the need for further additional institutional checks and balances, as elections per se are insufficient for constraining the executive in the absence of an effective legislature and an independent judiciary, a rich and diverse civil society and news media, and decentralized levels of governance.[8] Peace-keeping processes and the initial stages of regime transitions often involve multiple tasks beyond elections, including constitutional negotiations and settlements, reform of the media and security forces, the strengthening of legislative bodies and the courts, the building of political parties, and so on. According to consociational theories, it is also essential to build inclusive power-sharing arrangements into any postwar democratic constitutional settlements, with institutions such as proportional representation electoral systems, inclusive multiparty parliaments with mechanisms for women and minority representation, coalition governments, prime ministerial executives, federalism, and decentralization.[9] Many scholars therefore agree that democratic institutions and procedures have the potential capacity to overcome many of the world's ills, including reducing the causes of deep-rooted civil conflict, with indirect benefits for international security among states, although theorists differ in their prescriptions for institutional reforms.

The broadest claim argues that the international community needs to be fully committed to democracy promotion and holding elections even under the most challenging circumstances, such as in Southern Sudan, Egypt, Libya, and

Afghanistan.[10] Several reasons can be suggested for why deeply divided societies emerging from civil conflict should hold credible elections at an early stage in any peace-building process.

First, unless regimes are founded on competitive elections meeting international standards, as a minimum, it is argued that rulers will fail to be regarded as legitimate by citizens, thus fostering enduring grievances, suppressing but not mitigating the deeper causes of conflict. Democracies provide participatory outlets for the expression of discontent, reducing the need for extreme violence and coercion and building trust.

Secondly, democratic political institutions reduce state repression.[11] This involves a wide range of actions that states use against their own citizens, ranging from curtailments of fundamental freedoms and the imprisonment of dissidents to outright violence and even genocide. The "domestic peace" argument by Christian Davenport suggests that, at minimum, this type of regime constrains governments from repressive acts against their own citizens and thus reduces the causes of homegrown conflict.[12] Democracy curtails these acts through the mechanism of voice, as elected governments can be voted out of office, and through the mechanism of veto, because institutions check executive power. Repressive acts against citizens also violate democratic cultural norms and values, such as tolerance and compromise.

"State-building first" is also regarded as a flawed strategy for those holding democratic values, because there is no long-term guarantee, and every reason to doubt, that regimes will eventually voluntarily loosen their grip on power to transition toward democracy. Democracy deferred may well prove to be democracy denied.

Lastly, beyond the beneficial consequences for reducing the causes of internal conflict, it is also claimed that important indirect benefits follow for interstate relations.[13] The well-known "democratic peace" proposition maintains that democratic states have never, or rarely, fought each other. One of the most widely quoted studies, by Bruce Russett, suggests that the spread of the democratic peace developed toward the end of the nineteenth century, and this pattern has been enduring since then: "There are no clear-cut cases of sovereign stable democracies waging war with each other in the modern international system."[14] The precise underlying mechanisms generating any democratic peace dividend remain difficult to establish, however, and alternative theories focus on the importance of institutions, political culture, and globalization.[15] If all these claims are valid, this suggests that *countries that have held multiparty elections meeting international standards of electoral integrity will be less vulnerable to the threat of internal armed violence and civil wars.*

Establish Power-Sharing Democracies First

Yet several scholars argue that not all types of democracy encourage accommodation; as discussed earlier, theories based on ideas of "consociational" or "consensus" democracy, long championed by Arend Lijphart, emphasize that inclusive power-sharing arrangements engaging all parties are critical.[16] Consociationalists argue that power-sharing constitutional settlements serve to dampen armed conflicts in deeply divided multi-ethnic societies and thereby produce a durable peace settlement, political stability, and the conditions under which sustainable democracy flourishes.[17] According to Lijphart, democracies that endure in plural societies are characterized by multiple democratic checks and balances to ensure that power is widely dispersed vertically and horizontally, typified by the adoption of proportional representation electoral systems, decentralized and devolved governance, and prime ministerial executives accountable to parliament.[18] Consociational theory suggests that power-sharing democratic institutions are especially important for political stability following conflict in divided societies, mainly by restoring trust among community leaders, as well as increasing confidence in the responsiveness of elected officials among their followers, and thereby establishing conditions favoring sustainable peace. Empirical studies have explored several aspects of this complex relationship. In previous work, I have demonstrated that states with power-sharing arrangements do display significantly greater progress in democratization than those with majoritarian institutions.[19] Others have reported that peace settlements involving power sharing are more likely to endure.[20] If these arguments are correct, *states with power-sharing institutional arrangements should prove most effective at limiting domestic conflict.*

Or State-Building First?

Nevertheless, despite much theorizing about the general effects of democracy and democratization on civil war, generating a substantial literature, the statistical relationship is not robust. Interpretation of the evidence is sensitive to issues of measurement error and problems of validity, systematic biases in missing data, problems of endogeneity in complex pathways of causation, nonlinear and skewed indices, and a partial set of cases. For all these reasons, evidence remains inconclusive and democracy promotion arguments – especially the most general claims – have always proved controversial. Critics charge that power-sharing democracies can freeze group boundaries, heighten latent ethnic identities, hinder rebuilding the state in the early stages of recovery from violent internal conflict, and thereby fail to facilitate stability in multi-ethnic societies.[21] Democratic institutions are also thought to have a limited impact on the risk of conflict recurrence in divided societies if they remain vulnerable to poor economic growth, lingering disagreements about power-sharing arrangements, and continued opportunities for insurgencies to organize.[22] The transition from absolute autocracy toward more open regimes and electoral democracies is regarded by James D. Fearon and David Laitin as a particularly dangerous period for multi-ethnic societies, when autocratic control is curtailed, providing greater opportunities for rebellion, but at the same time new regimes have not engendered feelings of political legitimacy and loyal support.[23]

As discussed in Chapter 2, the primary counterpart to theories of democracy promotion derives from the state-building perspective, originating in the classic work of Samuel P. Huntington in his seminal book, *Political Order in Changing Societies* (1968).[24] These ideas are back in vogue among diverse commentators, such as Robert Kaplan, Francis Fukuyama, Edward Mansfield, and Jack Snyder.[25] For Huntington, regime transitions should be understood as a sequential process. The first priority following internal conflict is state-building, a process designed to expand governance capacity and establish conditions of social cohesion, order and stability, national unity, the rule of law, and the exercise of effective authority. State-building is understood as an essential precondition for subsequent industrialization and societal modernization so that, in the due course of time, nations eventually become ready to transition toward democracy, through the usual mechanisms of holding competitive elections, strengthening legislatures, and establishing independent checks and balances on the executive. Effective development is understood by Huntington to be a series of strategic steps where societies first need to build well-functioning states capable of maintaining order and security before they can subsequently expand processes of economic development. Only further down the road, once these preconditions are met, Huntington suggests, should societies seek to transition in the next stage to democratic regimes. If the steps are reversed, then Huntington anticipates heightened risks of political instability, coup d'états, violent rebellions, and guerrilla wars.[26]

Ideas of state-building and sequencing fell out of fashion during the early third wave era, in the years following the fall of the Berlin Wall. Contemporary debates about these notions revived again following experience of elections in post-Saddam Iraq and also in Afghanistan. American commentators were frequently dismayed by the results of reform efforts in these countries, exemplified by corruption that was reported to be pervasive throughout the Hamid Karzai administration and the fraudulent practices surrounding elections in Afghanistan, leading the Electoral Commission to discard one-fifth of all ballots cast for the 2010 Afghan parliamentary elections. Doubts about the fruits of democracy-promotion were further fueled by the outcome of the initial liberalization of many repressive regimes in the Middle East and North Africa. Multiparty elections led to popular gains for Islamist parties, which were often assumed by Western observers to be radical and antidemocratic forces, including the Islamic Party of Justice and Development (JDP) in Morocco in 2002, the Justice and Development Party in Turkey (2002 and 2007), the Muslim Brotherhood (the Freedom and Justice Party) and Al-Nour in Egypt (2012), and the Islamic Resistance Movement (Hamas) in Palestine (2006).[27] Meanwhile, some fragile gains for third wave electoral democracies during the 1990s subsequently faltered in Sub-Saharan Africa, notably in Gabon, Kenya, Niger, Sierra Leone, and Madagascar. In Eastern Europe, improvements in human rights during the early 1990s were reversed under Vladimir Putin's leadership in Russia.

Moreover, in recent decades the international community has become increasingly engaged in peace-building operations.[28] Since the early 1990s, there have been almost two dozen attempts at state-building by the international community, led by the United Nations. Yet these have had a mixed record of success; the outcome in some cases (such as Namibia, El Salvador, and Croatia) has resulted in durable peace settlements and legitimate governments. Elsewhere, other states continue to struggle with these challenges, as exemplified by intermittent conflict and instability in Somalia, Sudan, and the Democratic Republic of Congo.

Troubled by these developments, several international relations scholars have argued that enthusiasm for democracy-promotion should be tempered by other considerations. State-building theorists do not usually question normative claims about the ultimate importance of democracy and human rights; rather, they suggest that the most effective and realistic strategy to achieve this long-term goal is indirect. Echoing Huntington, such scholars suggest that countries afflicted with deep-rooted conflict need first to establish the foundations of a well-functioning state, rebuilding the fabric of society and the economic infrastructure and restoring intercommunal trust, before rushing headlong into elections and democracy.

Perhaps the most sustained challenge to democracy promotion has been articulated by Mansfield and Snyder.[29] These scholars warn that states holding elections as part of the process of transition from autocracy are far *more* susceptible to ethnic conflict, not less. The need for political parties and leaders to mobilize electoral support and compete for votes is thought to provide incentives for political polarization, nationalist rhetoric, and tribal appeals. Moreover, the transition from autocracy entails uncertain shifts in power that can increase the perceived threats facing out-groups who fail to gain representation. Mansfield and Snyder argue that elections are particularly dangerous if held early in any transition process, before the mechanisms of political accountability, institutional checks and balances, and a democratic culture have had time to consolidate.[30] They argue:

> In general, transitions are smoothest when the preconditions of democracy develop in a sequence that begins with the state's construction of an orderly administrative powerbase, followed by development of the rule of law and institutions of public debate. Only after successful completion of the first two steps can the state effectively confront the challenges of integrating the conflicting interests unleashed by universal suffrage.[31]

In particular, regime transitions from absolute autocracy to electoral democracy, or vice versa, are thought to heighten the risk of violence. Nevertheless, any estimates are sensitive to issues of measurement, timing, the severity and type of conflict, and the model specification, with complex interaction effects arising when analyzing this relationship.[32] Electoral competition for votes on the basis of heightened rhetoric and tribal appeals can heighten ethnic tensions, although the outcome is contingent on a range of issues such as sequencing, timing, mechanics, and administration.[33] Attempts to replicate Mansfield and Snyder's empirical evidence has raised several challenges, however; with the results contingent on measurement and methodological issues.[34] The empirical evidence for state-building claims therefore needs reexamining, including comparison of different types of regimes.

Therefore, commentators differ in many important regards, but those advocating state-building generally share the belief that the most effective and coherent strategy in failed or collapsed states is to follow a step-by-step sequential process, where the first priority is establishing effective governance. Once the foundation of order and stability is established in any society, then, it is hoped, this will be followed eventually by processes of societal development, market liberalization, and democratic elections. If this general account is true, then it follows that, all other things being equal, *states with strong and effective governance capacity will be less vulnerable to domestic violence and civil wars.*

Unified Theory

It is also possible that the debate, although heated, is based on a false dichotomy, if armed conflict is reduced most effectively where the formal institutions of liberal democracy are strengthened simultaneously with governance capacity, separately and in tandem. A number of scholars assume that states need to "do it all" – building effective law and order as well as holding competitive elections, improving the quality of public administration as well as bolstering human rights – rather than regarding these priorities as clear-cut alternatives. Hence Thomas Carothers suggests that the process of gradually strengthening democracy needs to accompany state-building initiatives, recognizing that both components are necessary for successful development.[35] The idea that these institutions working together will strengthen stable and accountable states is common in the literature, and its popularity rests in part on the way that the idea of "governance" is often so fuzzily defined and poorly conceptualized that it is sometimes equated automatically with "democracy."

The most common and recognizable feature of representative democracy is the holding of competitive multiparty elections. These contests are now a standard component in negotiated settlements for divided societies emerging from conflict, as part of the international peace-building process.[36] Yet this strategy may ultimately elect governments that fail and thus have the capacity to spread long-term public disillusionment with electoral democracy, the theory suggests, in states where regime authorities lack the military, financial, or administrative capacity or will to improve the lives of their citizens. Weak states have rulers who lack the ability to prevent bloodshed (as in the Democratic Republic of Congo), alleviate deep-rooted poverty (as in Liberia), maintain security (as in Somalia), or protect citizens against the ravages of humanitarian or natural disasters (as in Haiti). It may thus be problematic to develop the electoral institutions of representative democracy, which facilitate the expression and mobilization of citizens' demands, where states lack governance capacity to deliver services meeting basic needs, including control by their security forces over their own territory against external threats and internal rebellions.

Yet expanding state capacity – for example, by strengthening the executive bureaucracy, bolstering tax collection agencies, or equipping the security forces – may be equally problematic without first establishing the accountability mechanisms and safeguards over executive power provided by representative democratic institutions. Once ruling elites are installed securely in office, with strong state capacity, there is no guarantee whatever that they will necessarily subsequently relinquish power voluntarily. They may install mechanisms that facilitate the peaceful rotation of leadership positions, as in China. Based on past experience elsewhere, however, there is every expectation that they will not do so, that the strong state will be used to control and repress dissent and opposition forces. Therefore, the book's theory suggests that, rather than facing a false dichotomy, the challenge for the international community is to strike a careful and delicate balance between *simultaneously* strengthening both representative democracy *and* bureaucratic governance. The argument suggests that *the combination of both democracy and governance working in tandem will reduce the risks of civil war and outbreaks of internal violence.*

Structural Explanations

Lastly skeptics argue that the type of regime does not function as an independent determinant of war and peace, because conflict is driven by a combination of fixed structural conditions. Besides focusing on regime types, many previous studies of internal conflict have emphasized the critical importance of economic conditions, including the role of economic development (measured here by logged per capita GDP in purchasing power parity) and changes in income (measured by rates of economic growth). Poor economic performance is widely believed to fuel a sense of grievance, in particular if the combination of low rates of income growth, youth unemployment, and enduring poverty foster popular discontent against the government. Rapid economic change (positive or negative) is expected to intensify group competition for scarce resources, leading groups to support rebellion.[37] Nevertheless, potential problems of reverse causality arise when interpreting any correlation; William Easterly and Ross Levine emphasize that domestic violence and instability deter foreign investment and destroy core infrastructure, thus depressing economic development.[38] The process of postwar reconstruction can also generate a sudden spurt in income growth, funded by the investment of recovery efforts and humanitarian aid, but this is not generally sustainable over the long term.

Geographic factors may also prove important for conflict. The location of countries closer to the equator may be important, because we have already observed that these nations typically experience problems of economic growth, vulnerability to tropical diseases, and distance from industrial markets. Sub-Saharan Africa is particularly prone to internal instability, ethnic violence, and civil wars, from Angola and Rwanda to Ethiopia, Sierra Leone, Liberia, and DRC.[39] Thus geographic latitude is included in the models as a control.

The size of any nation-state – both in terms of population and physical span – is also likely to effect the difficulties of maintaining order and security. One of the basic problems of state capacity in Afghanistan and the Democratic Republic of Congo is the vast size of each country, coupled with the exceptionally poor transportation and communication infrastructure, and difficult physical terrain, generating security challenges from regional warlords who rival the control of the central government isolated in capital cities. In particular, larger countries that are also plural societies, such as Indonesia, India, Nigeria, and Russia, are potentially vulnerable to ethnic groups demanding succession or autonomy, thus increasing the risks of violent rebellion.

The well-known "resource curse" has often been blamed for fueling a sense of greed (providing opportunities to grab wealth such as diamonds and gold) and grievance (among those excluded from the patronage spoils). Nevertheless, the evidence remains under dispute.[40] The notion of a "resource curse" has been most commonly applied to explaining why many countries apparently blessed with abundant reserves of nonrenewable mineral resources, such as Nigerian oil, the Democratic Republic of Congo's gold, or Sierra Leone's diamonds, in fact are commonly blighted with less transparency and probity, economic stability, economic diversification, social equality, and investment in human capital. In these conditions, the heightened danger of state capture and rent seeking by ruling elites is thought to generate poorer prospects for the transition from autocracy and the consolidation of stable democracies. Lootable mineral resources, in particular, are thought to make a country particularly vulnerable to criminality, corruption, civil war, insurgency, and rebellion. Paul Collier and Nicholas Sambanis argue that rebel groups are often organized to profit financially, such as from pillage, piracy, control of trade, the transfer of land, or appropriation of humanitarian aid, even if leaders exploit the language of grievance.[41] Following Michael L. Ross, the role of natural resources is measured in this book by oil and gas rents per capita in constant dollars.[42]

Ethnic fractionalization and communal polarization are also commonly regarded as some of the most critical factors capable of triggering intercommunal violence.[43] In particular, ethnicity can be mobilized to fuel a sense of grievance focused around group oppression, social injustice, and the violation of rights.[44] This process is exemplified by the struggle for self-determination and independence in East Timor; the movement to gain UN recognition of a Palestinian state; conflict among the Sunni, Shi'ite, and Kurdish communities in post-Saddam Iraq; and tribal identities dividing rebels and supporters of Colonel Muammar Gaddafi in Libya. In practice, the theoretical bright line distinguishing economic opportunities ("greed") and subjective perceptions of group rights ("grievance") remains complex and ambiguous; it is difficult to identify when claims for community self-determination shade into claims for a fairer distribution of state entitlements or economic redistribution. The measurement of ethnicity also remains a complex matter. Studies most often gauge the proportion of ethnic minorities within any population. This measure is not equivalent to polarization, however, and the geographic distribution of communities within society is also likely to prove important. Moreover, all types of ethnic identities, such as those defined by race, tribe, language, religious faith, and nationalism, are not necessarily equivalent in terms of the capacity of communities to be mobilized into acts of hatred and violence. The distribution of each type of ethnicity also varies among global regions. Constructivist theory also suggests that endogeneity can operate here, if conflict heightens latent ethnic identities, so that social cleavages based on language, religion, race, or nationality are not endogenous to the regime.[45] In this book, societal levels of linguistic and religious ethnic fractionalization are derived from estimates provided by Alberto Alesina and his colleagues, the source providing the most comprehensive cross-national coverage.[46] The proxy measure assumes that high levels of ethnic polarization are most likely to occur in the most fractionalized societies.

The historical legacy of colonial backgrounds is also thought important for internal conflict. Some studies suggest that countries with a British colonial past have a better track record of democratization and stability, through the administrative and cultural legacy that was established by Britain.[47] Nevertheless, European colonial legacies have also been blamed for drawing territorial boundaries that created artificial nation-states, combining diverse ethnic and tribal identities, leading to long-term instability and succession. To test the evidence, models include a variable identifying a British colonial legacy. Therefore, many structural factors are believed to contribute toward internal violence and armed conflict, and a skeptical perspective suggests that the type of regime can be understood as the consequence of these factors as much as their cause. If structural explanations are correct, then it would be expected that *economic, geographic, social, and cultural factors will outweigh the impact of democratic governance.*

II. DATA AND EVIDENCE

The theories reviewed from the research literature suggest several empirically testable alternative propositions. To operationalize and test these alternative propositions, measures of civil wars are derived from the UCDP/PRIO Armed Conflict Dataset Version 4.0, providing a comprehensive accounting of all forms of major armed conflicts in the world over the contemporary period, 1946 to 2007.[48] UCDP defines conflict as "a contested incompatibility that concerns government and/or territory where the use of armed force between two parties, of which at least one is the government of a state, results in at least 25 battle-related deaths." The dataset identifies incidents of "internal armed conflict," or civil war, defined as that which occurs between the government of a state and one or more internal opposition groups without intervention from other states. The UCDP measure of civil war is coded on a four-point scale depending on the incidence and magnitude of conflict (measured by the number of battle-related deaths): (0) no internal conflict; (1) minor internal armed conflict; (2) moderate internal armed conflict; and (4) major internal armed conflict.

In addition, the dataset recognizes several other types of conflict that can be compared with incidents of internal armed conflict, including *extra-systemic* armed conflict, which occurs between a state and a nonstate group outside its own territory; *interstate* armed conflict, which occurs between two or more states; and finally *internationalized* internal armed conflict, which occurs between the government of a state and one or more internal opposition groups with intervention from other states. To replicate standard approaches in the research literature, the dependent variables derived from this dataset are the annual incidents of internal armed conflict. The country-year panel includes up to 2,631 observations across the whole period. This produces a large enough time series to model the dynamics for each unit. Given limits on data availability, the analysis is limited to 133 contemporary nation states (excluding dependent territories and states that dissolved during this period). Descriptive statistics are examined and then binary logistic regression is used to measure the impact of the independent variables on the duration of internal armed conflict in each society with the full battery of multivariate controls, as deployed in previous chapters.

Assessing the Impact of Democratic Governance on Conflict

The descriptive comparison of types of conflict (dichotomized to represent any instances of conflict, irrespective of the magnitude) can first be observed across regime types, without any controls. As shown in Figure 7.1 and Table 7.1, as predicted, patronage autocracies display by far the highest levels of internal conflict. The lack of state capacity to maintain effective security, coupled with lack of peaceful outlets for the expression of grievance in autocratic states, proves a deadly combination. This type of regime also displays the highest frequency of interstate and internationalized wars. Patronage democracies also experience moderately strong risks of domestic political violence, although not interstate wars. Lastly, bureaucratic democracies and bureaucratic autocracies are least prone to suffer from armed violence, with both regimes displaying a similar profile. Nevertheless, these similarities in outcomes are probably attributable to different underlying mechanisms. Bureaucratic autocracies have the capacity to use repressive mechanisms against their own citizens to silence popular criticism, prevent potential rebellions, and deter social instability from opposition movements. By contrast, bureaucratic democracies have the capacity to lower grievance by providing peaceful mechanisms for dissent, as well as generating stronger feelings of political legitimacy.

For a global comparison, Table 7.1 classifies the distribution of the different types of internal conflict occurring during 2004 by each of the four types of regime. Out of thirty-seven states experiencing internal conflict during this

TABLE 7.1. *Internal conflict by type of regime, 2004*

	No Internal Conflict	Internal Minor Armed Conflict	Internal Intermediate Armed Conflict	Internal War	Total N
Patronage autocracy	81	9	2	9	47
Patronage democracy	91	2	7	0	43
Bureaucratic autocracy	100	0	0	0	6
Bureaucratic democracy	95	0	3	3	37
Total	88	4	4	4	113

Note: The occurrence of internal conflict experienced by type of regime, 2004.
Source: Calculated from ECDP/PRIO. 2010. *The ECDP/PRIO Armed Conflict Dataset Codebook Version 4*. Uppsala: ECDP/PRI.

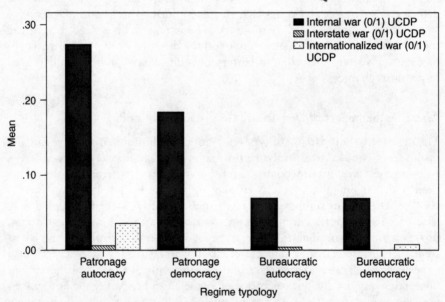

FIGURE 7.1. Conflict by type of regime, 1984–2004.
Note: The mean levels of internal, interstate, and internationalized conflict experienced by type of regime, 1984–2004.
Source: Calculated from ECDP/PRIO. 2010. *The ECDP/PRIO Armed Conflict Dataset Codebook Version 4*. Uppsala: ECDP/PRI.

year, nine were patronage autocracies, including four of the five cases classified as civil wars, defined in terms of the magnitude of fatalities. Therefore, this type of regime is not just particularly prone to incidents of internal conflict; they are also subject to the most severe type of internal violence. In addition, in

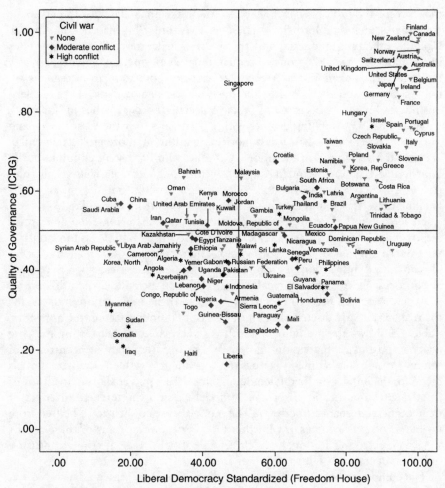

FIGURE 7.2. Civil wars by type of regime, 1984–2007.

Note: The mean levels of civil wars, measured by the incidents and intensity of internal armed conflict, by type of regime, 1984–2004.

Source: Calculated from ECDP/PRIO. 2010. *The ECDP/PRIO Armed Conflict Dataset Codebook Version 4.* Uppsala: ECDP/PRI.

this year, four of the patronage democracies were also subject to intermediate armed conflict and less severe minor conflict. None of the bureaucratic autocracies had any outbreaks of internal conflict, while three of the states classified as bureaucratic democracies experienced intermediate armed conflict (Israel, Turkey, and India).

To look at the specific cases, Figure 7.2 illustrates the societal contrasts in the experience of civil wars (the incidents and severity of armed internal conflict) during the period under comparison (1984–2007) by type of regime. Many of the most severe and prolonged civil wars are among regimes classified as patronage autocracies, including Iraq, Somalia, Sudan, Myanmar/Burma, Algeria, Angola, Uganda, Ethiopia, Indonesia, and the Russian Federation. Many other states in this category are also prone to moderate levels of internal violence, notably Haiti, Nigeria, Lebanon, and Yemen. Nevertheless, others types of regimes are not immune to conflict. Among the bureaucratic democracies, the most serious internal conflicts occurred in India (especially border clashes in Kashmir), Israel (in the long-standing dispute with Palestinians over the West Bank), and Turkey (concerning the Kurdish minority). In addition, more moderate conflict is evident, involving disorder among Catholics and Protestant communities in Northern Ireland in the United Kingdom; strife in Croatia following the dissolution of Yugoslavia and war in the Balkans; racial conflict and the end of apartheid in South Africa; and instability and unrest occurring in Thailand.

Nevertheless, before drawing any hard and fast conclusions, any descriptive results must be treated extremely cautiously, because multiple factors contribute toward internal violence. For example, many bureaucratic democracies are also advanced industrialized economies and affluent societies, whereas patronage autocracies are often ethnically heterogeneous societies. Structural control variables therefore need to be incorporated into the multivariate models, for the reasons already discussed, with the measures summarized in the appendix. Table 7.2 shows the preliminary results of successive models testing the core propositions, using regression analysis where the frequency of occurrence of internal armed conflict in any state is the dependent variable. Successive models compare the impact of liberal democracy (model 1), power-sharing institutions (model 2), bureaucratic governance (model 3), and the interaction effect of democratic governance (model 4). The models were confirmed to be free from problems of multicollinearity. Further tests for the robustness of these results were conducted in additional models, using Polity IV as an alternative measure of liberal democracy, but this did not substantially alter the key findings.

The comparison of the results across all the models is presented in Table 7.2. The impact of the structural control variables can be examined first. Levels of economic development were not consistently associated with levels of conflict across all the models, although a stronger economic performance was significantly correlated with lower conflict. Thus the results suggest that problems of economic growth encourage popular discontent, such as a sudden economic crisis or recession that can spill over into domestic violence, although absolute levels of economic development appear less important. The role of regional conflict served to increase internal instability to a modest degree, although not significantly in all models. The type of ethnic fractionalization also proved to matter; as expected, multilingual societies were more prone to internal violence, while those with high levels of religious fractionalization had significantly less conflict. Other scholars have reported similar findings,[49] although the precise reasons for these contrasts are not clear, and further robustness checks are required before having confidence in the findings. The remaining control variables behave mostly as expected; violence-prone societies tend

TABLE 7.2. *The impact of democratic governance on internal conflict*

Model	1 Liberal Democracy			2 Power-Sharing Institutions			3 Bureaucratic Governance			4 Democratic Governance		
	b	p	PCSE	b	p	PCSE	b	p	PCSE	b	p	PCSE
Regime Effects												
Liberal democracy (FH)	-.001	N/s	.001	-.001	***	.001				.001	N/s	.001
Bureaucratic governance							-.004	***	.001	-.004	***	.001
Federal state (1) Unitary (0)				.039	***	.007						
Parliamentary executive (1)/ other (0)				.048	***	.012						
PR electoral systems (1)/ majoritarian or mixed (0)				.142	***	.011						
Controls												
Economic												
Income (log GDP/capita)	-.001	***	.001	-.001	***	.001	.001	***	.001	.001	**	.001
Economic growth	-.001	**	.001	-.001	*	.001	.002	*	.001	-.002	*	.001
Geographic												
Location (latitude)	-.224	***	.021	-.263	***	.028	-.186	***	.029	-.184	***	.028
Area size (sq km)	.001	***	.001	.001	***	.001	.001	***	.001	.001	***	.001
Natural resources (oil/gas rents)	-.001	N/s	.001	.001	N/s	.001	-.001	***	.001	-.000	***	.001

(*continued*)

TABLE 7.2. (cont.)

Model	1 Liberal Democracy			2 Power-Sharing Institutions			3 Bureaucratic Governance			4 Democratic Governance		
	b	p	PCSE	b	p	PCSE	b	p	PCSE	b	p	PCSE
Social Structure												
Linguistic fractionalization	.182	***	.028	.162	***	.027	.266	***	.038	.268	***	.037
Religious fractionalization	-.306	***	.031	-.232	***	.032	-.434	***	.030	-.434	***	.031
Logged population size	.151	***	.003	.189	***	.004	.143	***	.006	.143	***	.006
Human capital (secondary schooling)	.001	N/s	.001	.001	N/s	.001	.001	*	.005	.001	*	.000
Cultural Traditions												
British colonial legacy	.095	***	.011	.107	***	.014	.109	***	.009	.109	***	.009
Year	.001	N/s	.001	.000	N/s	.001	-.005	***	.001	-.005	***	.001
R²	.175			.208			.250			.250		
Number of observations	4,469			4,138			2,338			2,338		
Number of countries	156			145			129			129		

Note: The models present the unstandardized beta coefficients and the statistical significance of ordinary least squares linear regression models with panel-corrected standard errors. The dependent variable is incidents of internal conflict. *** $p < 0.001$, ** $p < 0.01$, * $p < 0.05$. For details of all the variables, see the technical appendix.

to be larger physically, more populous, and less well integrated into political forms of global governance; moreover, both a British and French colonial legacy was associated with greater violence. Overall, each of the models explains a considerable degree of variance in societal violence (measured by the R^2).

Turning to the core propositions, democratic theories provide a series of reasons that liberal democracy is expected to be associated with the accommodation of grievances and checks on the repressive powers of the executive, thereby reducing the underlying causes of conflict. Nevertheless, the result of the analysis in Table 7.2 shows that by itself *the strength of liberal democracy is not significantly related to the degree of internal armed conflict in a society.* This confirms the descriptive results already examined. Overall, the analysis provides no support for the first hypothesis suggesting that countries that have built strong institutions of liberal democracy will be less vulnerable to internal violence and civil wars. This process is illustrated by well-known cases such as long-standing internal conflict among Palestinians demanding statehood and independence from Israel, the Kurds within Turkey, extreme drug-cartel violence in Mexico, and sporadic outbreaks of ethnic conflict in several states within India. Many of the regimes classified as patronage democracies, such as Guatemala, Sri Lanka, and the Philippines, also have experience of continuing civil war and internal violence.

Consociational theory predicts that democracy alone is insufficient to prevent dissent; instead, power-sharing institutions in democratic states are thought important for reducing societal conflict. The results of the analysis in Table 7.2 support this claim. Across all the models, significantly less societal conflict was evident in federal states and decentralized unions, countries with proportional electoral systems for the lower house of national parliaments, and those with parliamentary executives. The consociational proposition suggests that power-sharing constitutions depress minority grievances and thus reduce the underlying causes of internal conflict, and this claim is supported by these findings. Moreover, once these variables are included, the strength of liberal democracy per se was also significant.

What of state-building? Overall, the core proposition arising from the state-building perspective also receives support from the analysis in Table 7.2: *Civil wars are minimized in states characterized by quality of governance,* understood in terms of strong administrative capacity in the public sector, low corruption, and effective law and order through the strength and impartiality of the legal system. By contrast, the claim that both liberal democracy and governance capacity need to be strengthened to reduce violence significantly is not supported; when both were added to the models in Table 7.2, only bureaucratic governance proved significant.

CONCLUSIONS

The issue of internal conflict and civil wars has clearly risen on the agenda of the international community in recent decades, especially in the post–Cold War era. Unfortunately, in practice the efforts toward peace building have often failed to live up to expectations; such efforts may result in a temporary hiatus in hostilities, but then societies commonly lapse back into conflict and blood-shed. Understanding what works in the peace-building process is therefore of vital importance. The evidence presented here suggests that two alternative strategies can be used to reduce internal conflict.

One strategy provides support for the state-building perspective: According to the results of the analysis, even after controlling for many factors, regimes with strong governance capacity are less vulnerable to armed internal conflict. Leaders who have an effective military, police services, and courts have the capacity to maintain order through rule of law, contain threats arising through internal violence and insurgency movements, and deter rebellious groups when they calculate the risks of using armed violence to challenge the state. In addi-tion to the techniques of legal sanctions and armed repression, strong states also have greater capacity to deliver effective public goods and services, gaining support through clientalism, and thus reduce some of the underlying causes sparking grievances and disaffection. Counter to this argument, however, there is an alternative strategy, because the evidence also suggests that power-sharing democracies, in particular, are an effective way to reduce internal conflict. In this regard, peace settlements built on constitutional arrangements that dis-perse decision making through decentralization and federalism, parliamen-tary or mixed executives, and proportional electoral systems provide outlets for inclusive representation, minority participation, and the building of inter-communal trust. Thus although general claims about the instrumental conse-quences of liberal democracies for internal peace receive no systematic support from the evidence scrutinized here, the results do provide further confirmation of consociational claims about the benefits of power-sharing democracies.

As argued elsewhere, in multi-ethnic societies divided into different linguis-tic, religious, or national communities, power-sharing institutions and proce-dures help to turn political opponents into cooperative partners by providing communal leaders with a guaranteed stake in the democratic process. By con-trast, power-concentrating regimes offer rival communities a zero-sum game where losers have fewer incentives to work within the conventional political rules.[50] Through inclusive processes in representative bodies, consociational democracies thereby help to manage and contain ethnic tensions, armed upris-ings, and intercommunal violence, building peace and stabilizing fragile states in plural societies. Rebel factions are encouraged to lay down their arms and to contest power as political parties, gradually becoming integrated into the conventional process of bargaining and compromise.

These assumptions are not simply theoretical as they have shaped consti-tutional agreements in many recent peace settlements, as exemplified by the Dayton agreement governing Bosnia-Herzegovina and the Good Friday agree-ment in Northern Ireland. They remain at the heart of constitutional talks and peace-building initiatives in many countries, such as Nepal, Southern Sudan, and Sri Lanka, which are currently searching for a solution to deep-rooted armed conflict.[51] Nevertheless, elsewhere, even within the same region, power-sharing has been judged to have very different degrees of success, such as in the West African cases of Rwanda and Burundi.[52] Given the mixed bag of positive and negative experiences in different nations, clearly power-sharing arrangements cannot be claimed to be *sufficient* for containing communal violence and preventing outbreaks of open hostility, as multiple other structural factors may outweigh the institutional arrangements. Not surprisingly, given the complexity of the challenge, there is no single solution that can automatically be applied to guarantee that peace-building operations will succeed. Constitutional design is more of an art than a science. Nor can it be claimed that power-sharing arrangements are *necessary* for containing potential sources of communal conflict; the outright suppression of ethnic identities and minority rights is another strategy employed by strong states, as illustrated by the containment of ethnic divisions in the Federal Republic of Yugoslavia prior to dissolution and the outbreak of the Balkan wars, the bloodiest conflicts in Europe since the end of World War II.[53] What the evidence in this book demonstrates, reinforcing the conclusions of previous studies, is that power-sharing democracies increase the probability of reducing conflict, even after controlling for factors such as economic development, ethnic heterogeneity, and colonial background, all of which are also significantly associated with patterns of peace and conflict.

PART IV

CONCLUSIONS

8

Conclusion

Why Regimes Matter

Have processes of democratization during the third wave era led to concrete gains in economic growth, human welfare, and security, as the proponents of democracy-promotion suggest? Alternatively, has the spread of "good governance" encouraged development, as state-builders argue? Should our understanding of these relationships be reversed, as skeptics claim, if gradually rising levels of societal modernization, or achieving a certain threshold of per capita GDP or human capital, provide the foundation for subsequent improvements in both democracy and governance? Or should we seek to disentangle the interlinked processes strengthening development through advances in both democracy and good governance, within the constraints of structural conditions?

As discussed throughout this book, the varied thinkers who subscribe to the democracy-promotion viewpoint commonly make two core claims favoring this type of regime. Firstly, idealists argue on normative grounds that legitimate governance should be based on the will of the people, as expressed through the institutions of liberal democracy. These claims are embodied in international conventions, agreed on by the world's governments, notably Article 21 of the 1948 Universal Declaration of Human Rights: "The will of the people shall be the basis of the authority of government." Human rights–based arguments reflect universal claims, hence it is believed essential to deepen liberal democratic institutions in *every* society, as exemplified by holding multiparty elections as part of the peace-building process to establish a legitimate government in fragile states such as the Democratic Republic of Congo, Sudan, Iraq, and Afghanistan. Rights-based arguments reflect powerful moral claims that resonate widely among those sharing democratic values.

Confronted by those who remain skeptical about these arguments, however, the second strand of the argument suggests that democratic governance is not only of intrinsic value but also has instrumental benefits. The way that leaders are chosen and held accountable by citizens, idealists believe, has important consequences for whether they act in the public interest. The institutions of free and fair multiparty elections are fundamental to all theories of representative democracy. Citizens can exercise an informed and effective choice at the ballot box, theories of liberal democracies suggest, only if these contests are under-girded by constitutional checks and balances limiting the powers of the executive branch. Thus, in addition to competitive elections, liberal democracy also requires strong legislatures, competitive political parties, widespread respect for political rights and civil liberties, government transparency, an independent judiciary, a flourishing civil society, decentralized governance, and an independent media. Unless leaders have a strong incentive to act in the public interest, through periodic multiparty contests where they can be removed from office, in the long term it is thought that societies will fail to achieve the broader development goals of prosperity, welfare, and peace.

The main alternative school of thought criticizing these claims arises from diverse commentators who subscribe to what can be termed a state-building perspective. This viewpoint does not usually seek to challenge the long-term desirability of establishing liberal democracy. Nevertheless, commentators question the most pragmatic and effective way to achieve this ultimate objective. The idea that all societies are ready for liberal democracy is not only naïve and foolish, several scholars suggest, but also dangerously destabilizing in countries with inhospitable conditions. Development is understood as a sequential process of steps. The first priorities facing the world's fragile states are to build the capacity of the governing authorities to protect citizens against external threats spilling over national borders; to establish conditions of national cohesion, social order, and security at home; and to manage the delivery of essential goods and services, such as providing schools, building health clinics, and alleviating poverty. In this view, state-building is the most critical goal for societies such as Somalia, Chad, the Central African Republic, and Haiti, suffering from a lethal combination of extreme poverty, humanitarian disasters, and enduring conflict. Moreover, a related stream of realist thinking among developmental economists suggests that "good governance" is also vital for prosperity and growth. Stamping out endemic corruption, establishing rule of law and contract compliance, and safeguarding private property rights from state predation are regarded in this view as vital for encouraging business confidence, inward investment, and the workings of free markets. Once the foundations of state-building and the conditions of good governance are established, the realist perspective suggests, then societies are ready to move toward the next stage of development, by transitioning from autocracy and building democratic institutions, including holding competitive elections.

This book has outlined the basis of these arguments and then offered an alternative, more unified perspective emphasizing the need for both liberal democracy (strengthening citizens' demands) *and* bureaucratic governance (expanding the capacity of the state to respond effectively to social needs).

SUMMARIZING THE KEY FINDINGS

Accordingly, it is important to establish whether democratic regimes do indeed deliver concrete benefits for developing nations, as many hope and expect, and in general it seems timely to take stock of the broader impact of democracy and state capacity on core components of human security.

Prosperity

The first dimension of human security concerns economic prosperity, providing the resources to facilitate protection against the more severe risks and threats to well-being arising from lack of the basic necessities of life. The evidence from selected cases suggests that the process of democratization has often been accompanied by a mixed economic performance. Thus during the 1990s, many Latin American nations experienced substantial gains in political rights and civil liberties following the introduction of multiparty competitive elections and democratic reforms. Nevertheless, the economic performance of Latin America proved uneven during this era, with worsening inequalities between rich and poor.[1] Similarly, elsewhere the sudden shock therapy following the fall of the Soviet Union, and the expansion of electoral democracies and free markets, was usually followed during the 1990s by dramatic drops in living standards, rising unemployment, and economic dislocation in Central and Eastern Europe. Certainly some postcommunist states subsequently recovered and experienced rapid economic gains, fueled in part by oil prices – but not all.[2] The growing consensus among developmental economists emphasizes that although democracy is not clearly linked to growth, several dimensions of "good governance" are thought to be important – in particular, property rights, control of corruption, and rule of law. These institutions are believed to strengthen the underlying conditions conducive to business confidence, attracting market investment and thus boosting economic growth.[3] The institutions of private property rights and rule of law are closely associated with liberal democracy but, as exemplified by Singapore's case, they are not exclusive to this type of regime.[4] Moreover, a social democratic understanding of "good governance" assumes that the state needs the capacity for effective macroeconomic management, and an effective public sector bureaucracy expands this capacity.[5] Thus, argues Francis Fukuyama, even if the *scope* of the state shrinks through neoliberal reforms such as privatization, the capacity of the state to regulate the marketplace still remains important.[6]

The analysis of the impact of a wide range of factors on economic growth in fully specified multivariate models demonstrated that when entered separately, there was no significant impact on growth from "good governance," bureaucratic governance, or liberal democracy. *When entered together, however, both liberal democracy and bureaucratic governance emerged as significant predictors of economic growth.* Overall, bureaucratic democracies achieved an annual rate of growth of around 2.49 percent per annum from 1984 to 2007, twice the level experienced by patronage autocracies. Moreover, growth in bureaucratic democracies was also more steady and consistent, without the sharp fluctuations that can destabilize economies. To put this in more concrete terms, during the period under analysis, in stable bureaucratic democracies, average per capita incomes (in purchasing power parity) rose from about $17,000 to $29,000. By contrast, people living in bureaucratic autocracies saw their average incomes shrink in these years.

Welfare

The second dimension concerns a range of aspects of welfare security that are essential for achieving the targets of the Millennium Development Goals (MDGs). Some societies have made rapid gains in human development, while others have faltered and struggled to expand primary schools, health clinics, clean water, and sanitation and to protect their populations against the ravages of extreme hunger and vulnerability to humanitarian and natural disasters. There are plausible reasons to expect that democracy will strengthen accountability and thus the responsiveness of leaders to social needs. Certainly some studies conclude that compared with autocracies, democratic regimes are more likely to promote economic redistribution beneficial for the poor, as civil liberties are positively linked to economic equality.[7] Joseph T. Siegle, Michael Weinstein, and Morton Halperin compared a range of poorer societies, reporting that although democracies do not spend more on public services, they are generally better than autocracies at delivering education, literacy, and healthcare.[8] Likewise "good governance" is advocated by the World Bank as essential for furthering social development, by stamping out corruption and improving the equitable delivery of essential public services such as housing, healthcare, and jobs. Nevertheless, the claim that the type of regime matters has been challenged on methodological grounds, and debate about the evidence continues. Empirical analysis is hindered by problems of missing data in many developmental indicators, a problem that is particularly common in many poorer autocracies, generating systematic bias in cross-national coverage in comparative studies. Michael Ross demonstrates that at least on certain healthcare indices – namely infant and maternal mortality – even though democracies invest more resources, they do not always achieve better social *outcomes*.[9] Others report that the type of regime has no influence on policies, nor on levels of education spending, pensions, or other social policy expenditure.[10] It is thus by no means evident that the type of regime per se necessarily matters for reducing illiteracy and poverty, tackling diseases, reducing gender inequalities, and improving longevity in impoverished nations.

The evidence analyzed in this book compared the impact of regimes on six indices of welfare security. Overall, *before controls are applied, bureaucratic democracies consistently outperform all other types of regimes on human development* – and by a large improvement. Similarly, patronage autocracies display the worst record. The results could be dismissed on the grounds that the gap simply reflects basic differences between rich and poor societies and thus the available resources that can be invested in welfare services. After multiple controls are used in multivariate models, however, including for levels of economic development, the results suggest that *liberal democracy still has a positive impact on three of the six indicators*, monitoring levels of human development, gender equality in education, and the expansion of educational opportunities. Moreover, *bureaucratic state capacity has even more consistently positive effects, by improving human development, average longevity, gender equality in education, and access to secondary education, as well as reducing child mortality.* The effect of regimes varies, however, across the different MDG targets, probably due, at least in part, to the complexity and scope of the development challenges involved in each of these goals and the capacity for relatively low-cost technical solutions to have a major impact on human security. Thus some problems are more responsive to simple and relatively cheap technical solutions, such as the provision of bed-nets or child immunization. Others pose tougher and more complex challenges.

Peace

Lastly, human security also depends on achieving lasting reductions in violent conflict and preventing all the attendant problems of civil war. The international community has become more active in peacekeeping operations during the postwar era, although its record of success at preventing further outbreaks of bloodshed remains mixed. Elections are often held at an early stage in the process of peace building in the attempt to reduce the causes of popular grievances and to build government legitimacy. Unless governments come to power through competitive contests meeting international standards, it is thought that they will fail to be regarded as legitimate. Democracies provide peaceful outlets for the expression of discontent. Nevertheless, the transition from autocracy is a hazardous process, and Edward D. Mansfield and Jack Snyder argue that in deeply divided societies, premature elections can stoke the flames of ethnic hatreds.[11]

The comparative evidence presented in this book suggests that certainly some long-standing bureaucratic democracies have continued to struggle with internal violence and conflict, exemplified by the simmering tensions in Israel between the Palestinian and the Jewish communities; problems of recurrent religious clashes and violence in India, especially in the Kashmir region; and violence between Catholics and Protestants in Northern Ireland prior to the Good Sunday Peace Accord. Patronage democracies proved even more vulnerable to internal conflict. Nevertheless, in general, patronage autocracies displayed by far the worst record of internal war and also internationalized war. The multivariate analysis showed that overall *bureaucratic governance dampened internal conflict*; the capacity to maintain law and order and to deploy security forces effectively deters outbreaks of civil rebellions, while the capacity of these states to administer and deliver basic public services should reduce the causes of grievance. By contrast, *liberal democracy did not have a significant impact on civil war, with the important exception of when the regime had power-sharing institutions.* Thus liberal democratic elections, by themselves, seem insufficient to ensure peace unless there are also moves toward more inclusive forms of consociational democracies in the aftermath of civil wars.

DETERMINING THE DRIVERS OF HUMAN SECURITY

Determining the correct diagnosis about these issues is important theoretically but also practically, not least because the international development community, national governments, and civil society organizations have devoted growing resources to strengthening democracy and governance. During the 1990s, for example, the United Nations Development Programme (UNDP) used to have a small number of advisers providing technical assistance to public administration reform. In 2002, the organization's mission shifted to prioritize "democratic governance." By 2009, UNDP devoted $1.4 billion annually to this program area, the largest proportion (35 percent) of the total organizational budget, more than was spent directly on poverty alleviation and the MDGs.[12] Similarly, in the United States the 2009 annual budget of the United States Agency for International Development (USAID) allocated $1.7 billion to promoting democracy, including rule of law, elections, civil society, governance, and independent media.[13] The European Union has also focused increased attention on issues of democratic governance, notably when setting the political conditions of entry for new member states.[14] Therefore, establishing "what works" is important for deepening our understanding of processes of regime change, as well as vital for human security around the world.

What do the key findings imply for agencies in the international community and for local reformers? The conclusions suggest that it is not sufficient to focus on only one type of area for reform, but rather it is preferable to balance resources and overall priorities, recognizing the need for both strengthening state capacity and democratic accountability. Thus typical programs in the standard menu designed to strengthen governance include reforming the public sector in the civil service; establishing anticorruption and transparency initiatives, such as freedom of information laws; expanding professional skills and training for local administrative bodies; and improving the capacity of the courts, judiciary, and police. Work designed to improve democracy includes strengthening the independence and professional skills of independent election agencies, establishing effective human rights watchdogs, setting standards through international conventions, building modern information and communication services for legislative representatives and their staff, designing procedures to make sure that the composition of parliaments reflect the societies from which they are drawn, working with political parties and civil society organizations, and encouraging the independent media. In all these activities and programs, a fine balance needs to be struck so that both democracy and state capacity are developed simultaneously. In practice, however, the international community has often poured considerable resources into holding multiparty elections in the aftermath of regime change and peace agreements, to legitimize national governments, without necessarily investing equivalent aid in the less visible and glamorous but equally vital task of building state capacity through public sector reform. In this context, holding multiparty elections meeting all the criteria of liberal democracy can prove an exercise that raises public expectations only to see elected governments fail to deliver.

Another reason that it is important to understanding these issues concerns public attitudes toward democracy and governance. There is now overwhelming evidence from many surveys that the public living in many contemporary societies around the world appears to endorse democratic ideals and principles. In this regard, at least, debate about the value of democracy appears to be over. Surveys have sought to tap public attitudes toward democratic principles and autocratic forms of governance in several ways. Perhaps the most common approach has relied on questions that ask the public to express their direct or overt preferences for democratic rule as a normative ideal, using the "*d* word" but without providing a more specific context or elaborating its meaning further. For example, surveys have typically asked people whether they approve of democracy as the "best form of government," whether democracy is "preferable to any other form of government," whether it is important "to live in a country that is government democratically," or whether they approve of having a democratic system "as a good or suitable way of governing their own country." The direct or overt approach allows survey respondents to respond to questions using their own understanding of these terms rather than imposing a common meaning.

Using this approach, survey-based studies have repeatedly confirmed overwhelming support for democratic principles, both in established democracies and elsewhere in the world, even in many "unlikely" cases. Hence the World Values Survey (WVS) monitored endorsement of democratic political systems and rejection of autocratic principles in dozens of societies around the globe. When the fifth wave of the WVS (2005–7) asked people to evaluate democracy as a way of governing their own country, about eight out of ten citizens responded positively that this was either "very" or "fairly" good. There was an overwhelming consensus about the value of democracy in long-established democracies, such as Sweden, Italy, and the Netherlands, but similarly positive responses were expressed in many younger liberal democracies, electoral democracies, and even in most autocracies (with the exception of Russia).[15] Similarly, the Globalbarometer surveys conducted in over sixty nations suggest that many citizens around the globe expressed widespread aspirations for democratic principles as the best system of government. Indeed, based on this evidence, Larry Diamond and Marc F. Plattner note that almost universal public approval for the abstract idea of democratic governance has been expressed even in some of the most rigid East Asian autocracies, including Communist China and Vietnam, where the public lacks any direct experience of living under this type of rule.[16] In the Middle East, the region that lags furthest behind the rest of the world in transitions from autocracy, it might be expected that support for democratic ideals and values would be relatively scarce. Yet the 2006 Arab Barometer survey reported that eight or nine out of ten respondents in Jordan, Algeria, Morocco, and Kuwait believe that "democracy is the best form of government" and that "having a democratic system of government would be good for our country."[17] As Diamond and Plattner summarized the Globalbarometer evidence: "Strikingly, the belief that democracy is (in principle at least) the best system is overwhelming and universal. While there is a slightly higher preference for the Western industrialized countries, in every region – even the former Soviet Union and the Muslim Middle East – an average of at least 80 percent of people polled say that democracy is best."[18] If taken at face value, this worldwide pattern could be celebrated as indicating widespread popular aspirations for democracy – indeed, possibly signaling the end of normative debate about the best type of governance.

If the normative arguments for democracy have won, even if not symbolizing the end of history, why return to rehash the old debates? One reason is that although general adherence to democratic ideals now seems to be widespread, this does not mean that everyone worldwide automatically endorses all the *principles and practices* associated with liberal democracy, nor indeed that these complex notions are well understood. The fifth wave of the World Values Survey asked people in many societies to identify several characteristics that they associated with democracy. For most people, democracy is indeed understood in terms of certain principles and procedures closely associated with liberal democracy, such as the need for free elections to choose political leaders and protection of civil liberties. People in countries with the longest historical experience of living under democratic regimes gave the greatest emphasis to these procedures. Yet many people offered an alternative understanding of the characteristics of democracy, associating this type of regime with economic growth and improved living standards. Instrumental conceptions proved particularly common among citizens living in many autocracies, such as China, Russia, Iraq, and Jordan, who lacked historical experience of liberal democracy. Thus the global endorsement of democracy often reflects instrumental support based largely on the image and perception of many established democracies that are also affluent, stable, and effective states.

There is also considerable evidence of a substantial democratic deficit where people's expectations of democracy run ahead of their evaluations of its performance. The tensions between unwavering support for democratic principles and skeptical evaluations about democratic practices can be interpreted as the rise of "critical citizens."[19] There are multiple causes of this phenomenon, but one main aspect concerns dissatisfaction with the process performance of democratic governance. Unless democratic regimes have the capacity to deliver effective public services, especially in societies without deep reservoirs of support for this type of regime, then their legitimacy will remain in question.

Therefore, the unified theory developed in this book predicts that the institutions of both liberal democracy *and* state capacity need to be strengthened in parallel for the most effective progress deepening human security, within the broader enduring fixed constraints posed by structural environments. Overall, the empirical evidence that we have uncovered highlights the complexity of the relationship between regimes and human security. Democracy and governance are rightly regarded as separate and distinct phenomena, not muddled together conceptually, but regimes reflecting *both* dimensions are necessary (although far from sufficient) to achieve many aspects of human security. The challenge for regime design is therefore not simply to strengthen downward electoral accountability, so that vote-seeking politicians have an incentive to pay attention to citizens' needs. It is equally important to provide the public sector with the capacity, technical skills, and resources so that elected leaders can deliver things that most citizens want: basic security, schools, clinics, and better living standards. Recognizing the need for both dimensions would provide a more comprehensive understanding of the drivers of human security and how these can be strengthened.

Appendix

Description of the Variables and Data Sources

Name	Description and Source
Liberal democracy index	The Gastil index, the 7-point scale used by Freedom House, measuring political rights and civil liberties annually since 1972. The index is standardized to a 100-point scale.
	Freedom House. *Freedom in the World*. http://www. Freedomhouse.com.
Governance capacity	Political Risk Service's Group (PRSG) International Country Risk Guide estimates of the quality of governance (QOG). Based on expert assessments, the PRSG's Quality of Government index combines three components: (1) bureaucratic quality; (2) corruption; and (3) law and order. The index is standardized to a 100-point scale.
	Source: QOG Institute. 2010. *The Quality of Government Dataset*. Goteborg: University of Goteborg.
Democratic governance	The liberal democracy and the governance capacity indexes are multiplied and standardized to a 100-point scale.
Dependent Variables	
Economic growth	Annual percentage growth rate of per capita GDP at market prices based on constant local prices.
	Source: Penn World Tables.
Life expectancy	Life expectancy at birth, total years.
	Source: World Bank. 2010. *World Development Indicators*. http://data.worldbank.org/data-catalog/world-development-indicators?cid=GPD_WDI.
Infant mortality	Infant mortality rate (per 1,000 live births)
	Source: World Bank. 2010. *World Development Indicators*. http://data.worldbank.org/data-catalog/world-development-indicators?cid=GPD_WDI.

(continued)

Name	Description and Source
Maternal mortality	Maternal mortality rate (per 100,000 live births).
	Source: World Bank. 2010. *World Development Indicators*. http://data.worldbank.org/data-catalog/world-development-indicators?cid=GPD_WDI.
Internal armed conflict	Internal armed conflict is defined as that which occurs between the government of a state and one or more internal opposition group(s) without intervention from other states. The Uppsala Conflict Data Program (UCDP) measure is coded on a 4-point ordinal scale depending on the incidence and magnitude of conflict (depending on the number of battle-related deaths): (0) no interstate conflict; (1) minor interstate armed conflict; (2) interstate intermediate armed conflict; and (4) interstate war. The measure indicates the incidence and severity of internal armed conflict.
	Source: ECDP/PRIO. 2010. *The ECDP/PRIO Armed Conflict Dataset Codebook Version 4, 1946–2007*. Uppsala: ECDP/PRI.

Controls

Name	Description and Source
Geographic location	The absolute value of the latitude from the equator of the capital city, divided by 90 (to take values between 0 and 1).
	Source: Rafael La Porta, Florencio Lopez-De-Silanes, Andre Shleifer and Robert Vishny. 1999. "The Quality of Government." *Journal of Law Economics & Organization* 15 (1): 222–79.
Economic development	Per capita GDP measured in constant international $ in purchasing power parity. Various years.
	Source: World Bank. 2010. *World Development Indicators*. http://data.worldbank.org/data-catalog/world-development-indicators?cid=GPD_WDI.
Area size	Area of the nation-state in kilometers.
	Source: Arthur S. Banks. 2008. *Cross-Polity Time-Series Database*. State University of New York–Binghampton. http://www.databanks.sitehosting.net.
Natural resources	Natural resources are operationalized as oil and gas rents per capita. This represents the total annual value of a country's oil and gas production, minus the extraction costs in each country, divided by its population to normalize the value of the rents, measured from 1960 to 2002 in constant 2000 U.S. dollars.
	Source: Michael Ross. 2004. "How Do Natural Resources Influence Civil War? Evidence from Thirteen Cases." *International Organization* 58 (1): 35–67.

Name	Description and Source
Education	Gross enrollment ratio is the ratio of total enrollment, regardless of age, to the population of the age group that officially corresponds to the secondary level of education. Secondary education completes the provision of basic education that began at the primary level and aims at laying the foundations for lifelong learning and human development by offering more subject- or skill-oriented instruction using more specialized teachers.
	Source: World Bank. 2010. *World Development Indicators*. http://data.worldbank.org/data-catalog/world-development-indicators?cid=GPD_WDI.
Ethno-linguistic fractionalization	The share of languages spoken as "mother tongues" in each country, generally derived from national census data, as reported in the *Encyclopedia Britannica 2001*. The fractionalization index is computed as one minus the Herfindahl index of ethnolinguistic group share, reflecting the probability that two randomly selected individuals from a population belonged to different groups.
	Source: Alberto Alesina, Arnaud Devleeschauwer, William Easterly, Sergio Kurlat, and Romain Wacziarg. 2003. "Fractionalization." *Journal of Economic Growth* 8: 155–94.
Religious fractionalization	The share of the population adhering to different religions in each country, as reported in the *Encyclopedia Britannica 2001* and related sources. The fractionalization index is computed as one minus the Herfindahl index of ethnoreligious group share, reflecting the probability that two randomly selected individuals from a population belonged to different groups.
	Source: Alberto Alesina, Arnaud Devleeschauwer, William Easterly, Sergio Kurlat, and Romain Wacziarg. 2003. "Fractionalization." *Journal of Economic Growth* 8: 155–94.
Population size	The estimates of total population per state (thousands).
	Source: World Bank. 2010. *World Development Indicators*. http://data.worldbank.org/data-catalog/world-development-indicators?cid=GPD_WDI.
BritCol	The past colonial history of countries was classified into those that shared a British colonial background (1), and all others (0).
	Source: CIA. *The World Factbook*. http://www.cia.gov.
FrenchCol	The past colonial history of countries was classified into those that shared a French colonial background (1), and all others (0).
	Source: CIA. *The World Factbook*. http://www.cia.gov.

(*continued*)

Name	Description and Source
Globalization index	The KOF Index of Political Globalization, 1970–2010. The 100-point index is constructed from a comprehensive range of two dozen variables, designed to gauge three dimensions: *social* globalization (the spread of personal contact, information flows, and cultural proximity); *economic* globalization (the actual long-distant flows of goods, investment capital, and commercial services, as well as restrictions through import barriers, taxes, and tariffs); and *political* globalization (measured by integration with international intergovernmental organizations, the number of embassies based in a country, and national engagement in UN peace missions). The latter is included in this book.
	Source: KOF. *KOF Index of Political Globalization.* http:// globalization.kof.ethz.ch/.
PR electoral systems	The type of electoral systems used for the lower house of the national parliament. Majoritarian formulas include first-past-the-post, second ballot, the block vote, the single non-transferable vote, and the alternative vote. Proportional formulas are defined to include party list as well as the single transferable vote systems. Combined (or "mixed") formulas use both majoritarian and proportional ballots for election to the same body. Countries using proportional formulas are coded into a dummy variable (1/0).
	Sources: International IDEA. 2005. *Handbook of Electoral System Design.* 2nd ed. Stockholm: International IDEA; Pippa Norris. 2008. *Driving Democracy.* New York: Cambridge University Press.
Federal state	Federal states (coded 1) are either federations or decentralized unions. Federations are defined as compound polities where the directly elected constituent units possess independent powers in the exercise of their legislative, fiscal, and administrative responsibilities. Decentralized unions are those where constituent units of government work through the common organs of government, although constitutionally protected subunits of government have some functional autonomy. All states that are not either federations or decentralized unions are coded as unitary states (coded 0).
	Sources: Pippa Norris. 2008. *Driving Democracy.* New York: Cambridge University Press; Ronald L. Watts. 1999. *Comparing Federal Systems.* 2nd ed. Kingston, Ontario: McGill-Queen's University Press; Arthur Banks, Thomas C. Muller, William R. Overstreet, Volkan Aytar, Kristin Broderick, Sean M. Phelan, Edward R. McMahon, and Elaine Tallman, eds. 2004. *Political Handbook of the World 2000–2002.* Revised ed. Washington, DC: CQ Press.

Notes

1. Does Democratic Governance Determine Human Security?

1. Nicholas Thomas and William T. Tow. 2002. "The Utility of Human Security: Sovereignty and Humanitarian Intervention." *Security Dialogue* 33 (2): 177–92; E. Burger. 2004. "Human Security and the Crisis of Public Health Care in Malawi." *Canadian Journal of Development Studies* 25 (2): 239–55; Taylor Owen. 2004. "Human Security – Conflict, Critique and Consensus: Colloquium Remarks and a Proposal for a Threshold-based Definition." *Security Dialogue* 35 (3): 373–87; Sandra J. MacLean, David R. Black, and Timothy M. Shaw, eds. 2006. *A Decade of Human Security: Global Governance and New Multilateralisms.* Aldershot, UK, and Burlington, VT: Ashgate; Ken Booth. 2007. *Theory of World Security.* New York and Cambridge: Cambridge University Press; Mary Kaldor. 2007. *Human Security.* Cambridge: Polity Press; Shahrbanou Tadjbakhsh and Anuradha M. Chenoy. 2007. *Human Security: Concepts and Implications.* New York: Routledge; Barry Buzan and Lena Hansen. 2009. *The Evolution of International Security Studies.* New York: Cambridge University Press; Derek S. Reveron and Kathleen A. Mahoney-Norris. 2011. *Human Security in a Borderless World.* Boulder, CO: Westview Press.

2. Larry Diamond. 1996. *Developing Democracy: Toward Consolidation.* Baltimore: Johns Hopkins University Press; Thomas Carothers. 1999. *Aiding Democracy Abroad: The Learning Curve.* Washington, DC: Carnegie Endowment for International Peace; Morton H. Halperin, Joseph T. Siegle, and Michael M. Weinstein. 2010. *The Democracy Advantage: How Democracies Promote Prosperity and Peace.* 2nd ed. New York: Routledge; Michael McFaul. 2010. *Advancing Democracy Abroad.* New York: Rowman & Littlefield.

3. Thomas Carothers. 1999. *Aiding Democracy Abroad.* Washington, DC: Carnegie Endowment for International Peace, chapter 5; Larry Diamond. 1999. *Developing Democracy: Toward Consolidation.* Baltimore: Johns Hopkins University Press.

4. Simon Chesterman. 2004. *You, the People: The United Nations, Transitional Administration, and State-Building.* New York: Oxford University Press; James D. Fearon and David D. Laitin. 2004. "Neo-trusteeship and the Problem of Weak States." *International Security* 29 (4): 5–43; Francis Fukuyama. 2004. *State-Building: Governance and World Order in the 21st Century.* Ithaca, NY: Cornell University Press; Stephen Krasner. 2004. "Sharing Sovereignty: New Institutions for Collapsed

and Failing States." *International Security* 29 (2): 85–120; Roland Paris. 2004. *At War's End: Building Peace after Civil Conflict*. Cambridge: Cambridge University Press.

5. An annual ranked Failed States Index is published by the Fund for Peace; see http://www.fundforpeace.org/global/?q=fsi. The 2011 index ranked Somalia, Chad, and Sudan in the worst positions. See also Monty G. Marshall and Benjamin R. Cole. 2011. *Global Report 2011: Conflict, Governance and State Fragility*. Maryland: University of Maryland, Center for Systemic Peace.

6. Francis Fukuyama. 2011. *The Origins of Political Order: From Prehuman Times to the French Revolution*. New York: Farrar, Straus & Giroux.

7. See Roland Paris and Timothy D. Sisk, eds. 2009. *The Dilemmas of Statebuilding*. New York: Routledge.

8. For a critical account of the conventional view of development, see Gilbert Rist. 2008. *The History of Development: From Western Origins to Global Faith*. London: Zed.

9. Seymour Martin Lipset. 1959. "Some Social Requisites of Democracy: Economic Development and Political Legitimacy." *American Political Science Review* 53: 69–105.

10. For example, this phrase was quoted in a speech by Jacob G. Zuma, president of South Africa, commenting on the growth of democracy in Africa, at a meeting of the World Economic Forum in May 2010.

11. Pippa Norris. 2011. *Democratic Deficit*. New York: Cambridge University Press.

12. Charles Tilly. 2007. *Democracy*. New York: Cambridge University Press, chapter 1. See also Roland Paris and Timothy D. Sisk, eds. 2009. *The Dilemmas of State-Building*. New York: Routledge.

13. Samuel P. Huntington. 1991. *The Third Wave: Democratization in the Late Twentieth Century*. Norman: University of Oklahoma Press.

14. Marco Verweij and Riccardo Pelizzo. 2009. "Singapore: Does Authoritarianism Pay?" *Journal of Democracy* 20 (2): 18–32; United Nations Development Programme. 2011. *2010 Human Development Report*. New York: UNDP/Oxford University Press. http://hdrstats.undp.org/en/indicators/49806.html.

15. For an account of Kim Jong Il's dictatorship, see Jasper Becker. 2006. *Rogue Regime Kim Jong Il and the Looming Threat of North Korea*. Oxford: Oxford University Press.

16. Human Rights Watch. 2009. *North Korea*. http://www.hrw.org/en/node/87398.

17. United Nations General Assembly. November 2009. Resolution 64/175. http://daccess-dds-ny.un.org/doc/UNDOC/GEN/N09/472/33/PDF/N0947233.pdf?OpenElement.

18. John Kie-chiang Oh. 1999. *Korean Politics: The Quest for Democratization and Economic Development*. Ithaca, NY: Cornell University Press.

19. The Polity IV Constitutional democracy index is a one hundred–point scale constructed from the autocracy-democracy index. See Chapter 2 and the appendix for details.

20. S. C. Yang. 1999. *The North and South Korean Political Systems: A Comparative Analysis*. Seoul: Hollym; Young Whan Kihl. 2005. *Transforming Korean Politics: Democracy, Reform, and Culture*. Armonk, NY: M. E. Sharpe.

21. For example, in the Corruption Perception Index published by Transparency International, South Korea has risen from being ranked forty-eighth worldwide in 2000 to thirty-ninth in 2010. http://www.transparency.org/policy_research/surveys_indices/cpi/2010/results.

22. Alice Amsden. 1989. *Asia's Next Giant*. Oxford: Oxford University Press; Robert Wade. 1990. *Governing the Market*. Princeton, NJ: Princeton University Press; Francis Fukuyama. 2007. "Liberalism versus State-Building." *Journal of Democracy* 18 (3):10–13.

23. Experts in the United Nations' World Food Programme estimate that the famine in the 1990s caused over one million deaths.

24. Stockholm International Peace Research Institute (SIPRI). 2010. http://www.sipri. org/; World Bank. 2010. *World Development Indicators*. http://data.worldbank. org/data-catalog/world-development-indicators?cid=GPD_WDI.

25. Oh Kongdan and Ralph Hassig. 2010. "North Korea in 2009: The Song Remains the Same." *Asian Survey* 50 (1): 89–96; CIA. *The World Factbook*. http://www.cia.gov.

26. Robert A. Dahl. 1989. *Democracy and Its Critics*. New Haven, CT: Yale University Press.

27. Anne Mette Krær. 2004. *Governance*. Cambridge: Polity Press.

28. For more technical details, see the discussion in Chapter 3, and also http://www. prsgroup.com.

29. A similar pattern has also been observed by others; see Hanna Back and Axel Hadenius. 2008. "Democracy and State Capacity: Exploring a J-shaped Relationship." *Governance* 21 (1): 1–24; Nicholas Charron and Victor Lapuente. 2010. "Does Democracy Produce Quality of Government?" *European Journal of Political Research* 49: 443–70.

30. For example, Beck and Katz's 1995 *American Political Science Review* (APSR) article on the topic has been selected as one of the most heavily cited in the history of the APSR. See Nathaniel Beck and Jonathan Katz. 1995. "What to Do (and Not to Do) with Time-Series Cross-Section Data." *American Political Science Review* 89 (3): 634–47; Nathaniel Beck, Jonathan Katz, and Richard Tucker. 1998. "Taking Time Seriously: Time-Series-Cross-Section Analysis with a Binary Dependent Variable." *American Journal of Political Science* 42 (4): 1260–88; Nathaniel Beck. 2001. "Time-Series/Cross-Section Data: What Have We Learned in the Past Few Years?" *Annual Review of Political Science* 4: 271–93.

31. Henry Brady and David Collier. 2004. *Rethinking Social Inquiry: Diverse Tools, Shared Standards*. New York: Rowman & Littlefield; Alexander L. George and Andrew Bennett. 2004. *Case Studies and Theory Development*. Cambridge, MA: MIT Press; Evan Lieberman. 2005. "Nested Analysis as a Mixed-Method Strategy for Comparative Research." *American Political Science Review* 99 (3): 435–52.

32. Adam Przeworski, Michael E. Alvarez, José Antonio Cheibub, and Fernando Limongi. 2000. *Democracy and Development: Political Institutions and Well-being in the World, 1950–1990*. New York: Cambridge University Press; Yi Feng. 2003. *Democracy, Governance and Economic Growth: Theory and Evidence*. Cambridge, MA: MIT Press.

33. Jonathan Krieckhaus. 2004. "The Regime Debate Revisited: A Sensitivity Analysis of Democracy's Economic Effect." *British Journal of Political Science* 34 (4): 635–55; Hristos Doucouliagos and Mehmet Ali Ulubasoglu. 2008. "Democracy and Economic Growth: A Meta-analysis." *American Journal of Political Science* 52 (1): 61–83.

34. Christopher J. Anderson. 1995. *Blaming the Government: Citizens and the Economy in Five European Democracies*. New York: M. E. Sharpe.

35. David S. Brown. 1999. "Democracy and Social Spending in Latin America, 1980–92." *American Political Science Review* 93 (4): 779; David S. Brown. 1999. "Reading, Writing, and Regime Type: Democracy's Impact on Primary School

Enrollment." *Political Research Quarterly* 52 (4): 681–707; Adam Przeworski, Michael E. Alvarez, Jose Antonio Cheibub, and Fernando Limongi. 2000. *Democracy and Development: Political Institutions and Well-Being in the World, 1950–1990.* New York: Cambridge University Press; David S. Brown and Wendy Hunter. 2004. "Democracy and Human Capital Formation." *Comparative Political Studies* 37 (7): 842–64.

36. David A. Lake and Matthew A. Baum. 2001. "The Invisible Hand of Democracy: Political Control and the Provision of Public Services." *Comparative Political Studies* 34 (6): 587–621.

37. Torsten Persson and Guido Tabellini. 2003. *The Economic Effects of Constitutions.* Cambridge, MA: MIT Press; Torsten Persson. 2004. "Constitutions and Economic Policy." *Journal of Economic Perspectives* 18: 75; Torsten Persson. 2006. "Democracy and Development: The Devil Is in the Details." *American Economic Review* 96: 319; Torsten Persson and Guido Tabellini. 2009. "Democratic Capital: The Nexus of Political and Economic Change." *American Economic Journal-Macroeconomics,* 1 (2): 88–126.

38. Carl Henrik Knutsen. 2011. "Which Democracies Prosper? Electoral Rules, Form of Government and Economic Growth." *Electoral Studies* 30 (1): 83–90.

39. Guillermo O'Donnell. 1979. *Modernization and Bureaucratic-Authoritarianism Studies in South American Politics.* Berkeley: Institute of International Studies, University of California.

40. Marco Verweij and Riccardo Pelizzo. 2009. "Singapore: Does Authoritarianism Pay?" *Journal of Democracy* 20 (2): 18–32.

41. Francis Fukuyama. 2004. "The Imperative of State-Building." *Journal of Democracy* 15 (2): 17–31.

42. James W. McGuire. 2010. *Wealth, Health, and Democracy in East Asia and Latin America.* New York: Cambridge University Press.

43. For useful literature reviews, see Michael Ross. 2006. "Is Democracy Good for the Poor?" *American Journal of Political Science* 50 (4): 860–74; Manus I. Midlarsky, ed. 1997. *Inequality, Democracy and Economic Development.* Cambridge: Cambridge University Press.

44. Carl Henrik Knutsen. 2011. "Which Democracies Prosper? Electoral Rules, Form of Government and Economic Growth." *Electoral Studies* 30 (1): 83–90.

45. A thorough review, summarizing the empirical literature analyzing the effects of democracy on social spending and social policy outcomes, is provided in Stephan Haggard and Robert R. Kaufman. 2008. *Development, Democracy, and Welfare States: Latin America, East Asia, and Eastern Europe.* Princeton, NJ: Princeton University Press, appendix 1.

46. Bruce Bueno de Mesquita, Alastair Smith, Randolph M. Siverson, and James D. Morrow. 2003. *The Logic of Political Survival.* Cambridge, MA: MIT Press.

47. Bruce Bueno de Mesquita, James D. Morrow, Randolph M. Siverson, and Alastair Smith. 1999. "An Institutional Explanation of the Democratic Peace." *American Political Science Review* 93 (4): 791–807; Bruce Bueno de Mesquita, Alastair Smith, Randolph M. Siverson, and James D. Morrow. 2003. *The Logic of Political Survival.* Cambridge, MA: MIT Press.

48. William J. Dixon. 1994. "Democracy and the Peaceful Settlement of International Conflict." *American Political Science Review* 88 (1): 14–32.

49. For further discussion, see Pippa Norris and Ronald Inglehart. 2009. *Cosmopolitan Communications.* New York: Cambridge University Press.

50. Edward D. Mansfield and Jack Snyder. 2007. *Electing to Fight: Why Emerging Democracies Go to War*. Cambridge, MA: MIT Press.
51. Samuel P. Huntington. 1968. *Political Order in Changing Societies*. New Haven, CT: Yale University Press; Ian Bremer. 2006. *The J Curve*. New York: Simon & Schuster.
52. Matthijs Bogaards. 2010. "Measures of Democratization: From Degree to Type to War." *Political Research Quarterly* 63 (2): 475–88.
53. Thomas Carothers. 1999. *Aiding Democracy Abroad*. Washington, DC: Carnegie Endowment for International Peace.
54. Merilee Grindle. 2004. "Good Enough Governance: Poverty Reduction and Reform in Developing Countries." *Governance* 17 (4): 525–48.

2. Theories of Regime Effects

1. Katie Willis. 2005. *Theories and Practice of Development*. London: Routledge; John Rapley. 2007. *Understanding Development*. Boulder, CO: Lynne Rienner; Gilbert Rist. 2008. *The History of Development: From Western Origins to Global Faith*. London: Zed.
2. See, for example, Adam Przeworski, Michael E. Alvarez, José Antonio Cheibub, and Fernando Limongi. 2000. *Democracy and Development: Political Institutions and Well-Being in the World, 1950–1990*. New York: Cambridge University Press; Hristos Doucouliagos and Mehmet Ali Ulubasoglu. 2008. "Democracy and Economic Growth: A Meta-analysis." *American Journal of Political Science* 52 (1): 61–83.
3. Michael Ross. 2006. "Is Democracy Good for the Poor?" *American Journal of Political Science* 50 (4): 860–74.
4. Edward D. Mansfield and Jack Snyder. 2007. *Electing to Fight: Why Emerging Democracies Go to War*. Cambridge, MA: MIT Press.
5. Seymour Martin Lipset. 1959. "Some Social Requisites of Democracy: Economic Development and Political Legitimacy." *American Political Science Review* 53: 69–105; Seymour Martin Lipset. 1960. *Political Man: The Social Basis of Politics*. New York: Doubleday; Seymour Martin Lipset and Jason M. Lakin. 2004. *The Democratic Century*. Norman: University of Oklahoma Press.
6. Adam Przeworski, Michael E. Alvarez, José Antonio Cheibub, and Fernando Limongi. 2000. *Democracy and Development: Political Institutions and Well-Being in the World, 1950–1990*. New York: Cambridge University Press.
7. Edward L. Glaeser, Rafael La Porta, Florencio Lopez-de-Silanes, and Andre Shleifer. 2004. "Do Institutions Cause Growth?" *Journal of Economic Growth* 9 (3): 271–303.
8. See Jon M. Carey. "Parchment, Equilibria, and Institutions." *Comparative Political Studies* 33 (6–7): 735–61.
9. Dani Rodrik, Arvind Subramanian, and Francesco Trebbi. 2004. "Institutions Rule: The Primacy of Institutions over Geography and Integration in Economic Development." *Journal of Economic Growth* 9 (2): 131–65; Dani Rodrik. 2007. *One Economics, Many Recipes*. Princeton, NJ: Princeton University Press.
10. Stephan Haggard and Robert R. Kaufman. 2008. *Development, Democracy, and Welfare States: Latin America, East Asia, and Eastern Europe*. Princeton, NJ: Princeton University Press.
11. Bruce Bueno de Mesquita, Alaistair Smith, Randolph M. Siverson, and James D. Morrow. 2003. *The Logic of Political Survival*. Cambridge, MA: MIT Press.

12. Michael McFaul. 2010. *Advancing Democracy Abroad*. New York: Rowman & Littlefield.

13. Joseph T. Siegle, Michael M. Weinstein, and Morton H. Halperin. 2004. "Why Democracies Excel." *Foreign Affairs* 83 (5): 57–72; Morton Halperin, Joseph T. Siegle, and Michael Weinstein. 2005. *The Democracy Advantage*. New York: Routledge.

14. Bruce M. Russett. 1993. *Grasping the Democratic Peace*. Princeton, NJ: Princeton University Press, p.11.

15. Christian Davenport. 2007. *State Repression and the Domestic Democratic Peace*. Cambridge: Cambridge University Press.

16. Arend Lijphart. 1999. *Patterns of Democracy*. New Haven, CT: Yale University Press.

17. For a stout and influential defense of these arguments, see Adam Przeworski. 1999. "Minimalist Conception of Democracy: A Defense." In Ian Shapiro and Casiano Hacker-Cordon, eds., *Democracy's Value*. Cambridge: Cambridge University Press; Adam Przeworski, Adam, Michael E. Alvarez, Jose Antonio Cheibub, and Fernando Limongi. 2000. *Democracy and Development: Political Institutions and Well-Being in the World, 1950–1990*. New York: Cambridge University Press.

18. A. H. Meltzer and S. F. Richard. 1981. "A Rational Theory of the Size of Government." *Journal of Political Economy* 89 (5): 914–27.

19. D. A. Lake and Mathew A. Baum. 2001. "The Invisible Hand of Democracy – Political Control and the Provision of Public Services." *Comparative Political Studies* 34 (6): 587–621; Daron Acemoglu and James A. Robinson. 2006. *Economic Origins of Dictatorship and Democracy*. New York: Cambridge University Press.

20. Andreas Schedler. 2002. "The Menu of Manipulation." *Journal of Democracy* 13 (2): 36–50; Steven Levitsky and Lucan A. Way. 2010. *Competitive Authoritarianism: Hybrid Regimes after the Cold War*. New York: Cambridge University Press.

21. Staffan Lindberg. 2006. *Democracy and Elections in Africa*. Baltimore: Johns Hopkins University Press; Staffan Lindberg, ed. 2009. *Democratization by Elections: A New Mode of Transition*. Baltimore: Johns Hopkins University Press.

22. Amartya Sen. 1981. *Poverty and Famines: An Essay on Entitlement and Deprivation*. Oxford: Clarendon Press.

23. Amartya Sen. 1999. *Development as Freedom*. Oxford: Oxford University Press; A. Adsera, Carles Boix, and M. Payne. 2003. "Are You Being Served? Political Accountability and Quality of Government." *Journal of Law Economics & Organization* 19: 445.

24. Arend Lijphart. 1999. *Patterns of Democracy*. New Haven, CT: Yale University Press.

25. Arend Lijphart. 1969. "Consociational Democracy." *World Politics* 21: 207–25; Arend Lijphart. 1975. *The Politics of Accommodation: Pluralism and Democracy in the Netherlands*. Berkeley: University of California Press; Arend Lijphart. 1999. *Patterns of Democracy: Government Forms and Performance in 36 Countries*. New Haven, CT: Yale University Press; Arend Lijphart. 2008. *Thinking about Democracy: Power Sharing and Majority Rule in Theory and Practice*. New York: Routledge.

26. Torsten Persson and Guido Tabellini. 2003. *The Economic Effects of Constitutions*. Cambridge, MA: MIT Press; Torsten Persson. 2004. "Constitutions and Economic Policy." *Journal of Economic Perspectives* 18: 75; Torsten Persson. 2006. "Democracy and Development: The Devil in the Details." *American Economic Review* 96: 319;

Carl Henrik Knutsen. 2011. "Which Democracies Prosper? Electoral Rules, Form of Government and Economic Growth." *Electoral Studies* 30 (1): 83–90.

27. For a review of the extensive literature, see Rudy B. Andweg. 2000. "Consociational Democracy." *Annual Review of Politics* 3: 509–36. For the development of alternative versions of this concept, see Gerhard Lehmbruch. 1967. *Proporzdemokratie. Politisches System und politische Kultur in der Schweiz und Osterreich.* Tubingen: Mohr; Jurg Steiner. 1974. *Amicable Agreement versus Majority Rule: Conflict Resolution in Switzerland.* Chapel Hill: University of North Carolina Press; Hans Daalder. 1974. "The Consociational Democracy Theme." *World Politics* 26: 604–21; Kenneth McRae, ed. 1974. *Consociational Democracy: Conflict Accommodation in Segmented Societies.* Toronto: McClelland and Stewart; Klaus Armingeon. 2002. "The Effects of Negotiation Democracy: A Comparative Analysis." *European Journal of Political Research* 41: 81; Arend Lijphart. 2002. "Negotiation Democracy versus Consensus Democracy: Parallel Conclusions and Recommendations." *European Journal of Political Research* 41 (1): 107–13; Wolf Linder and Andre Baechtiger. 2005. "What Drives Democratization in Asia and Africa?" *European Journal of Political Research* 44: 861–80; Pippa Norris. 2009. *Driving Democracy.* New York: Cambridge University Press; Andrew Reynolds. 2011. *Designing Democracy in a Dangerous World.* Oxford: Oxford University Press.

28. Samuel P. Huntington. 1968. *Political Order in Changing Societies.* New Haven, CT: Yale University Press.

29. Daniel Lerner. 1958. *The Passing of Traditional Society.* Glencoe, IL: Free Press.

30. Samuel P. Huntington. 1968. *Political Order in Changing Societies.* New Haven, CT: Yale University Press, p. 5.

31. Robert Kaplan. 2001. *The Coming Anarchy: Shattering the Dreams of the Post-Cold War.* New York: Vintage.

32. Fareed Zakaria. 2003. *The Future of Freedom: Illiberal Democracy at Home and Abroad.* New York: W. W. Norton.

33. Edward D. Mansfield and Jack Snyder. 1995. "Democratization and the Danger of War." *International Security* 20 (1): 5–38; Edward D. Mansfield and Jack Snyder. 2007. *Electing to Fight: Why Emerging Democracies Go to War.* Cambridge, MA: MIT Press; Edward D. Mansfield and Jack Snyder. 2007. "The Sequencing 'Fallacy'." *Journal of Democracy* 18 (3): 5–9.

34. Francis Fukuyama. 2004. "The Imperative of State-Building." *Journal of Democracy* 15 (2): 17–31; Francis Fukuyama. 2004. "Stateness First." *Journal of Democracy* 16 (1): 84–8; Francis Fukuyama. 2007. "Liberalism versus State-Building." *Journal of Democracy* 18 (3): 10–13; Francis Fukuyama. 2011. *The Origins of Political Order.* New York: Farrar, Straus, and Giroux.

35. Simon Chesterman. 2004. *You, the People: The United Nations, Transitional Administration, and Statebuilding.* New York: Oxford University Press. For related arguments, see also James Fearon and David Laitin. 2004. "Neo-trusteeship and the Problem of Weak States." *International Security* 29 (4): 5–43; Roland Paris. 2004. *At War's End: Building Peace after Civil Conflict.* Cambridge: Cambridge University Press.

36. Amy Chua. 2004. *World on Fire: How Exporting Free Market Democracy Breeds Ethnic Hatred and Global Instability.* New York: Anchor.

37. Kofi Annan, United Nations Secretary General. 2002. "Preface." In United Nations. 2002 *Human Development Report.* New York: UNDP.

38. John Williamson coined the term "Washington Consensus." See John Williamson. 1990. "What Washington Means for Policy Reform." In John Williamson, ed., *Latin American Adjustment: How Much Has Happened?* Washington, DC: Institute for International Economics, chapter 2; J. Marangos. 2009. "The Evolution of the Term 'Washington Consensus'." *Journal of Economic Surveys* 23 (2): 350–84.

39. L. Fraile. 2009. "Lessons from Latin America's Neo-liberal Experiment: An Overview of Labour and Social Policies since the 1980s." *International Labour Review* 148 (3): 215–33; Luis F. Lopez-Calva and Nora Lustig, eds. 2010. *Declining Inequality in Latin America.* New York: UNDP.

40. Joseph E. Stigletz. 1989. *The Economic Role of the State.* Oxford: Blackwell; Joseph E. Stigletz. 2003. *Globalizations and Its Discontents.* New York: W. W. Norton; Joseph E. Stigletz. 2006. *Making Globalization Work.* New York: W. W. Norton.

41. James Manor. 2007. *Aid that Works: Successful Development in Fragile States.* Washington, DC: World Bank.

42. Dani Rodrik. 2007. *One Economics, Many Recipes.* Princeton, NJ: Princeton University Press.

43. Stephen Kosack. 2003. "Effective Aid: How Democracy Allows Development Aid to Improve the Quality of Life." *World Development* 31 (1): 1–22.

44. Dani Rodrik, Arvind Subramanian, and Francesco Trebbi. 2004. "Institutions Rule: The Primacy of Institutions over Geography and Integration in Economic Development." *Journal of Economic Growth* 9 (2): 131–65.

45. OECD. 2009. *Donor Approaches to Governance Assessments: 2009 Sourcebook.* Paris: OECD.

46. Edwards R. McMahon and Scott H. Baker. 2006. *Piecing a Democratic Quilt? Regional Organizations and Universal Norms.* West Hartford, CT: Kumarian Press; OECD. 2009. *Donor Approaches to Governance Assessments: 2009 Sourcebook.* Paris: OECD.

47. Peter Evans and J. E. Rauch. 1999. "Bureaucracy and Growth: A Cross-National Analysis of the Effects of 'Weberian' State Structures on Economic Growth." *American Sociological Review* 64 (5): 748–65. For a recent project updating this approach, see Carl Dahlström, Victor Lapuente, and Jan Teorell. 2011. *Dimensions of Bureaucracy II: A Cross-National Dataset on the Structure and Behavior of Public Administration.* Gothenburg: QoG Working Paper Series 2011:6, Quality of Government Institute, University of Gothenburg.

48. Bo Rothstein. 2011. *The Quality of Government.* Chicago: University of Chicago Press.

49. Thomas Carothers. 2007. "The 'Sequencing' Fallacy." *Journal of Democracy* 18 (1): 12–27.

50. Some, although not all, donor and multilateral agencies regard "good governance" and democracy as equivalent. See OECD. 2009. *Donor Approaches to Governance Assessments: 2009 Sourcebook.* Paris: OECD, pp.22–4. For example, this approach is emphasized by the Sweden International Development Agency: "On the whole, good governance implies an efficient and predictable public sector incorporating participation and the rule of law, i.e. with the characteristics of democratic governance." Similar conceptualizations are offered by GTZ in Germany and Austria and USAID. Other agencies treat democracy and governance as separate phenomena.

51. David Easton. 1965. *A Framework for Political Analysis.* Eaglewood Cliffs, NJ: Prentice Hall; John W. Kingdon. 1984. *Agendas, Alternatives, and Public Policies.*

Boston: Little Brown; Thomas R. Dye. 1995. *Understanding Public Policy.* 8th ed. Eaglewood Cliffs, NJ: Prentice Hall.

52. Anna Jarstad and Timothy D. Sisk, eds. 2007. *From War to Democracy.* Cambridge: Cambridge University Press.

53. Sheri Berman. 2007. "The Vain Hope of 'Correct' Timing." *Journal of Democracy* 18 (3): 14–17.

3. The Regime Typology

1. David Easton. 1965. *A Framework for Political Analysis.* Englewood Cliffs, NJ: Prentice Hall.

2. Anne Mette Kjaer. 2010. *Governance.* Cambridge: Polity Press.

3. Merilee Grindle. 2004. "Good Enough Governance: Poverty Reduction and Reform in Developing Countries." *Governance* 17 (4): 525–48.

4. Merilee Grindle. 2004. "Good Enough Governance: Poverty Reduction and Reform in Developing Countries." *Governance* 17 (4): 525–48; Derick W. Brinkerhoff and Arthur A. Goldsmith. 2005. "Institutional Dualism and International Development: A Revisionist Interpretation of Good Governance." *Administration and Society* 37 (2): 199–225; Merilee Grindle. 2007. "Good Enough Governance Revisited." *Development Policy Review* 25: 553; Marcus J. Kurtz and Andrew Schrank. 2007. "Growth and Governance: Models, Measures, and Mechanisms." *Journal of Politics* 69 (2): 538–54; C. R. Apaza. 2009. "Measuring Governance and Corruption through the Worldwide Governance Indicators: Critiques, Responses, and Ongoing Scholarly Discussion." *PS – Political Science & Politics* 42 (1): 139–43.

5. Nicholas Charron and Victor Lapuente. 2010. "Does Democracy Produce Quality of Governance?" *European Journal of Political Research* 49: 443–70.

6. Hanna Back and Axel Hadenius. 2008. "Democracy and State Capacity: Exploring a J-shaped Relationship." *Governance* 21 (1): 1–24.

7. Michael Mann. 1993. *The Sources of Social Power.* Cambridge: Cambridge University Press. See also Hanna Back and Axel Hadenius. 2008. "Democracy and State Capacity: Exploring a J-shaped Relationship." *Governance* 21 (1): 1–24.

8. Max Weber. 1958. "Politics as a Vocation." In *From Max Weber: Essays in Sociology,* edited by H. H. Gerth and C. Wright Mills. New York: Galaxy, p. 212.

9. Jack A. Goldstone, Robert H. Bates, David L. Epstein, Ted Robert Gurr, Michael B. Lustik, Monty G. Marshall, Jay Ulfelder, and Mark Woodward. 2010. "A Global Model for Forecasting Political Instability." *American Journal of Political Science* 54 (1): 190–208.

10. Max Weber. 1997. *The Theory of Social and Economic Organization,* ed. Talcott Parsons. New York: Free Press.

11. Max Weber. [1904]. 1968. *Economy and Society,* ed. Guenter Roth and Claus Wittich. New York: Bedmaster. For further discussion, see Gili S. Droro, Yong Suk Jang, and John W. Meyer. 2006. "Sources of Rationalized Governance: Cross-National Longitudinal Analysis, 1985–2002." *Administrative Science Quarterly* 51 (2): 205–29.

12. For an alternative argument, see Bo Rothstein. 2011. *The Quality of Government.* Chicago: University of Chicago Press.

13. Max Weber. [1904]. 1968. *Economy and Society,* ed. Guenter Roth and Claus Wittich. New York: Bedmaster, chapter 8, "Bureaucracy."

14. Hans A. G. M. Bekke and Frits M. van der Meer, eds. 2000. *Civil Service Systems in Western Europe*. Edward Elgar: Cheltenham, UK.

15. Samuel N. Eisenstadt. 1973. *Traditional Patrimonialism and Modern Neopatrimonialism*. Beverly Hills, CA: Sage; Robin Theobald. 1982. "Patrimonialism." *World Politics* 34: 548–59; Anne Pitcher, Mary H. Moran, and Michael Johnston. 2009. "Rethinking Patrimonialism and Neopatrimonialism in Africa." *African Studies Review* 52 (1): 125–56.

16. Elaine C. Kamarck. 2007. *The End of Government...as We Know It*. Boulder, CO: Lynne Rienner.

17. David Osborne and Ted Gaebler. 1993. *Reinventing Government: How the Entrepreneurial Spirit Is Transforming the Public Sector*. New York: Plume.

18. Michael Barzelay. 2001. *The New Public Management: Improving Research and Policy Dialogue*. University of California Press; Christopher Pollitt and Geert Bouckaert. 2004. *Public Management Reform: A Comparative Analysis*. Oxford: Oxford University Press; R. Laking and R. Norman. 2007. "Imitation and Inspiration in Public Sector Reform: Lessons from Commonwealth Experiences." *International Review of Administrative Sciences* 73 (4): 517–30; B. Guy Peters. 2009. *The Politics of Bureaucracy: An Introduction to Comparative Public Administration*, 6th ed. New York: Routledge.

19. Christopher Pollitt and Geert Bouckaert. 2004. *Public Management Reform: A Comparative Analysis*. Oxford: Oxford University Press.

20. Cullen S. Hendrix. 2010. "Measuring State Capacity: Theoretical and Empirical Implications for the Study of Civil Conflict." *Journal of Peace Research* 47 (3): 273–85.

21. Cullen S. Hendrix. 2010. "Measuring State Capacity: Theoretical and Empirical Implications for the Study of Civil Conflict." *Journal of Peace Research* 47 (3): 273–85.

22. Data are available from International Monetary Fund. *Government Finance Statistics*. Table 7: Outlays by Function: General and Central Government. http://www2.imfstatistics.org/GFS/.

23. International Monetary Fund. *Government Finance Statistics*. Table 7: Outlays by Function: General and Central Government. http://www2.imfstatistics.org/GFS/.

24. Peter Evans and J. E. Rauch. 1999. "Bureaucracy and Growth: A Cross-National Analysis of the Effects of 'Weberian' State Structures on Economic Growth." *American Sociological Review* 64 (5): 748–65.

25. Carl Dahlstrom, Victor Lapuente, and Jan Teorell. 2010. *Dimensions of Bureaucracy: A Cross National Dataset on the Structure and Behavior of Public Administration*. Stockholm: Quality of Governance Institute Working Paper Series 2010: 13.

26. Stephen Knack and Philip Keefer. 1995. "Institutions and Economic Performance: Cross-Country Tests Using Alternative Institutional Measures." *Economics and Politics* 7 (3): 207–27; Gili S. Droro, Yong Suk Jang, and John W. Meyer. 2006. "Sources of Rationalized Governance: Cross-National Longitudinal Analysis, 1985–2002." *Administrative Science Quarterly* 51 (2): 205–29.

27. Details about the Political Risk Services Group's (PRSG) International Country Risk Guide are available from http://www.prsgroup.com/. It should be noted that the concept of political risk drives this measure of bureaucratic quality, which therefore emphasizes *continuity* of public policies rather than responsiveness. "Bureaucratic quality" is described by PRSG as follows: "High points are given to

countries where the bureaucracy has the strength and expertise to govern without drastic changes in policy or interruptions in government services. In these low-risk countries, the bureaucracy tends to be somewhat autonomous from political pressure and to have an established mechanism for recruitment and training. Countries that lack the cushioning effect of a strong bureaucracy receive low points because a change in government tends to be traumatic in terms of policy formulation and day-to-day administrative functions." http://www.prsgroup.com/ICRG_Methodology.aspx#PolRiskRating.

28. Nicholas Charron and Victor Lapuente. 2010. "Does Democracy Produce Quality of Governance?" *European Journal of Political Research* 49: 443–70.

29. Others have also included the PRSG measure of whether countries are seen to have a favorable investment profile, but this seems to confuse an indicator about economic markets with indicators about bureaucratic administration. See Gili S. Droro, Yong Suk Jang, and John W. Meyer. 2006. "Sources of Rationalized Governance: Cross-National Longitudinal Analysis, 1985–2002." *Administrative Science Quarterly* 51 (2): 205–29.

30. Daniel Kaufmann, Aart Kraay, and Massimo Mastruzzi. 2007. *Governance Matters VI: Aggregate and Individual Governance Indicators, 1996–2006.* Washington, DC: World Bank, Policy Research Working Paper; Daniel Kaufmann, Aart Kraay, and Massimo Mastruzzi. 2010. "The Worldwide Governance Indicators: Methodology and Analytical Issues." Washington, DC: Brookings Institute. www.govindicators.org.

31. David Collier. 1997. "Democracy with Adjectives." *World Politics* 49 (3): 430–51. For a discussion, see also David Held. 2006. *Models of Democracy.* 3rd ed. Stanford, CA: Stanford University Press.

32. This book is limited to comparing governance within nation-states, but governance is not necessarily confined to this level, by any means. A useful definition has been offered by Keohane and Nye: "By governance we mean the processes and institutions, both formal and informal, that guide and restrain the collective activities of a group. Government is the subset that acts with authority and creates formal obligations. Governance need not necessarily be conducted exclusively by governments. Private firms, associations of firms, nongovernmental organizations (NGOs), and associations of all NGOs engage in it; sometimes without governance authority." Robert Keohane and Joseph S. Nye, eds. 2000. *Governance in a Globalized World.* Washington, DC: Brookings Institution.

33. Joseph A. Schumpeter. 1947. *Capitalism, Socialism, and Democracy.* 2nd ed. New York: Harper.

34. Robert A. Dahl. 1971. *Polyarchy: Participation and Opposition.* New Haven, CT: Yale University Press; Robert A. Dahl. 1989. *Democracy and Its Critics.* New Haven, CT: Yale University Press.

35. Robert Dahl. 1989. *Democracy and its Critics,* New Haven, CT: Yale University Press, p. 221.

36. Larry Diamond. 1996. *Developing Democracy: Toward Consolidation.* Baltimore: Johns Hopkins University Press; Robert J. Barro. 1999. "Determinants of Democracy." *Journal of Political Economy* 107 (6): 158–83; Ronald Inglehart and Christian Welzel. 2005. *Modernization, Cultural Change, and Democracy: The Human Development Sequence.* New York: Cambridge University Press.

37. Diego Giannone. 2010. "Political and Ideological Aspects in the Measurement of Democracy: The Freedom House Case." *Democratization* 17 (1): 68–97.

38. David Collier and Robert Adcock. 1999. "Democracy and Dichotomies: A Pragmatic Approach to Choices about Concepts." *Annual Review of Political Science* 1: 537–65.

39. Freedom House. 2010. *Freedom in the World 2010.* Washington, DC: Freedom House. http://www.freedomhouse.org.

40. Geraldo L. Munck and Jay Verkuilen. 2002. "Conceptualizing and Measuring Democracy: Evaluating Alternative Indices." *Comparative Political Studies.* 35 (1): 5–34.

41. See, for example, R. E. Burkhart. 2000. "Economic Freedom and Democracy: Post–Cold War Tests." *European Journal of Political Research* 37 (2): 237–53; Diego Giannone. 2010. "Political and Ideological Aspects in the Measurement of Democracy: The Freedom House Case." *Democratization* 17 (1): 68–97.

42. For a disaggregated approach, see Bruce Bueno De Mesquita, G. W. Downs, Alistair Smith, and F. M. Cherif. 2005. "Thinking Inside the Box: A Closer Look at Democracy and Human Rights." *International Studies Quarterly* 49 (3): 439–57.

43. Diego Giannone. 2010. "Political and Ideological Aspects in the Measurement of Democracy: The Freedom House Case." *Democratization* 17 (1): 68–97.

44. Ted Robert Gurr. 1974. "Persistence and Change in Political Systems." *American Political Science Review* 74: 1482–1504.

45. Monty Marshall and Keith Jaggers. 2003. *Polity IV Project: Political Regime Characteristics and Transitions, 1800–2003.* http://www.cidcm.umd.edu/inscr/polity/; Monty Marshall, Ted Robert Gurr, Christian Davenport, and Keith Jaggers. 2002. "Polity IV, 1800–1999: Comments on Munck and Verkuilen." *Comparative Political Studies* 35 (1): 40–5.

46. Monty G. Marshall, Ted Robert Gurr, Christian Davenport, and Keith Jaggers. 2002. "Polity IV, 1800–1999: Comments on Munck and Verkuilen." *Comparative Political Studies* 35 (1): 40–5; Geraldo L. Munck and Jay Verkuilen. 2002. "Conceptualizing and Measuring Democracy: Evaluating Alternative Indices." *Comparative Political Studies.* 35 (1): 5–34.

47. Amy C. Alexander and Christian Welzel. 2011. "Measuring Effective Democracy: The Human Empowerment Approach." *Comparative Politics* 43 (3): 271–89.

48. Daniel Kaufmann, Aart Kraay, and Massimo Mastruzzi. 2003. "Governance Matters III: Governance Indicators 1996–2002." Washington, DC: World Bank; Daniel Kaufmann, Aart Kraay, and Massimo Mastruzzi. 2007. *Governance Matters VI: Aggregate and Individual Governance Indicators, 1996–2006.* Washington, DC: World Bank, Policy Research Working Paper 4280; Daniel Kaufmann, Aart Kraay, and Massimo Mastruzzi. 2010. *The Worldwide Governance Indicators: Methodology and Analytical Issues.* Washington, DC: World Bank, Policy Research Working Paper 5430.

49. Hanna Back and Axel Hadenius. 2008. "Democracy and State Capacity: Exploring a J-shaped Relationship." *Governance* 21 (1): 1–24; Nicholas Charron and Victor Lapuente. 2010. "Does Democracy Produce Quality of Governance?" *European Journal of Political Research* 49: 443–70.

50. Alan Angell. 2007. *Democracy after Pinochet: Politics, Parties and Elections in Chile.* London: University of London Press.

51. Peter H. Smith. 2005. *Democracy in Latin America: Political Change in Comparative Perspective.* Oxford: Oxford University Press; Scott Mainwaring and

Timothy Scully, eds. 2009. *Democratic Governance in Latin America*. Stanford, CA: Stanford University Press.

52. *Report of the Chilean National Commission on Truth and Reconciliation*. 1993. Notre Dame, IN: University of Notre Dame Press.

53. Peter H. Smith. 2005. *Democracy in Latin America: Political Change in Comparative Perspective*. Oxford: Oxford University Press; Pablo Policzer. 2009. *The Rise and Fall of Repression in Chile*. Notre Dame, IN: University of Notre Dame Press; Mary Helen Spooner. 2011. *The General's Slow Retreat: Chile after Pinochet*. Berkeley: University of California Press.

54. Ramon M. Alvarez and Gabriel Katz. 2009. "Structural Cleavages, Electoral Competition and Partisan Divide: A Bayesian Multinomial Probit Analysis of Chile's 2005 Election." *Electoral Studies* 28 (2): 177–89.

55. M. A. Garreton and R. Garreton. 2010. "Incomplete Democracy in Chile: Reality behind International Rankings." *Revista De Ciencia Politica* 30 (1): 115–48.

56. Maxwell A. Cameron. 2010. "The State of Democracy in the Andes." *Revista De Ciencia Politica* 30 (1): 5–20.

57. See World Bank. Worldwide Governance Indicators. Washington, DC: World Bank. http://info.worldbank.org/governance/wgi/index.asp.

58. Joseph Aye. 2000. *Deepening Democracy in Ghana*. Oxford: Freedom.

59. Naomi Chazan. 1988. "Democracy and Democratic Rule in Ghana." In Larry Diamond, Juan Linz, and Seymour Martin Lipset, eds., *Democracy in Developing Countries: Africa*. Boulder, CO: Lynne Rienner; Naomi Chazan, Peter Lewis, Robert Mortimer, Donald Rothchild, and Steven Stedman. 1999. *Politics and Society in Contemporary Africa*. Boulder, CO: Lynne Rienner, and London: Macmillan.

60. United Nations Development Programme. 2008. "Human Development Indices 2008." http://hdr.undp.org/en/statistics/data/.

61. Freedom House. "Freedom around the World 2009." http://www.freedomhouse.org.

62. Kwame Boafo-Arthur, ed. 2007. *Ghana: One Decade of the Liberal State*. London: Zed.

63. UNDP Ghana. 2010. "MDG Progress for All." http://www.undp-gha.org/mainpages. php?page=MDG%20Progress.

64. UNDP Ghana. 2004. "Common Country Assessment: Ghana." http://www.undp-gha.org/Ghana_CCA.pdf.

65. Marco Verweij and Riccardo Pelizzo. 2009. "Singapore: Does Authoritarianism Pay?" *Journal of Democracy* 20 (2): 18–32.

66. For more details about the historical development and contemporary nature of the political system, see Diane K. Mauzy and R. S. Milne. 2002. *Singapore Politics under the People's Action Party*. New York: Routledge; Carl A. Trocki. 2006. *Singapore: Wealth, Power and the Culture of Control*. New York: Routledge.

67. Michael Haas, ed. 1999. *The Singapore Puzzle*. Westport, CT: Praeger.

68. Hussin Mutalib, ed. 2003. *Parties and Politics: A Study of Opposition Parties and PAP in Singapore*. Singapore, New York: Eastern Universities Press.

69. For details of the electoral system, see http://www.elections.gov.sg/index.html.

70. Diane K. Mauzy. 2002. "Electoral Innovation and One-Party Dominance in Singapore." In John Fuh-Sheng Hsieh and David Newman, eds., *How Asia Votes*. London: Chatham House, pp. 235–54.

71. Jorgen Elkit and Palle Svensson. 1997. "What Makes Elections Free and Fair?" *Journal of Democracy* 8 (3): 32–46.

4. Analyzing Regime Effects

1. See Sebastian Dellepiane-Avellaneda. 2009. "Review Article: Good Governance, Institutions and Economic Development: Beyond the Conventional Wisdom." *British Journal of Political Science* 40: 195–224; Matthijs Bogaards. 2010. "Measures of Democratization: From Degree to Type to War." *Political Research Quarterly* 63 (2): 475–88.

2. See, for example, Robert Adcock and David Collier. 2001. "Measurement Validity: A Shared Standard for Qualitative and Quantitative Research." *American Political Science Review* 95 (3): 529–46; Merilee Grindle. 2004. "Good Enough Governance: Poverty Reduction and Reform in Developing Countries." *Governance* 17 (4): 525–48.

3. See discussions in Nicholas Thomas and William T. Tow. 2002. "The Utility of Human Security: Sovereignty and Humanitarian Intervention." *Security Dialogue* 33 (2): 177–92; E. Burger. 2004. "Human Security and the Crisis of Public Health Care in Malawi." *Canadian Journal of Development Studies* 25 (2): 239–55; Taylor Owen. 2004. "Human Security – Conflict, Critique and Consensus: Colloquium Remarks and a Proposal for a Threshold-based Definition." *Security Dialogue* 35 (3): 373–87; Sandra J. MacLean, David R. Black, and Timothy M. Shaw, eds. 2006. *A Decade of Human Security: Global Governance and New Multilateralisms.* Aldershot, UK, and Burlington, VT: Ashgate; Shahrbanou Tadjbakhsh and Anuradha M. Chenoy. 2007. *Human Security: Concepts and Implications.* New York: Routledge; Ken Booth. 2007. *Theory of World Security.* New York: Cambridge: Cambridge University Press; Mary Kaldor. 2007. *Human Security.* Cambridge: Polity Press; Barry Buzan and Lena Hansen. 2009. *The Evolution of International Security Studies.* New York: Cambridge University Press; Derek S. Reveron and Kathleen A. Mahoney-Norris. 2011. *Human Security in a Borderless World.* Boulder, CO: Westview Press.

4. S. Neil MacFarlane and Yuen Foong Khong. 2006. *Human Security and the UN: A Critical History.* Bloomington: Indiana University Press.

5. United Nations Development Programme. 1994. *Human Development Report.* New York: UNDP, p. 22.

6. United Nations Development Programme. 1994. *Human Development Report.* New York: UNDP. http://hdr.undp.org/en/humandev/.

7. Franklin D. Roosevelt. 1941. *State of the Union,* January 6.

8. Flavio Comim, Mozaffar Qizilbash, and Sabina Alkire, eds. 2008. *The Capabilities Approach: Concepts, Measures and Applications.* New York: Cambridge University Press.

9. United Nations Development Programme. 1991. *Human Development Report.* New York: UNDP.

10. Amartya Sen. 1999. *Development as Freedom.* Oxford: Oxford University Press.

11. See, for example, Jean-Pierre Chauffour. 2009. *The Power of Freedom: Uniting Human Rights and Development.* New York: Cato Institute.

12. Craig N. Murphy. 2006. *The United Nations Development Programme: A Better Way?* Cambridge: Cambridge University Press; Sabina Alikre. 2010. "Human Development: Definitions, Critiques and Related Concepts." *UNDP Human Development Research Paper 2010/01.* New York: UNDP.

13. United Nations Development Programme. 2010. *Human Development Report.* New York: UNDP. http://hdr.undp.org/en/reports/global/hdr2010/.

14. United Nations Development Programme. 1994. *Human Development Report.* New York: UNDP. http://hdr.undp.org/en/humandev/.

15. Sabina Alkire. 2010. "Human Development: Definitions, Critiques and Related Concepts." Human Development Research Paper 2010/01. New York: UNDP.

16. For details, see http://www.un.org/millenniumgoals/reports.shtml. For critical discussions, see Michael A. Clemens, Charles J. Kenny, and Todd J. Moss. 2007. "The Trouble with the MDGs: Confronting Expectations of Aid and Development Success." *World Development* 35 (5): 735–51; Jan Vandemoortele. 2009. "The MDG Conundrum: Meeting the Targets without Missing the Point." *Development Policy Review* 27 (4): 355–71.

17. See United Nations. 2000. UN General Assembly Resolution 55/2. *United Nations Millennium Declaration*. http://www.un.org/millennium/declaration/ares552e.pdf. Clause 6: "Freedom. Men and women have the right to live their lives and raise their children in dignity, free from hunger and from the fear of violence, oppression or injustice. Democratic and participatory governance based on the will of the people best assures these rights."

18. United Nations. 1948. *Universal Declaration of Human Rights*. New York: United Nations. http://www.un.org/en/documents/udhr/.

19. Nevertheless, a handful of countries such as Mongolia have expanded the core list by adding a locally defined ninth goal concerning governance, human rights, and democracy. For more details about current debates, see Andy Sumner and Meera Tiwari. 2009. "After 2015: What Are the Ingredients of an 'MDG-plus' Agenda for Poverty Reduction?" *Journal of International Development* 21 (6): 834–43.

20. The "drivers of change" phrase comes from the Department for International Development (DFID) in the UK. DFID. 2003. "Drivers Of Change." London. DFID. http://www.dfid.gov.uk/Contracts/files/ojec_5512_background.pdf.

21. World Bank. 1998. *Assessing Aid: What Works, What Doesn't and Why*. Washington, DC: World Bank.

22. Millennium Challenge Corporation. http://www.mcc.gov/mcc/selection/index.shtml.

23. Larry Diamond. 2008. *The Spirit of Democracy: The Struggle to Build Free Societies throughout the World*. New York: Times Books, p. 323; Michael McFaul. 2010. *Advancing Democracy Abroad*. New York: Rowman & Littlefield, p. 193.

24. T. Addison, G. Mavrotas, and M. McGillivray. 2005. "Development Assistance and Development Finance: Evidence and Global Policy Agendas." WIDER Research Paper 23. Helsinki: WIDER; Roger C. Riddell. 2007. *Does Foreign Aid Really Work?* New York: Oxford University Press.

25. William Easterly. 2006. *The White Man's Burden*. New York: Penguin Press.

26. A. Ebrahim. 2003. "Accountability in Practice: Mechanisms for NGOs." *World Development* 31 (5): 813–29.

27. Freedom House. http://www.freedomhouse.org.

28. Sakiko Fukuda-Parr. 2005 "Millennium Development Goals: Why They Matter." *Global Governance* 10: 395–402; David Hulme. 2010. "The Making of the Millennium Development Goals: Human Development Meets Results-based Management in an Imperfect World." *IDS Bulletin* 41: 15–25; Sakiko Fukuda-Parr. 2011. "Theory and Policy in International Development: Human Development and Capability Approach and the Millennium Development Goals." *International Studies Review* 13 (1): 122–32.

29. Michael A. Clemens, Charles J. Kenny, and Todd Moss. 2007. "The Trouble with the MDGs: Confronting Expectations of Aid and Development Success." *World Development* 35 (5): 735–51; Andy Sumner and Meera Tiwari. 2009. "After 2015:

What Are the Ingredients of an 'MDG-Plus' Agenda for Poverty Reduction?" *Journal of International Development* 21 (6): 834–43; Jan Vandemoortele. 2009. "The MDG Conundrum: Meeting the Targets without Missing the Point." *Development Policy Review* 27 (4): 355–71.

30. United Nations. 2011. *The Millennium Development Goals Report 2011*. New York: United Nations. http://www.un.org/millenniumgoals/11_MDG%20Report_EN.pdf.

31. United Nations Development Programme. 2011. *2010 Human Development Report*. New York: UNDP/Oxford University Press. http://hdrstats.undp.org/en/indicators/49806.html.

32. Ted Robert Gurr, Joseph Hewitt, and Jonathan Wilkenfeld. 2011. *Peace and Conflict 2010*. Maryland: CIDCM/University of Maryland/ Paradigm.

33. For a recent study of these developments, see Jan Teorell. 2010. *Determinants of Democratization: Explaining Regime Change in the World, 1972–2006*. New York: Cambridge University Press.

34. Samuel P. Huntington. 1991. *The Third Wave: Democratization in the Late Twentieth Century*. Norman: University of Oklahoma Press.

35. In 1973, Freedom House reported that forty countries were free, compared with eighty-seven in 2011, rising from 29 to 45 percent of all countries worldwide. See Freedom House. 2011. *Freedom in the World 2011 Country Rankings*. http://www.freedomhouse.org/images/File/fiw/historical/CountryStatusRatingsOverview 1973–2011.pdf.

36. Larry J. Diamond. 2008. *The Spirit of Democracy: The Struggle to Build Free Societies throughout the World*. New York: Times Books. Freedom House estimates that democratic losses outweighed gains annually from 2007 to 2010. Freedom House. *Freedom in the World 2010*. New York: Freedom House.

37. Jason Brownlee. 2007. *Authoritarianism in an Age of Democratization*. New York: Cambridge University Press; Steven Levitsky and Lucan A. Way. 2010. *Competitive Authoritarianism: Hybrid Regimes after the Cold War*. New York: Cambridge University Press.

38. Staffan Lindburg, ed. 2009. *Democratization by Elections: A New Mode of Transition*. Baltimore: Johns Hopkins University Press.

39. Freedom House. 2012. *Freedom around the World*. http://www.freedomhouse.org.

40. Francis Fukuyama. 1992. *The End of History and the Last Man*. New York: Free Press.

41. Samuel P. Huntington. 1991. *The Third Wave: Democratization in the Late Twentieth Century*. Norman: University of Oklahoma Press.

42. International Monetary Fund. 2009. *Government Finance Statistics*. http://www.imf.org/.

43. David A. Hastings. 2011. "The Human Security Index: An Update and a New Release." http://www.HumanSecurityIndex.org; Sascha Werthes, Corinne Heaven, and Sven Vollnhals. 2011. *Assessing Human Security Worldwide: The Way to a Human (In)Security Index*. Essen: University of Essen, Institut fur Entwickland und Frieden (INEF) Report 102. http://inef.uni-due.de.

44. Gary King and Christopher J. L. Murray. 2001. "Rethinking Human Security." *Political Science Quarterly* 116 (4): 585–610.

45. Roland Paris. 2001. "Human Security: Paradigm Shift or Hot Air?" *International Security* 26 (2): 87–102.

46. United Nations. 2011. *The Millennium Development Goals Report 2011*. New York: United Nations.

47. See the Uppsala Conflict Data Program. http://www.ucdp.uu.se.

48. *Pwt_rgdpch* measures PPP converted GDP per capita (chain series) at 2005 constant prices. Real GDP per capita (chain) is a chain index obtained by first applying the component growth rates between each pair of consecutive years, *t-l* and *t* (*t* = 1951 to 2007), to the current price component shares in year *t-1* to obtain the domestic absorption (DA) growth rate for each year. This DA growth rate for each year *t* is then applied backward and forward from 2005 and summed to the constant price net foreign balance to obtain the chain GDP series. Alan Heston, Robert Summers, and Bettina Aten. 2011. *Penn World Table* Version 7.0. Philadelphia: University of Pennsylvania, Center for International Comparisons of Production, Income and Prices. http://pwt.econ.upenn.edu/php_site/pwt_index.php.

49. United Nations. *UN Millennium Development Goals*. New York: United Nations. http://www.un.org/millenniumgoals/.

50. UN General Assembly. 2010. *Keeping the Promise: United to Achieve the Millennium Development Goals*. New York: United Nations. http://www.un.org/en/mdg/summit2010/pdf/mdg%20outcome%20document.pdf.

51. For all technical details, see the Uppsala Conflict Data Program. 2010. http://www.ucdp.uu.se; ECDP/PRIO. 2010. *The ECDP/PRIO Armed Conflict Dataset Codebook Version 4*. Uppsala: ECDP/PRIO.

52. Uppsala Conflict Data Program. 2010. http://www.ucdp.uu.se; ECDP/PRIO. 2010. *The ECDP/PRIO Armed Conflict Dataset Codebook Version 4*. Uppsala: ECDP/PRIO.

53. For example, in Transparency International's Corruption Perception Index, Singapore ranks third highest out of 180 nations worldwide, compared to the Philippines, which ranks 139th. http://www.transparency.org/policy_research/surveys_indices/cpi/2009/cpi_2009_table.

54. Barbara Geddes. 2003. *Paradigms and Sand Castles: Theory Building and Research Design in Comparative Politics*. Ann Arbor: University of Michigan Press; Alexander L. George and Andrew Bennett. 2004. *Case Studies and Theory Development*. Cambridge, MA: MIT Press.

55. For a discussion of the advantages of mixed research designs, see Henry Brady and David Collier. 2004. *Rethinking Social Inquiry: Diverse Tools, Shared Standards*. New York: Rowman & Littlefield.

56. To illustrate the range of indicators, see the datasets assembled by the Quality of Governance Institute at the University of Gothenburg. http://www.qog.pol.gu.se/.

57. Robert J. Barro. 1997. *Determinants of Economic Growth: A Cross-Country Empirical Study*. Cambridge, MA: MIT Press; Michael Ross. 2006. "Is Democracy Good for the Poor?" *American Journal of Political Science* 50 (4): 860–74.

58. James A. Stimson. 1985. "Regression in Time and Space: A Statistical Essay." *American Journal of Political Science* 29: 914–47; Cheng M. Hsiao. 1986. *Analysis of Panel Data*. Cambridge: Cambridge University Press.

59. Cheng M. Hsiao. 1986. *Analysis of Panel Data*. New York: Cambridge University Press.

60. Nathaniel Beck and Jonathan Katz. 1995. "What to Do (and Not to Do) with Time-Series Cross-Section Data." *American Political Science Review* 89: 634–47; Nathaniel Beck and Jonathan Katz. 1996. "Nuisance vs. Substance: Specifying and Estimating Time-Series Cross-Sectional Models." In J. Freeman, ed., *Political Analysis*. Ann Arbor: University of Michigan Press.

61. Cheng M. Hsaio. 1986. *Analysis of Panel Data*. New York: Cambridge University Press.
62. Nathaniel Beck and Jonathan Katz. 1995. "What to Do (and Not to Do) with Time-Series Cross-Section Data." *American Political Science Review* 89: 634–47.
63. Nicholas Charron and Victor Lapuente. 2010. "Does Democracy Produce Quality of Government?" *European Journal of Political Research* 49: 443–70.
64. Seymour Martin Lipset. 1959. "Some Social Requisites of Democracy: Economic Development and Political Legitimacy." *American Political Science Review* 53: 69–105.
65. See, for example, Kevin R. Cox and Tohit Negi. 2010. "The State and the Question of Development in Sub-Saharan Africa." *Review of African Political Economy* 37 (123): 71–85.
66. See Sven E. Wilson and David M. Butler. 2007. "A Lot More to Do: The Sensitivity of Time-Series Cross-Section Analyses to Simple Alternative Specifications." *Political Analysis* 15 (2): 101–23.
67. John Gerring, Philip Bond, William T. Barndt, and Carola Moreno. 2005. "Democracy and Economic Growth: A Historical Perspective." *World Politics* 57 (3): 323–64.
68. Paul D. Allison. 2009. *Fixed Effects Regression Models*. London: Sage.
69. Allison J. Sovey and Donald P. Green. 2011. "Instrumental Variables Estimation in Political Science: A Readers' Guide." *American Journal of Political Science* 55 (1): 188–200.
70. See Daron Acemoglu, Simon Johnson, and James A. Robinson. 2001. "The Colonial Origins of Comparative Development: An Empirical Investigation." *American Economic Review* 91 (5): 1369–1401; Daron Acemoglu, Simon Johnson, and James A. Robinson. 2002. "Reversal of Fortune: Geography and Institutions in the Making of the Modern Income Distribution." *Quarterly Journal of Econometrics* 118: 1231–94; Daron Acemoglu and James A. Robinson. 2006. *Economic Origins of Dictatorship and Democracy*. New York: Cambridge University Press.
71. See also Dani Rodrik, Arvind Subramanian, and Francesco Trebbi. 2004. "Institutions Rule: The Primacy of Institutions over Geography and Integration in Economic Development." *Journal of Economic Growth* 9 (2): 131–65.
72. Edward L. Glaeser, Rafael La Porta, Florencio Lopez-de-Silanes, and Andre Shleifer. 2004. "Do Institutions Cause Growth?" *Journal of Economic Growth* 9 (3): 271–303.
73. United Nations. *List of Member States*. New York: United Nations. http://www.un.org/en/members/growth.shtmlchael.
74. Alberto Alesina and Enrico Spolaore. 2003. *The Size of Nations*. Cambridge, MA: MIT Press.
75. Jared Diamond. 1997 *Guns, Germs, and Steel: The Fates of Human Societies*. New York: W. W. Norton.
76. Michael L. Ross. 2001. "Does Oil Hinder Democracy?" *World Politics* 53: 325–61; Michael L. Ross. 2004. "How Do Natural Resources Influence Civil War? Evidence from Thirteen Cases." *International Organization* 58 (1): 35–67; Paul Collier and Nicholas Sambanis, eds. 2005. *Understanding Civil War*. Washington, DC: World Bank; M. Humphreys. 2005. "Natural Resources, Conflict, and Conflict Resolution: Uncovering the Mechanisms." *Journal of Conflict Resolution* 49 (4): 508–37. For a critique, however, see Pauline Jones Luong and Erika Weithal. 2010. *Oil Is Not a Curse: Ownership Structure and Institutions in Soviet Successor States*. New York: Cambridge University Press.

77. William Easterly. 1997. "Africa's Growth Tragedy: Policies and Ethnic Divisions." *Quarterly Journal of Economics* 112: 1203; S. G. Simonsen. 2005. "Addressing Ethnic Divisions in Post-Conflict Institution-Building: Lessons from Recent Cases." *Security Dialogue* 36 (3): 297–318; Edward D. Mansfield and Jack Snyder. 2007. *Electing to Fight: Why Emerging Democracies Go to War.* Cambridge, MA: MIT Press; Paul Collier, Anke Hoeffler, and Dominic Rohner. 2009. "Beyond Greed and Grievance: Feasibility and Civil War." *Oxford Economic Papers* 61: 1–27.

78. Ronald Inglehart and Christian Welzel. 2005. *Modernization, Cultural Change, and Democracy: The Human Development Sequence.* New York: Cambridge University Press.

5. Prosperity

1. Robert E. Hall and Charles I. Jones. 1999. "Why Do Some Countries Produce So Much More Output per Worker than Others?' *Quarterly Journal of Economics* 114 (1): 83–116; Dani Rodrik, Arvind Subramanian, and Francesco Trebbi. 2004. "Institutions Rule: The Primacy of Institutions over Geography and Integration in Economic Development." *Journal of Economic Growth* 9 (2): 131–65; Dani Rodrik. 2007. *One Economics, Many Recipes.* Princeton, NJ: Princeton University Press.

2. John Geering and Strom C. Thacker. 2004. "Political Institutions and Corruption: The Role of Unitarism and Parliamentarism." *British Journal of Political Science* 34: 295–330; H. E. Sung. 2004. "Democracy and Political Corruption: A Cross-National Comparison." *Crime, Law and Social Change* 41: 179.

3. Vasudha Chhotray and David Hulme. 2009. "Contrasting Visions for Aid and Governance in the 21st Century: The White House Millennium Challenge Account and DFID's Drivers of Change." *World Development* 37 (1): 36–49.

4. Edward Newman and Roland Rich, eds. 2004. *The UN Role in Promoting Democracy.* New York: United Nations University Press.

5. United Nations Development Programme. 2011. *Annual Report 2011.* New York: United Nations. http://www.undp.org/annualreport2011/democratic_governance. html.

6. For literature reviews, see Hristos Doucouliagos and Mehmet Ali Ulubasoglu. 2008. "Democracy and Economic Growth: A Meta-analysis." *American Journal of Political Science* 52 (1): 61–83; Sebastian Dellepiane-Avellaneda. 2009. "Review Article: Good Governance, Institutions and Economic Development: Beyond the Conventional Wisdom." *British Journal of Political Science* 40: 195–224.

7. See, for example, Dani Rodrik, Arvind Subramanian, and Francesco Trebbi. 2004. "Institutions Rule: The Primacy of Institutions over Geography and Integration in Economic Development." *Journal of Economic Growth* 9 (2): 131–65.

8. See, for example, Edward L. Glaeser, Rafael La Porta, Florencio Lopez-de-Silanes, and Andre Shleifer. 2004. "Do Institutions Cause Growth?" *Journal of Economic Growth* 9 (3): 271–303; Marcus J. Kurtz and Andrew Schrank. 2007. "Growth and Governance: Models, Measures, and Mechanisms." *Journal of Politics* 69 (2): 538–54; Daron Acemoglu, Simon Johnson, and James A. Robinson. 2008. "Income and Democracy." *American Economic Review* 98 (3): 808–42; Nicholas Charron and Victor Lapuente. 2010. "Does Democracy Produce Quality of Government?" *European Journal of Political Research* 49: 443–70.

9. R. Levine and D. Renelt. 1992. "A Sensitivity Analysis of Cross-Country Growth Regressions." *American Economic Review* 82 (4): 942–63; James L. Butkiewicz and Halit Yanikkaya. 2006. "Institutional Quality and Economic Growth: Maintenance of the Rule of Law or Democratic Institutions, or Both?" *Economic Modelling* 23 (4): 648–61.

10. For textbook approaches, see Robert J. Barro and Xavier Sala-i-Martin. 2003. *Economic Growth*. 2nd ed. Cambridge, MA: MIT Press; Rick Szostak. 2009. *The Causes of Economic Growth: Interdisciplinary Perspectives*. Heidelberg: Springer.

11. Douglas North. 1990. *Institutions, Institutional Change and Economic Performance*. Cambridge: Cambridge University Press; Dani Rodrik, Arvind Subramanian, Francesco Trebbi. 2004. "Institutions Rule: The Primacy of Institutions over Geography and Integration in Economic Development." *Journal of Economic Growth* 9 (2): 131–65; R. Rigobon and Dani Rodrik. 2005. "Rule of Law, Democracy, Openness, and Income: Estimating the Interrelationships." *Economics of Transition* 13 (3): 533–64.

12. See Daron Acemoglu, Simon Johnson, and James A. Robinson. 2001. "The Colonial Origins of Comparative Development: An Empirical Investigation." *American Economic Review* 91 (5): 1369–1401; Daron Acemoglu, Simon Johnson, and James A. Robinson. 2002. "Reversal of Fortune: Geography and Institutions in the Making of the Modern Income Distribution." *Quarterly Journal of Econometrics* 118: 1231–94; Daron Acemoglu and James A. Robinson. 2006. *Economic Origins of Dictatorship and Democracy*. New York: Cambridge University Press.

13. Marcus J. Kurtz and Andrew Schrank. 2007. "Growth and Governance: Models, Measures, and Mechanisms." *Journal of Politics* 69 (2): 538–54.

14. Edward L. Glaeser, Rafael La Porta, Florencio Lopez-de-Silanes, and Andre Shleifer. 2004. "Do Institutions Cause Growth?" *Journal of Economic Growth* 9 (3): 271–303.

15. See Nicholas Charron and Victor Lapuente. 2010. "Does Democracy Produce Quality of Government?" *European Journal of Political Research* 49: 443–70.

16. Sebastian Dellepiane-Avellaneda. 2009. "Review Article: Good Governance, Institutions and Economic Development: Beyond the Conventional Wisdom." *British Journal of Political Science* 40: 195–224.

17. Robert J. Barro. 1996. "Democracy and Growth." *Journal of Economic Growth* 1 (1): 1–27; Robert J. Barro. 1997. *Determinants of Economic Growth: A Cross-Country Empirical Study*. Cambridge: MIT Press.

18. Adam Przeworski, Michael E. Alvarez, José Antonio Cheibub, and Fernando Limongi. 1996. "What Makes Democracies Endure?" *Journal of Democracy* 7 (1): 39–55; Adam Przeworski and F. Limongi. 1997. "Modernization: Theories and Facts." *World Politics* 49: 155–83; Adam Przeworski, Michael E. Alvarez, José Antonio Cheibub, and Fernando Limongi. 2000. *Democracy and Development: Political Institutions and Well-Being in the World, 1950–1990*. New York: Cambridge University Press.

19. Adam Przeworski, Michael E. Alvarez, José Antonio Cheibub, and Fernando Limongi. 2000. *Democracy and Development: Political Institutions and Well-Being in the World, 1950–1990*. New York: Cambridge University Press.

20. Hristos Doucouliagos and Mehmet Ali Ulubasoglu. 2008. "Democracy and Economic Growth: A Meta-analysis." *American Journal of Political Science* 52 (1): 61–83.

21. See, for example, William Easterly. 2002. *The Elusive Quest for Growth.* Cambridge, MA: MIT Press, chapters 11 and 12.

22. John Williamson. 1990. "What Washington Means by Policy Reform." In John Williamson, ed., *Latin American Adjustment: How Much Has Happened?* Washington, DC: Institute for International Economics, chapter 2; J. Marangos. 2009. "The Evolution of the Term 'Washington Consensus.'" *Journal of Economic Surveys* 23 (2): 350–84.

23. John Williamson and Pedro-Pablo, eds. 2003. *After the Washington Consensus: Restarting Growth and Reform in Latin America.* Washington, DC: Peterson Institute; Francisco Panizz. 2009. *Contemporary Latin America: Development and Democracy beyond the Washington Consensus.* London: Zed.

24. Ian Marsh, Jean Blondel, and Takashi Inoguchi, eds. 1999. *Democratic Governance and Economic Performance.* New York: United Nations University Press; H. Z. Li and Z. H. Xu. 2007. "Economic Convergence in Seven Asian Economies." *Review of Development Economics* 11 (3): 531–49; F. K. W. Loh. 2008. "Procedural Democracy, Participatory Democracy and Regional Networking: The Multi-Terrain Struggle for Democracy in Southeast Asia." *Inter-Asia Cultural Studies* 9 (1): 127–41.

25. Joseph E. Stigletz. 2010. *Freefall: America, Free Markets, and the Sinking of the World Economy.* New York: W. W. Norton.

26. John Williamson. 1990. "What Washington Means by Policy Reform." In John Williamson, ed., *Latin American Adjustment: How Much Has Happened?* Washington, DC: Institute for International Economics, chapter 2; J. Marangos. 2009. "The Evolution of the Term 'Washington Consensus.'" *Journal of Economic Surveys* 23 (2): 350–84.

27. Douglas North. 1990. *Institutions, Institutional Change and Economic Performance.* Cambridge: Cambridge University Press.

28. Paulo Mauro. 1995. "Corruption and Growth." *Quarterly Journal of Economics* 110: 681–712.

29. P. Bardhan. 1997. "Corruption and Development: A Review of Issues." *Journal of Economic Literature* 35 (3): 1320–46; Susan Rose-Ackerman. 1999. *Corruption and Government: Causes, Consequences and Reform.* New York: Cambridge University Press; A. Brunetti and B. Weder. 2003. "A Free Press Is Bad News for Corruption." *Journal of Public Economics* 87 (7–8): 1801–24; Alan Doig. 2000. *Corruption and Democratization.* London: Frank Cass.

30. Stephen Knack and Philip Keefer. 1995. "Institutions and Economic Performance: Cross-Country Tests Using Alternative Institutional Measures." *Economics and Politics* 7 (3): 207–27.

31. Daniel Kaufmann, Aart Kraay, and Massimo Mastruzzi. 2010. *The Worldwide Governance Indicators: Methodology and Analytical Issues.* Washington, DC: Brookings Institute. http://www.govindicators.org.

32. Daniel Kaufmann, Aart Kraay, and Massimo Mastruzzi. 2007. *Governance Matters VI: Aggregate and Individual Governance Indicators, 1996–2006.* Washington, DC: World Bank, Policy Research Working Paper; Daniel Kaufmann, Aart Kraay, and Massimo Mastruzzi. 2007. "Growth and Governance: A Rejoinder." *Journal of Politics* 69 (2): 570–2.

33. Dani Rodrik, Arvind Subramanian, Francesco Trebbi. 2004. "Institutions Rule: The Primacy of Institutions over Geography and Integration in Economic Development." *Journal of Economic Growth* 9 (2): 131–65; R. Rigobon and Dani

Rodrik. 2005. "Rule of Law, Democracy, Openness, and Income: Estimating the Interrelationships." *Economics of Transition* 13 (3): 533–64.

34. Joseph E. Stigletz. 1989. *The Economic Role of the State*. Oxford: Blackwell; Joseph E. Stigletz. 2006. *Making Globalization Work*. New York: W. W. Norton.

35. Francis Fukuyama. 2004. *State-Building: Governance and World Order in the 21st Century*. Ithaca, NY: Cornell University Press.

36. Francis Fukuyama. 2004. *State-Building: Governance and World Order in the 21st Century*. Ithaca, NY: Cornell University Press, pp. 26–9.

37. Peter Evans and J. E. Rauch. 1999. "Bureaucracy and Growth: A Cross-National Analysis of the Effects of 'Weberian' State Structures on Economic Growth." *American Sociological Review* 64 (5): 748–65.

38. Alice Amsden. 1989. *Asia's Next Giant*. Oxford: Oxford University Press; Robert Wade. 1990. *Governing the Market: Economic Theory and the Role of Government in East Asian Industrialization*. Princeton, NJ: Princeton University Press; Alice Amsden. 2001. *The Rise of the "Rest": Challenges to the West from Late-industrializing Economies*. Oxford: Oxford University Press; Young Whan Kihl. 2005. *Transforming Korean Politics: Democracy, Reform, and Culture*. Armonk, NY: M. E. Sharpe; Francis Fukuyama. 2007. "Liberalism versus State-Building." *Journal of Democracy* 18 (3): 10–13.

39. See Diane K. Mauzy and R. S. Milne. 2002. *Singapore Politics under the People's Action Party*. New York: Routledge; Carl A. Trocki. 2006. *Singapore: Wealth, Power and the Culture of Control*. New York: Routledge.

40. Gross domestic product based on purchasing power parity (PPP) per capita GDP, current international dollars, as estimated by the IMF. IMF. 2010. *World Economic Outlook Database*. http://www.imf.org/external/pubs/ft/weo/2010/01/weodata/index.aspx.

41. Martin King Whyte. 2009. "Paradoxes of China's Economic Boom." *Annual Review of Sociology* 35: 371–92.

42. David Kang. 2002. *Crony Capitalism: Corruption and Development in South Korea and the Philippines*. New York: Cambridge University Press. The 2010 Corruption Perceptions Index by Transparency International, however, ranks the Republic of Korea as 39th (best) out of 178 countries worldwide, placed in a similar ranking to Malta and Costa Rica. Transparency International. 2010. *The 2010 Corruption Perceptions Index*. http://www.transparency.org/policy_research/surveys_indices/cpi/2010/results.

43. Morton H. Halperin, Joseph T. Siegle, and Michael M. Weinstein. 2010. *The Democracy Advantage: How Democracies Promote Prosperity and Peace*. 2nd ed. New York: Routledge, p. 15.

44. Francis Fukuyama. 2004. *State-Building: Governance and World Order in the 21st Century*. Ithaca, NY: Cornell University Press, p. 28.

45. Morris Fiorina. 1981. *Retrospective Voting in American National Elections*. New Haven, CT: Yale University Press; Michael S. Lewis-Beck. 1988. *Economics and Elections: The Major Western Democracies*. Ann Arbor: University of Michigan Press; Anthony Downs. 1997. *An Economic Theory of Democracy*. New York: Addison Wesley.

46. Michael S. Lewis-Beck. 1990. *Economics and Elections: The Major Western Democracies*. Ann Arbor: University of Michigan Press; G. Bingham Powell and G. D. Whitten. 1993. "A Cross-National Analysis of Economic Voting: Taking Account of the Political Context." *American Journal of Political Science* 37 (2):

391–414; Christopher J. Anderson. 1995. *Blaming the Government: Citizens and the Economy in Five European Democracies*. New York: M. E. Sharpe; G. Bingham Powell. 2000. *Elections as Instruments of Democracy*. New Haven, CT: Yale University Press.

47. Wouter van der Brug, Cees van der Eijk, and Mark Franklin. 2007. *The Economy and the Vote: Economic Conditions and Elections in Fifteen Countries*. Cambridge: Cambridge University Press.

48. Donald Wittman. 1995. *The Myth of Democratic Failure*. Chicago: University of Chicago Press.

49. Morton H. Halperin, Joseph T. Siegle, and Michael M. Weinstein. 2010. *The Democracy Advantage: How Democracies Promote Prosperity and Peace*. 2nd ed. New York: Routledge, p. 48.

50. Morton H. Halperin, Joseph T. Siegle, and Michael M. Weinstein. 2010. *The Democracy Advantage: How Democracies Promote Prosperity and Peace*. 2nd ed. New York: Routledge, p. 32.

51. Guillermo O'Donnell. 1979. *Modernization and Bureaucratic-Authoritarianism Studies in South American Politics*. Berkeley: Institute of International Studies, University of California.

52. Robert J. Barro. 1997. *Determinants of Economic Growth: A Cross-Country Empirical Study*. Cambridge, MA: MIT Press.

53. Matthew A. Baum and David A. Lake. 2003. "The Political Economy of Growth: Democracy and Human Capital." *American Journal of Political Science* 47 (2): 333–47; David S. Brown and Wendy Hunter. 2004. "Democracy and Human Capital Formation." *Comparative Political Studies* 37 (7): 842–64.

54. Morton H. Halperin, Joseph T. Siegle, and Michael M. Weinstein. 2010. *The Democracy Advantage: How Democracies Promote Prosperity and Peace*. 2nd ed. New York: Routledge, p. 39.

55. Robert J. Barro. 2001. "Human Capital and Growth." *American Economic Review* 91 (2): 12–17.

56. Robert J. Barro. 1999. "Determinants of Democracy." *Journal of Political Economy* 107 (6): 158–83.

57. Pippa Norris. 2004. *Electoral Engineering*. New York: Cambridge University Press, chapter 4; Pippa Norris. 2009. *Driving Democracy*. New York: Cambridge University Press.

58. Arend Lijphart. 1999. *Patterns of Democracy*. New Haven, CT: Yale University Press; Peter Cowhey and Stephen Haggard. 2001. *Presidents, Parliaments and Policy*. Cambridge: Cambridge University Press; Torsten Persson and Guido Tabellini. 2003. *The Economic Effects of Constitutions*. Cambridge, MA: MIT Press; Carl Henrik Knutsen. 2011. "Which Democracies Prosper? Electoral Rules, Form of Government and Economic Growth." *Electoral Studies* 30 (1): 83–90; Stefan Voigt. 2011. "Positive Constitutional Economics II: A Survey of Recent Developments." *Public Choice* 146 (1–2): 205–56.

59. Torsten Persson and Guido Tabellini. 2003. *The Economic Effects of Constitutions*. Cambridge, MA: MIT Press; Torsten Persson and Guido Tabellini. 2004. "Constitutions and Economic Policy." *Journal of Economic Perspectives* 18: 75–98; Torsten Persson. 2006. "Democracy and Development: The Devil in the Details." *American Economic Review* 96: 319.

60. Carl Henrik Knutsen. 2011. "Which Democracies Prosper? Electoral Rules, Form of Government and Economic Growth." *Electoral Studies* 30 (1): 83–90.

61. Pippa Norris. 2004. *Electoral Engineering*. New York: Cambridge University Press.

62. John Geering and Strom C. Thacker. 2004. "Political Institutions and Corruption: The Role of Unitarism and Parliamentarism." *British Journal of Political Science* 34: 295–330.

63. Christopher D. Anderson. 2006. "Economic Voting and Multilevel Governance: A Comparative Individual-level Analysis." *American Journal of Political Science* 50: 449–63; M. A. Kayser and Christopher Wlezien. 2011. "Performance Pressure: Patterns of Partisanship and the Economic Vote." *European Journal of Political Research* 50 (3): 365–94.

64. Arend Lijphart. 1999. *Patterns of Democracy*. New Haven, CT: Yale University Press.

65. Yi Feng. 2003. *Democracy, Governance and Economic Growth: Theory and Evidence*. Cambridge, MA: MIT Press.

66. Daron Acemoglu, Simon Johnson, and James A. Robinson. 2008. "Income and Democracy." *American Economic Review* 98 (3): 808–42.

67. Seymour Martin Lipset. 1959. "Some Social Requisites of Democracy: Economic Development and Political Legitimacy." *American Political Science Review* 53: 69–105.

68. See also Dankwart Rustow. 1970. "Transitions to Democracy." *Comparative Politics* 2: 337–63.

69. Daron Acemoglu, Simon Johnson, and James A. Robinson. 2008. "Income and Democracy." *American Economic Review* 98 (3): 808–42. See also Edward L. Glaeser, Rafael La Porta, Florencio Lopez-de-Silanes, and Andre Shleifer. 2004. "Do Institutions Cause Growth?" *Journal of Economic Growth* 9 (3): 271–303.

70. David Dollar and V. Levine. "The Increasing Selectivity of Foreign Aid, 1984–2003." *World Development* 34 (12): 2034–46.

71. See, however, Torsten Persson and Guido Tabellini. 2003. *The Economic Effects of Constitutions*. Cambridge, MA: MIT Press; Torsten Persson. 2006. "Democracy and Development: The Devil in the Details." *American Economic Review* 96: 319.

72. Geraldo L. Munck. 2009. *Measuring Democracy: A Bridge between Scholarship and Politics*. Baltimore: Johns Hopkins University Press.

73. Anne Mette Kjaer. 2010. *Governance*. Cambridge: Polity Press.

74. Marcus J. Kurtz and Andrew Schrank. 2007. "Growth and Governance: Models, Measures, and Mechanisms." *Journal of Politics* 69 (2): 538–54; C. R. Apaza. 2009. "Measuring Governance and Corruption through the Worldwide Governance Indicators: Critiques, Responses, and Ongoing Scholarly Discussion." *PS – Political Science & Politics* 42 (1): 139–43.

75. Stephen Haggard and Lydia Tiede. 2011. "The Rule of Law and Economic Growth: Where Are We?" *World Development* 39 (5): 673–85.

76. Alan Heston, Robert Summers, and Bettina Aten. 2011. *Penn World Table* Version 7.0. Philadelphia: Center for International Comparisons of Production, Income and Prices, University of Pennsylvania. http://pwt.econ.upenn.edu/php_site/pwt_index.php.

77. Institutions are classified from Pippa Norris. 2009. *Driving Democracy*. New York: Cambridge University Press.

78. Nicholas Charron and Victor Lapuente. 2010. "Does Democracy Produce Quality of Government?" *European Journal of Political Research* 49: 443–70.

79. Jared M. Diamond. 1999. *Guns, Germs, and Steel: The Fates of Human Societies.* New York: W.W. Norton.

80. William Easterly and R. Levine.1997. "Africa's Growth Tragedy: Policies and Ethnic Divisions." *Quarterly Journal of Economics* 111 (4): 1203–50.

81. Macartan Humphreys, Jeffrey D. Sachs, and Joseph E. Stiglitz, eds. 2007. *Escaping the Resource Curse.* New York: Columbia University Press.

82. William Easterly. 2002. *The Elusive Quest for Growth.* Cambridge, MA: MIT Press, chapter 4.

83. Peter Evans and J. E. Rauch. 1999. "Bureaucracy and Growth: A Cross-National Analysis of the Effects of 'Weberian' State Structures on Economic Growth." *American Sociological Review* 64 (5): 748–65.

84. Morton H. Halperin, Joseph T. Siegle, and Michael M. Weinstein. 2010. *The Democracy Advantage: How Democracies Promote Prosperity and Peace.* 2nd ed. New York: Routledge, p. 39.

85. Robert J. Barro. 1997. *Determinants of Economic Growth: A Cross-Country Empirical Study.* Cambridge: MIT Press; Adam Przeworski, Michael E. Alvarez, José Antonio Cheibub, and Fernando Limongi. 2000. *Democracy and Development: Political Institutions and Well-Being in the World, 1950–1990.* New York: Cambridge University Press; Hristos Doucouliagos and Mehmet Ali Ulubasoglu. 2008. "Democracy and Economic Growth: A Meta-analysis." *American Journal of Political Science* 52 (1): 61–83.

86. Jose Maria Maravall and Ignacio Sanchez-Cuenca, eds. 2008. *Controlling Governments: Voters, Institutions and Accountability.* New York: Cambridge University Press.

87. Isabella Alcaniz and Timothy Hellwig. 2011. "Who's to Blame? The Distribution of Responsibility in Developing Democracies." *British Journal of Political Science* 41: 389–411.

88. Torsten Persson and Guido Tabellini. 2004. "Constitutions and Economic Policy." *Journal of Economic Perspectives* 18 (1): 75–98.

89. Henrik Knutsen. 2011. "Which Democracies Prosper? Electoral Rules, Form of Government and Economic Growth." *Electoral Studies* 30 (1): 83–90.

90. William Easterly. 2002. *The Elusive Quest for Growth.* Cambridge, MA: MIT Press, chapter 4.

91. Adam Przeworski, Michael E. Alvarez, José Antonio Cheibub, and Fernando Limongi. 2000. *Democracy and Development: Political Institutions and Well-Being in the World, 1950–1990.* New York: Cambridge University Press.

92. For other recent comparative studies of these issues, see Laura Jaramillo and Cemile Sancak. 2007. *Growth in the Dominican Republic and Haiti: Why Has the Grass Been Greener on One Side of Hispaniola?* IMF Working Paper 07/63; Cecilia Ann Winters and Robert Derrell. 2010. "Divided Neighbors on an Indivisible Island: Economic Disparity and Cumulative Causation on Hispaniola." *Journal of Economic Issues* 44 (3): 597–613.

93. Philippe R. Girard. 2010. *Haiti: The Tumultuous History: From Pearl of the Caribbean to Broken Nation.* New York: Palgrave Macmillan.

94. Daron Acemoglu and James A. Robinson. 2006. *Economic Origins of Dictatorship and Democracy.* New York: Cambridge University Press.

95. Cecilia Ann Winters and Robert Derrell. 2010. "Divided Neighbors on an Indivisible Island: Economic Disparity and Cumulative Causation on Hispaniola." *Journal of Economic Issues* 44 (3): 597–613.

96. Robert A. Dahl and Edwards R. Tufte. 1973. *Size and Democracy*. Stanford, CA: Stanford University Press; Alberto Alesina and Enrico Spolaore. 2003. *The Size of Nations*. Cambridge, MA: MIT Press.

97. Jared Diamond. 2005. *Collapse: How Societies Choose to Fail or Succeed*. New York: Viking/Penguin.

98. William Easterly and R. Levine.1997. "Africa's Growth Tragedy: Policies and Ethnic Divisions." *Quarterly Journal of Economics* 111 (4): 1203–50.

99. Erica Caple James. 2010. *Democratic Insecurities: Violence, Trauma, and Intervention in Haiti*. Berkeley: University of California Press.

100. Mats Lundahl and Claudio Vedovato. 1989. "The State and Economic Development in Haiti and the Dominican Republic." *Scandanavian Economic History Review* 37: 39–59.

101. Francis Fukuyama, ed. 2011. *Falling Behind: Explaining the Development Gap Between Latin America and the United States*. New York: Oxford University Press.

102. See also Laura Jaramillo and Cemile Sancak. 2007. *Growth in the Dominican Republic and Haiti: Why Has the Grass Been Greener on One Side of Hispaniola?* IMF Working Paper 07/63.

6. Welfare

1. Jarad Diamond. 1999. *Guns, Germs and Steel: The Fates of Human Societies*. New York: W. W. Norton.

2. Sakiko Fukuda-Parr. 2011. "Theory and Policy in International Development: Human Development and Capability Approach and the Millennium Development Goals." *International Studies Review* 13 (1): 122–32.

3. See, for example, P. Navia and T. D. Zweifel. 2003. "Democracy, Dictatorship, and Infant Mortality Revisited." *Journal of Democracy* 14 (3): 90–103; David Stasavage. 2005. "Democracy and Education Spending in Africa." *American Journal of Political Science* 49 (2): 343–58; Michael Ross. 2006. "Is Democracy Good for the Poor?" *American Journal of Political Science* 50 (4): 860–74.

4. David S. Brown. 1999. "Reading, Writing, and Regime Type: Democracy's Impact on Primary School Enrollment." *Political Research Quarterly* 52 (4): 681–707; David A. Lake and Matthew A. Baum. 2001. "The Invisible Hand of Democracy: Political Control and the Provision of Public Services." *Comparative Political Studies* 34 (6): 587–621; Morton H. Halperin, Joseph T. Siegle, and Michael M. Weinstein. 2010. *The Democracy Advantage: How Democracies Promote Prosperity and Peace*. 2nd ed. New York: Routledge, p. 39.

5. Charles Seymour. 1970. *Electoral Reform in England and Wales*. London: David & Charles; Daron Acemoglu and James A. Robinson. 2000. "Why Did the West Extend the Franchise? Democracy, Inequality and Growth in Historical Perspective." *Quarterly Journal of Economics* 115 (4): 1167–99; Carles Boix. 2003. *Democracy and Redistribution*. New York: Cambridge University Press; Daron Acemoglu and James A. Robinson. 2006. *Economic Origins of Dictatorship and Democracy*. New York: Cambridge University Press.

6. Allan H. Meltzer and Scott F. Richard. 1981. "A Rational Theory of the Size of Government." *Journal of Political Economy* 89 (5): 914–27.

7. David A. Lake and Matthew A. Baum. 2001. "The Invisible Hand of Democracy: Political Control and the Provision of Public Services." *Comparative Political Studies* 34 (6): 587–621.

8. A thorough review summarizing the empirical literature analyzing the effects of democracy on social spending and social policy outcomes is provided in Stephan Haggard and Robert R. Kaufman. 2008. *Development, Democracy, and Welfare States: Latin America, East Asia, and Eastern Europe.* Princeton, NJ: Princeton University Press, appendix 1. See also Kenneth A. Bollen and Robert W. Jackman. 1985. "Political Democracy and the Size Distribution of Income." *American Sociological Review* 50: 438–58; Kenneth A. Bollen and Robert W. Jackman. 1995. "Income Inequality and Democratization Revisited: Comment on Muller." *American Sociological Review* 60: 983–9.

9. Joseph T. Siegle, Michael Weinstein, and Morton Halperin. 2004. "Why Democracies Excel." *Foreign Affairs* 83 (5): 57–72; Morton Halperin, Joseph T. Siegle, and Michael Weinstein. 2010. *The Democracy Advantage.* 2nd ed. New York: Routledge.

10. Morton Halperin, Joseph T. Siegle, and Michael Weinstein. 2010. *The Democracy Advantage.* 2nd ed. New York: Routledge, p. 22.

11. C. B. Mulligan, R. Gil, and Xavier Sala-i-Martin. 2004. "Do Democracies Have Different Public Policies than Non-democracies?" *Journal of Economic Perspectives* 18 (1): 52–74; P. Nel. 2005. "Democratization and the Dynamics of Income Distribution in Low- and Middle-Income Countries." *Politikon* 32 (1): 17–43; Michael McFaul. 2010. *Advancing Democracy Abroad.* New York: Rowman & Littlefield.

12. David S. Brown. 1999. "Reading, Writing, and Regime Type: Democracy's Impact on Primary School Enrollment." *Political Research Quarterly* 52 (4): 681–707; David S. Brown and Wendy Hunter. 1999. "Democracy and Social Spending in Latin America, 1980–92." *American Political Science Review* 93: 779–90.

13. David A. Lake and Matthew A. Baum. 2001. "The Invisible Hand of Democracy: Political Control and the Provision of Public Services." *Comparative Political Studies* 34 (6): 587–621; G. Avelino, David S. Brown, and Wendy Hunter. 2005. "The Effects of Capital Mobility, Trade Openness, and Democracy on Social Spending in Latin America, 1980–1999." *American Journal of Political Science* 49 (3): 625–41.

14. David Stasavage. 2005. "Democracy and Education Spending in Africa." *American Journal of Political Science* 49 (2): 343–58.

15. Steven Kosack. 2003. "Effective Aid: How Democracy Allows Development Aid to Improve the Quality of Life." *World Development* 31 (1): 1–22.

16. P. Navia and T. D. Zweifel. 2003. "Democracy, Dictatorship, and Infant Mortality Revisited." *Journal of Democracy* 14 (3): 90–103.

17. Isabella Alcaniz and Timothy Hellwig. 2011. "Who's to Blame? The Distribution of Responsibility in Developing Democracies." *British Journal of Political Science* 41 (2): 389–411.

18. D. Bradley, Evelyn Huber, Susan Moller, F. Nielsen, and J. D. Stephens. 2003. "Distribution and Redistribution in Post-Industrial Democracies." *World Politics* 55 (2): 193–228.

19. Francis Fukuyama. 2004. *State-Building: Governance and World Order in the 21st Century.* Ithaca, NY: Cornell University Press.

20. William Easterley. 2001. *The Elusive Quest for Growth.* Cambridge, MA: MIT Press; William Easterley. 2006. *The White Man's Burden.* New York: Penguin.

21. Michael Ross. 2006. "Is Democracy Good for the Poor?" *American Journal of Political Science* 50 (4): 860–74.

22. Timothy Powell-Jackson, Sanjay Basu, Dina Balabanova, Martin McKee, and David Stuckler. 2011. "Democracy and Growth in Divided Societies: A Health-Inequality Trap?" *Social Science & Medicine* 73 (1): 33–41.

23. United Nations Development Programme. 2002. *Human Development Report 2002.* New York: UNDP/Oxford University Press.

24. Gøsta Esping-Andersen. 1990. *The Three Worlds of Welfare Capitalism.* Princeton, NJ: Princeton University Press.

25. Haejoo Chung and Carles Muntaner. 2006. "Political and Welfare State Determinants of Infant and Child Health Indicators: An Analysis of Wealthy Countries." *Social Science & Medicine* 63 (3): 829–42.

26. Peter A. Hall and David Soskice, eds. 2001. *Varieties of Capitalism: The Institutional Foundations of Comparative Advantage.* Oxford: Oxford University Press.

27. For a range of cases, see James W. McGuire. 2010. *Wealth, Health, and Democracy in East Asia and Latin America.* New York: Cambridge University Press.

28. Thomas Carothers. 2005. "The Backlash against Democracy Promotion." *Foreign Affairs* March/April: 55–68.

29. Morton Halperin, Joseph T. Siegle, and Michael Weinstein. 2010. *The Democracy Advantage.* 2nd ed. New York: Routledge, p. 22.

30. Ross E. Burkhart. 1997. "Comparative Democracy and Income Distribution: Shape and Direction of the Causal Arrow." *Journal of Politics* 59 (1): 148–64; Robert J. Barro. 1999. "Determinants of Democracy." *Journal of Political Economy* 107 (6): 158–83; Matthew A. Baum and David A. Lake. 2003. "The Political Economy of Growth: Democracy and Human Capital." *American Journal of Political Science* 47 (2): 333–47.

31. Sakiko Fukuda-Parr. 2011. "Theory and Policy in International Development: Human Development and Capability Approach and the Millennium Development Goals." *International Studies Review* 13 (1): 122–32.

32. United Nations. *Data Availability.* http://mdgs.un.org/unsd/mdg/DataAvailability.aspx.

33. Flavio Comim, Mozaffar Qizilbash, and Sabina Alkire, eds. 2008. *The Capabilities Approach: Concepts, Measures and Applications.* New York: Cambridge University Press.

34. United Nations. 2011. *The Millennium Development Goals Report 2011.* New York: UN.

35. Robert J. Barro. 2001. "Human Capital and Growth." *American Economic Review* 91 (2): 12–17.

36. United Nations. 2011. *The Millennium Development Goals Report 2011.* New York: UN.

37. Ronald Inglehart and Pippa Norris. 2003. *Rising Tide: Gender Equality & Cultural Change around the World.* New York: Cambridge University Press.

38. See Antonio Davoia, Joshy Easaw, and Andrew MacKay. 2004. "Inequality, Democracy and Institutions: A Critical Review of Recent Research." *World Development* 38: 2.

39. Robert J. Barro. 2000. "Inequality and Growth in a Panel of Countries." *Journal of Economic Growth* 5 (1): 5–32.

40. Jared M. Diamond. 1999. *Guns, Germs, and Steel: The Fates of Human Societies.* New York: W.W. Norton; William Easterly and Ross Levine. 2003. "Tropics, Germs, and Crops: How Endowments Influence Economic Development." *Journal of Monetary Economics* 50: 3–39.

41. Daron Acemoglu, Simon Johnson, and James A. Robinson. 2002. "Reversal of Fortune: Geography and Institutions in the Making of the Modern Income Distribution." *Quarterly Journal of Econometrics* 118: 1231–94.

42. William Easterly and Ross Levine. 1997. "Africa's Growth Tragedy: Policies and Ethnic Divisions." *Quarterly Journal of Economics* 111 (4): 1203–50.

43. David S. Brown. 1999. "Reading, Writing, and Regime Type: Democracy's Impact on Primary School Enrollment." *Political Research Quarterly* 52 (4): 681–707; David A. Lake and Matthew A. Baum. 2001. "The Invisible Hand of Democracy: Political Control and the Provision of Public Services." *Comparative Political Studies* 34 (6): 587–621; Morton H. Halperin, Joseph T. Siegle, and Michael M. Weinstein. 2010. *The Democracy Advantage: How Democracies Promote Prosperity and Peace.* 2nd ed. New York: Routledge, p. 39.

44. David S. Brown. 2004. "Democracy and Gender Inequality in Education: A Cross-National Examination." *British Journal of Political Science* 34: 137–92.

45. http://www.gatesfoundation.org/global-health/Pages/global-health-strategies.aspx.

46. http://africanelections.tripod.com/recent.html.

47. United Nations Development Programme/Zambian Ministry of Finance and National Planning. 2011. *Zambia Millennium Development Goals Report, 2011.* UNDP: Lusaka.

48. Steven C. Radelet. 2010. *Emerging Africa: How 17 Countries Are Leading the Way.* Washington, DC: Brookings Institution Press.

49. Robin Theobald and Robert Williams. 2000. "Combating Corruption in Botswana: Regional Role Model or Deviant Case?" In A. Doig and R. Williams, eds., *Corruption and Democratisation* (London: Frank Cass), pp. 117–34.

50. Michael L. Ross. 2001. "Does Oil Hinder Democracy?" *World Politics* 53: 325–61; Michael L. Ross. 2004. "How Do Natural Resources Influence Civil War? Evidence from Thirteen Cases." *International Organization* 58 (1): 35–67; Hazel M. McFerson. 2009. "Governance and Hyper-corruption in Resource-rich African Countries." *Third World Quarterly* 30 (8): 1529–48; Limi Atsushi. 2011. "Escaping from the Resource Curse: Evidence from Botswana and the Rest of the World." *IMF Staff Papers* 54 (4): 663–99.

51. Michael L. Ross. 2006. "A Closer Look at Oil, Diamonds, and Civil War." *Annual Review of Political Science.* 9: 265–300.

52. See also Pauline Jones Luong and Erika Weinthal. 2010. *Oil Is Not a Curse.* New York: Cambridge University Press.

53. Paresh Kumar Narayan, Seema Narayan, and Russell Smyth. 2011. "Does Democracy Facilitate Economic Growth or Does Economic Growth Facilitate Democracy? An Empirical Study of Sub-Saharan Africa." *Economic Modelling* 28 (3): 900–10.

7. Peace

1. The expansion in peacekeeping activities and the settlement of civil wars has attracted a substantial literature. See, for example, Roland Paris, 2004. *At War's End: Building Peace after Civil Conflict.* Cambridge: Cambridge University Press; Paul Collier and Nicholas Sambanis, eds. 2005. *Understanding Civil War.* Washington, DC: World Bank; James Dobbins, Seth G. Jones, Keith Crane, Andrew Rathmell, Brett Steele, Richard Teltschik, and Anga R. Timilsina. 2005. *The UN's Role in Nation-Building: From the Congo to Iraq.* Santa Monica: RAND; Ho-Won

Jeong. 2005. *Peace-Building in Post-Conflict Societies*. Boulder, CO: Lynne Rienner; Michael W. Doyle and Nicholas Sambanis. 2006. *Making War and Building Peace*. Princeton, NJ: Princeton University Press; Anna K. Jarsad and Timothy D. Sisk, eds. 2008. *From War to Democracy*. New York: Cambridge University Press; Lise Morjé Howard. 2009. *UN Peacekeeping in Civil Wars*. New York: Cambridge University Press; Monica Toft. 2010. *Securing the Peace: The Durable Settlement of Civil Wars*. Princeton, NJ: Princeton University Press.

2. Roland Paris and Timothy D. Sisk, eds. 2009. *The Dilemmas of State-Building*. New York: Routledge.

3. Virginia Page Fortna. 2004. "Does Peacekeeping Keep Peace? International Intervention and the Duration of Peace after Civil War." *International Studies Quarterly* 48 (2): 269–92; Virginia Page Fortna and Lise Morjé Howard. 2008. "Pitfalls and Prospects in the Peacekeeping Future." *Annual Review of Political Science* 11: 283–301.

4. Michael W. Doyle and Nicholas Sambanis. 2006. *Making War and Building Peace*. Princeton, NJ: Princeton University Press.

5. These three states scored highest on the State Fragility Index 2009; see Monty G. Marshall and Benjamin R. Cole. 2009. *State Fragility Index and Matrix 2009*. College Park: University of Maryland, Center for Systemic Peace. http://www.systemicpeace.org/SFImatrix2009c.pdf.

6. J. Joseph Hewitt, Jonathan Wilkenfeld, and Ted Robert Gurr. 2011. *Peace and Conflict 2011*. College Park: University of Maryland, Center for Systemic Peace. http://www.systemicpeace.org/SFImatrix2009c.pdf.

7. Joseph A. Schumpeter, 1947. *Capitalism, Socialism, and Democracy*. 2nd ed. New York: Harper.

8. Robert A. Dahl, 1971. *Polyarchy: Participation and Opposition*. New Haven, CT: Yale University Press.

9. See, for example, Thomas Carothers. 2007. "The 'Sequencing' Fallacy." *Journal of Democracy* 18 (1): 12–27; Michael McFaul. 2010. *Advancing Democracy Abroad*. New York: Rowman & Littlefield.

10. Michael McFaul. 2010. *Advancing Democracy Abroad*. New York: Rowman & Littlefield.

11. Bruce Bueno de Mesquita, Alistair Smith, Randolph M. Siverson, and James D. Morrow. 2003. *The Logic of Political Survival*. Cambridge, MA: MIT Press.

12. Christian Davenport. 2007. "State Repression and Political Order." *Annual Review of Political Science* 10: 1–23; Christian Davenport. 2007. *State Repression and the Domestic Democratic Peace*. Cambridge: Cambridge University Press.

13. Bruce M. Russett. 1993. *Grasping the Democratic Peace: Principles for a Post–Cold War World*. Princeton, NJ: Princeton University Press, p. 11.

14. Bruce M. Russett. 1993. *Grasping the Democratic Peace: Principles for a Post–Cold War World*. Princeton, NJ: Princeton University Press, p. 11.

15. Michael W. Doyle. 2005. "Three Pillars of the Liberal Peace." *American Political Science Review* 99: 463–6.

16. Arend Lijphart. 1999. *Patterns of Democracy*. New Haven, CT: Yale University Press.

17. For a review of the extensive literature, see Rudy B. Andweg. 2000. "Consociational Democracy." *Annual Review of Politics* 3: 509–36. For the development of alternative versions of this concept, see Gerhard Lehmbruch. 1967. *Proporzdemokratie. Politisches System und politische Kultur in der Schweiz und Osterreich*. Tubingen:

Mohr; Hans Daalder. 1974. "The Consociational Democracy Theme." *World Politics* 26: 604–21; Kenneth McRae, ed. 1974. *Consociational Democracy: Conflict Accommodation in Segmented Societies*. Toronto: McClelland and Stewart; Jurg Steiner. 1974. *Amicable Agreement versus Majority Rule: Conflict Resolution in Switzerland*. Chapel Hill: University of North Carolina Press; Klaus Armingeon. 2002. "The Effects of Negotiation Democracy: A Comparative Analysis." *European Journal of Political Research* 41: 81; Arend Lijphart. 2002. "Negotiation Democracy versus Consensus Democracy: Parallel Conclusions and Recommendations." *European Journal of Political Research* 41 (1): 107–13; Wolf Linder and Andre Baechtiger. 2005. "What Drives Democratization in Asia and Africa?" *European Journal of Political Research* 44: 861–80; Pippa Norris. 2009. *Driving Democracy*. New York: Cambridge University Press; Andrew Reynolds. 2011. *Designing Democracy in a Dangerous World*. Oxford: Oxford University Press.

18. Arend Lijphart. 1969. "Consociational Democracy." *World Politics* 21: 207–25; Arend Lijphart. 1975. *The Politics of Accommodation: Pluralism and Democracy in the Netherlands*. Berkeley: University of California Press; Arend Lijphart. 1999. *Patterns of Democracy: Government Forms and Performance in 36 Countries*. New Haven, CT: Yale University Press; Arend Lijphart. 2008. *Thinking about Democracy: Power Sharing and Majority Rule in Theory and Practice*. New York: Routledge.

19. Pippa Norris. 2009. *Driving Democracy*. New York: Cambridge University Press. See also Virginia Page Fortna. 2008. "Peacekeeping and Democratization." In Anna K. Jarsad and Timothy D. Sisk, eds., *From War to Democracy*. New York: Cambridge University Press, pp. 39–79; Andrew Reynolds. 2011. *Designing Democracy in a Dangerous World*. Oxford: Oxford University Press.

20. C. Hartzell and M. Hoddie. 2004. "Institutionalizing Peace: Power Sharing and Post–Civil War Conflict Management." *American Journal of Political Science* 47 (2): 318–32.

21. S. G. Simonsen. 2005. "Addressing Ethnic Divisions in Post-Conflict Institution-Building: Lessons from Recent Cases." *Security Dialogue* 36 (3): 297–318.

22. Håvard Hegre and Hanne Fjelde. 2010. "Democratization and Post-Conflict Transitions." In J. Joseph Hewitt, Jonathan Wilkenfeld, and Ted Robert Gurr, eds., *Peace and Conflict*. 2010. Maryland: Center for Systemic Peace, University of Maryland, chapter 8.

23. James D. Fearon and David Laitin. "Ethnicity, Insurgency, and Civil War." *American Political Science Review*. 97 (1): 75–90.

24. Samuel P. Huntington. 1968. *Political Order in Changing Societies*. New Haven, CT: Yale University Press.

25. Simon Chesterman. 2004. *You, the People: The United Nations, Transitional Administration, and State-Building*. New York: Oxford University Press; James D. Fearon and David D. Laitin. 2004. "Neo-trusteeship and the Problem of Weak States." *International Security* 29 (4): 5–43; Francis Fukuyama. 2004. *State-Building: Governance and World Order in the 21st Century*. Ithaca, NY: Cornell University Press; Stephen Krasner. 2004. "Sharing Sovereignty: New Institutions for Collapsed and Failing States." *International Security* 29 (2): 85–120; Roland Paris. 2004. *At War's End: Building Peace after Civil Conflict*. Cambridge: Cambridge University Press.

26. Samuel P. Huntington. 1968. *Political Order in Changing Societies*. New Haven, CT: Yale University Press, p. 5.

27. C. Garcia-Rivero and H. Kotze. 2007. "Electoral Support for Islamic Parties in the Middle East and North Africa." *Party Politics* 13 (5): 611–36. For evidence that many Islamic parties are actually moderate, see Charles Kurzman and Ijlal Naqvi. 2010. "Do Muslims Vote Islamic?" *Journal of Democracy* 21 (2): 50–63.

28. Roland Paris and Timothy D. Sisk, eds. 2009. *The Dilemmas of State-Building*. New York: Routledge.

29. Edward D. Mansfield and Jack Snyder. 1995. "Democratization and the Danger of War." *International Security* 20 (1): 5–38; Edward D. Mansfield and Jack Snyder. 2007. *Electing to Fight: Why Emerging Democracies Go to War*. Cambridge, MA: MIT Press; Edward D. Mansfield and Jack Snyder. 2007. "The Sequencing 'Fallacy'." *Journal of Democracy* 18 (3): 5–9.

30. Edward D. Mansfield and Jack Snyder. 2007. *Electing to Fight: Why Emerging Democracies Go to War*. Cambridge, MA: MIT Press.

31. Edward D. Mansfield and Jack Snyder. 2007. *Electing to Fight: Why Emerging Democracies Go to War*. Cambridge, MA: MIT Press, p. 59.

32. J. Joseph Hewitt, Jonathan Wilkenfeld, and Ted Robert Gurr. 2010. *Peace and Conflict*. College Park: Center for Systemic Peace, University of Maryland.

33. Benjamin Reilly. 2007. "Post-War Elections: Uncertain Turning Points of Transition." In Anna Jarstad and Timothy D. Sisk, eds., *From War to Democracy*. Cambridge: Cambridge University Press, pp. 157–80.

34. Matthijs Bogaards. 2010. "Measures of Democratization: From Degree to Type to War." *Political Research Quarterly* 63 (2): 475–88.

35. Thomas Carothers. 2007. "The 'Sequencing' Fallacy." *Journal of Democracy* 18 (1): 12–27.

36. Anna Jarstad and Timothy D. Sisk, eds. 2007. *From War to Democracy*. Cambridge: Cambridge University Press.

37. Saul Newman. 1991. "Does Modernization Breed Ethnic Conflict?" *World Politics* 43 (3): 451–78.

38. William Easterly and Ross Levine. 1997. "Africa's Growth Tragedy: Policies and Ethnic Divisions." *Quarterly Journal of Economics* 111 (4): 1203–50.

39. J. Joseph Hewitt, Jonathan Wilkenfeld, and Ted Robert Gurr. 2011. *Peace and Conflict 2011*. College Park: Center for Systemic Peace, University of Maryland.

40. Ibrahim Elbadawi and Nicholas Sambanis. 2002. "How Much War Will We See? Estimating the Prevalence of Civil War, 1960–1999." *Journal of Conflict Resolution* 46: 307–44; Paul Collier and Nicholas Sambanis, eds. 2005. *Understanding Civil War*. Washington, DC: World Bank; M. Humphreys. 2005. "Natural Resources, Conflict, and Conflict Resolution: Uncovering the Mechanisms." *Journal of Conflict Resolution* 49 (4): 508–37.

41. Paul Collier and Nicholas Sambanis, eds. 2005. *Understanding Civil War*. Washington, DC: World Bank.

42. Michael L. Ross. 2001. "Does Oil Hinder Democracy?" *World Politics* 53: 325–61; Michael L. Ross. 2004. "How Do Natural Resources Influence Civil War? Evidence from Thirteen Cases." *International Organization* 58 (1): 35–67; Michael L. Ross. 2006. "A Closer Look at Oil, Diamonds, and Civil War." *Annual Review of Political Science* 9: 265–300.

43. S. G. Simonsen. 2005. "Addressing Ethnic Divisions in Post-Conflict Institution-Building: Lessons from Recent Cases." *Security Dialogue* 36 (3): 297–318; Edward D. Mansfield and Jack Snyder. 2007. *Electing to Fight: Why Emerging Democracies Go to War*. Cambridge, MA: MIT Press; Paul Collier, Anke Hoeffler, and Dominic

Rohner. 2009. "Beyond Greed and Grievance: Feasibility and Civil War." *Oxford Economic Papers* 61: 1–27.

44. Stuart J. Kaufman. 2001. *Modern Hatreds: The Symbolic Politics of Ethnic War.* Ithaca, NY: Cornell University Press.

45. Stuart J. Kaufman. 2001. *Modern Hatreds: The Symbolic Politics of Ethnic War.* Ithaca, NY: Cornell University Press; Dan Posner. 2004. "The Political Salience of Cultural Difference: Why Chewas and Tumbukas Are Allies in Zambia and Adversaries in Malawi." *American Political Science Review* 98 (4): 529–46.

46. Alberto Alesina, Arnaud Devleeschauwer, William Easterly, Sergio Kurlat, and Romain Wacziarg. 2003. "Fractionalization." *Journal of Economic Growth* 8: 155–94.

47. David Beetham, ed. 1994. *Defining and Measuring Democracy.* London: Sage; Paul Collier, Anke Hoeffler, and Dominic Rohner. 2009. "Beyond Greed and Grievance: Feasibility and Civil War." *Oxford Economic Papers* 61: 1–27.

48. For all technical details, see Uppsala Conflict Data Program. 2010. http://www.ucdp.uu.se; ECDP/PRIO. 2010. *The ECDP/PRIO Armed Conflict Dataset Codebook Version 4.* Uppsala: ECDP/PRIO.

49. Paul Collier, Anke Hoeffler, and Dominic Rohner. 2009. "Beyond Greed and Grievance: Feasibility and Civil War." *Oxford Economic Papers* 61: 1–27.

50. For further discussion, see Pippa Norris. 2010. *Driving Democracy.* New York: Cambridge University Press.

51. See, for example, V. K. Nanayakkara. 2006. "From Dominion to Republican Status: Dilemmas of Constitution Making in Sri Lanka." *Public Administration and Development* 26 (5): 425–37; Andrew Reynolds, ed. 2002. *The Architecture of Democracy: Constitutional Design, Conflict Management and Democracy.* Oxford: Oxford University Press.

52. Rene Lemarchand. 2007. "Consociationalism and Power Sharing in Africa: Rwanda, Burundi, and the Democratic Republic of the Congo." *African Affairs* 106 (422): 1–20. For an alternative interpretation, see also D. P. Sullivan. 2005. "The Missing Pillars: A Look at the Failure of Peace in Burundi through the Lens of Arend Lijphart's Theory of Consociational Democracy." *Journal of Modern African Studies* 43 (1): 75–95.

53. G. Vuckovic. 1997. *Ethnic Cleavages and Conflict: The Sources of National Cohesion and Disintegration. The Case of Yugoslavia.* Aldershot, UK: Ashgate.

8. Conclusion: Why Regimes Matter

1. Terry Lynn Karl. 2003. "The Vicious Cycle of Inequality in Latin America." In Susan Eva Eckstein and Timothy P. Wickham-Crowley, eds., *The Politics of Injustice in Latin America.* Berkeley: University of California Press, pp. 133–57; J. Krieckhaus. 2006. "Democracy and Economic Growth: How Regional Context Influences Regime Effects." *British Journal of Political Science* 36 (2): 317–40.

2. Timothy Frye. 2002. "The Perils of Polarization: Economic Performance in the Post-Communist World." *World Politics* 54 (3): 308.

3. Stephen Knack and Philip Keefer. 1995. "Institutions and Economic Performance: Cross-Country Tests Using Alternative Institutional Measures." *Economics and Politics* 7 (4): 207–27; Daron Acemoglu, Simon Johnson, and James A. Robinson. 2001. "The Colonial Origins of Comparative Development: An Empirical Investigation." *American Economic Review* 91 (5): 1369–1401; William Easterly and Ross Levine. 2003. "Tropics, Germs, and Crops: How Endowments Influence

Economic Development." *Journal of Monetary Economic* 50: 3–39; Dani Rodrik, Arvind Subramanian, and Francesco Trebbi. 2004. "Institutions Rule: The Primacy of Institutions over Geography and Integration in Economic Development." *Journal of Economic Growth* 9 (2): 131–65; Daron Acemoglu and James A. Robinson. 2006. *Economic Origins of Dictatorship and Democracy*. New York: Cambridge University Press.

4. Stephen Haggard and Lydia Tiede. 2011. "The Rule of Law and Economic Growth: Where Are We?" *World Development* 39 (5): 673–85.

5. Peter Evans and J. E. Rauch. 1999. "Bureaucracy and Growth: A Cross-National Analysis of the Effects of 'Weberian' State Structures on Economic Growth." *American Sociological Review* 64 (5): 748–65; M. J. Kurtz and A. Schrank. 2007. "Growth and Governance: Models, Measures, and Mechanisms." *Journal of Politics* 69 (2): 538–54; J. Henderson, D. Hulme, H. Jalilian, and R. Phillips. 2007. "Bureaucratic Effects: 'Weberian' State Agencies and Poverty Reduction." *Sociology: The Journal of the British Sociological Association* 41 (3): 515–32.

6. Francis Fukuyama. 2004. *State-Building: Governance and World Order in the 21st Century*. Ithaca, NY: Cornell University Press.

7. H. Li, L. Squire, and H. F. Zou. 1998. "Explaining International and Inter-temporal Variations in Income Inequality." *Economic Journal* 108: 26–43.

8. Joseph T. Siegle, Michael Weinstein, and Morton Halperin. 2004. "Why Democracies Excel." *Foreign Affairs* 83 (5): 57–72; Morton Halperin, Joseph T. Siegle, and Michael Weinstein. 2005. *The Democracy Advantage*. New York: Routledge; Morton Halperin, Joseph T. Siegle, and Michael Weinstein. 2010. *The Democracy Advantage*. 2nd ed. New York: Routledge.

9. Michael Ross. 2006. "Is Democracy Good for the Poor?" *American Journal of Political Science* 50 (4): 860–74.

10. Casey B. Mulligan, R. Gil, and X. Sala-a-martin. 2004. "Do Democracies Have Different Public Policies Than Non-democracies?" *Journal of Economic Perspectives* 18 (1): 51–74.

11. Edward D. Mansfield and Jack Snyder. 2007. *Electing to Fight: Why Emerging Democracies Go to War*. Cambridge, MA: MIT Press.

12. UNDP. 2007. *Democratic Governance Annual Report*. New York: UNDP; UNDP. 2009. *Annual Report*. New York: UNDP. For more details of the historical shift from public administration to democratic governance, see Edward Neuman and Roland Rich, eds. 2004. *The UN Role in Promoting Democracy: Between Ideals and Reality*. Tokyo: UN University Press; Craig N. Murphy. 2006. *The United Nations Development Programme: A Better Way?* Cambridge: Cambridge University Press.

13. USAID. 2010. "Where Does USAID's Money Go?" http://www.usaid.gov/policy/budget/money/. See also Steven E. Finkel, Anibal S. Perez-Linan, and Mitchell A. Seligson. 2006. *Effects of U.S. Foreign Assistance on Democracy Building: Results of a Cross-National Quantitative Study*. Nashville, TN: USAID/Vanderbilt University; Steven E. Finkel, Aníbal S. Pérez Liñan, and Mitchell A. Seligson. 2007. "The Effects of U.S. Foreign Assistance on Democracy Building, 1990–2003." *World Politics* 59 (3): 404–40.

14. Richard Youngs. 2002. *The European Union and the Promotion of Democracy*. Oxford: Oxford University Press.

15. Pippa Norris. 2011. *Democratic Deficits*. New York: Cambridge University Press, table 5.3

16. Larry Diamond and Marc F. Plattner. 2008. "Introduction." In Larry Diamond and Marc F. Plattner, eds. *How People View Democracy*. Baltimore: Johns Hopkins University Press.

17. Mark Tessler. 2002. "Do Islamic Orientations Influence Attitudes toward Democracy in the Arab World? Evidence from Egypt, Jordan, Morocco, and Algeria." *International Journal of Comparative Sociology* 43 (3–5): 229–49; Mark Tessler and E. Gao. 2005. "Gauging Arab Support for Democracy." *Journal of Democracy* 16 (3): 83–97; Amaney Jamal and Mark Tessler. 2008. "The Arab Aspiration for Democracy." In Larry Diamond and Marc F. Plattner, eds., *How People View Democracy*. Baltimore: Johns Hopkins University Press, table 1.

18. Larry Diamond and Marc F. Plattner, eds. 2008. "Introduction." In Larry Diamond and Marc F. Plattner, eds., *How People View Democracy*. Baltimore: Johns Hopkins University Press.

19. Pippa Norris. 2011. *Democratic Deficit*. New York: Cambridge University Press.

Select Bibliography

Acemoglu, Daron and Simon Johnson. 2005. "Unbundling Institutions." *Journal of Political Economy* 113 (5): 949–95.

Acemoglu, Daron, Simon Johnson, and James A. Robinson. 2001. "The Colonial Origins of Comparative Development: An Empirical Investigation." *American Economic Review* 91 (5): 1369–1401.

2002. "Reversal of Fortune: Geography and Institutions in the Making of the Modern Income Distribution." *Quarterly Journal of Econometrics* 118: 1231–94.

2008. "Income and Democracy." *American Economic Review* 98 (3): 808–42.

Acemoglu, Daron and James A. Robinson. 2000. "Why Did the West Extend the Franchise? Democracy, Inequality and Growth in Historical Perspective." *Quarterly Journal of Economics* 115 (4): 1167–99.

2001. "A Theory of Political Transitions." *American Economic Review* 91 (4): 938–63.

2006. *Economic Origins of Dictatorship and Democracy.* New York: Cambridge University Press.

Adcock, Robert and David Collier. 2001. "Measurement Validity: A Shared Standard for Qualitative and Quantitative Research." *American Political Science Review* 95 (3): 529–46.

Alcaniz, Isabella and Timothy Hellwig. 2011. "Who's to Blame? The Distribution of Responsibility in Developing Democracies." *British Journal of Political Science* 41 (2): 389–411.

Alesina, Alberto, Arnaud Devleeschauwer, William Easterly, Sergio Kurlat, and Romain Wacziarg. 2003. "Fractionalization." *Journal of Economic Growth* 8: 155–94.

Alesina, Alberto and Eliana La Ferrara. 2005. "Ethnic Diversity and Economic Performance." *Journal of Economic Literature* 43 (3): 762–800.

Alesina, Alberto and Enrico Spolaore. 2003. *The Size of Nations.* Cambridge, MA: MIT Press.

Alexander, Amy C. and Christian Welzel. 2011. "Measuring Effective Democracy: The Human Empowerment Approach." *Comparative Politics* 43 (3): 271–89.

Allison, Graham T. and R. P. Beschel. 1992. "Can the United States Promote Democracy?" *Political Science Quarterly* 107 (1): 81–98.

Almond, Gabriel A. and Sidney Verba. 1963. *The Civic Culture: Political Attitudes and Democracy in Five Nations.* Princeton, NJ: Princeton University Press.

eds. 1980. *The Civic Culture Revisited.* Boston: Little Brown.

Alonso, Sonia, John Keane, Wolfgang Merkel, and Maria Fotou, eds. 2011. *The Future of Representative Democracy.* New York: Cambridge University Press.

Alvarez, R. Michael, José Antonio Cheibub, Fernando Limongi, and Adam Przeworski. 1996. "Classifying Political Regimes." *Studies in International Comparative Development* 31: 3–36.

Alvarez, R. Michael, Thad E. Hall, and Susan D. Hyde, eds. 2008. *Election Fraud: Detecting and Deterring Electoral Manipulation.* Washington, DC: Brookings Institute.

Ames, Barry. 2001. *The Deadlock of Democracy in Brazil.* Ann Arbor: University of Michigan Press.

Amsden, Alice. 2001. *The Rise of the 'Rest': Challenges to the West from Late-industrializing Economies.* Oxford: Oxford University Press.

Anckar, D. and C. Anckar. 2000. "Democracies without Parties." *Comparative Political Studies* 33 (2): 225–47.

Anderson, Christopher J. 1995. *Blaming the Government: Citizens and the Economy in Five European Democracies.* New York: M. E. Sharpe.

Anderson, Christopher J. and Christine A. Guillory. 1997. "Political Institutions and Satisfaction with Democracy." *American Political Science Review* 91 (1): 66–81.

Andweg, Rudy B. 2000. "Consociational Democracy." *Annual Review of Politics* 3: 509–36.

Apaza, C. R. 2009. "Measuring Governance and Corruption through the Worldwide Governance Indicators: Critiques, Responses, and Ongoing Scholarly Discussion." *PS: Political Science & Politics* 42 (1): 139–43.

Arat, Zehra. 1988. "Democracy and Economic Development: Modernization Theory Revisited." *Comparative Politics* 21: 21–36.

Armingeon, Klaus. 2002. "The Effects of Negotiation Democracy: A Comparative Analysis." *European Journal of Political Research* 41: 81.

Armony, Ariel C. and Hector E. Schamis. 2005. "Babel in Democratization Studies." *Journal of Democracy* 16 (4): 113–28.

Avelino, George, David S. Brown, and Wendy Hunter. 2005. "The Effects of Capital Mobility, Trade Openness, and Democracy on Social Spending in Latin America 1980–1999." *American Journal of Political Science* 49 (3): 625–41.

Avritzer, Leonardo. 2009. *Participatory Institutions in Democratic Brazil.* Baltimore: Johns Hopkins University Press.

Back, Hanna and Axel Hadenius. 2008. "Democracy and State Capacity: Exploring a J-shaped Relationship." *Governance* 21 (1): 1–24.

Banducci, Susan A., Todd Donovan, and Jeffrey A. Karp. 2004. "Minority Representation, Empowerment, and Participation." *Journal of Politics* 66 (2): 534–56.

Banerjee, Abhijit and Ester Duflo. 2011. *Poor Economics: A Radical Rethinking of the Way to Fight Global Poverty.* New York: PublicAffairs.

Banks, Arthur S. 2008. *Cross-Polity Time-Series Database.* State University of New York–Binghampton. http://www.databanks.sitehosting.net.

Bardhan P. 1997. "Corruption and Development: A Review of Issues." *Journal of Economic Literature* 35 (3): 1320–46.

Barnes, Samuel and Max Kaase. 1979. *Political Action: Mass Participation in Five Western Democracies.* Beverley Hills, CA: Sage.

Barnes, Samuel and Janos Simon, eds. 1998. *The Post-Communist Citizen.* Budapest: Erasmus Foundation.

Baron, Stephen, John Field, and Tom Schuller, eds. 2000. *Social Capital: Critical Perspectives.* Oxford: Oxford University Press.

Barria, Lilian A. and Steven D. Roper. 2011. *The Development of Institutions of Human Rights: A Comparative Study*. New York: Palgrave Macmillan.

Barro, Robert J. 1996. "Democracy and Growth." *Journal of Economic Growth* 1 (1): 1–27.

1997. *Determinants of Economic Growth: A Cross-Country Empirical Study*. Cambridge, MA: MIT Press.

1999. "Determinants of Democracy." *Journal of Political Economy* 107 (6): 158–83.

2000. "Inequality and Growth in a Panel of Countries." *Journal of Economic Growth* 5 (1): 5–32.

2001. "Human Capital and Growth." *American Economic Review* 91 (2): 12–17.

Barry, Brian. 1975. "Review Article: Political Accommodation and Consociational Democracy." *British Journal of Political Science* 5 (4): 194.

Bartolini, Stephano and Peter Mair. 1990. *Identity, Competition, and Electoral Availability: The Stabilization of European Electorates, 1885–1985*. Cambridge: Cambridge University Press.

Bates, Robert H. 2009. *When Things Fall Apart: State Failure in Late-Century Africa*. Cambridge: Cambridge University Press.

Baum, Jeeyang Rhee. 2011. *Responsive Democracy: Increasing State Accountability in East Asia*. New York: Cambridge University Press.

Baum, Matthew A. and David A. Lake. 2003. "The Political Economy of Growth: Democracy and Human Capital." *American Journal of Political Science* 47 (2): 333–47.

Beck, Nathaniel. 2001. "Time-Series/Cross-Section Data: What Have We Learned in the Past Few Years?" *Annual Review of Political Science* 4: 271–93.

Beck, Nathaniel and Jonathan Katz. 1995. "What to Do (and Not to Do) with Time-Series Cross-Section Data." *American Political Science Review* 89 (3): 634–47.

1996. "Nuisance vs. Substance: Specifying and Estimating Time-Series Cross-Sectional Models." In J. Freeman, ed., *Political Analysis*. Ann Arbor: University of Michigan Press.

Beck, Nathaniel, Jonathan Katz, and Richard Tucker. 1998. "Taking Time Seriously: Time-Series-Cross-Section Analysis with a Binary Dependent Variable." *American Journal of Political Science* 42 (4): 1260–88.

Beetham, David. 1994. *Defining and Measuring Democracy*. London: Sage.

2001. *International IDEA Handbook of Democracy Assessment*. New York: Kluwer.

Bell, Daniel. 1999. *The Coming of Post-Industrial Society: A Venture in Social Forecasting*. New York: Basic.

Bendix, Reinhard. 1978. *Kings or People: Power and the Mandate to Rule*. Berkeley: University of California Press.

Berendsen, Bernard and Paul H. Collier. 2008. *Democracy and Development*. Amsterdam: KIT.

Berglund, Sten and Jan A. Dellenbrant. 1994. *The New Democracies in Eastern Europe: Party Systems and Political Cleavages*. Aldershot: Edward Elgar.

Berg-Schlosser, Dietrich and Gisèle De Meur. 1994. "Conditions of Democracy in Interwar Europe: A Boolean Test of Major Hypotheses." *Comparative Politics* 26 (3): 253–80.

Berman, Sheri. 2007. "The Vain Hope of 'Correct' Timing'." *Journal of Democracy* 18 (3): 14–17.

Bermeo, Nancy. 2002. "The Import of Institutions." *Journal of Democracy* 13 (12): 96–110.

2003. *Ordinary People in Extraordinary Times: The Citizenry and the Breakdown of Democracy.* Princeton, NJ: Princeton University Press.

Bernhard, Michael, Christopher Reenock, and Timothy Nordstrom. 2004. "The Legacy of Western Overseas Colonialism on Democratic Survival." *International Studies Quarterly* 48 (1): 225–50.

Besley, Timothy and R. Burgess. 2002. "The Political Economy of Government Responsiveness: Theory and Evidence from India." *Quarterly Journal of Economics* 117 (4): 1415–51.

Besley, Timothy and Rajshri Jayaraman. 2011. *Institutional Microeconomics of Development.* Cambridge, MA: MIT Press.

Besley, Timothy and Andrea Prat. 2006. "Handcuffs for the Grabbing Hand? Media Capture and Government Accountability." *American Economic Review* 96 (3): 720–36.

Bevir, Mark. 2010. *Democratic Governance.* Princeton, NJ: Princeton University Press.

Bickel, Robert. 2007. *Multilevel Analysis for Applied Research: It's Just Regression!* New York: Guilford Press.

Bielasiak, Jack. 2002. "The Institutionalization of Electoral and Party Systems in Post-Communist States." *Comparative Politics* 34 (2): 189.

Birdsall Nancy, Dani Rodrik, and Arvind Subramanian. 2005. "How to Help Poor Countries." *Foreign Affairs* 84 (4): 136–52.

Blais, André. 1988. "The Classification of Electoral Systems." *European Journal of Political Research* 16: 99–110.

2000. *To Vote or Not to Vote? The Merits and Limits of Rational Choice Theory.* Pittsburgh, PA: University of Pittsburgh Press.

Blais, André and R. Kenneth Carty. 1991. "The Psychological Impact of Electoral Laws: Measuring Duverger's Elusive Factor." *British Journal of Political Science* 21 (1): 79–93.

Blais, André, Louis Massicote, and Agnieszka Dobrzynska. 1997. "Direct Presidential Elections: A World Summary." *Electoral Studies* 16 (4): 441–55.

Blais, André, Louis Massicote, and A. Yoshinaka. 2001. "Deciding Who Has the Right to Vote: A Comparative Analysis of Election Laws." *Electoral Studies* 20 (1): 41–62.

Blanton, Shannon L. 2000. "Promoting Human Rights and Democracy in the Developing World: U.S. Rhetoric versus U.S. Arms Exports." *American Journal of Political Science* 44 (1): 123–31.

Bogaards, Matthijs. 2010. "Measures of Democratization: From Degree to Type to War." *Political Research Quarterly* 63 (2): 475–88.

Bogaards, Matthijs and Fransoise Boucek. 2011. *Dominant Political Parties and Democracy: Concepts, Measures, Cases, and Comparisons.* New York: Routledge.

Bogdanor, Vernon and David Butler, eds. 1983. *Democracy and Elections.* Cambridge: Cambridge University Press.

Boix, Carles. 1999. "Setting the Rules of the Game: The Choice of Electoral Systems in Advanced Democracies." *American Political Science Review* 93 (3): 609–24.

2001. "Democracy, Development and the Public Sector." *American Journal of Political Science* 45: 1–17.

2003. *Democracy and Redistribution.* Cambridge: Cambridge University Press.

Bollen, Kenneth A. 1979. "Political Democracy and the Timing of Development." *American Sociological Review* 44: 572–87.

1980. "Issues in the Comparative Measurement of Political Democracy." *American Sociological Review* 45: 370–90.

1983. "World System Position, Dependency and Democracy: The Cross-National Evidence." *American Sociological Review* 48: 468–79.

1991. "Political Democracy: Conceptual and Measurement Traps." In Alex Inkeles, ed., *On Measuring Democracy: Its Consequences and Concomitants*. New Brunswick, NJ: Transaction, pp. 3–20.

1993. "Liberal Democracy: Validity and Method Factors in Cross-National Measures." *American Journal of Political Science* 37: 1207–30.

Bollen, Kenneth A. and Robert W. Jackman. 1985. "Political Democracy and the Size Distribution of Income." *American Sociological Review* 50: 438–58.

1989. "Democracy, Stability and Dichotomies." *American Sociological Review* 54: 612–21.

1995. "Income Inequality and Democratization Revisited: Comment on Muller." *American Sociological Review* 60: 983–9.

Bollen, Kenneth A. and Pamela Paxton. 2000. "Subjective Measures of Liberal Democracy." *Comparative Political Studies* 33 (1): 58–86.

Boone, P. 1996. "Politics and the Effectiveness of Foreign Aid." *European Economic Review* 40: 289–329.

Booth, David. 2011. "Aid, Institutions and Governance: What Have We Learned?" *Development Policy Review*, 29 (5): 26.

Bourdieu, Pierre. 1970. *Reproduction in Education, Culture and Society*. London: Sage.

Brady, David, Andrew S. Fullerton, and Jennifer Moren Cross. 2009. "Putting Poverty in Political Context: A Multi-Level Analysis of Adult Poverty across 18 Affluent Democracies." *Social Forces* 88 (1): 271–99.

Brady, Henry and David Collier. 2004. *Rethinking Social Inquiry: Diverse Tools, Shared Standards*. New York: Rowman & Littlefield.

Brancati, Dawn. 2006. "Decentralization: Fueling the Fire or Dampening the Flames of Ethnic Conflict and Secessionism?" *International Organization* 60 (3): 651–85.

2007. *Design over Conflict: Managing Ethnic Conflict and Secessionism through Decentralization*. New York: Cambridge University Press.

Bratton, Michael and Nicholas van de Walle. 1997. *Democratic Experiments in Africa*. Cambridge: Cambridge University Press.

Brautigam, Deborah. 1992. "Governance, Economy, and Foreign Aid." *Studies in Comparative International Development* 27 (3): 325.

2000. *Aid Dependence and Governance*. Stockholm: Almqvist and Wiksell International.

Bremer, Ian. 2006. *The J Curve*. New York: Simon & Schuster.

Brenner, Y. S., Hartmut Kaelble, and Mark Thomas, eds. 1991. *Income Distribution in Historical Perspective*. Cambridge: Cambridge University Press.

Brown, David S. 1999. "Democracy and Social Spending in Latin America, 1980–92." *American Political Science Review* 93 (4): 779–90.

1999. "Reading, Writing, and Regime Type: Democracy's Impact on Primary School Enrollment." *Political Research Quarterly* 52 (4): 681–707.

2004. "Democracy and Gender Inequality in Education: A Cross-National Examination." *British Journal of Political Science* 34: 137–92.

Brown, David S. and Wendy Hunter. 2004. "Democracy and Human Capital Formation." *Comparative Political Studies* 37 (7): 842–64.

Brown, Michael E., ed. 2001. *Nationalism and Ethnic Conflict*. Cambridge, MA: MIT Press.

Brown, Nathan J. *The Dynamics of Democratization: Dictatorship, Development, and Diffusion*. Baltimore: Johns Hopkins University Press.

Brownlee, Jason. 2007. *Authoritarianism in an Age of Democratization*. New York: Cambridge University Press.

Brunetti, A. and B. Weder. 2003. "A Free Press Is Bad News for Corruption." *Journal of Public Economics* 87 (7–8): 1801–24.

Brunk, Gregory C., Gregory A. Caldeira, and Michael S. Lewis-Beck. 1987. "Capitalism, Socialism, and Democracy: An Empirical Inquiry." *European Journal of Political Research* 15: 459–70.

Bueno de Mesquita, Bruce and Hilton Root. 2000. *Governing for Prosperity*. New Haven, CT: Yale University Press.

Bueno de Mesquita, Bruce, Alastar Smith, Randolph M. Siverson, and James D. Morrow. 2003. *The Logic of Political Survival*. Cambridge, MA: MIT Press.

Bunch, Valerie and Sharon I. Wolchik. 2006. "International Diffusion and Post-Communist Electoral Revolutions." *Communist and Post-Communist Studies* 39 (3): 283–304.

Burgoon, B. 2006. "On Welfare and Terror: Social Welfare Policies and Political-Economic Roots of Terrorism." *Journal of Conflict Resolution* 50 (2): 176–203.

Burkhart, Ross E. 1997. "Comparative Democracy and Income Distribution: Shape and Direction of the Causal Arrow." *Journal of Politics* 59 (1): 148–64.

Burkhart, Ross E. and Michael S. Lewis-Beck. 1994. "Comparative Democracy: The Economic Development Thesis." *American Political Science Review* 88: 903–10.

Burnell, Peter, ed. 2000. *Democracy Assistance: International Co-operation for Democratization*. London: Frank Cass.

Burnside, Craig and David Dollar. 2000. "Aid, Policies, and Growth." *American Economic Review* 90 (4): 847–68.

Butkiewicz, James L. and Halit Yanikkaya. 2006. "Institutional Quality and Economic Growth: Maintenance of the Rule of Law or Democratic Institutions, or Both?" *Economic Modelling* 23 (4): 648–61.

Byman, Daniel L. 2002. *Keeping the Peace: Lasting Solutions to Ethnic Conflict*. Baltimore: Johns Hopkins University Press.

Cain, Bruce E., Russell J. Dalton, and Susan E. Scarrow. 2004. *Democracy Transformed? Expanding Political Opportunities in Advanced Industrial Democracies*. Oxford: Oxford University Press.

Call, Charles T. and Vanessa Wyeth. 2008. *Building States to Build Peace*. Boulder, CO: Lynne Rienner.

Campbell, Colin and M.J. Wyszimirski, eds. 1991. *Executive Leadership in Anglo-American Systems*. Pittsburgh, PA: University of Pittsburgh Press.

Caplan, Richard D. 2005. *International Governance of War-Torn Territories: Rule and Reconstruction*. Oxford and New York: Oxford University Press.

Caraway, Teri L. 2004. "Inclusion and Democratization: Class, Gender, Race, and the Extension of Suffrage." *Comparative Politics* 36 (4): 443–60.

Cardoso, Fernando Henrique and Enzo Faletto. 1979. *Dependency and Development in Latin America*. Berkeley: University of California Press.

Carothers, Thomas. 1999. *Aiding Democracy Abroad*. Washington, DC: Carnegie Endowment for International Peace.

2002. "The End of the Transition Paradigm." *Journal of Democracy* 13: 5–21.

2003. "Promoting Democracy and Fighting Terror." *Foreign Affairs* 82 (1): 84–97.

2004. *Critical Mission: Essays on Democracy Promotion.* Washington, DC: Carnegie Endowment for International Peace.

2007. "The 'Sequencing' Fallacy." *Journal of Democracy* 18 (1): 12–27.

Carothers, Thomas and Marina Ottaway, eds. 2005. *Uncharted Journey: Promoting Democracy in the Middle East.* Washington, DC: Carnegie Endowment for International Peace.

Cederman, Lars-Erik, Simon Hug, and Andreas Wenger. 2008. "Democratization and War in Political Science." *Democratization* 15 (3): 509–24.

Chan, Sylvia. 2002. *Liberalism, Democracy and Development.* New York: Cambridge University Press.

Chandra, Kanchan. 2001. "Ethnic Bargains, Group Instability, and Social Choice Theory." *Politics & Society* 29 (3): 337–62.

2004. *Why Ethnic Parties Succeed: Patronage and Ethnic Headcounts in India.* Cambridge: Cambridge University Press.

2005. "Ethnic Parties and Democratic Stability." *Perspectives on Politics.* 3 (2): 235–52.

Charron, Nicholas and Victor Lapuente. 2010. "Does Democracy Produce Quality of Government?" *European Journal of Political Research* 49: 443–70.

Chase-Dunn, Christopher. 1975. "The Effects of International Economic Dependence on Development and Inequality: A Cross-National Study." *American Sociological Review* 40: 720–38.

Cheibub, José. 2002. "Minority Governments, Deadlock Situations, and the Survival of Presidential Democracies." *Comparative Political Studies* 35 (3): 284–312.

2002. "Presidentialism and Democratic Performance." In Andrew Reynolds, ed., *Constitutional Design: Institutional Design, Conflict Management, and Democracy in the Late Twentieth Century.* Oxford: Oxford University Press, pp. 104–40.

2007. *Presidentialism, Parliamentarism, and Democracy.* New York: Cambridge University Press.

Cheibub, José and Jennifer Gandhi. 2004. "A Six-fold Measure of Democracies and Dictatorships." Paper presented at the Annual Meeting of the American Political Science Association.

Cheibub, José and Fernando Limongi. 2002. "Democratic Institutions and Regime Survival: Parliamentary and Presidential Democracies Reconsidered." *Annual Review of Political Science* 5: 151–79.

Cheibub, José, Adam Przeworski, and S. M. Saiegh. 2004. "Government Coalitions and Legislative Success under Presidentialism and Parliamentarism." *British Journal of Political Science* 34: 565–87.

Chesterman, Simon. 2004. *You, the People: The United Nations, Transitional Administration, and State-Building.* New York: Oxford University Press.

Chirot, Daniel. 1981. "Changing Fashions in the Study of the Social Causes of Economic and Political Change." In J. F. Short, ed., *The State of Sociology: Problems and Prospects.* London: Sage, pp. 259–82.

2001. "A Clash of Civilizations or of Paradigms? Theorizing Progress and Social Change." *International Sociology* 16 (3): 341–60.

Chong, Alberto and Mark Gradstein. 2007. "Inequality and Institutions." *Review of Economics and Statistics* 89 (3): 454–65.

Chu, Yin-wah and Siu-lun Wong. *East Asia's New Democracies: Deepening, Reversal, Non-Liberal Alternatives.* New York: Routledge.

Chua, Amy. 2004. *World on Fire: How Exporting Free Market Democracy Breeds Ethnic Hatred and Global Instability*. New York: Anchor.

Cingranelli, David L. and Thomas E. Pasquarello. 1985. "Human Rights Practices and the Distribution of U.S. Foreign Aid to Latin America." *American Journal of Political Science* 29 (3): 539–63.

Clague, Christopher, Suzanne Gleason, and Stephen Knack. 2001. "Determinants of Lasting Democracy in Poor Countries: Culture, Development, and Institutions." *Annals of the American Academy of Political and Social Science* 573: 16–41.

Clarke, Harold D., Alan Kornberg, C. McIntyre, P. Bauer-Kaase, and Max Kaase. 1999. "The Effect of Economic Priorities on the Measurement of Value Change: New Experimental Evidence." *American Political Science Review* 93 (3): 637–47.

Clarke, Kevin A. and Randall W. Stone. 2008. "Democracy and the Logic of Political Survival." *American Political Science Review* 102 (3): 387–92.

Coakley, John, ed. 1993. *The Territorial Management of Ethnic Conflict*. London: Frank Cass.

Cohen, Frank. 1997. "Proportional versus Majoritarian Ethnic Conflict Management in Democracies." *Comparative Political Studies* 30 (5): 607–30.

Collier, David and Robert Adcock. 1999. "Democracy and Dichotomies: A Pragmatic Approach to Choices about Concepts." *Annual Review of Political Science* 1: 537–65.

Collier, Paul. 2009. *Wars, Guns, and Votes: Democracy in Dangerous Places*. New York: Harper Collins.

  2010. *Conflict, Political Accountability, and Aid*. New York: Routledge.

Collier, Paul, Anke Hoeffler, and Dominic Rohner. 2009. "Beyond Greed and Grievance: Feasibility and Civil War." *Oxford Economic Papers* 61: 1–27.

Collier, Paul and Nicholas Sambanis, eds. 2005. *Understanding Civil War*. Washington, DC: World Bank.

Collier, Ruth Berins. 1999. *Paths toward Democracy: Working Class and Elites in Western Europe and South America*. New York: Cambridge University Press.

Colomer, Joseph M., ed. 2004. *Handbook of Electoral System Choice*. New York: Palgrave Macmillan.

Cooper, Andrew F. and Thomas Legler. 2007. *Intervention without Intervening? The OAS Defense and Promotion of Democracy in the Americas*. New York: Palgrave Macmillan.

Coppedge, Michael. 1999. "Thickening Thin Concepts and Theories: Combining Large N and Small in Comparative Politics." *Comparative Politics* 31 (4): 465–76.

Coppedge, Michael and Wolfgang Reinicke. 1990. "A Scale of Polyarchy." *Studies in Comparative and International Development* 25 (1): 51–72.

  1991. "Measuring Polyarchy." In Alex Inkeles, ed., *On Measuring Democracy*. New Brunswick, NJ: Transaction, pp. 47–68.

Coulter, Philip B. 1975. *Social Mobilization and Democracy: A Macro-quantitative Analysis of Global and Regional Models*. Lexington, KY: Lexington.

Cox, Gary. 1997. *Making Votes Count*. Cambridge: Cambridge University Press.

Cox, Kevin R. and Tohit Negi. 2010. "The State and the Question of Development in Sub-Saharan Africa." *Review of African Political Economy* 37 (123): 71–85.

Cox, Michael, G. John Ikenberry and Takashi Inoguchi. 2002. *American Democracy Promotion*. New York: Oxford University Press.

Crawford, Gordon. 1997. "Foreign Aid and Political Conditionality: Issues of Effectiveness and Consistency." *Democratization* 4 (3): 69–108.

Creevey, Lucy, Paul Ngomo, and Richard Vergroff. 2005. "Party Politics and Different Paths to Democratic Transitions: A Comparison of Benin and Senegal." *Party Politics* 11 (4): 471–93.

Cutright, Phillips. 1963. "National Political Development: Measurement and Analysis." *American Sociological Review* 28: 253–64.

Daalder, Hans. 1974. "The Consociational Democracy Theme." *World Politics* 26: 604–21.

Dahl, Robert A. 1971. *Polyarchy: Participation and Opposition.* New Haven, CT: Yale University Press.

   1989. *Democracy and Its Critics.* New Haven, CT: Yale University Press.

   1998. *On Democracy.* New Haven, CT: Yale University Press.

Dahlstrom, Carl, Victor Lapuente, and Jan Teorell. 2010. *Dimensions of Bureaucracy: A Cross National Dataset on the Structure and Behavior of Public Administration.* Stockholm: Quality of Governance Institute Working Paper Series 2010: 13.

Dalton, Russell J. and Martin P. Wattenberg, eds. 2000. *Parties without Partisans: Political Change in Advanced Industrial Democracies.* Oxford: Oxford University Press.

Dashti-Gibson, Jaleh, Patricia Davis, and Benjamin Radcliff. 1997. "On the Determinants of the Success of Economic Sanctions: An Empirical Analysis." *American Journal of Political Science* 41 (2): 608–18.

Database of Political Institutions. 2010. http://www.worldbank.org/research/bios/pkeefer.htm.

Davenport, Christian. 2007. "State Repression and Political Order." *Annual Review of Political Science* 10: 1–23.

   2007. *State Repression and the Domestic Democratic Peace.* Cambridge: Cambridge University Press.

Davoia, Antonio, Joshy Easaw, and Andrew MacKay. 2004. "Inequality, Democracy and Institutions: A Critical Review of Recent Research." *World Development* 38: 2.

Della Porta, Donnatella. 1999. *Corrupt Exchanges.* New York: Aldine de Gruyter.

Della Porta, Donnatella and Yves Meny. 1996. *Democracy and Corruption in Europe.* New York: Pinter.

Dellepiane-Avellaneda, Sebastian. 2009. "Review Article: Good Governance, Institutions and Economic Development: Beyond the Conventional Wisdom." *British Journal of Political Science* 40: 195–224.

Denters, Bas and Lawrence Rose, eds. 2005. *Comparing Local Governance: Trends and Developments.* London: Palgrave/Macmillan.

Deutsch, Karl W. 1964. "Social Mobilization and Political Development." *American Political Science Review* 55: 493–514.

Deutscher, Irwin. 2002. *Accommodating Diversity: National Policies that Prevent Conflict.* Lanham, MD: Lexington.

Di Palma, Guiseppe. 1990. *To Craft Democracies: An Essay on Democratic Transitions.* Berkeley: University of California Press.

Diamond, Jared, 2005. *Collapse: How Societies Choose to Fail or Succeed.* New York: Viking, Penguin Group.

Diamond, Larry. 1992. "Economic Development and Democracy Reconsidered." *American Behavioral Scientist* 35: 450–99.

   1992. "Economic Development and Democracy Reconsidered." In Gary Marks and Larry Diamond, eds., *Reexamining Democracy.* Newbury Park: Sage, pp. 93–139.

1996. *Developing Democracy: Toward Consolidation.* Baltimore: Johns Hopkins University Press.

2002. "Thinking about Hybrid Regimes." *Journal of Democracy* 13 (2): 21–35.

Diamond, Larry and Richard Gunther. 2001. *Political Parties and Democracy.* Baltimore: Johns Hopkins Press.

Diamond, Larry, Mark Plattner, and Daniel Brumberg, eds. 2003. *Islam and Democracy in the Middle East.* Baltimore: Johns Hopkins Press.

Dixon, William J. 1994. "Democracy and the Peaceful Settlement of International Conflict." *American Political Science Review* 88 (1): 14–32.

Dobbins, James, Seth G. Jones, Keith Crane, Andrew Rathmell, Brett Steele, Richard Teltschik, and Anga R. Timilsina. 2005. *The UN's Role in Nation-Building: From the Congo to Iraq.* Santa Monica, CA: Rand Corporation.

Doig, Alan. 2000. *Corruption and Democratization.* London: Frank Cass.

Dollar, David and Lant Pritchett. 1998 *Assessing Aid: What Works, What Doesn't, and Why.* New York: Oxford University Press.

Dollar, David and V. Levine. "The Increasing Selectivity of Foreign Aid, 1984–2003." *World Development* 34 (12): 2034–46.

Domingues, Jorge and Michael Shifter, eds. 2003. *Constructing Democratic Governance in Latin America.* 2nd ed. Baltimore: Johns Hopkins University Press.

Doorenspleet, Renske. 1997. "Political Democracy: A Cross-National Quantitative Analysis of Modernization and Dependency Theories." *Acta Politica* 32: 349–74.

2000. "Reassessing the Three Waves of Democratization." *World Politics* 52: 384–406.

2002. "Development, Class and Democracy: Is There a Relationship?" In G. Hyden and O. Elgstrom, eds., *Development and Democracy.* London: Routledge, pp. 48–64.

2005. *Democratic Transitions: Exploring the Structural Sources during the Fourth Wave.* Boulder, CO: Lynne Rienner.

Doucouliagos, Hristos and Mehmet Ali Ulubasoglu. 2008. "Democracy and Economic Growth: A Meta-analysis." *American Journal of Political Science* 52 (1): 61–83.

Doyle, Michael W. 2005. "Three Pillars of the Liberal Peace." *American Political Science Review* 99: 463–6.

Doyle, Michael W. and Nicholas Sambanis. 2006. *Making War and Building Peace.* Princeton, NJ: Princeton University Press.

Dunleavy, Patrick and Brendan O'Leary. 1987. *Theories of the State.* Basingstoke, UK: Macmillan.

Easterly, William. 2001. *The Elusive Quest for Growth.* Cambridge, MA: MIT Press.

2006. *The White Man's Burden.* New York: Penguin.

Easterly, William and Ross Levine. 1997. "Africa's Growth Tragedy: Policies and Ethnic Divisions." *Quarterly Journal of Economics* 111 (4): 1203–50.

2003. "Tropics, Germs, and Crops: How Endowments Influence Economic Development." *Journal of Monetary Economics* 50: 3–39.

Ehtisham, Ahmad, ed. 2002. *Fiscal Decentralization.* London: Routledge.

Eisenstadt, Samuel N. 1973. *Traditional Patrimonialism and Modern Neopatrimonialism.* Beverly Hills, CA: Sage.

Elazar, Daniel. 1994. *Federal Systems of the World: A Handbook of Federal, Confederal and Autonomy Arrangements.* Essex, UK: Longman.

Elbadawi, Ibrahim and Nicholas Sambanis. 2002. "How Much War Will We See? Estimating the Prevalence of Civil War, 1960–1999." *Journal of Conflict Resolution* 46: 307–44.

Elgstram, Ole and Goran Hydan. 2002. *Development and Democracy: What Have We Learned and How?* New York: Routledge.

Elkins, Zachary. 2000. "Gradations of Democracy? Empirical Tests of Alternative Conceptualizations." *American Journal of Political Science* 44 (2): 293–300.

Elkins, Zachary and John Sides. 2007. "Can Institutions Build Unity in Multiethnic States?" *American Political Science Review* 101 (4): 1–16.

Elkit, Jorgen and Palle Svensson. 1997. "What Makes Elections Free and Fair?" *Journal of Democracy* 8 (3): 32–46.

Engerman, Stanley L. and Kenneth L. Sokoloff. 2008. "Debating the Role of Institutions in Political and Economic Development: Theory, History, and Findings." *Annual Review of Political Science* 11: 119–35.

Erk, Jan. 2006. "Does Federalism Really Matter?" *Comparative Politics* 39 (1): 103.

Esping-Andersen, Gøsta. 1990. *The Three Worlds of Welfare Capitalism.* Princeton, NJ: Princeton University Press.

Esposito, John L., ed. 1997. *Political Islam: Revolution, Radicalism or Reform?* Boulder, CO: Lynne Reinner.

Esposito, John L. and John O. Voll. 1996. *Islam and Democracy.* Oxford: Oxford University Press.

Eubank, William Lee and Leonard Weinberg. 2001. "Terrorism and Democracy: Perpetrators and Victims." *Terrorism and Political Violence* 13 (1): 108–18.

Evans, Peter and James E. Rauch. 1999. "Bureaucracy and Growth: A Cross-National Analysis of the Effects of 'Weberian' State Structures on Economic Growth." *American Sociological Review* 64 (5): 748–65.

Fearon, James D. and David D. Laitin. 1996. "Explaining Interethnic Cooperation." *American Political Science Review* 90 (4): 715–35.

2003. "Ethnicity, Insurgency, and Civil War." *American Political Science Review* 97 (1): 75–90.

2004. "Neo-trusteeship and the Problem of Weak States." *International Security* 29 (4): 5–43.

Feng, Yi. 1997. "Democracy, Political Stability and Economic Growth." *British Journal of Political Science* 27: 391–418.

2003. *Democracy, Governance and Economic Growth: Theory and Evidence.* Cambridge, MA: MIT Press.

Feng, Yi and I. Gizelis. 2002. "Building Political Consensus and Distributing Resources: A Trade-off or Compatible Choice?" *Economic Development and Cultural Change* 51 (1): 217–36.

Feng, Yi and P. J. Zak. 1999. "Determinants of Democratic Transitions." *Journal of Conflict Resolution* 43 (2): 162–77.

Filmer, Deon and Lant Pritchett. 1999. "The Impact of Public Spending on Health: Does Money Matter?" *Social Science and Medicine* 49 (10): 1309–23.

Finkel, Steven E., Anibal Perez-Linan, and Mitchell A. Seligson. 2006. *Effects of U.S. Foreign Assistance on Democracy Building: Results of a Cross-National Quantitative Study.* Nashville, TN: USAID/Vanderbilt University.

Fish, M. Stephen. 2006. "Stronger Legislatures, Stronger Democracies." *Journal of Democracy* 17 (1): 5–20.

Fisher, Steven D. and Sara B. Hobolt. 2010. "Coalition Government and Electoral Accountability." *Electoral Studies* 29 (3): 358–69.

Foley, Michael and Bob Edwards. 1998. "Beyond Tocqueville: Civil Society and Social Capital in Comparative Perspective." *American Behavioral Scientist* 42 (1): 5–20.

Fortin, Jessica. 2010. "A Tool to Evaluate State Capacity in Post-Communist Countries, 1989–2006." *European Journal of Political Research* **49** (5): 654–86.

Fortna, Virginia Page. 2004. "Does Peacekeeping Keep Peace? International Intervention and the Duration of Peace after Civil War." *International Studies Quarterly* **48** (2): 269–92.

Fortna, Virginia Page and Lise Morjé Howard. 2008. "Pitfalls and Prospects in the Peacekeeping Future." *Annual Review of Political Science* **11**: 283–301.

Foweraker, Joe and Roman Krznaric. 2000. "Measuring Liberal Democratic Performance: An Empirical and Conceptual Critique." *Political Studies* **48**: 759–87.

Fox, Jonathan. 2001. "Two Civilizations and Ethnic Conflict: Islam and the West." *Journal of Peace Research* **38** (4): 459–72.

Fraile, L. 2009. "Lessons from Latin America's Neo-Liberal Experiment: An Overview of Labour and Social Policies since the 1980s." *International Labour Review* **148** (3): 215–33.

Franco, A., C. Alvarez-Dardet, and M. T. Ruiz. 2004. "Effect of Democracy on Health." *British Medical Journal* **329**: 1421–3.

Freedom House. *Democracy's Century.* http://www.freedomhouse.org/reports/century. html.

   Various years. *Freedom in the World.* www.freedomhouse.org.

Frey, R. S. and A. Al-Raumi. 1999. "Political Democracy and the Physical Quality of Life: The Cross-National Evidence." *Social Indicators Research* **47** (1): 73–98.

Friedman, Milton. 1958. "Foreign Economic Aid: Means and Objectives." *Yale Review* **47** (4): 500–16.

Frye, Timothy. 1997. "A Politics of Institutional Choice: Post-Communist Presidencies." *Comparative Political Studies* **30**: 523.

Fukuyama, Francis. 1992. *The End of History and the Last Man.* New York: Free Press.
   1995. *Trust: The Social Virtues and the Creation of Prosperity.* New York: Free Press.
   2004. "The Imperative of State-Building." *Journal of Democracy* **15** (2): 17–31.
   2004. *State-Building: Governance and World Order in the 21st Century.* Ithaca, NY: Cornell University Press.
   2004. "Stateness First." *Journal of Democracy* **16** (1): 84–8.
   2007. "Liberalism versus State-Building." *Journal of Democracy* **18** (3): 10–13.
   2011. *The Origins of Political Order: From Prehuman Times to the French Revolution.* New York: Farrar, Straus & Giroux.

Gagnon, Alain-G. and James Tully, eds. 2001. *Multinational Democracies.* New York: Cambridge University Press.

Gallagher, Michael and Paul Mitchell, eds. 2005. *The Politics of Electoral Systems.* Oxford: Oxford University Press.

Gasiorowski, Mark J. 1995. "Economic Crisis and Political Regime Change: An Event History Analysis." *American Political Science Review* **89** (4): 882–97.

Gasiorowski, Mark J. and Timothy J. Power. 1997. "Institutional Design and Democratic Consolidation in the Third World." *Comparative Political Studies* **30** (2): 123–55.
   1998. "The Structural Determinants of Democratic Consolidation." *Comparative Political Studies* **31**: 740–71.

Gastil, Raymond D. 1979. *Freedom in the World: Political Rights and Civil Liberties.* Washington, DC: Freedom House.
   1991. "The Comparative Survey of Freedom: Experiences and Suggestions." In A. Inkeles, ed., *On Measuring Democracy.* New Brunswick, NJ: Transaction, pp. 21–46.

Geddes, Barbara. 2003. *Paradigms and Sand Castles: Theory Building and Research Design in Comparative Politics.* Ann Arbor: University of Michigan Press.

Geering, John and Strom C. Thacker. 2004. "Political Institutions and Corruption: The Role of Unitarism and Parliamentarism." *British Journal of Political Science* 34: 295–330.

George, Alexander L. and Andrew Bennett. 2004. *Case Studies and Theory Development.* Cambridge, MA: MIT Press.

Gerges, Fawaz A. 1999. *America and Political Islam: Clash of Cultures or Clash of Interests?* New York: Cambridge University Press.

Gerring, John, Philip Bond, William T. Barndt, and Carola Moreno. 2005. "Democracy and Economic Growth: A Historical Perspective." *World Politics* 57 (3): 323–64.

Ghani, Ashraf and Claire Lockhart. 2008. *Fixing Failed States: A Framework for Rebuilding a Fractured World.* Oxford: Oxford University Press.

Ghobarah, Hazem, Paul Huth, and Bruce Russett. 2004. "Comparative Public Health: The Political Economy of Human Misery and Well-being." *International Studies Quarterly* 48: 73–94.

Giannone, Diego. 2010. "Political and Ideological Aspects in the Measurement of Democracy: The Freedom House Case." *Democratization* 17 (1): 68–97.

Gill, Graeme. 2003. *The Nature and Development of the Modern State.* Basingtoke, UK: Palgrave.

Ginsburg, Thomas and Tamir Moustafa. 2008. *Rule by Law: The Politics of Courts in Authoritarian Regimes.* New York: Cambridge University Press.

Glaeser, Edward L., Rafael La Porta, Florencio Lopez-de-Silanes, and Andre Shleifer. 2004. "Do Institutions Cause Growth?" *Journal of Economic Growth* 9 (3): 271–303.

Gleditsch, Kristian and Michael D. Ward. 1997. "Double Take: A Re-examination of Democracy and Autocracy in Modern Polities." *Journal of Conflict Resolution* 41: 361–83.

2000. "War and Peace in Space and Time: The Role of Democratization." *International Studies Quarterly* 44 (1): 1–29.

Gleditsch, Kristian Skrede and Michael D. Ward. 2006. "Diffusion and the International Context of Democratization." *International Organization* 60: 911–33.

Goldner, Matthew. 2004. *Codebook: Democratic Electoral Systems Around the World 1945–2000.* https://files.nyu.edu/mrg217/public/codebook_es1.pdf.

2005. "Democratic Electoral Systems around the World, 1946–2000." *Electoral Studies* 24 (2): 103–21.

Goldsmith, Arthur A. 2007. "Is Governance Reform a Catalyst for Development?" *Governance* 20 (2): 165–86.

Goldsmith, Michael. 2002. "Central Control over Local Government: A Western European Comparison." *Local Government Studies* 28 (3): 91.

Goldstone, Jack A., Robert H. Bates, David L. Epstein, Ted Robert Gurr, Michael B. Lustik, Monty G. Marshall, Jay Ulfelder, and Mark Woodward. 2010. "A Global Model for Forecasting Political Instability." *American Journal of Political Science* 54 (1): 190–208.

Gonick, Lev S. and Robert M. Rosh. 1988. "The Structural Constraints of the World-Economy on National Political Development." *Comparative Political Studies* 21: 171–99.

Goodman, David S. G. 2009. "Sixty Years of the People's Republic: Local Perspectives on the Evolution of the State in China." *Pacific Review* 22 (4): 429–50.

Griffiths, Ann L., ed. 2005. *Handbook of Federal Countries, 2005*. Montreal: Forum of Federations/McGill University Press.

Grindle, Merilee. 2004. "Good Enough Governance: Poverty Reduction and Reform in Developing Countries." *Governance* 17 (4): 525–48.

Grossman, Herschel I. 1991. "A General Equilibrium Theory of Insurrections." *American Economic Review* 81: 912–21.

    1992. "Foreign Aid and Insurrection." *Defense Economics* 3: 275–88.

Grugel, Jean. 1999. *Democracy without Borders: Transnationalisation and Conditionality in New Democracies*. London: Routledge.

Guelke, Adrian, ed. 2004. *Democracy and Ethnic Conflict*. New York: Palgrave.

Gunther, Richard, Jose Ramon Montero, and Joan J. Linz. 2002. *Political Parties: Old Concepts and New Challenges*. Oxford: Oxford University Press.

Gurr, Tedd Robert. 1970. *Why Men Rebel*. Princeton, NJ: Princeton University Press.

    1974. "Persistence and Change in Political Systems." *American Political Science Review* 74: 1482–1504.

    ed. 1980. *Handbook of Political Conflict*. New York: Free Press.

    2000. "Ethnic Conflict on the Wane." *Foreign Affairs* 79 (3): 52–64.

    2000. *Peoples versus States: Minorities at Risk in the New Century*. Washington, DC: US Institute for Peace Press.

Gurr, Ted Robert, Keith Jaggers, and Will H. Moore. 1989. *Polity II Codebook*. Unpublished manuscript. Boulder: University of Colorado.

    1990. "Transformation of the Western State: The Growth of Democracy, Autocracy and State Power since 1800." *Studies in Comparative International Development* 25 (1): 73–108.

    1991. "The Transformation of the Western State: The Growth of Democracy, Autocracy and State Power since 1800." In Alex Inkeles, ed., *On Measuring Democracy*. New Brunswick, NJ: Transaction, pp. 68–104.

Gurr, Ted Robert, Monty G. Marshall, and Deepa Khosla. 2010. *Peace and Conflict 2010*. College Park: University of Maryland, Center for International Development and Conflict Management (CIDCM).

Hadenius, Axel. 1992. *Democracy and Development*. New York: Cambridge University Press.

    1997. *Democracy's Victory and Crisis*. Cambridge: Cambridge University Press.

Haerpfer, Christian W., Patrick Bernhagen, Ronald F. Inglehart, and Christian Welzel. 2009. *Democratization*. Oxford: Oxford University Press.

Haggard, Stephen and Robert R. Kaufman. 1995. *The Political Economy of Democratic Transitions*. Princeton, NJ: Princeton University Press.

    2008. *Development, Democracy, and Welfare States: Latin America, East Asia, and Eastern Europe*. Princeton, NJ: Princeton University Press.

Haggard, Stephen and Lydia Tiede. 2011. "The Rule of Law and Economic Growth: Where Are We?" *World Development* 39 (5): 673–85.

Hagopian, Frances and Scott Mainwaring, eds. 2005. *The Third Wave of Democratization in Latin America: Advances and Setbacks*. New York: Cambridge University Press.

Hale, Henry E. 2004. "Divided We Stand: Institutional Sources of Ethno-Federal State Survival and Collapse." *World Politics* 56: 165–93.

Hall, Peter A. and David Soskice. 2001. *Varieties of Capitalism: The Institutional Foundations of Comparative Advantage*. Oxford: Oxford University Press.

Hall, Robert E. and Charles I. Jones. 1999. "Why Do Some Countries Produce So Much More Output per Worker than Others?" *Quarterly Journal of Economics* 114 (1): 83–116.

Halperin, Morton H., Joseph T. Siegle, and Michael M. Weinstein. 2010. *The Democracy Advantage: How Democracies Promote Prosperity and Peace*. 2nd ed. New York: Routledge.

Hannan, Michael T. and Glenn R. Carroll. 1981. "Dynamics of Formal Political Structure: An Event-History Analysis." *American Sociological Review* 46: 19–35.

Harrison, Lawrence E. and Samuel P. Huntington, eds. 2000. *Culture Matters*. New York: Basic.

Hartzell, Caroline A. and Matthew Hoddie. 2004. "Institutionalizing Peace: Power Sharing and Post–Civil War Conflict Management." *American Journal of Political Science* 47 (2): 318–32.

2007. *Crafting Peace: Power Sharing and Negotiated Settlements of Civil Wars*. Philadelphia: Penn State Press.

Hechter, Michael. 1992. "The Dynamics of Secession." *Acta Sociologica* 35 (4): 267–83.

Hegre, Håvard and Hanne Fjelde. 2010. "Democratization and Post-Conflict Transitions." In J. Joseph Hewitt, Jonathan Wilkenfeld, and Ted Robert Gurr, eds., *Peace and Conflict 2010*. College Park: Center for Systemic Peace, University of Maryland, pp. 79–90.

Heidenheimer, Arnold, ed. 2002. *Political Corruption: Concepts and Contexts*. New Brunswick, NJ: Transaction.

Held, David. 2006. *Models of Democracy*. 3rd ed. Stanford, CA: Stanford University Press.

Helliwell, John F. 1994. "Empirical Linkages between Democracy and Economic Growth." *British Journal of Political Science* 24 (2): 225–48.

Henderson, Errol A. and Richard Tucker. 2001. "Clear and Present Strangers: The Clash of Civilizations and International Politics." *International Studies Quarterly* 45 (2): 317–38.

Henderson, J., D. Hulme, H. Jalilian, and R. Phillips. 2007. "Bureaucratic Effects: 'Weberian' State Agencies and Poverty Reduction." *Sociology: The Journal of The British Sociological Association* 41 (3): 515–32.

Hendrix, Cullen S. 2010. "Measuring State Capacity: Theoretical and Empirical Implications for the Study of Civil Conflict." *Journal of Peace Research* 47 (3): 273–85.

Hewitt, J. Joseph, Jonathan Wilkenfeld, and Ted Robert Gurr. 2010. *Peace and Conflict 2010*. College Park: Center for Systemic Peace, University of Maryland.

Hibbing, John R. and Elizabeth Theiss-Morse. 2003. *Stealth Democracy: Americans' Beliefs about How Government Should Work*. Cambridge: Cambridge University Press.

Hoeffler, Anke and Verity Outram. 2011. "Need, Merit, or Self-Interest: What Determines the Allocation of Aid?" *Review of Development Economics* 15 (2): 237–50.

Holmberg, Sören, Bo Rothstein, and Naghmeh Nasiritousi. 2008. *Quality of Government: What You Get*. Gothenberg: Quality of Governance Institute QoG Working Paper Series 2008:21.

Honaker, James and Gary King. 2010. "What to Do about Missing Values in Time-Series Cross-Section Data." *American Journal of Political Science* 54 (2): 561–81.

Horowitz, Donald L. 1985. *Ethnic Groups in Conflict*. Berkeley: University of California Press.

1991. *A Democratic South Africa? Constitutional Engineering in a Divided Society.* Berkeley: University of California Press.

2003. *The Deadly Ethnic Riot.* Berkeley: University of California Press.

2003. "Electoral Systems: A Primer for Decision-makers." *Journal of Democracy* 14 (4): 116–27.

Hossain, Akhtar. 2000. "Anatomy of Hartal Politics in Bangladesh." *Asian Survey* 40 (3): 508–29.

Hout, Wil. 2010. "Governance and Development: Changing EU Policies." *Third World Quarterly* 31 (1): 1–12.

Hsiao, Cheng M. 1986. *Analysis of Panel Data.* Cambridge: Cambridge University Press.

Huber, Evelyne, Dietrich Rueschmeyer, and John D. Stephens. 1993. "The Impact of Economic Development on Democracy." *Journal of Economic Perspectives* 7 (3): 71–85.

Humphreys, M. 2005. "Natural Resources, Conflict, and Conflict Resolution: Uncovering the Mechanisms." *Journal of Conflict Resolution* 49 (4): 508–37.

Hunter, Shireen T. 1998. *The Future of Islam and the West: Clash of Civilizations or Peaceful Coexistence?* Westport, CT: Praeger.

Huntington, Samuel P. 1968. *Political Order in Changing Societies.* New Haven, CT: Yale University Press.

1991. *The Third Wave: Democratization in the Late Twentieth Century.* Norman: University of Oklahoma Press.

1996. *The Clash of Civilizations and the Remaking of World Order.* New York: Simon & Schuster.

1997. "The Clash of Civilizations: A Response." *Millennium: Journal of International Studies* 26 (1): 141–2.

Hyden, Goran. 2007. "Governance and Poverty Reduction in Africa." *Proceedings of the National Academy of Sciences of the USA* 104 (43): 16751–6.

Inglehart, Ronald. 1977. *The Silent Revolution: Changing Values and Political Styles among Western Publics.* Princeton, NJ: Princeton University Press.

1988. "The Renaissance of Political Culture." *American Political Science Review* 82: 1203–30.

1990. *Culture Shift in Advanced Industrial Society.* Princeton, NJ: Princeton University Press.

1997. *Modernization and Post-Modernization: Cultural, Economic and Political Change in 43 Societies.* Princeton, NJ: Princeton University Press.

2003. "How Solid Is Mass Support for Democracy and How Do We Measure It?" *PS: Political Science and Politics* 36 (1): 51–7.

ed. 2003. *Islam, Gender, Culture, and Democracy.* Ontario: De Sitter.

Inglehart, Ronald and Paul Abramson. 1999. "Measuring Post-Materialism." *American Political Science Review* 93 (3): 665–77.

Inglehart, Ronald and Wayne E. Baker. 2000. "Modernization, Globalization and the Persistence of Tradition: Empirical Evidence from 65 Societies." *American Sociological Review* 65: 19–55.

Inglehart, Ronald and Pippa Norris. 2003. "Muslims and the West: A Clash of Civilizations?" *Foreign Policy* 135: 63–70.

Inglehart, Ronald and Christian Welzel. 2003. "Political Culture and Democracy: Analyzing Cross-Level Linkages." *Comparative Politics* 36 (1): 61–79.

2005. *Modernization, Cultural Change, and Democracy: The Human Development Sequence.* New York: Cambridge University Press.

2010. "Changing Mass Priorities: The Link between Modernization and Democracy." *Perspectives on Politics* 8 (2): 551–67.

Inkeles, Alex, ed. 1991. *On Measuring Democracy: Its Consequences and Concomitants.* New Brunswick, NJ: Transaction.

International IDEA. *State of Democracy Project.* http://www.idea.int.

Isham, Jonathan, Daniel Kaufmann, and Lant Pritchett. 1997. "Civil Liberties, Democracy, and the Performance of Government Projects." *World Bank Economic Review* 11 (2): 219–42.

Jackman, Robert W. 1973. "On the Relation of Economic Development and Democratic Performance." *American Journal of Political Science* 17: 611–21.

Jackman, Robert W. and Ross A. Miller. 1995. "Voter Turnout in Industrial Democracies during the 1980s." *Comparative Political Studies* 27: 467–92.

Jaggers, Keith and Tedd Gurr. 1995. "Tracking Democracy's Third Wave with the Polity III Data." *Journal of Peace Research* 32: 469–82.

Jaramillo, Laura and Cemile Sancak. 2007. *Growth in the Dominican Republic and Haiti: Why Has the Grass Been Greener on One Side of Hispaniola?* IMF Working Paper 07/63.

Jarstad, Anna and Timothy D. Sisk, eds. 2007. *From War to Democracy.* Cambridge: Cambridge University Press.

Jelen, Ted Gerard, and Clyde Wilcox, eds. 2002. *Religion and Politics in Comparative Perspective.* Cambridge: Cambridge University Press.

Jensen N. M. 2003. "Democratic Governance and Multinational Corporations: Political Regimes and Inflows of Foreign Direct Investment." *International Organization* 57 (3): 587–616.

Jensen, N. M. and L. Wantchekon. 2004. "Resource Wealth and Political Regimes in Africa." *Comparative Political Studies* 37: 816–41.

Jeong, Ho-Won. 2005. *Peace-Building in Post-Conflict Societies.* Boulder, CO: Lynne Reinner.

Jesse, Neal G. and Kristen P. Williams. 2005. *Identity and Institutions: Conflict Reduction in Divided Societies.* Albany: State University of New York Press.

Jolly, Richard. 2009. *UN Ideas that Changed the World.* United Nations Intellectual History Project Series. Bloomington: Indiana University Press.

Jones, Mark P. 1995. *Electoral Laws and the Survival of Presidential Democracies.* Notre Dame, IN: University of Notre Dame Press.

Kabuli, Niaz Faizi. 1994. *Democracy According to Islam.* Pittsburgh, PA: Dorrance.

Kaiser, Andre, Matthias Lehnert, Bernhard Miller, and Ulrich Sieberer. 2002. "The Democratic Quality of Institutional Regimes: A Conceptual Framework." *Political Studies* 50: 313–31.

Kaplan, Robert. 2001. *The Coming Anarchy: Shattering the Dreams of the Post Cold War.* New York: Vintage.

Kaplan, Seth. 2008. *Fixing Fragile States: A New Paradigm for Development.* New York: Praeger.

Karl, Terry L. 1991. "Dilemmas of Democratization in Latin America." In D. A. Rustow and K. P. Erickson, eds., *Comparative Political Dynamics: Global Research Perspectives.* New York: Harper Collins, pp. 163–91.

1997. *The Paradox of Plenty: Oil Booms and Petro-States.* Berkeley: University of California Press.

Kasza, Gregory. 1996. "War and Comparative Politics." *Comparative Politics* 28 (3): 355–73.

Katz, Richard S. 1997. *Democracy and Elections*. New York: Oxford University Press.

Kaufman, Stuart J. 2001. *Modern Hatreds: The Symbolic Politics of Ethnic War*. Ithaca, NY: Cornell University Press.

Kaufmann, Chaim. 1996. "Possible and Impossible Solutions to Ethnic Civil Wars." *International Security* 20 (4): 136–75.

Kaufmann, Daniel, Aart Kraay, and Massimo Mastruzzi. 2003. *Governance Matters III: Governance Indicators 1996–2002*. Washington, DC: World Bank. http://www.worldbank.org/wbi/governance/pubs/govmatters3.html.

2007. *Governance Matters VI: Aggregate and Individual Governance Indicators, 1996–2006*. Washington, DC: World Bank, Policy Research Working Paper.

2007. "Growth and Governance: A Rejoinder." *Journal of Politics* 69 (2): 570–2.

2010. *The Worldwide Governance Indicators: Methodology and Analytical Issues*. Washington, DC: Brookings Institute. http://www.govindicators.org.

Kaufmann, Daniel and Pablo Zoido-Lobatón. 1999. *Governance Matters*. Washington, DC: World Bank. http://www.worldbank.org/wbi/governance/pubs/govmatters.htm.

Kay, Cristobal. 2011. "Contemporary Latin America: Development and Democracy beyond the Washington Consensus." *Journal of Latin American Studies* 43: 180–2.

Kayser, M. A. and Christopher Wlezien. 2011. "Performance Pressure: Patterns of Partisanship and the Economic Vote." *European Journal of Political Research* 50 (3): 365–94.

Keck, Margaret E. and Kathryn Sikkink. 1998. *Activists beyond Borders: Advocacy Networks in International Politics*. Ithaca, NY: Cornell University Press.

Keefer, Philip. 2005. *Database of Political Institutions, 2004*. Washington, DC: World Bank.

2007. "Clientelism, Credibility, and the Policy Choices of Young Democracies." *American Journal of Political Science* 51: 804.

Kennedy, Randall. 2009. "Survival and Accountability: An Analysis of the Empirical Support for 'Selectorate Theory'." *International Studies Quarterly* 53 (3): 695–714.

Kier, Elizabeth and Ronald R. Krebs. *In War's Wake: International Conflict and the Fate of Liberal Democracy*. New York: Cambridge University Press.

Kitschelt, Herbert. 1992. "Political Regime Change: Structure and Process-Driven Explanations." *American Political Science Review* 86: 1028–34.

Klingemann, Hans-Dieter and Dieter Fuchs. 1995. *Citizens and the State*. Oxford: Oxford University Press.

Kloti, U. "Consensual Government in a Heterogeneous Polity." *West European Politics* 24 (2): 19–25.

Knack, Stephen. 2001. "Aid Dependence and the Quality of Governance." *Southern Economic Journal* 68 (2): 310–29.

2004. "Does Foreign Aid Promote Democracy?" *International Studies Quarterly* 48 (1): 251–66.

Knack, Stephen and Philip Keefer. 1995. "Institutions and Economic Performance: Cross-Country Tests Using Alternative Institutional Measures." *Economics and Politics* 7 (3): 207–27.

Knutsen, Carl Henrik. 2010. "Measuring Effective Democracy." *International Political Science Review* 31 (2): 109–28.

2011. "Which Democracies Prosper? Electoral Rules, Form of Government and Economic Growth." *Electoral Studies* 30 (1): 83–90.

Kochanek, Stanley A. 2000. "Governance, Patronage Politics, and Democratic Transition in Bangladesh." *Asian Survey* 40 (3): 530–50.

Kornai, János, Bo Rothstein, and Susan Rose-Ackerman, eds. 2004. *Creating Social Trust in Post-Socialist Transitions*. New York: Palgrave Macmillan.

Kosack, Stephen. 2003. "Effective Aid: How Democracy Allows Development Aid to Improve the Quality of Life." *World Development* 31 (1): 1–22.

Kotzian, Peter. 2011. "Public Support for Liberal Democracy." *International Political Science Review* 32 (1): 23–41.

Krær, Anne Mette. 2004. *Governance*. Cambridge: Polity Press.

Krieckhaus, Jonathan. 2004. "The Regime Debate Revisited: A Sensitivity Analysis of Democracy's Economic Effect." *British Journal of Political Science* 34 (4): 635–55.
  2006. "Democracy and Economic Growth: How Regional Context Influences Regime Effects." *British Journal of Political Science* 36 (2): 317–40.

Kurrild-Klitgaard, Peter, Morgens K. Jutesen, and Robert Klemmensen. 2006. "The Political Economy of Freedom, Democracy and Transnational Terrorism." *Public Choice* 128: 289–315.

Kurtz, Marcus J. and Andrew Schrank. 2007. "Growth and Governance: Models, Measures, and Mechanisms." *Journal of Politics* 69 (2): 538–54.

Kurzman, C., R. Werum, and R. E. Burkhart. 2002. "Democracy's Effect on Economic Growth: A Pooled Time-Series Analysis, 1951–1980." *Studies in Comparative International Development* 37 (1): 3–33.

Laakso, Marku and Rein Taagepera. 1979. "The 'Effective' Number of Parties: A Measure with Application to Western Europe." *Comparative Political Studies* 12: 3–28.

Lake, David A. and Matthew A. Baum. 2001. "The Invisible Hand of Democracy: Political Control and the Provision of Public Services." *Comparative Political Studies* 34 (6): 587–621.

Leblang, David A. 1997. "Political Democracy and Economic Growth: Pooled Cross-Sectional and Time-Series Evidence." *British Journal of Political Science* 27 (3): 453–66.

La Porta, Rafael, Florencio Lopez-De-Silanes, Andre Shleifer and Robert Vishny. 1999. "The Quality of Government." *Journal of Law Economics & Organization* 15 (1): 222–79.

LeDuc, Lawrence, Richard G. Niemi, and Pippa Norris, eds. 2002. *Comparing Democracies 2: Elections and Voting in Global Perspective*. London: Sage.

Leftwich, Adrian. 1996. *Democracy and Development: Theory and Practice*. Cambridge: Blackwell.

Lehmbruch, Gerhard. 1967. *Proporzdemokratie. Politisches System und politische Kultur in der Schweiz und Osterreich*. Tubingen: Mohr.

Lerner, Daniel. 1958. *The Passing of Traditional Society*. Glencoe, IL: Free Press.

Levi, Margaret. 2006. "Why We Need a New Theory of Government." *Perspectives on Politics* 4 (1): 5–19.

Levine, R. and D. Renelt. 1992. "A Sensitivity Analysis of Cross-Country Growth Regressions." *American Economic Review* 82 (4): 942–63.

Levitsky, Steven and Lucan A. Way. 2002. "The Rise of Competitive Authoritarianism." *Journal of Democracy* 13 (2): 51–65.
  2010. *Competitive Authoritarianism: Hybrid Regimes after the Cold War*. New York: Cambridge University Press.

Lewis, Arthur W. 1965. *Politics in West Africa*. London: Allen & Unwin.

Lewis, Bernard. 2002. *What Went Wrong? Western Impact and Middle Eastern Response*. New York: Oxford University Press.

Li, Q. 2005. "Does Democracy Promote or Reduce Transnational Terrorist Incidents?" *Journal of Conflict Resolution* 49 (2): 278–97.

Lijphart, Arend. 1969. "Consociational Democracy." *World Politics* 21: 207–25.

1975. *The Politics of Accommodation: Pluralism and Democracy in the Netherlands.* Berkeley: University of California Press.

1977. *Democracy in Plural Societies: A Comparative Exploration.* New Haven, CT: Yale University Press.

1984. *Democracies.* New Haven, CT: Yale University Press.

1991. "Constitutional Choices for New Democracies." *Journal of Democracy* 2: 72–84.

1994. *Electoral Systems and Party Systems: A Study of Twenty-Seven Democracies, 1945–1990.* Oxford: Oxford University Press.

ed. 1996. *Presidential v. Parliamentary Government.* Oxford: Oxford University Press.

1997. "Unequal Participation: Democracy's Unresolved Dilemma." *American Political Science Review* 91: 1–14.

1999. *Patterns of Democracy: Government Forms and Performance in 36 Countries.* New Haven, CT: Yale University Press.

2002. "Negotiation Democracy versus Consensus Democracy: Parallel Conclusions and Recommendations." *European Journal of Political Research* 41 (1): 107–13.

2004. "Constitutional Design for Divided Societies." *Journal of Democracy* 15 (2): 96–109.

2008. *Thinking about Democracy: Power Sharing and Majority Rule in Theory and Practice.* New York: Routledge.

Lindberg, Staffan. 2006. *Democracy and Elections in Africa.* Baltimore: Johns Hopkins University Press.

ed. 2009. *Democratization by Elections: A New Mode of Transition.* Baltimore: Johns Hopkins University Press.

Linder, Wolf and Andre Baechtiger. 2005. "What Drives Democratization in Asia and Africa?" *European Journal of Political Research* 44: 861–80.

Linz, Juan J. and Alfred Stepan. 1978. *The Breakdown of Democratic Regimes.* Baltimore: Johns Hopkins University Press.

1996. *Problems of Democratic Transition and Consolidation: Southern Europe, South America and Post-Communist Europe.* Baltimore: Johns Hopkins Press.

Linz, Juan J. and Arturo Valenzuela, eds.1994. *The Failure of Presidential Democracy.* Baltimore: Johns Hopkins Press.

Lipset, Seymour Martin. 1959. "Some Social Requisites of Democracy: Economic Development and Political Legitimacy." *American Political Science Review* 53: 69–105.

1960. *Political Man: The Social Basis of Politics.* New York: Doubleday.

1994. "The Social Requisites of Democracy Revisited." *American Sociological Review* 59: 1–22.

1995. "Economic Development." In Seymour Martin Lipset, ed., *The Encyclopedia of Democracy.* London: Routledge.

Lipset, Seymour Martin and Jason M. Lakin. 2004. *The Democratic Century.* Norman: University of Oklahoma Press.

Lipset, Seymour Martin, Kyoung-Ryung Seong, and John Charles Torres. 1993. "A Comparative Analysis of the Social Requisites of Democracy." *International Social Science Journal* 45 (2): 154–75.

Lonti, Zsuzsanna and Matt Woods. 2008. "Towards Government at a Glance: Identification of Core Data and Issues Related to Public Sector Efficiency." *OECD Working Papers on Public Governance, No. 7,* Paris: OECD. doi:10.1787/ 245570167540.

Lublin, David. 1997. *The Paradox of Representation: Racial Gerrymandering and Minority Interests.* Princeton, NJ: Princeton University Press.

Lustik, Ian S., Dan Miodownik, and Roy J. Eidelson. 2004. "Secessionism in Multicultural States: Does Sharing Power Prevent or Encourage It?" *American Political Science Review* 98 (2): 209–29.

Lynch, Gabrielle and Gordon Crawford. 2011. "Democratization in Africa 1990–2010: An Assessment." *Democratization* 18 (2): 275–310.

Mainwaring, Scott. 1993. "Presidentialism, Multipartism, and Democracy: The Difficult Combination." *Comparative Political Studies* 26 (2): 198–228.

Mainwaring, Scott, Guillermo O'Donnell, and J. Samuel Valenzuela, eds. 1992. *Issues in Democratic Consolidation: The New South American Democracies in Comparative Perspective.* Notre Dame, IN: University of Notre Dame Press.

Mainwaring, Scott and Matthew Soberg Shugart. 1997. *Presidentialism and Democracy in Latin America.* New York: Cambridge University Press.

Mair, Peter. 2001. "Party Membership in Twenty European Democracies 1980–2000." *Party Politics* 7 (1): 5–22.

Malloy, James M. and Mitchell A. Seligson, eds. *Authoritarians and Democrats: Regime Transition in Latin America.* Pittsburgh, PA: University of Pittsburgh Press.

Manor, James. 1999. *The Political Economy of Democratic Decentralization.* Washington, DC: World Bank.

2007. *Aid that Works: Successful Development in Fragile States.* Washington, DC: World Bank.

Mansfield, Edward D. and Jack Snyder. 1995. "Democratization and the Danger of War." *International Security* 20 (1): 5–38.

2007. *Electing to Fight: Why Emerging Democracies Go to War.* Cambridge, MA: MIT Press.

2007. "The Sequencing 'Fallacy'." *Journal of Democracy* 18 (3): 5–9.

Maravall, J. M. 2010. "Accountability in Coalition Governments." *Annual Review of Political Science* 13: 81–100.

Maren, Michael. 1997. *The Road to Hell: The Ravaging Effects of Foreign Aid and International Charity.* New York: Free Press.

Marenco, Andre. 2010. "When Laws Fail to Produce the Expected Results: Election Finance from a Comparative Perspective." *Dados-Revista De Ciencias Sociais* 53 (4): 821–53.

Marshall, Monty G. and Benjamin R. Cole. 2009. *State Fragility Index and Matrix 2009.* College Park: University of Maryland, Center for Systemic Peace. http://www.systemicpeace.org/SFImatrix2009c.pdf.

Marshall, Monty G. and Ted Robert Gurr. 2006. *Peace and Conflict 2005.* Baltimore: University of Maryland, Center for International Development and Conflict Management (CIDCM).

Marshall, Monty G., Ted Robert Gurr, Christian Davenport, and Keith Jaggers. 2002. "Polity IV, 1800–1999: Comments on Munck and Verkuilen." *Comparative Political Studies* 35 (1): 40–5.

Marshall, Monty G. and Keith Jaggers. 2002. *Polity IV Project: Political Regime Characteristics and Transitions, 1800–2002: Dataset Users' Manual.* College Park: University of Maryland. http://www.bsos.umd.edu/cidcm/polity/.

Maseland, Robert and Andre van Hoorn. 2011. "Why Muslims Like Democracy Yet Have So Little of It." *Public Choice* 147 (3–4): 481–96.

Mauro, Paulo. 1995. "Corruption and Growth." *Quarterly Journal of Economics* 110: 681–712.

McCormick, James M. and Neil Mitchell. 1988. "Is U.S. Aid Really Linked to Human Rights in Latin America?" *American Journal of Political Science* 32 (1): 231–9.

McCrone, Donald J. and Charles F. Cnudde. 1967. "Toward a Communications Theory of Democratic Political Development: A Causal Model." *American Political Science Review* 61: 72–9.

McDonald, Michael P. and Samuel L. Popkin. 2001. "The Myth of the Vanishing Voter." *American Political Science Review* 95 (4): 963–74.

McFaul, Michael. 2010. *Advancing Democracy Abroad: Why We Should and How We Can*. Stanford, CA.: Stanford University Press.

McGrew, Anthony and David Held, eds. 2007. *Globalization Theory: Approaches and Controversies*. Cambridge: Polity Press.

McGuire, James W. 2001. "Social Policy and Mortality Decline in East Asia and Latin America." *World Development* 29 (10): 1673–97.

  2006. "Basic Health Care Provision and Under-5 Mortality: A Cross-National Study of Developing Countries." *World Development* 34 (3): 405–25.

  2010. *Wealth, Health, and Democracy in East Asia and Latin America*. New York: Cambridge University Press.

McRae, Kenneth, ed. 1974. *Consociational Democracy: Conflict Accommodation in Segmented Societies*. Toronto: McClelland and Stewart.

Meernik, James, Eric L. Krueger, and Stephen C. Poe. 1998. "Testing Models of U.S. Foreign Policy: Foreign Aid during and after the Cold War." *Journal of Politics* 60: 63–85.

Mehta, Pratap Bhanu. 2010. "India: Governance and Growth in State Capacity." *Governance* 23 (3): 381–4.

Meltzer, A. H. and S. F. Richard. 1981. "A Rational Theory of the Size of Government." *Journal of Political Economy* 89 (5): 914–27.

Mesquita, Bruce Bueno de, Alastair Smith, Randolph M. Siverson, and James D. Morrow. 2003. *The Logic of Political Survival*. Cambridge, MA: MIT Press.

Midgley, John. 1995. *Social Development: The Development Perspective in Social Welfare*. London: Sage.

Midlarsky, Manus I., ed. 1997. *Inequality, Democracy and Economic Development*. Cambridge: Cambridge University Press.

  1998. "Democracy and Islam: Implications for Civilizational Conflict and the Democratic Process." *International Studies Quarterly* 42 (3): 485–511.

Milner, Henry. 2002. *Civic Literacy: How Informed Citizens Make Democracy Work*. Hanover, MA: Tufts University.

Minier, J. A. 1998. "Democracy and Growth: Alternative Approaches." *Journal of Economic Growth* 3 (3): 241–66.

Monten, Jonathan. 2005. "The Roots of the Bush Doctrine: Power, Nationalism and Democracy Promotion in U.S. Strategy." *International Security* 29 (4): 112–56.

Montinola, G. R. 2002. "Sources of Corruption: A Cross-Country Study." *British Journal of Political Science* 32: 147.

Moon, B. E. and W. J. Dixon. 1985. "Politics, the State, and Basic Human Needs: A Cross-National Study." *American Journal of Political Science* 29 (4): 661–94.

Moore, Barrington. 1966. *Social Origins of Dictatorship and Democracy*. Boston: Beacon Press.

Moore, Mick. 1998. "Death without Taxes: Democracy, State Capacity, and Aid Dependence in the Fourth World." In G. White and M. Robinson, eds., *Towards a Democratic Developmental State.* Oxford: Oxford University Press, pp. 84–121.

Moriconi, Marcelo. 2009. "Critical Review: The Need to Incorporate Good Rhetorical Thinking into the Construction of Good Governance." *Revista De Estudios Politicos* 145 (3): 119–55.

Morjé Howard, Lise. 2009. *UN Peacekeeping in Civil Wars.* New York: Cambridge University Press.

Morlino, Leonardo. 1998. *Democracy between Consolidation and Crisis: Parties, Groups, and Citizens in Southern Europe.* New York: Oxford University Press.

Most, Benjamin A. and Harvey Starr. 1980. "Diffusion, Reinforcement, Geopolitics, and the Spread of War." *American Political Science Review* 74: 932–46.

Mozaffar, Shaheen, James R. Scarritt, and Glen Galaich. 2003. "Electoral Institutions, Ethno-Political Cleavages, and Party Systems in Africa's Emerging Democracies." *American Political Science Review* 97: 379–90.

Muller, Edward N. 1988. "Democracy, Economic Development, and Income Inequality." *American Sociological Review* 53 (2): 50–68.

1995. "Economic Determinants of Democracy." *American Sociological Review* 60 (4): 966–82.

1995. "Income Inequality and Democratization: Reply to Bollen and Jackman." *American Sociological Review* 60 (4): 990–6.

Muller, Edward N. and Mitch A. Seligson. 1994. "Civic Culture and Democracy: The Question of Causal Relationships." *American Political Science Review* 88: 635–52.

Mulligan, Casey B., R. Gil, and X. Sala-a-martin. 2004. "Do Democracies Have Different Public Policies Than Non-democracies?" *Journal of Economic Perspectives* 18 (1): 51–74.

Munck, Geraldo L. 2001. "The Regime Question: Theory Building in Democratic Societies." *World Politics* 54: 119–44.

2009. *Measuring Democracy: A Bridge between Scholarship and Politics.* Baltimore: Johns Hopkins University Press.

2010. "The Origins and Durability of Democracy in Latin America: Advances and Challenges of a Research Agenda." *Revista De Ciencia Politica* 30 (3): 573–97.

Munck, Geraldo L. and Jay Verkuilen. 2002. "Conceptualizing and Measuring Democracy: Evaluating Alternative Indices." *Comparative Political Studies* 35 (1): 5–34.

2002. "Generating Better Data: A Response to Discussants." *Comparative Political Studies* 35 (1): 52–7.

Murphy, Craig N. 2006. *The United Nations Development Programme: A Better Way?* Cambridge: Cambridge University Press.

Myagkov, Mikhail, Peter C. Ordeshook, and Dimitri Shakin. 2009. *The Forensics of Election Fraud: Russia and Ukraine.* New York: Cambridge University Press.

Narayan, P. K. S. Narayan, and R. Smyth. 2011. "Does Democracy Facilitate Economic Growth or Does Economic Growth Facilitate Democracy? An Empirical Study of Sub-Saharan Africa." *Economic Modelling* 28 (3): 900–10.

Navia, P. and T. D. Zweifel. 2003. "Democracy, Dictatorship, and Infant Mortality Revisited." *Journal of Democracy* 14 (3): 90–103.

Nel, P. 2005. "Democratization and the Dynamics of Income Distribution in Low- and Middle-Income Countries." *Politikon* 32 (1): 17–43.

Nelson, J. 2007. "Elections, Democracy and Social Services." *Studies in Comparative Democratic Politics* 41 (4): 79–97.

Neubauer, Deane E. 1967. "Some Conditions of Democracy." *American Political Science Review* 61: 1002–9.

Neuman, Edward and Roland Rich, eds. 2004. *The UN Role in Promoting Democracy: Between Ideals and Reality.* Tokyo: UN University Press.

Neumayer, E. 2002. "Do Democracies Exhibit Stronger International Environmental Commitment? A Cross-Country Analysis." *Journal of Peace Research* 39: 139. New York: Cambridge University Press.

Newman, Saul. 1991. "Does Modernization Breed Ethnic Conflict?" *World Politics* 43 (3): 451–78.

Noel, Sid, ed. 2005. *From Power Sharing to Democracy: Post-Conflict Institutions in Ethnically Divided Societies.* Montreal/Ithaca, NY: McGill-Queen's University Press.

Norris, Pippa, ed. 1998. *Critical Citizens: Global Support for Democratic Government.* New York: Oxford University Press.

  2000. *A Virtuous Circle.* New York: Cambridge University Press.

  2001. *Digital Divide.* New York: Cambridge University Press.

  2002. *Democratic Phoenix: Reinventing Political Activism.* New York: Cambridge University Press.

  2004. *Electoral Engineering.* New York: Cambridge University Press.

  2008. *Driving Democracy.* New York: Cambridge University Press.

  ed. 2010. *Public Sentinel.* Washington, DC: World Bank.

  2011. *Democratic Deficit.* New York: Cambridge University Press.

Norris, Pippa and Ronald Inglehart. 2004. *Sacred and Secular.* New York: Cambridge University Press.

North, Douglas. 1990. *Institutions, Institutional Change and Economic Performance.* Cambridge: Cambridge University Press.

North, Douglas C. 2005. *Understanding the Process of Economic Change.* Princeton, NJ: Princeton University Press.

Nussbaum, Martha C. 2011. *Creating Capabilities: The Human Development Approach.* Cambridge, MA: Harvard University Press.

O'Donnell, Guillermo. 1979. *Modernization and Bureaucratic-Authoritarianism Studies in South American Politics.* Berkeley: Institute of International Studies, University of California.

  ed. 2004. *The Quality of Democracy: Theory and Applications.* Notre Dame, IN: University of Notre Dame Press.

O'Donnell, Guillermo and Phillippe Schmitter. 1986. *Transitions from Authoritarian Rule: Tentative Conclusions about Uncertain Transitions.* Baltimore: Johns Hopkins University Press.

Ohmae, K. 1995. *The End of the Nation State.* New York: Free Press.

O'Loughlin, John, Michael D. Ward, Corey L. Lofdahl, Jordin S. Cohen, David S. Brown, David Reilly, Kristian Gledistch, and Michael Shin. 1998. "The Diffusion of Democracy, 1946–1994." *Annals of the Association of American Geographers* 88: 545–74.

Olsen, Mancur E. 1968. "Multivariate Analysis of National Political Development." *American Sociological Review* 33: 699–712.

Organization for Economic Cooperation and Development. 2007. "Towards Better Measurement of Government." *OECD Working Papers on Public Governance,* 2007/1. Paris: OECD.

  2009. *Government at a Glance.* Paris: OECD.

Ottaway, Marina and Thomas Carothers, eds. 2000. *Funding Virtue: Civil Society Aid and Democracy Promotion*. Washington, DC: Brookings Institution.

Page, C. and Michael Goldsmith. 1987. *Central and Local Government Relations*. London: Sage.

Page, Ed C. 1991. *Localism and Centralism in Europe*. Oxford: Oxford University Press.

Painter, Martin and B. Guy Peters, eds. 2010. *Tradition and Public Administration*. London: Palgrave Macmillan.

Papadopoulos, Y. and P. Warin. 2007. "Are Innovative, Participatory and Deliberative Procedures in Policy Making Democratic and Effective?" *European Journal of Political Research* 46: 445–72.

Paris, Roland. 2004. *At War's End: Building Peace after Civil Conflict*. Cambridge: Cambridge University Press.

Paris, Roland and Timothy D. Sisk, eds. 2009. *The Dilemmas of State-Building*. New York: Routledge.

Paxton, Pamela. 2000. "Women's Suffrage in the Measurement of Democracy: Problems of Operationalization." *Studies in Comparative International Development* 35 (3): 92–111.

2002. "Social Capital and Democracy: An Interdependent Relationship." *American Sociological Review* 67 (2): 254–77.

Paxton, Pamela, Kenneth A. Bollen, Deborah M. Lee, and Hyo Joung Kim. 2003. "A Half Century of Suffrage: New Data and a Comparative Analysis." *Studies in Comparative International Development* 38 (1): 93–122.

Pérez-Liñán, Aníbal. 2001. "Neo-institutional Accounts of Voter Turnout: Moving beyond Industrial Democracies." *Electoral Studies* 20 (2): 281–97.

Persson, Torsten. 2004. "Constitutions and Economic Policy." *Journal of Economic Perspectives* 18: 75.

2006. "Democracy and Development: The Devil Is in the Details." *American Economic Review* 96: 319.

Persson, Torsten and Guido Tabellini. 2003. *The Economic Effects of Constitutions*. Cambridge, MA: MIT Press.

2009. "Democratic Capital: The Nexus of Political and Economic Change." *American Economic Journal—Macroeconomics* 1 (2): 88–126.

Petersen, Roger. 2002. *Understanding Ethnic Violence: Fear, Hatred and Resentment in Twentieth-Century Eastern Europe*. Cambridge: Cambridge University Press.

Pevehouse, Jon C. 2002. "Democracy from the Outside-In? International Organizations and Democratization." *International Organization* 56 (3): 515–49.

2002. "With a Little Help from My Friends? Regional Organizations and the Consolidation of Democracy." *American Journal of Political Science* 46 (3): 611–26.

2004. *Democracy from Above: Regional Organizations and Democratization*. New York: Cambridge University Press.

Piazza, James A. 2007. "Draining the Swamp: Democracy Promotion, State Failure, and Terrorism in 19 Middle Eastern Countries." *Studies in Conflict and Terrorism* 30: 521–39.

Piccone, Ted and Richard Youngs, eds. 2006. *Strategies for Democratic Change: Assessing the Global Response*. Washington, DC: Democracy Coalition.

Pintor, Rafael Lopez and Maria Gratschew. *Voter Turnout since 1945: A Global Report*. Stockholm: International IDEA. http://www.idea.int.

Pitcher, Anne, Mary H. Moran, and Michael Johnston. 2009. "Rethinking Patrimonialism and Neo-patrimonialism in Africa." *African Studies Review* 52 (1): 125–56.

Ponzio, Richard J. 2007. "Transforming Political Authority: UN Democratic Peace-Building in Afghanistan." *Global Governance* 13 (2): 255–75.

Posner, Daniel. 2004. "Measuring Ethnic Fractionalization in Africa." *American Journal of Political Science* 48 (4): 849–63.

2004. "The Political Salience of Cultural Difference: Why Chewas and Tumbukas Are Allies in Zambia and Adversaries in Malawi." *American Political Science Review* 98 (4): 529–46.

2005. *Institutions and Ethnic Politics in Africa.* Cambridge University Press.

Potter, Daniel, David Goldblatt, Margaret Kiloh, and Paul Lewis, eds. 1997. *Democratization.* Cambridge: Polity Press.

Powell, Derek. 2010. "The Role of Constitution Making and Institution Building in Furthering Peace, Justice and Development: South Africa's Democratic Transition." *International Journal of Transitional Justice* 4 (2): 230–50.

Powell, G. Bingham. 1982. *Contemporary Democracies.* New Haven, CT: Yale University Press.

1986. "American Turnout in Comparative Perspective." *American Political Science Review* 80: 17–43.

2000. *Elections as Instruments of Democracy.* New Haven, CT: Yale University Press.

Pridham, Geoffrey, ed. 1995. *Transitions to Democracy: Comparative Perspectives from Southern Europe, Latin America and Eastern Europe.* Brookfield, VT, and Aldershot, UK: Dartmouth.

Pridham, Geoffrey and Tatu Vanhanen, eds. 1994. *Democratization in Eastern Europe: Domestic and International Perspectives.* London: Routledge.

Prudhomme, Remy. 1995. "The Dangers of Decentralization." *World Bank Research Observer* 10 (2): 201–20.

Przeworski, Adam. 1991. *Democracy and the Market: Political and Economic Reforms in Eastern Europe and Latin America.* Cambridge: Cambridge University Press.

1999. "Minimalist Conception of Democracy: A Defense." In Ian Shapiro and Casiano Hacker-Cordon, eds., *Democracy's Value.* Cambridge: Cambridge University Press, pp. 23–55.

Przeworski, Adam, Michael Alvarez, José Antonio Cheibub, and Fernando Limongi. 1996. "What Makes Democracies Endure?" *Journal of Democracy* 7 (1): 39–55.

2000. *Democracy and Development: Political Institutions and Well-Being in the World, 1950–1990.* New York: Cambridge University Press.

Przeworski, Adam, and Fernando Limongi. 1993. "Political Regimes and Economic Growth." *Journal of Economic Perspectives* 7 (3): 51–69.

1997. "Modernization: Theories and Facts." *World Politics* 49: 155–83.

Putnam, Robert D. 1993. *Making Democracy Work: Civic Traditions in Modern Italy.* Princeton, NJ: Princeton University Press.

2000. *Bowling Alone.* New York: Simon & Schuster.

Putnam, Robert D. and Lewis Feldstein. 2003. *Better Together: Restoring the American Community.* New York: Simon & Schuster.

Radelet, Steven C. 2010. *Emerging Africa: How 17 Countries Are Leading the Way.* Washington, DC: Brookings Institution Press.

Rauch, James E. 2000. "Bureaucratic Structure and Bureaucratic Performance in Less Developed Countries." *Journal of Public Economics* 75 (1): 49–71.

Reed, W. Robert and Haichun Ye. 2011. "Which Panel Data Estimator Should I Use?" *Applied Economics* 43 (8): 985–1000.

Regan, P. and E. Henderson. 2002. "Democracy, Threats and Political Repression in Developing Countries: Are Democracies Internally Less Violent?" *Third World Quarterly* 23 (1): 119–36.

Reilly, Ben. 2001. *Democracy in Divided Societies: Electoral Engineering for Conflict Management.* Cambridge: Cambridge University Press.

Reilly, Ben and Andrew Reynolds. 1998. *Electoral Systems and Conflict in Divided Societies.* Washington, DC: National Academy Press.

Reilly, Benjamin. 2007. "Post-War Elections." In Anna Jarstad and Timothy D. Sisk, eds., *From War to Democracy.* Cambridge: Cambridge University Press, pp. 157–80.

Remmer, Karen L. 1996. "The Sustainability of Political Democracy." *Comparative Political Studies* 296: 611–34.

Reynolds, Andrew, ed. 2002. *The Architecture of Democracy: Constitutional Design, Conflict Management and Democracy.* Oxford: Oxford University Press.

2005. "Reserved Seats in National Legislatures." *Legislative Studies Quarterly* 30 (2): 301–10.

2007. *Minority MPs in National Legislatures: Existing Research and Data Gaps.* New York: Minority Rights Group International/ UNDP.

2011. *Designing Democracies in a Dangerous World.* New York: Oxford University Press.

Reynolds, Andrew and Ben Reilly. 1997. *The International IDEA Handbook of Electoral System Design.* Stockholm: International Institute for Democracy and Electoral Assistance.

Rigobon, R. and Dani Rodrik. 2005. "Rule of Law, Democracy, Openness, and Income: Estimating the Interrelationships." *Economics of Transition* 13 (3): 533–64.

Riker, William H. 1964. *Federalism: Origins, Operations, Significance.* Boston: Little Brown.

Rist, Gilbert. 2008. *The History of Development: From Western Origins to Global Faith.* London: Zed.

Roberts, Adam and Timothy Garton Ash, eds. 2009. *Civil Resistance and Power Politics.* Oxford: Oxford University Press.

Rodden, Jonathan. 2004. "Comparative Federalism and Decentralization: On Meaning and Measurement." *Comparative Politics* 36 (4): 481.

Rodrik, Dani. 2007. *One Economics, Many Recipes.* Princeton, NJ: Princeton University Press.

Rodrik, Dani and Arvind Subramanian. 2003. "The Primacy of Institutions." *Finance and Development.* 3: 31–4.

Rodrik, Dani, Arvind Subramanian, and Francesco Trebbi. 2004. "Institutions Rule: The Primacy of Institutions over Geography and Integration in Economic Development." *Journal of Economic Growth* 9 (2): 131–65.

Roeder, Philip and Donald Rothschild. 2005. *Sustainable Peace: Power and Democracy after Civil Wars.* Ithaca, NY: Cornell University Press.

Rose, Richard. 2001. *The International Encyclopedia of Elections.* Washington, DC: CQ Press.

Rose-Ackerman, Susan. 1999. *Corruption and Government: Causes, Consequences and Reform.* New York: Cambridge University Press.

Ross, Michael L. 2001. "Does Oil Hinder Democracy?" *World Politics* 53: 325–61.

2004. "How Do Natural Resources Influence Civil War? Evidence from Thirteen Cases." *International Organization* 58 (1): 35–67.

2006. "A Closer Look at Oil, Diamonds, and Civil War." *Annual Review of Political Science* 9: 265–300.

2006. "Is Democracy Good for the Poor?" *American Journal of Political Science* 50 (4): 860–74.

Rostow, Walt W. 1960. *The Stages of Economic Growth*. Cambridge: Cambridge University Press.

Rotberg, Robert, ed. 2003. *When States Fail: Causes and Consequences*. Princeton, NJ: Princeton University Press.

Rothchild, Donald. 1997. *Managing Ethnic Conflict in Africa: Pressures and Incentives for Cooperation*. Washington, DC: Brookings Institution.

Rothstein, Bo. 2011. *The Quality of Government*. Chicago: University of Chicago Press.

Rothstein, Bo and Jan Teorell. 2008. "What Is Quality of Government? A Theory of Impartial Government Institutions." *Governance* 21 (2): 165–90.

Rucht, Dieter, Ruud Koopmans, and F. Niedhart. 1998. *Acts of Dissent: New Developments in the Study of Protest*. Berlin: Sigma Edition.

Rudra, N. and Stephen Haggard. 2005. "Globalization, Democracy and Effective Welfare Spending in the Developing World." *Comparative Political Studies* 38 (9): 1015–49.

Rueschemeyer, Dietrich. 1991. "Different Methods, Contradictory Results? Research on Development and Democracy." *International Journal of Comparative Sociology* 32 (1–2): 9–38.

2008. "Democracy and Social Welfare." *Contemporary Sociology* 37 (5): 407–10.

Rueschemeyer, Dietrich, Evelyne H. Stephens, and John D. Stephens. 1992. *Capitalist Development and Democracy*. Cambridge: Polity Press.

Russett, Bruce M. 1993. *Grasping the Democratic Peace: Principles for a Post-Cold War World*. Princeton, NJ: Princeton University Press.

Russett, Bruce M., John R. O'Neal, and Michael Cox. 2000. "Clash of Civilizations, or Realism and Liberalism Déjà Vu? Some Evidence." *Journal of Peace Research* 37 (5): 583–608.

Rustow, Dankwart. 1970. "Transitions to Democracy: Toward a Dynamic Model." *Comparative Politics* 2: 337–63.

Sacks, A. and Margaret Levi. 2010. "Measuring Government Effectiveness and Its Consequences for Social Welfare in Sub-Saharan African Countries." *Social Forces* 88 (5): 2325–51.

Saha, Jean. C. 2011. "Legislative Democracy, Economic Growth and Multi-dimensional Poverty in Sub-Sahara Africa." *Journal of International Development* 23 (3): 443–60.

Sahin, Selver B. 2011. "Building the Nation in Timor-Leste and Its Implications for the Country's Democratic Development." *Australian Journal of International Affairs* 65 (2): 220–42.

Sartori, Giovani. 1987. *The Theory of Democracy Revisited*. Chatham, UK: Chatham House.

1994. *Comparative Constitutional Engineering: An Inquiry into Structures, Incentives, and Outcomes*. New York: Columbia University Press.

Saward, Michael, ed. 2000. *Democratic Innovation: Deliberation, Representation and Association*. London: Routledge.

Scarritt, James R. and Shaheen Mozaffar. 1999. "The Specification of Ethnic Cleavages and Ethnopolitical Groups for the Analysis of Democratic Competition in Contemporary Africa." *Nationalism and Ethnic Politics* 5: 82–117.

Schedler, Andreas, ed. 2005. *Electoral Authoritarianism: The Dynamics of Unfree Competition*. Boulder, CO: Lynne Reinner.

Scherrer, Christian P. 2002. *Structural Prevention of Ethnic Violence*. New York: Palgrave Macmillan.

Schmitz, Hans Peter. 2004. "Domestic and Transnational Perspectives on Democratization." *International Studies Review* 6: 403–26.

Schneckener, Ulrich. 2002. "Making Power-Sharing Work: Lessons from Successes and Failures in Ethnic Conflict Regulation." *Journal of Peace Research* 39 (2): 203–28.

Schneckner, Ulrich and Stefan Wolff, ed. 2004. *Managing and Settling Ethnic Conflicts: Perspectives on Successes and Failures in Europe, Africa and Asia*. London: C. Hurst.

Schneider, Aaron. 2003. "Decentralization: Conceptualization and Measurement." *Studies in Comparative International Development* 38 (3): 32–56.

Scholdan, Bettina. 2000. "Democratization and Electoral Engineering in Post-Ethnic Conflict Societies." *Javnost* 7 (1).

Schumpeter, Joseph A. 1947. *Capitalism, Socialism, and Democracy*. 2nd ed. New York: Harper.

Scott, James M. and Carie Steele. 2011. "Sponsoring Democracy: The United States and Democracy Aid to the Developing World, 1988–2001." *International Studies Quarterly* 55 (1): 47–69.

Segura-Ubiergo, Alex. 2007. *The Political Economy of the Welfare State in Latin America: Globalization, Democracy and Development*. New York: Cambridge University Press.

Seligson, Mitchell A. 2002. "The Renaissance of Political Culture or the Renaissance of the Ecological Fallacy?" *Comparative Politics* 34 (3): 273.

Sen, Amartya. 1999. *Development as Freedom*. New York: Knopf.

Shepherd, A. 2000. "Governance, Good Government and Poverty Reduction." *International Review of Administrative Sciences* 66: 269.

Shin, Doh C. 1994. "On the Third Wave of Democratization: A Synthesis and Evaluation of Recent Theory and Research." *World Politics* 47: 135–70.

Siegle, Joseph T., Michael M. Weinstein, and Morton H. Halperin. 2004. "Why Democracies Excel." *Foreign Affairs* 83 (5): 57–72.

Simeon, Richard and Daniel-Patrick Conway. 2001. "Federalism and the Management of Conflict in Multinational Societies." In Alain-G. Gagnon and James Tully, ed., *Multinational Democracies*. New York: Cambridge University Press, pp. 338–65.

Simonsen, S. G. 2005. "Addressing Ethnic Divisions in Post-Conflict Institution-Building: Lessons from Recent Cases." *Security Dialogue* 36 (3): 297–318.

Sirowy, Larry and Alex Inkeles. 1990. "The Effects of Democracy on Economic Growth and Inequality: A Review." *Studies in Comparative International Development* 25 (2): 126–57.

Sisk, Timothy. 1996. *Power-Sharing and International Mediation in Ethnic Conflicts*. Washington, DC: U.S. Institute of Peace Press.

Sisk, Timothy and Andrew Reynolds, eds. 1998. *Elections and Conflict Management in Africa*. Washington, DC: U.S. Institute of Peace.

Smith, Gordon. 2009. *Democratic Innovations*. Cambridge: Cambridge University Press.

Smith, Peter. 2005. *Democracy in Latin America: Political Change in Comparative Perspective*. New York: Oxford University Press.

Snyder, David and Edward L. Kick. 1979. "Structural Position in the World System and Economic Growth, 1955–1970: A Multiple-Network Analysis of Transnational Interactions." *American Journal of Sociology* 84: 1096–1126.

Snyder, Jack. 2000. *From Voting to Violence: Democratization and Nationalist Conflict.* New York: W. W. Norton.

Snyder, Richard. 2006. "Does Lootable Wealth Breed Disorder? A Political Economy of Extraction Framework." *Comparative Political Studies* 39 (8): 943–68.

Soifer, Hillel. 2008. "State Infrastructural Power: Approaches to Conceptualization and Measurement." *Studies in Comparative International Development* 43 (3–4): 231–51.

Soifer, Hillel and Mathias vom Hau. 2008. "Unpacking the Strength of the State: The Utility of State Infrastructural Power." *Studies in Comparative International Development* 43 (3–4): 219–30.

Spicker, Paul. 2008. "Government for the People: The Substantive Elements of Democracy." *International Journal of Social Welfare* 17 (3): 251–9.

Starr, Harvey and Christina Lindborg. 2003. "Democratic Dominoes: Diffusion Approaches to the Spread of Democracy in the International System." *Journal of Conflict Resolution* 35 (2): 356–81.

Stasavage, D. 2005. "Democracy and Education Spending in Africa." *American Journal of Political Science* 49 (2): 343–58.

Stegarescu, Dan. 2005. "Public Sector Decentralisation: Measurement Concepts and Recent International Trends." *Fiscal Studies* 26 (3): 301–33.

Steiner, Jurg. 1974. *Amicable Agreement versus Majority Rule: Conflict Resolution in Switzerland.* Chapel Hill: University of North Carolina Press.

Stepan, Alfred. 1986. "Paths toward Redemocratization: Theoretical and Comparative Considerations." In Guillermo O'Donnell, Phillippe Schmitter, and Laurence Whitehead, eds. *Transitions from Authoritarian Rule*, vol. III. Baltimore: Johns Hopkins University Press, pp. 64–84.

  1999. "Federalism and Democracy: Beyond the U.S. Model." *Journal of Democracy* 10 (4): 19–34.

Stepan, Alfred and Cindy Skach. 1993. "Constitutional Frameworks and Democratic Consolidation: Parliamentarism and Presidentialism." *World Politics* 46 (1): 1–22.

Stimson, James A. 1985. "Regression in Time and Space: A Statistical Essay." *American Journal of Political Science* 29: 914–47.

Stroup, Michael D. 2006. "Economic Freedom, Democracy, and the Quality of Life." *World Development* 35 (1): 52–66.

Sung, H. E. 2004. "Democracy and Political Corruption: A Cross-National Comparison." *Crime, Law and Social Change* 41: 179.

Svensson, Jakob. 1999. "Aid, Growth and Democracy." *Economics and Politics* 11: 275–97.

Taagepera, Rein and Matthew Shugart. 1989. *Seats and Votes: The Effects and Determinants of Electoral Systems.* New Haven, CT: Yale University Press.

Taras, Raymond and Rajat Ganguly. 1998. *Understanding Ethnic Conflict.* New York: Longman.

Teorell, Jan. 2010. *Determinants of Democratization: Explaining Regime Change in the World, 1972–2006.* New York: Cambridge University Press.

Theobald, Robin. 1982. "Patrimonialism." *World Politics* 34: 548–59.

Thies, Cameron G. 2010. "Of Rulers, Rebels and Revenue: State Capacity, Civil War Onset and Primary Commodities." *Journal of Peace Research* 47 (3): 321–32.

Tilly, Charles. 2007. *Democracy.* New York: Cambridge University Press.

Timmons, J. F. 2010. "Does Democracy Reduce Economic Inequality?" *British Journal of Political Science* 40 (4): 741–57.

Toft, Monica. 2010. *Securing the Peace: The Durable Settlement of Civil Wars*. Princeton, NJ: Princeton University Press.

Tornquist, Olle. 2011. "Dynamics of Peace and Democratization: The Aceh Lessons." *Democratization* 18 (3): 823–46.

Transparency International. *The Corruption Perception Index*. http://www.transparency.org/surveys/index.html#cpi.

Global Corruption Barometer. http://www.transparency.org/.

Treisman, Daniel. 2007. *The Architecture of Government: Rethinking Political Decentralization*. New York: Cambridge University Press.

Tsai, Ming-Chang. 2006. "Does Political Democracy Enhance Human Development in Developing Countries?" *American Journal of Economics and Sociology* 65 (2): 233–68.

Tsebelis, George. 2002. *Veto Players: How Political Institutions Work*. Princeton, NJ: Princeton University Press.

Tull, Denis M. and Andreas Mehler. 2005. "The Hidden Costs of Power-Sharing: Reproducing Insurgent Violence in Africa." *African Affairs* 104: 375–98.

United Nations Development Programme (UNDP). 2004. *Arab Human Development Report 2004*. New York: UNDP/Oxford University Press.

University of Maryland, Center for International Development and Conflict Management (CIDCM). *Minorities at Risk* (database). http://www.cidcm.umd.edu/inscr/mar/.

Uppsala Conflict Data Program. 2010. *The ECDP/PRIO Armed Conflict Dataset Codebook Version 4*. www.ucdp.uu.se.

Van Rijckeghem, C. and B. Weder. 2001. "Bureaucratic Corruption and the Rate of Temptation: Do Wages in the Civil Service Affect Corruption, and by How Much?" *Journal of Development Economics* 65: 307–31.

Vanhanen, Tatu. 1990. *The Process of Democratization: A Comparative Study of 147 States. 1980–88*. New York: Crane Russak.

1997. *Prospects for Democracy: A Study of 172 Countries*. New York: Routledge.

2000. "A New Dataset for Measuring Democracy, 1810–1998." *Journal of Peace Research* 37 (2): 251–65.

Varshney, Ashutosh. 2000. "Why Have Poor Democracies Not Eliminated Poverty?" *Asian Survey* 40 (5): 718.

2003. *Ethnic Conflict and Civic Life: Hindus and Muslims in India*. New Haven, CT: Yale University Press.

Vincent, Andrew. 1987. *Theories of the State*. Oxford: Blackwell.

Wade, Robert. 1990. *Governing the Market: Economic Theory and the Role of Government in East Asian Industrialization*. Princeton, NJ: Princeton University Press.

Wallerstein, Peter and Margareta Sollenberg. 1997. "Armed Conflicts, Conflict Termination, and Peace Agreements, 1989–96." *Journal of Peace Research* 34 (3): 339–58.

Walter, Barbara and Jack Snyder, eds. 1999. *Civil Wars, Insecurity and Intervention*. New York: Columbia University Press.

Watts, Ronald L. 1999. *Comparing Federal Systems*. 2nd ed. Kingston, Ontario: McGill-Queen's University Press.

2006. *Models of Federal Power-Sharing*. Washington, DC: National Democratic Institute.

Weber, Max. [1904]. 1968. *Economy and Society*. Edited by Guenter Roth and Claus Wittich. New York: Bedmaster.

Weiss, Thomas G., David P. Forsythe, and Roger A. Coate. 2004. *United Nations and Changing World Politics.* Boulder, CO: Westview Press.

Weller, Marc and Stefan Wolff, eds. 2005. *Autonomy, Self-Governance and Conflict Resolution: Innovative Approaches to Institutional Design in Divided Societies.* London and New York: Routledge.

Welzel, Christian. 2008. "The Role of Ordinary People in Democratization." *Journal of Democracy* 19: 126.

2011. "The Asian Values Thesis Revisited: Evidence from the World Values Surveys." *Japanese Journal of Political Science* 12: 1–31.

Welzel, Christian, Ronald Inglehart, and Hans-Dieter Klingemann. 2003. "The Theory of Human Development: A Cross-Cultural Analysis." *European Journal of Political Research* 42 (3): 341–79.

Whitehead, Laurence. 1986. "International Aspects of Democratization." In Guillermo O'Donnell, Phillippe Schmitter, and Laurence Whitehead, eds., *Transitions from Authoritarian Rule: Comparative Perspectives.* Baltimore: Johns Hopkins University Press, pp. 3–46.

Wibbels, Erik. 2005. *Federalism and the Market: Intergovernmental Conflict and Economic Reform in the Developing World.* New York: Cambridge University Press.

Willis, Katie. 2011. *Theories and Practices of Development.* Routledge Perspectives on Development. New York: Routledge.

Wilson, Sven E. and Daniel M. Butler. 2007. "A Lot More to Do: The Sensitivity of Time-Series Cross-Section Analyses to Simple Alternative Specifications." *Political Analysis* 15: 101–23.

Wittman, D. 1989. "Why Democracies Produce Efficient Results." *Journal of Political Economy* 97 (6): 1395–1424.

Wolff, Jonas and Iris Wurm. 2011. "Towards a Theory of External Democracy Promotion: A Proposal for Theoretical Classification." *Security Dialogue* 42 (1): 77–96.

Wolff, Stefan. 2003. *Disputed Territories: The Transnational Dynamics of Ethnic Conflict Settlement.* New York: Berghahn.

Wooldridge, J. M. 2002. *Econometric Analysis of Cross Section and Panel Data.* Cambridge, MA: MIT Press.

World Bank. *World Bank Governance Indicators.* http://www.worldbank.org/wbi/governance.

1999. "Can Corruption Be Measured? Bank Offers Diagnostic Tools to Measure and Combat Corruption in Member Countries." http://www.worldbank.org/wbi/governance/pubs/measurecor.htm.

Zakaria, Fareed. 1997. "The Rise of Illiberal Democracy." *Foreign Affairs* 76 (6): 22–41.

2003. *The Future of Freedom: Illiberal Democracy at Home and Abroad.* New York: W. W. Norton.

Zartman, I. William, ed. 1995. *Collapsed States: The Disintegration and Restoration of Legitimate Authority.* Boulder, CO: Lynne Rienner.

Zielonka, Jan, ed. 2001. *Democratic Consolidation in Eastern Europe.* Oxford: Oxford University Press.

Zweifel, T. D. and P. Navia. 2000. "Democracy, Dictatorship and Infant Mortality." *Journal of Democracy* 11: 99–114.

Index

Afghanistan
   armed conflict in, 80
   public service issues in, 81
   state-building in, 4–5
Africa, welfare systems in, after
      democratization, 138. *See also specific
      nations*
African Union, 33
Akufo-Addo, Nana, 62
al-Abidine Ben Ali, Zine, xi
Allende, Salvador, 60
Alvarez, Michael, 100
American Political Science Association
      Taskforce on Indicators of Democracy
      and Governance, xi
anarchy, 44–5
Annan, Kofi, 32
Arab Spring, xi
   long-term effects of, 81
Aristide, Jean-Bertrand, 131
Australia
   macroeconomic policy stability in, 108
authoritarian advantage model, 19–20
authoritarian regimes
   economic development under, 19–20
   human development under, 11–12
   welfare outcomes under, 20
authorities, in regimes, 43
   legal-rational, 45–6
autocratic regimes
   bureaucratic, 16
   economic development in, 105–6
   patronage, 16
   political benevolence of, 38
   transition to democracy, 170–1
   welfare outcomes under, 20
Aylwin, Patricio, 60

Bahrain
   Arab Spring in, long-term effects of, 81
   armed conflict in, 80
   suppression of protests in, xi
Balaguer, Joaquin, 130
Banda, Rupiah, 157
Bangladesh, 5
Barre, Mohamed Siad, 65
Barro, Robert, 100
BDP. *See* Botswana Democratic Party
Belgium, public administration policy in, 48
Benin, natural crisis management in, 4
blood diamonds, 162
Botswana, 159–63
   anticorruption policies in, 161–2
   human development failures in, 159
   resource curse in, 162
   Zambia compared to, 154–5, 160–1
Botswana Democratic Party (BDP), 161
Brady, Henry, xi
Brazil
   economic influences on democratic
      development, 11
   as patronage state, 48
bureaucratic autocracies, 16.
      See also Singapore
   Chile as, 60
   economic development in, 117
   educational access in, 148
   gender parity in education in, 148–50
   human development in, 136
   income levels in, 117
   longevity in, 146–8
   types of civil conflicts in, 175–81
bureaucratic democracies, 16. *See also* Chile
   educational access in, 148
   gender parity in education in, 148–50

CPSIA information can be obtained at www.ICGtesting.com
Printed in the USA
LVOW11s1714201013

357763LV00006B/10/P